Population Geography

Published by Rowman & Littlefield Publishers, Inc.
A wholly owned subsidiary of The Rowman & Littlefield Publishing Group, Inc.
4501 Forbes Boulevard, Suite 200, Lanham, Maryland 20706
http://www.rowmanlittlefield.com

Estover Road, Plymouth PL6 7PY, United Kingdom

British Library Cataloguing in Publication Information Available

Library of Congress Cataloging-in-Publication Data

Newbold, K. Bruce, 1964–
Population geography : tools and issues / K. Bruce Newbold.
    p.   cm.
   Includes bibliographical references and index.
   ISBN 978-0-7425-5753-6 (cloth : alk. paper)
   ISBN 978-0-7425-5754-3 (pbk. : alk. paper)
   ISBN 978-0-7425-5755-0 (electronic)
   1. Population geography.   I. Title.
HB1951.N47   2009
304.6—dc22

2009038560

Printed in the United States of America

To Christine

Contents

Acknowledgments

I gratefully acknowledge the mapping and GIS assistance of Adam Drackley, School of Geography and Earth Sciences, McMaster University. Finally, my thanks to the team at Rowman & Littlefield Publishers.

Figures and Tables

FIGURES

TABLES

Population Geography:
An Introduction

FOR MOST OF humanity's history, the global population was small and grew at a slow pace. Estimates of the world's population at the start of the seventeenth century, on the eve of a faster population growth regime, are about 500 million. Since then, advances in medicine, sanitation, and nutrition have allowed the world's population to grow at a faster rate. By 1900, the world's population was approximately 2 billion, growing to over 6.8 billion in 2009,[1] with the last billion people added in just fourteen years. Most of that growth has occurred in the developing world[2]—Africa, large parts of Asia, and South and Central America. Moreover, much of the future growth of the world's population is expected to occur in the developing world, fueled by comparably high birth rates, reduced death rates, and young populations.

To view population processes, including fertility, mortality, and population movement, at work across the globe is to begin to understand many of the underlying issues in today's society, including conflict, resource use, environmental degradation, and relations between countries and their peoples. Societies around the world are characterized by or shaped by their population processes and characteristics. We may characterize, for example, populations and regions by differences in mortality and fertility processes. For instance, the infant mortality rate (IMR), which measures the number of deaths to infants less than one year of age per one thousand births, was six in developed countries, compared to a world average of forty-six in 2009. Life expectancy at birth, which measures the number of years an individual is expected to live, averaged seventy-seven years in developed countries, but only sixty-seven in developing countries. In many cases, the poor life expectancy outcomes and high death rates reflect poor or inadequate health care, the failure of governments to provide basic necessities, or educational differences. In sub-Saharan Africa, the HIV/AIDS epidemic has reshaped population profiles and reduced life expectancies.

Countries or regions are also tied together by population movement. War, refugee movements, and simple geographic interaction across space perpetuate poor health and disease. Population movement includes local residential changes as housing needs change; domestic migration associated with, for example, employment opportunities or amenities; or international migration. While local or domestic migration is rarely controlled, most countries, including many in the developing world, tightly control international movements, often restricting entry to those who qualify under specific programs. With population mobility and migration typically selecting the young and those with skills, who moves is just as important as the origins and destinations of migrants. Most developed countries actively promote the entry of individuals who are able to invest in the host country or embody the education or skills that are demanded by developed countries.

While the movement of legal immigrants is not inconsequential, illegal immigrants and refugees dominate the international movement of people. For those seeking a better life elsewhere, illegal immigration may be a desperate, but the only, option. Exemplified by the sagas of Mariel Cubans and Indochinese boat people and recent events in Afghanistan, Darfur, and Congo, refugees and displaced populations have become an increasingly visible issue. Defined by the United Nations, refugees are persons who are outside their country of nationality and are unable to return owing to fear of persecution for reason of race, religion, nationality, or association in a social or political group.[3] Major refugee-producing countries by mid-2008 included Sudan (Darfur), Iraq, Afghanistan, and Somalia. Overall, the United Nations High Commissioner on Refugees (UNHCR) estimated that there were more than 67 million individuals of concern worldwide in 2007, including some 9.6 million refugees.[4]

The importance of considering fertility, mortality, and population movement is realizing the multiple interconnections with population, such that population underlies many of the issues facing the world today, including resource and environmental issues. Packaged with understanding population processes is the ability to understand and interpret their measurement. The primary motivation of this text is to provide the reader with a set of functional tools—measuring or describing population processes, data, and population composition—for studying population geography, while linking to population issues such as fertility, mortality, and immigration. Although the study of population is interdisciplinary in its scope, the geographical perspective is valued through its emphasis on the role of space and place, location, regional differences, and diffusion and its ability to provide insight and bridge disparate issues. Second, the book is motivated by the need to understand population processes. In other words, in addition to introducing population studies, it also makes available to readers an overview of current and future issues related to population by drawing linkages to economic, political, and resource issues.

WHAT IS POPULATION GEOGRAPHY AND WHY STUDY IT?

Population geography is the study of the human population with respect to size, composition, spatial distribution, and changes in the population that occur over time. Populations are altered by three basic processes: fertility (births), mortality (deaths), and migration (movement of people across space), topics that this book explores in greater detail in subsequent chapters. Population geographers, like others interested in population, seek to understand the society around them, the structure of a population, and how it changes through births, deaths, and migrations. This interest is reflected in a number of professional organizations, including the Association of American Geographers (AAG) and its Population Geography Specialty Group, the Canadian Association of Geographers (CAG), and the United Kingdom's Royal Geographical Society—Institute of British Geographers. Outside of geography, the Population Association of America (PAA) is also an important venue for population geographers (table I.1).

Population research draws on many disciplines and research traditions, a multidisciplinarity that is reflected in its various titles. For instance, economists, geographers, sociologists, planners, and anthropologists regularly contribute to population studies, and their methods, perspectives, and findings crossfertilize other disciplinary perspectives. More formally, *demography*, with its roots in the analysis of mortality and fertility statistics, is the statistical analysis of population, while *population studies* is often used to describe other approaches to looking at population issues, including non-statistical approaches. *Population geography* is the geographical study of population, with an emphasis on location and spatial processes.

While population geography as a formal field of study only dates from the 1950s and is therefore relatively new,[5] this work has assumed an important

Table I.1.   Professional Geographical Organizations and Leading Journals in Geography and Related Disciplines

Group name	Journal(s)	Web resources
Academic groups		
Association of American Geographers (AAG)	*The Professional Geographer* *Annals of the AAG*	www.aag.org www.pop.psu.edu/aag/ psg.html
Canadian Association of Geographers (CAG)	*The Canadian Geographer*	www.cag-acg.ca
Royal Geographical Society–Institute of British Geographers (RGS-IBG)	*Area* *Transactions* *The Geographical Journal*	www.rgs.org/HomePage .htm
Other groups		
Population Association of America (PAA)	*Demography*	www.popassoc.org
Population Reference Bureau (PRB)	*Population Bulletin*	www.prb.org
UN Population Division		www.un.org/esa/ population/

For a more complete list of web resources, including data sources, please refer to the websites section at the back of the book.

role within the discipline of geography. Interestingly, although there are some geographers that consider fertility and mortality differences across space, migration and the study of population mobility have assumed prominence amongst geographers. Perhaps it is the very nature and outcome of population movement, which has an ability to rapidly alter the population structure and characteristics of a region, that has focused geographer's attention. That is, population mobility is inherently spatial, connecting places both local and international. For instance, interest in movement between cities in the United States has demonstrated the impact of out-migration from the northeastern Rust Belt and the astonishing growth of the South and Southwest over the past few decades as people move in search of both employment opportunities and amenities. Complementing this movement has been that of retirees heading southward as well.

More recently, population geographers have turned their attention to international migrations. Geographers have, for instance, analyzed the economic, social, and political effects associated with international movement into the United States and other countries. Others have focused on the movement of labor between countries in the developing world. In both cases, various theoretical approaches, including gendered studies, political-economic theory, Marxist theories, and/or utility-maximizing theories, have been brought to bear on the questions and issues, all highlighting the diversity of the field and its research.

Populations are governed by various natural laws—we are all born, age, and must ultimately die. On that journey from birth to death, we may go to university, be married, have children, change jobs and occupations, and move. Understanding the population around us and the transitions that are occurring within it is key. All levels of governments, for example, are interested in the structure of their populations: What percentage is over sixty-five? What proportion can vote? What proportion is less than fifteen years old? How many move and who moves or changes residential location or moves nationally or internationally in a year? What is the ethnic or racial composition of an area? From this information, governments can direct program delivery to ensure that the needs of their constituents are met. Consequently, an understanding of the composition of a population, its distribution, and how it changes over time is important and needed for planning purposes as well as the private and public sectors. For example, school boards and universities will wish to be able to project enrollment or participation in schooling. Service organizations will want to know about the elderly or immigrant populations—their size, age structure, and location—so that the appropriate services may be delivered. Likewise, retailers will wish to know similar information about the population so that they can target specific segments with their products or learn more about the buying power or retail needs of a particular group.

At an international scale, governments and other international bodies such as the United Nations and the UNHCR are interested in issues, including population growth, fertility, and the movement of people. Encompassing legal and illegal immigration, refugees, and internally displaced people, interest focuses on where people are moving from and to, the reasons for movement, and the implications for the individual, the receiving community, and the sending community. Much international immigration is prompted by economic issues and the dream of a better life.

WHAT IS THE GEOGRAPHICAL PERSPECTIVE?

As Gober and Tyner note in *Geography in America at the Dawn of the Twenty-First Century,* "geographic issues loom large."[6] Legal and illegal immigration; assimilation and adjustment of new arrivals to the host country; economic, social, and political responses to population movement; and population aging are among the relevant topics that are addressed by population geographers.

Moreover, these are not just "American" issues, but ones that are faced throughout the developed and developing world. Although the study of population is interdisciplinary in scope, with contributions by sociologists, economists, and anthropologists, the geographic perspective is especially valuable. Geography, by its nature, offers an integrative framework through which to view population (or other) issues. The disciplinary concerns of geography—space, regional variations, diffusion, and place, and their role in human and natural processes—provide this unique framework for looking at population issues. Space is not a unique concern to geography, and geographers do not deal exclusively with space, but it is the understanding of spatial processes, such as the diffusion of ideas associated with small families or birth control techniques, which is of interest. Whether we are interested in population issues related to fertility or immigration, spatial processes are implied as states and their governments alter the demographic makeup of nations through policies related to, for example, immigration or families. Similarly, economic systems will determine fertility behavior, and the mortality of populations and environmental crises related to pollution, deforestation, and water scarcity provide examples of the linkage between regions. These are also dynamic processes, changing over time and across the landscape, and a geographical approach enables the explanation of past, present, and future relationships and patterns.

Population geography first rose to prominence as a field of study in geography with Glenn T. Trewartha's call for its increased study at the 1953 AAG annual meeting.[7] Trewartha envisioned population geography as a separate subdiscipline, along with physical geography and cultural geography. Since then, geography has more commonly been divided into physical and human geography, with population geography a component of the latter.[8]

Population geography initially dealt with the geographic character of places, content to describe the location of a population and its characteristics and to explain the spatial configuration of these numbers. Wilbur Zelinsky's 1966 book on population geography[9] helped to further cement the field of population geography, including the description of populations, explanation for the spatial configuration of populations, and the geographical analysis of population phenomena. Reflecting population geography's close ties to formal demography, many population geographers relied on logical positivism (combining empirical study with mathematics and scientific inquiry), quantitative methods, and the analysis of large data sources through the 1970s and 1980s. Moreover, there was a corresponding increase in computational abilities. The emergence of desktop computing and statistical software packages greatly increased the flexibility and tools at the disposal of researchers, including the ability to test hypotheses through inferential techniques and apply more complex multivariate statistical analysis.

Since Trewartha, population geography has grown in importance and scope, and many geographers have made important contributions to the field, with the field growing to draw upon a multiplicity of methods and theoretical approaches. Qualitative approaches offer detailed insights, and geographic information systems (GIS) and spatial analytical techniques offer newer insights into population processes. Most writers and researchers now place population within a broader context, recognizing the importance of place and drawing upon the diverse insights provided by geography and related social science disciplines. The diversity of conceptual approaches provided by geography provides a framework through which to view complex phenomena. Economic and cultural geography provide insights into fertility choices, which may reflect the economic needs of the family, including a trade-off between children as labor or "pension plans" and the ability to provide an education or the larger cultural expectations of society. Similarly, political, social, and cultural geography provide insight into the potential for conflict by bridging disparate issues, enabling the recognition of the interrelationships between resources, environment, politics, and policy within the realm of population geography.

CURRENT RESEARCH THEMES AND CONTRIBUTIONS OF POPULATION GEOGRAPHERS

We cannot hope to completely enumerate the variety of research subjects (or researchers!) that are included within the fold of population geography, particularly when, as Ogden notes,[10] some geographers who do population-related work do not call themselves population geographers. Instead, they may describe their work through cultural, ethnic, or rural geography. The 2005 publication *Geography in America at the Dawn of the Twenty-First Century*[11] identified six research themes in population geography: (1) internal migration and residential mobility, (2) international migration and transnationalism, (3) immigrant assimilation and adjustment and the emergence of ethnic enclaves, (4) regional demographic variation, (5) social theory and population processes, and (6) public policy.

Amongst these, internal migration and residential mobility has largely defined population geography, and includes the work of geographers such as Plane, Brown, Moore, Rogerson, Long, Clark, and Cushing. Research themes include the relationship between migration and economic cycles and restructuring, the effects of demographic cycles (i.e., population aging and the baby boom cohort) on migration, life course perspectives on population mobility, and ethnographic approaches to migration.

Research associated with international migration, transnationalism, immigrant assimilation, adjustment, and ethnic enclaves remains important for population geographers. Edited volumes such as *EthniCity*[12] and *Migration and Restructuring in the US*[13] highlight the varied contributions of geographers to this area. Other individual researchers have explored the evolution of immigrant settlements and enclaves over time,[14] residential dispersion,[15] circular migration,[16] and the economic integration of new arrivals.[17] David Ley[18] has explored concepts of transnationalism, particularly in the context of Canada. In a similar way, Crush and McDonald[19] have explored the role of transnationalism in Africa.

Research evaluating regional demographic variation highlights such questions as differential population aging, fertility rates, and migration propensities. Geographers have long noted significant variations in migration rates between US states, particularly with respect to retirement migration, aging in place, and poverty migration.[20] Other population processes have not escaped geography's attention, with, for example, Franklin[21] exploring regional variations in Italian fertility levels, while many "health geographers" study mortality and morbidity patterns within populations.

Social theorists, including Blue,[22] Findlay,[23] McHugh,[24] Silvey,[25] and others, have sought to incorporate issues such as gender and race into alternative approaches to the study of population geography. This approach has often included greater emphasis on ethnographic and qualitative methods. Finally, public policy has been engaged by researchers including Morrill[26] and Clark and Morison,[27] who explore the intersection between population structure (i.e., race, ethnicity), legislative redistricting, and voting.

The use of diverse quantitative and qualitative techniques including GIS and spatial analysis techniques builds upon the tradition of spatial population geography.[28] This has meant that population geographers have applied themselves and their work outside the traditional domains of population research, engaging in health, transportation, and economic analyses. Concurrently, newly emergent themes and research directions include more active links to environmental geography. Although population issues frequently lie at the heart of environmental issues, as with the relationship between human migration and environmental degradation, social and ethnic unrest, or food security,[29] there has been relatively little attention to the shared research agendas, although this is now changing.[30] Arguably, nongeographers, including Homer-Dixon,[31] have been quicker to realize population-environment linkages, while other nongeographers have noted the relationships between population and health[32] and population and economic growth.[33] This is not to say geographers have not contributed to these debates, but rather that there is much room for additional geographical insight. Similarly, population geographers need to further address the relationship between population and economic development.[34] Additionally, increased ties are emerging between population geography, GIS, and spatial analysis, reflecting the increased integration of these tools into geography in general.

OVERVIEW OF THE BOOK

The primary motivation of this text is to identify and discuss population issues such as fertility, mortality, and immigration, while also providing the reader with a set of functional tools—measuring or describing population processes, data, and population composition—for studying population geography. The book is structured into substantive chapters that focus on particular population processes and related issues. Each of the substantive chapters also have "Focus" and "Methods, Measures, and Tools" boxes embedded in the text. The intent is to weave the overall discussion of each chapter into more specific examples, including issues or areas of particular interest as well as a discussion of how population geography research is performed. While measures and tools that population geographers frequently use are presented in the text, the intent is not necessarily to provide full explanation and descriptions—existing software programs, basic statistical analysis packages, and the increased use of the World Wide Web essentially mean that many of the tools are easily and quickly automated. Instead, the intent is to provide an understanding of the tools and link their use to issues. As such, "Focus" boxes will present "real-world" examples to illustrate the concepts discussed in each chapter, including their use and interpretation. Methods, Measures, and Tools boxes will illustrate methods and measures commonly used by population geographers (i.e., population projection techniques).

FOCUS: THE IMPORTANCE OF SPATIAL SCALE

It is important to realize that spatial phenomena, such as population movement, do not occur at just one geographic scale. The phenomena of interest for the geographer may occur at a variety of spatial scales ranging from the individual to the international. For instance, people may move between houses within their immediate neighborhood, within the same city, across the country, or internationally, with each move potentially explained by a different set of factors. For the household moving locally, for example, the move may be driven by the need for more (or less) space as the family size changes, while they want to remain in the same area where friendships have been established. For the household moving across the country, the move may reflect starting a new job or going to school, the search for employment, or retirement to a location with greater amenities or that is closer to family. Similarly, at one scale fertility choices may reflect the particulars of that place—its ethnic or religious makeup, for example, details which may be "washed out" at larger scales as larger populations are averaged together.

For this reason, we must be aware of the implications that our choice of spatial scale has on the outcome and its interpretation. First, changing the scale of analysis often implies that a different set of questions (and potentially methods) must be applied to the problem. For the researcher interested in local issues, questions may focus more on neighborhood and household/family effects, while economic and amenity effects may dominate larger-scale analyses.

Second, changing spatial scale often changes what we can physically observe. For the migration analyst, this is particularly acute, given the well-known fact that people are more likely to move over short distances than they are over longer ones, a conclusion that dates back to the writings of Ravenstein in the 1800s.[1] More generally, the number of observed migrants depends on the size, shape, population distribution, and characteristics of the population (i.e., older populations are less likely to move than younger populations) within the study area.[2]

Third, the so-called modifiable areal unit problem (MAUP) has been an issue that has

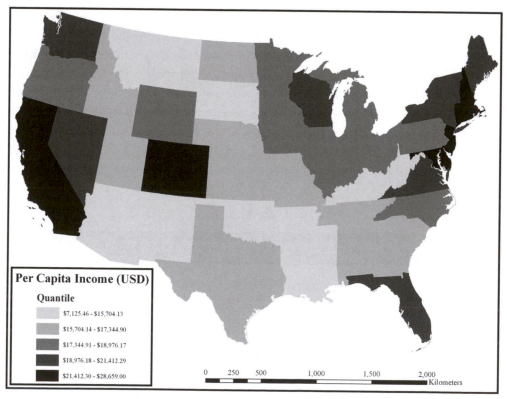

Figure IF.1   Per-capita Income by State, 1999.

Compare this figure with that in 1MMT.1b, which maps the same data at the county scale. The detail in the latter map is missing in this one.

Source: Author.

concerned geographers and cartographers alike. MAUP is a potential source of error that can affect studies that utilize aggregate data sources and is closely related to ecological fallacy, or the errors in allowing inferences about individual behavior when the analysis is based on group or area statistics. In order to present results, geographical data are often aggregated and mapped to spatial objects such as census tracts, providing an illustration of the spatial phenomena. However, these zones and their boundaries are often arbitrary in nature, defined by statistical organizations such as the Census Bureau. While changing the geographical scale (i.e., moving from the census tract to an enumeration area) can be just as meaningful for the presentation of the data, the revisualization may also provide a different representation of the information. For instance, the appearance of spatial clustering at one scale may not be visible at another. Moreover, different processes may be responsible for the outcome of interest.

Clearly, these issues of spatial scale are not mutually exclusive. However, the choice of the spatial zones that are to be used must be given careful consideration, with a preference to use the smallest, and most meaningful, spatial scale possible. However, it should also be noted that this preference only holds when the data at that scale is reliable and when any processes at smaller scales are stable. Failing either of these, the analyst should turn to the geographic scale that does meet these requirements. This is not to say that the impact of spatial scale should be avoided and that comparisons across spatial scales are inappropriate. In fact, complementary results based on analyses at different scales are often noted, and comparisons yield important insights into underlying spatial processes, with an understanding of the process at one scale aiding the analysis at another scale.

METHODS, MEASURES, AND TOOLS: TOOLS OF THE POPULATION GEOGRAPHER

Population geography, like demography in general, has traditionally been strongly rooted in empiricism and statistical analysis. As a field of study, population geography does not have its own set of analytical tools that define the field of research, although geographic information systems come close. Instead, the tools of the population geographer reflect those of related disciplines, including cartography, demography, economics, anthropology, and sociology. As such, population geographers rely on a variety of tools and methods that are shared across disciplinary fields. These tools can be broadly summarized under data, methods, and presentation.

DATA

Clearly, any analysis or insight into population processes is dependent on data. If, for example, we wish to gauge the fertility of a population, we need to know such things as the number of children born to each woman, the age of the mother at the time of the child's birth, and the total population of women eligible to give birth. In considering these population counts, we do not want to attribute births to males or to individuals who are either too young or too old to conceive, although we also need to make some assumptions, including that most births occur to women between the ages of 15 and 49. While births can (and do) happen to either younger or older women, these are a numerically small proportion of all births, and are not typically included in formal measures.

Data are therefore an important part of the population geographer's toolbox. Researchers often turn to large, publicly available data sources such as those collected by the US Census Bureau or other statistical agencies. These large surveys are typically representative of the total population, are geographically extensive, and include demographic, economic, and social data pertaining to a specific time on all persons in a country. Alternatively, researchers may conduct their own surveys and data collection. These are typically associated with more specialized research questions or geographic areas, may include a qualitative component, and capture information that may not be available in larger surveys.

Data can be divided into two main types: qualitative and quantitative. *Qualitative data* consists of nonnumerical information such as text, images, or verbal descriptions. Qualitative data may be obtained through case studies, open-ended interviews, focus groups, participant observation, or diary methods. *Quantitative data* is numerical and includes counts, rates, or scales reflecting experimental outcomes or data collected from questionnaires. Quantitative data provide information to which statistical analysis can be applied, including population projection methods such as the cohort component model, life tables from demography, and other multivariate methods including regression analysis. These methods commonly provide an indication of statistical significance and therefore either prove or disprove hypotheses.

METHODS

Methodology is also important, with methods often reflecting data sources and how data is collected. Both qualitative and quantitative data have different assumptions and reflect different theoretical approaches to the analysis and questions that are brought to bear on population issues. How population processes are defined and measured may alter the empirical measurement and the derived conclusions. How, for example, are the data operationalized and interpreted? What analytical methods are to be used?

Echoing the two broad types of data, *qualitative methods* are concerned with describing meaning rather than with drawing statistical inferences. While qualitative methods (e.g., case studies and interviews) lose generalizability and reliability, they provide greater depth of analysis along with typically rich descriptions of the process being studied. Qualitative analysis is aided by computer programs, including Nvivo (www.qsrinternational.com/). *Quantitative methods*, on the other hand, are those methods that focus on numbers and frequencies rather than on meaning and experience. Methods including descriptive, inferential, and multivariate statistical techniques such as regression analysis allow the researcher to understand and model the outcome of interest, and are aided by the many statistical packages that are available. Common packages include SAS (www.sas.com), STATA (www.stata.com), and SPSS (www.spss.com). Quantitative methods are associated with the scientific and experimental approach and are criticized for not providing an in-depth description. The use of large data files such as those generated by the US Census Bureau has often been accompanied by positivistic theoretical approaches, the goal of which is to verify (or falsify) empirical observations and to construct laws that can be generalized to a wide variety of models and theories.[1]

Population geographers also have at their disposal a series of other measures that can be used to describe population composition, fertility, mortality, and movement. For instance, the total fertility rate provides a numerical representation of the number of children born to a woman over her reproductive life, migration rates capture the propensity to move or likelihood of moving relative to some geographic area within a population, and mortality rates define death processes within a society. Such measures are defined in greater detail elsewhere in this book.

The wealth of data sources, including census products, has enabled population geographers and other social scientists to understand population trends and their spatial consequences. Their widespread use, and the use of related data files, is due in large part to their validity and the detail found in data sources such as the census.

At the same time, increasing emphasis has been placed on the use of qualitative methods within population geography.[2] The ongoing reliance on empirical analyses has led some researchers to charge that too much emphasis has been placed on empirical data, with the data influencing the choice of methods and approaches while missing or failing to give adequate attention to questions of theoretical development and relationships. In other words, research questions have been limited by and, in many cases, defined by the availability of data such as the census.[3]

PRESENTATION

Presentation of the data and final results is also important. While tabular or written (report) formats are common, the amount of data and its geographical nature means that maps are frequently used to easily and conveniently display information. The emergence and availability of mapping tools and geographic information systems (GIS) over the past two decades have enabled the storage, presentation, and analysis of large amounts of geographical data. The Methods, Measures, and Tools discussion in chapter 1 covers this material in greater depth.

Chapter One

World Population

HOW QUICKLY has the world's population grown? Where is it growing the fastest? How can we characterize world population growth and transitions from high to low mortality and fertility? What are the implications of population growth and what is the ultimate size of the world's population? Starting with a brief review of world population growth, these and other issues are explored in this chapter. The "Focus" section contrasts the current growth regimes in the United States, Germany, and India, and the "Methods, Measures, and Tools" sections explore the graphical presentation of population data and population projection techniques.

A BRIEF HISTORY OF WORLD POPULATION GROWTH

For much of humanity's history, world population was small and population growth was slow (see figure 1.1). Aided by food security, the shift from hunter-gatherer societies to agricultural-based societies (around 8000 BC and 5000 BC) allowed the population to grow, but the population was still probably only slightly more than 200 million around 1 AD. Still, high birthrates were offset

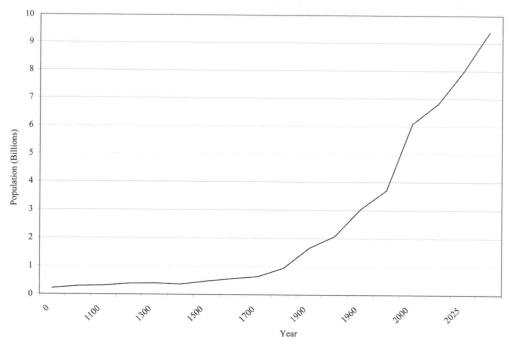

Figure 1.1.   World Population Growth

Source: US Census Bureau.

by high death rates from famine, war, and epidemics. It is estimated, for example, that the bubonic plague reduced the populations of Europe and China by one-third to one-half in the fourteenth century.[1] Even by 1600, the world's population was estimated to be only 500 million—not all that much larger than the population of the United States.[2]

Beginning in the mid-1600s, the world's population started to grow more rapidly as life expectancy slowly increased with improvements in commerce, food production and security, and nutrition, with the world's population reaching approximately one billion by 1800. The nineteenth century would, however, bring a surge in population growth, particularly in Europe. Coinciding with the Industrial Revolution, the population of Europe doubled between 1800 and 1900. Fueled by European immigration, North America's population multiplied by twelve in the same period.[3] The population of developing countries grew more slowly during this time, but they already held the bulk of the world's population. Advances in medicine and sanitation increased survival and life expectancies. By 1900, world population was approximately 1.7 billion, increasing to two billion by 1930. The mid-twentieth century saw unprecedented population growth, with the world's population reaching three billion by 1960 and four billion by 1974. The fifth billion was reached just twelve years later. By mid-2009, the total population was over 6.8 billion, and is projected to reach 7 billion by 2012.[4] Up-to-date world and US population figures can be found at www.census.gov/main/www/popclock.html.

Between 1960 and 1998, the world's population doubled from three to six billion. Demographers often refer to the amount of time it would take for a population to double in size, assuming that the growth rate remained constant into the future. A simple way to determine the doubling time is

$$DoublingTime = \ln 2/r$$

where ln 2 is the mathematical notation for the natural logarithm of 2 and r is the annual percentage growth rate, expressed as a decimal. So, given that Egypt is growing at 1.9 percent, it would take just 36 years for its population to double (from 78.6 million in 2009)! For the United States, the doubling period would be over 116 years, given its 2009 natural growth rate of 0.6 percent. This assumes, however, that the growth rate (r) remains unchanged by shifts in fertility and mortality over the period.

Regional Growth

The population growth patterns that we observe around the world are not the same. We can roughly divide the world into two broad regions, namely the developed world and the developing world. The developed world includes the United States, Canada, western Europe, Japan, and Australia, and the developing world can be roughly identified as all other countries. Most of the world's population growth originates in the developing world, which represents over 80 percent of the world's population and where 98 percent of the world's population growth is now occurring. Put in another perspective, over 121 million children were born in the developing world in 2008, compared to about 13.3 million in developed, industrialized countries.[5]

Even within the developing world, however, there are great differences in terms of population growth regimes. China, currently the world's most populous country, has a growth rate of just 0.5 percent, meaning that while its population continues to grow, it is growing at a much slower rate and could ultimately be faced with population decline. It is already grappling with issues of population aging because of its one-child policy, issues that are explored further in chapter 10. China also has an impressive impact on population statistics. For instance, if China is included in population statistics for the developing world, the fertility rate is just 2.7, compared to 3.1 when China is excluded. As a result, the Population Reference Bureau (PRB) regularly provides statistics that both include and exclude China.

As the world's second-largest country, India has a population growth rate of 1.6 percent and a fertility rate of 2.7, meaning that its population continues to expand rapidly, and it will soon overtake China as the world's most populous country. Elsewhere in the developing world, Africa, and in particular sub-Saharan Africa, has growth rates in excess of 2.5 percent, and fertility rates that exceed 5.0. In short, population growth rates remain high and long-term population growth is ensured. Population growth rates are much lower in Central America, South America, and the Caribbean, although fertility rates remain in excess of 2.1, so that the population continues to grow as well.

In most of the developed world, population growth rates are much lower. The natural growth rate in the United States is just 0.6 percent, and its fertility level hovers near replacement (2.1). Even this, however, is comparatively fast when compared to Japan and some of the western and Eastern European nations, where growth rates are much less. As a whole, Europe's growth rate was zero percent in 2009. In other words, its population was stable—neither growing nor declining. At the same time, several Eastern European countries, including Hungary, Romania, and Russia, had negative growth rates, while the population of western Europe, including France, barely managed to grow. Population decline brings with it multiple questions of state identity, political power, and economic growth that are further discussed later in this chapter.

Urban Growth

Accompanying the world's population explosion has been the explosion in the size and number of urban areas. As recently as 1975, only 33 percent of the world's population lived in urban areas, with most of these living in relatively small cities of less than one million.[6] In 2009, approximately 50 percent of the world's population lived in urban areas. While the developing world lags the developed world in the proportion urbanized (44 percent to 75 percent, respectively), the urban population in the developing world is expected to grow rapidly in the coming decades, with upwards of 61 percent of the world's population living in urban areas by 2030.[7] Placing urban growth in another perspective, the number of cities in the developing world with populations in excess of one million is expected to jump from 345 in 2000 to 480 by 2015. The number of megacities (cities with populations in excess of ten million) has also grown from 8 in 1985 to 20 in 2007, and the number of these superlarge cities is projected to grow to 22 by 2015. Most of these new megacities will be in the developing world, as it becomes home to an increasing proportion of the world's population, with their growth driven by natural increase,[8] net rural to urban migration, and urban reclassification.

THE DEMOGRAPHIC TRANSITION

The population explosion in Western countries during the 1800s marked the beginning of the shift from high to low mortality and high to low fertility, known to demographers as the demographic transition, and formalized by the demographic transition theory (DTT) (figure 1.2). The theory argues that prior to transition, birth and death rates are high, and largely cancel each other's effect, meaning that populations grow slowly. As a society develops and modernizes, death rates decline, but fertility remains high, corresponding to the period of rapid population growth. At the conclusion of the demographic transition, birth and death rates are again comparable, but at a much lower level than prior to transition, and population growth again stabilizes.

Within this theory, the most important determinants of population growth are the pretransition fertility rate and the time lag between the decline in mortality and fertility. That is, while fertility rates remain high and death rates are low, the population can grow quickly. The former captures how far fertility rates must fall, with high fertility reflecting a large demand for children in a society and with fertility reduction generally taking longer in high-fertility societies. The latter effect (the lag between mortality and fertility declines) captures the length of time over which rapid population growth can occur, with longer

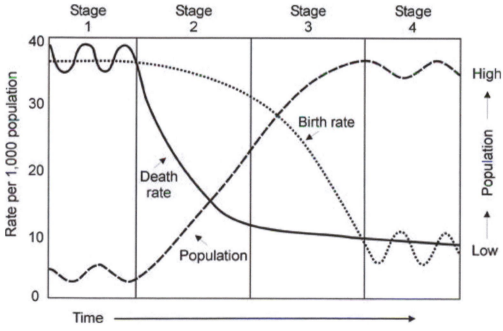

Figure 1.2   The Demographic Transition Theory.

Rapid population growth occurs when births exceed deaths (stages two and three), with total growth reflecting the length of time over which these two stages occur and the difference between the maximum birth and death rates (stage one) and the minimum rates (stage four).

Source: Author.

time periods translating to a longer time period over which the population can grow rapidly.

Although the concept of demographic transition can be roughly applied to all countries, with a decline in mortality rates followed by an eventual decline in fertility rates, the timing, pace, and triggers of the transition vary. Within the developed world, shifts in mortality and fertility occurred in the later parts of the nineteenth century and early twentieth centuries as the Industrial Revolution progressed and as major public health improvements led to declines in infant mortality rates and increased life expectancy. Fertility rates were somewhat slower to change since social and behavioral change defining the desired family size tend to be slower, but fell rapidly after 1900 as more children survived to adulthood, marriage patterns changed, women moved into paid work, and parents placed greater value on the education their children received. In the United States, the total fertility rate dropped from an average of four or five children in 1900 to approximately two children per woman by the 1930s. Canadian and European rates followed a similar pattern.

This demographic transition has generally not yet finished in the developing world, where rapid population growth continues. On the one hand, mortality rates in the developing world have generally fallen rapidly from the 1950s onward, particularly with the introduction of antibiotics, immunizations, and better medical care and nutrition. On the other hand, fertility rates largely remain above replacement level, and average approximately three children per woman in the developing world, with higher rates in sub-Saharan Africa. Even as mortality and fertility rates in the developed world stabilized and low and stable rates of population growth were realized, much of Africa, Asia, and Latin America were still experiencing relatively high mortality and fertility levels.

As countries in the developing world started their demographic transition, they frequently had higher levels of birth and death rates than those observed in developed countries a century earlier, with fertility rates in many countries continuing to average more than six children per woman. Fertility reduction in the developing world has also typically been slower than experienced in the developed world (i.e., the lag between the decline in mortality and fertility has been longer). Instead, it varied across countries, defined by differences in social, cultural, and religious expectations; literacy rates; female participation in the workforce; family and economic considerations; and the availability and acceptability of family-planning programs. Rates of natural increase (the birthrate minus the death rate, indicating the annual rate of population growth) remain high in much of the developing world.

Although the demographic transition theory has been widely applied, it has also been extensively criticized because of its Western-centric biases. It was, for all intents and purposes, validated on the demographic experiences of Europe and assumes that all other countries would progress similarly through its stages. In the developing world, the triggers for fertility reduction differ, including differential access to education and employment and differential roles for women within society. It is also relatively unable to account for myriad variations such as higher fertility levels, alternative forces associated with the decline in mortality, or social and cultural issues.[9]

FUTURE POPULATION SCENARIOS: WHO GAINS AND WHO LOSES?

At the dawn of the twenty-first century, there was some evidence that the developing world was finally transitioning from high to low fertility, evidenced by a 2009 total fertility rate (TFR) of 2.7 (3.1 if China is excluded), a rate that is considerably lower than that observed just a quarter of a century earlier.[10] With the expectation that fertility rates will continue to decline, some analysts have concluded that the risk of population growth has been greatly diminished.[11] Indeed, some authors have suggested that the new problem is a population *deficit* and an aging of the world's population,[12] and others have suggested that the threat of world population growth is now more regional than global and of consequence only in countries such as Pakistan and India where high fertility regimes remain.

While the world's population growth rate did peak in the 1960s and has declined since then, the global population is still rapidly expanding, evidenced by a global growth rate of 1.2 percent. In effect, to say that it is a regional problem allows the Western world to ignore the problem, but only at its peril. The current fertility rate in the developing world translates to a growth rate of 1.4 percent (1.7 percent excluding China). This allows the population in the developing world to double in approximately forty-nine years (assuming growth continues at its current rates) or forty years if China is excluded. Even as fertility rates have dropped in Asia, Latin America, and the Caribbean, they remain stubbornly high in the world's least developed countries, with a 2009 TFR of 4.6. In sub-Saharan Africa, the 2009 TFR was 5.3. Moreover, in countries where fertility rates have dropped quickly, the young age structure of the population will ensure growth for the next two to three decades. Put another way, a huge proportion of the world's population have not started having children. Instead, they *are* children. Consequently, a total world population of 8 billion by 2025 likely cannot be avoided, and most projections place world population between 7.3 and 10.7 billion by 2050, with nearly all of this growth occurring in the developing world (table 1.1). So, while population growth is indeed slowing, we must still feed, clothe, and shelter a growing population, a task that it is unclear whether the world can accomplish.

Table 1.1.   Current Population Statistics by Selected World Regions, 2009

	Population mid-2009 (millions)	Total fertility rate	Natural increase (annual, %)	Doubling time (years)	Projected population 2025 (millions)
World	6,810	2.6	1.2	58	8,087
North America	341	2.0	0.6	116	395
Central America	152	2.5	1.7	41	179
South America	386	2.2	1.3	53	443
Caribbean	41	2.5	1.2	58	46
Oceania	36	2.5	1.1	65	45
Northern Europe	99	1.9	0.3	231	109
Western Europe	189	1.6	0.1	693	192
Eastern Europe	295	1.5	-0.2	—	278
Southern Europe	155	1.4	0.1	693	157
Asia (excludes China)	2,786	2.7	1.5	46	3,382
Asia (includes China)	4,117	2.3	1.2	58	4,858
Western Asia	231	3.1	1.9	36	293
South Central Asia	1,726	2.8	1.7	41	2,148
Southeast Asia	597	2.5	1.4	50	712
East Asia	1,564	1.6	0.5	139	1,704
Sub-Saharan Africa	836	5.3	2.4	29	1,184
Northern Africa	205	3.0	1.9	36	257
Western Africa	297	5.5	2.7	26	420
Eastern Africa	313	5.4	2.6	27	455
Middle Africa	125	6.1	2.8	25	189
Southern Africa	58	2.8	0.9	77	63

(—) indicates data not available or applicable.

Source: Population Reference Bureau, *2009 World Population Data Sheet*.

While many developing countries in Asia still have above-replacement TFRs, China, South Korea, Taiwan, and Thailand have fertility levels lower than replacement. China is, in fact, an important exception to the generally high fertility rates of the developing world. With a population of 1,331 million in mid-2009 and an annual growth rate of 0.5 percent, China is the world's most populous country. Despite fertility levels that exceeded 7.0 recorded as recently as the 1950s, China's fertility rate has plunged to below replacement level (1.6), largely attributed to its one-child policy, which has artificially lowered fertility levels since its inception. India, too, has attempted fertility control policies, but has had much less success.[13] Although it has a smaller population (1,171 million), India is growing at a rate of 1.6 percent, meaning it will surpass China's population by the middle of the twenty-first century. In other parts of Asia, there has been little change in fertility in places such as Iraq and Pakistan. In

Africa, the transition to a lower fertility regime is still in progress. Total fertility rates still exceed 6.0 in countries including Mali, Uganda, Somalia, and Malawi, and there is little evidence that a downward shift in fertility is about to occur. Throughout much of Africa, infant mortality rates remain high (74 per 1,000), and life expectancies are short (fifty-five years). In contrast, most developed countries are experiencing slow growth or even population decline, long life expectancies, and low infant mortality rates.

At a very general scale, the developed world is largely characterized by relatively slow rates of population growth, low fertility levels, and controlled immigration. With a current growth rate of 0.2 percent per year, it will take approximately three hundred and fifty years to double the current population, assuming a constant rate of natural increase. Some countries in Europe, and especially Eastern Europe, are experiencing negative population growth rates, meaning that their populations are declining. For example, the Population Reference Bureau projects Latvia's current population of 2.3 million to decline to 1.9 million by 2050, attributed to extremely low fertility levels. Germany's population, currently 82 million, is projected to decline to 71.4 million by 2050.

What do these population trends mean and what are their implications? We will briefly explore issues related to overall population growth. While many are expanded in later chapters, their discussion contextualizes world population growth. For instance, high fertility in much of the developing world ensures population growth, while low fertility in the developing world points to population decline. Urban growth, population aging, and immigration also spill out of these broader trends.

Continued Population Growth

The current distribution of the world's population (figure 1.3), coupled with high fertility in much of the developing world, means that the global population will continue to grow into the near future before leveling off between 7.3 and 10.7 billion later this century, despite falling fertility rates and slowing population growth rates since the 1960s. Rapid population growth in the second half of the twentieth century has meant that the share of the world's population residing in the developing world climbed from 68 to 82 percent. According to United Nations projections, the percentage residing in the developing world will grow to 86 percent by 2050.

The certainty of continued global population growth is grounded in three assumptions. First, improvements in life expectancy (reduced mortality) will contribute to population growth, as individuals survive longer. Longer life expectancies increase a child's likelihood of surviving infancy and childhood and completing his or her reproductive years. Second, the age structure of a

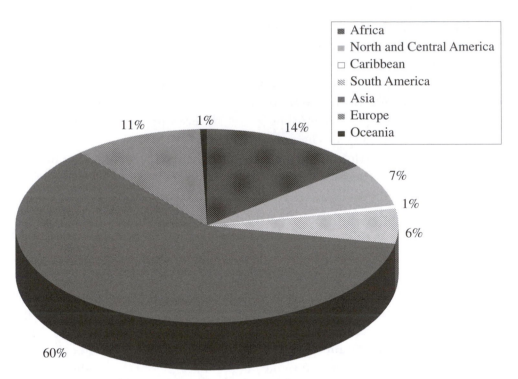

- Africa
- North and Central America
- Caribbean
- South America
- Asia
- Europe
- Oceania

11%   1%   14%

7%

1%

6%

60%

Figure 1.3   World Population Distribution by Major Region, 2009.
Data derived from 2008 *World Population Data Sheet* (Washington, DC: Population Reference Bureau, 2009).

Source: Author.

Table 1.2.   The Ten Most Populous Countries in the World, 2009 and 2050 (Projected)

	2009		2050	
Country	Population (millions)	Country	Population (millions)
China	1,331	India	1,748
India	1,171	China	1,437
United States	307	United States	439
Indonesia	243	Indonesia	343
Brazil	192	Pakistan	335
Pakistan	181	Bangladesh	223
Bangladesh	162	Nigeria	285
Nigeria	153	Brazil	215
Russia	142	Congo (Kinshasa)	189
Japan	128	Ethiopia	150

Source: Population Reference Bureau, *2009 World Population Data Sheet.*

population is key to the expected future growth, with populations having a greater number of individuals in their childbearing years tending to grow faster irrespective of the fertility rate. Women may have fewer children than in the past, but there are more women having children. Excluding China, which has seen a shift in its age structure associated with its one-child policy, 33 percent of the population in the developing world is less than fifteen years old. In sub-Saharan Africa, 43 percent of the population is aged less than fifteen years. The young age profile of the developing world means that this population still has to enter its reproductive years. Even if fertility rates decline, population momentum will ensure sustained population growth. In comparison, only 17 percent of the population in the developed world is less than fifteen years old, a proportion that continues to decline.

Third, most demographers expect that fertility rates will eventually decline below replacement, ending the population explosion. Yet, fertility rates continue to remain above replacement in many regions of the world. Declines have been noted, but it is unknown whether further declines in fertility can be expected, with recent surveys in both Bangladesh and Egypt pointing to the danger in assuming that fertility will drop below the level needed to replace the population. Despite early successes in reducing fertility in Bangladesh, with fertility rates dropping from over six children per woman in the early 1970s, fertility rates have remained relatively unchanged since the 1990s. Similarly, Egypt's birthrate has remained equal to or greater than 3.0 since 1993. This trend is far from isolated, with Argentina's birthrate remaining at about 3 children for nearly fifty years, although by 2009 it had fallen to 2.4.[14]

A look at worldwide demographic data quickly highlights the fact that differential population growth regimes are occurring around the world. The combined impact of slowing population growth or decline in some countries and continued growth in others leads to issues associated with population aging and immigration, discussed below.

Population Aging and Decline

It is rather paradoxical that while we talk of continued population growth at the global scale, we also observe population decline in some regions or countries where population aging and fertility decline have emerged as new issues.[15] Globally, the proportion of the population over sixty-five has grown from 5 percent in 1950 to 8 percent in 2009. While seemingly a small change, it is in many ways the tip of the iceberg. By 2050, for example, the Population Reference Bureau expects that approximately 18 percent of Asia's population will be sixty-five or older. In large part, this is driven by China, where its one-child policies have resulted in a dramatic aging of the population, so much so that there was renewed discussion in 2008 of further relaxing its fertility policies.

Likewise, 19 percent of Latin America's population is expected to be aged sixty-five or greater by 2050.

In much of the developed world, population aging is further advanced. Japan as well as much of Europe already have some of the highest proportions of older populations (aged sixty-five-plus). In 2009, Japan's older population share was 23 percent, amongst the highest in the world. The United States, Canada, Australia, and New Zealand are not far behind, as their baby boomers age into retirement and fertility rates remain low. At the same time, numerous countries were already experiencing negative rates of natural increase, including Estonia, Latvia, Germany, Hungary, Russia, and Ukraine. Countries such as Japan and Canada had growth rates that were near zero and were experiencing slowing population growth.

Consequently, population *deficits*, and the economic and social consequences of these, have increasingly emerged as an important issue for some developed countries, with commentators openly worried about the consequences of aging populations and declining population growth.[16] In particular, while it is unclear what impacts aging societies will have, most commentators assume negative consequences, including declining national and international political influence, loss of national identity, altered political agendas that favor older populations at the expense of younger cohorts, slower economic growth, and increasing demands on health and social welfare programs at the same time that the labor force and economically active population is shrinking. Concurrently, countries have looked to policies to actively promote population growth through increased fertility and/or increased immigration.

Immigration

Human populations have been inherently mobile throughout history. In 2005, the PRB estimated that there were 191 million international migrants, meaning that 3 percent of the world's people had left their country of birth or citizenship for a year or more. For the developed world, the number of international migrants stood at 120 million, while approximately 61 million migrants moved within the developing world.[17] Most of these migrations are closely linked to economic opportunities and are encouraged by globalization, which has linked economies and employment around the world, encouraging the use of low-skilled and low-cost workers worldwide. While most countries now attempt to control entry through various pieces of legislation, immigration remains a potentially large source of population change. For developed countries such as Canada and the United States, most immigrants arrive from the developing world, and immigration policies are typically structured to attract "the best and the brightest" immigrants. While benefiting the receiving country, such policies have been criticized because they skim talented individuals from developing-world countries that need them.

The international movement of people has raised concerns within many countries. While not denying past immigration policies that were openly racist and exclusionary, both the United States and Canada have historically been receptive to immigration. In the United States, this history may be in danger, illustrated by the fear of demographic "Balkanization," welfare reform, and the tightening of immigration and refugee policies in a post-9/11 world. Anti-immigrant sentiments are especially visible in Europe, coloring national political debates and economic opportunities. European countries have only recently shifted from being labor exporters to importers of labor, a shift that is difficult to digest. Yet, the demographic realities of low fertility and an aging population mean that European countries are faced with a crisis in their labor force. Increased immigration may be the only option for meeting employment requirements, but it remains an option that carries significant political, social, and cultural problems, since most Europeans continue to associate the foreign-born with unskilled work and unemployment. Most likely, Europe will ultimately need to address its new role as a receiver of immigrants. In addition, both North America and Europe are grappling with illegal immigration, imposing burdens upon local service providers at the same time that illegal immigrants sustain the economy by working for low pay and in positions or conditions that few others are willing to tolerate.

Most governments in the developed world have moved to control immigration, limiting the type of immigrant (i.e., family reunification and economic), origin, and overall number allowed entry over any given year. Despite their efforts through both legislation as well as active enforcement of borders, most countries have found it increasingly difficult to control the entry of immigrants, creating an immigration crisis reflected in what has been described as the "gap" between immigration control policies and their outcomes. The emerging reality is that governments are less able to control immigration now than in the past. Globalization and the increasing flow of labor and capital, the emergence of civil rights and liberalism, and the domestic need for inexpensive labor, which legitimized immigration flows, have contributed to this inability to control both illegal and legal migration flows.

Immigration is also a significant source of labor in the developing world. Laborers from countries such as Indonesia, India, and Pakistan are, for example, attracted to Persian Gulf states for work in the construction and oil industries. These migrants become an important source of income for their families through the money sent back home, which is then invested in new housing or other goods. This money, or remittances, has become an important source of income for families and countries alike.[18] Typically, movement is into a richer developing country for temporary work. Although entry is often unregulated, states in the developing world are increasingly moving to tighten their own entry requirements. Another source of population change is the movement of refugees across international borders.

CONCLUSION

The current rapid pace of world population growth reflects comparatively low mortality levels, fertility rates that remain high in much of the developing world, and the impact of a young population that remains in its childbearing years. The end result is that the world's population will continue to grow for the foreseeable future. While we may be content in this realization, it is only the beginning of our discussion. Why, for instance, are fertility rates relatively slow to decline, while mortality rates declined early and rapidly? What is the outlook for mortality, particularly in the face of HIV/AIDS? How does immigration shift populations from country to country or within countries? What does population growth mean for the development and growth of urban areas and the potential for conflict? These, and other related issues, are explored more fully in the following pages.

FOCUS: POPULATION GROWTH REGIMES IN INDIA, GERMANY, AND THE UNITED STATES

It is easy to recognize that different regions, and indeed different countries, face alternate population growth regimes, with some growing rapidly while others are in decline. We focus here on three different countries: India, a rapidly growing country; Germany, a country faced with population decline; and the United States, a country that is experiencing modest population growth but that has also completed the demographic transition (see table 1F.1).

Like other countries in the developing world, India's population growth exploded in the twentieth century. Between 1900 and 2000, its population grew fourfold, from approximately 238 million to one billion.[1] With a 2009 population of 1,171 million, India's population is growing at a rate of 1.6 percent per year, adding some 18 million to its population each year.[2] Fueled by high total fertility (2.7), a relatively young population (32 percent are aged fifteen years or less), and increasing life expectancies, its population is expected to grow to 1,755 million by 2050, surpassing China's population by 2030. On its own, the country's young age structure will ensure that its population continues to grow due to demographic momentum, given that so many women have yet to enter their childbearing ages. Fertility decline since the 1960s has slowed population growth in India, but there are wide dis-

Table 1F.1.   Population Growth in India, Germany, and the United States

| | Population 2009 (millions) | Growth rate (%) | Total fertility rate | Projected population (millions) | | Projected population change (%) | Percent of population aged | |
				2025	2050	2007–2050	<15	>65
India	1171.0	1.6	2.7	1407.7	1755.2	53	32	5
Germany	82.0	− 0.2	1.3	79.6	71.4	− 13	14	20
United States	306.8	0.6	2.1	355.7	438.2	44	20	13

Source: Derived from Population Reference Bureau (PRB), *2009 World Population Data Sheet,* www.prb.org.

parities in birth rates between the northern and southern states, with northern states characterized by high birth rates (approximately four children), and the southern states, where, additionally, life expectancy is greater. Fertility is also higher and life expectancy lower in rural rather than urban areas.[3]

Germany presents almost the mirror image to India, having completed its demographic transition. With a much smaller (2009) population of 82 million, its growth rate is -0.2 percent, such that its population is in decline. By 2050, its population is expected to have shrunk to 71.4 million, or a decrease of approximately 13 percent. This population decline is exacerbated by limited immigration and a low total fertility rate (1.3), meaning neither immigration nor natural increase are sources of population growth. Germany's changing population structure also means that its population is rapidly aging, with 20 percent already aged sixty-five and over, with this proportion expected to grow as its population continues to age. In contrast, just 14 percent of its population is less than fifteen years, and the youngest generation (aged zero to four) is half the size of the forty to forty-four year age group.[4] Its age and population structure are similar to those of other western and Eastern European countries, where debates over population trends and policies have focused on increasing immigration levels or increased fertility.[5] Immigration provides a short-term solution, although Germany does not see itself as a destination for immigrants, with some fearing the erosion of culture and nationality, reflecting both Germany's history and experiences with the guest worker program, which imported workers for German factories.[6] Changes to fertility rates, however, are much more difficult to encourage.[7]

While the United States has also completed its demographic transition, population growth has been comparatively rapid relative to other developed countries: its population was just 100 million in 1915, with the next hundred million added by 1967, and 300 million in 2006. As of 2009, its population was 306.8 million, and it is expected to grow to 438.2 million by 2050. Its population growth can be partially attributed to high immigration levels, with approximately one million new arrivals each year. In addition, fertility remains relatively high and approximately equal to the replacement level (2.1). In fact, the fertility rates of ethnic minorities and the foreign-born population—especially Hispanic immigrants—in the United States tends to be somewhat higher than that of the native-born population, pushing the national average rate upward.[8] Fertility rates amongst Hispanics, for instance, were 3.2, compared to 1.9 amongst non-Hispanic whites.[9] Even amongst whites, this is a relatively high fertility rate in comparison to fertility rates observed in other developed countries. While foreign-born Hispanics have higher fertility rates than their native-born counterparts, immigrant fertility rates have been found to decrease sharply in the second generation, related to improved education and income.[10] Although the aging baby boom population is increasing the proportional share of those aged sixty-five and over, this group still only represented 13 percent of the population in 2009, a comparatively low share relative to other countries in the developed world.

Population geographers are frequently faced with a large volume of data that must be presented. What is the best way to portray population statistics? One of the clearest ways to display population information is through mapping, largely because of maps' visual impact and their ability to easily communicate information, along with identifying and illustrating spatial patterns. Maps are used in multiple ways, including in public health (i.e., disease surveillance), transportation (i.e., optimal vehicle routing or analysis of pollution along major arteries), site locations for stores and services, disaster planning, and so on. In many cases, maps are used to highlight the presence of a spatial relationship that can then be explored further through modeling and other techniques.

MAP TYPES

Population *dot maps* provide a simple way to graphically represent the distribution of a population. The basic idea of this sort of map is straightforward: a dot is used to symbolize the location of a person (or group of people or other object) of interest. An early use of this sort of map is John Snow's mapping of London's cholera epidemic around the Broad Street pump in 1854.[1] Snow mapped the locations of the homes of those who died during the outbreak, observing that the majority of cases were located close to the pump, which acted as the contaminant source and was ultimately closed. Dot density maps are most useful for showing where particular data occur. However, caution should be exercised as the dot location does not always indicate the precise location of the data of interest. Instead, they often represent data occurring within a geographical area such as a census tract, zone improvement plan (zip) code, or county.

Choropleth maps, whereby regions are shaded corresponding to the value of interest, provide an alternative representation and are frequently part of the geographer's toolbox. While commonly used, choropleth maps can be misleading due to the artificial boundaries, such as borders between census tracts or counties, that are used to define the map. The fixed geography of these imposed boundaries creates an artificial order on the data. In addition, differences in the size of units in the map can lead to visual distortion. Moreover, choice of class interval (i.e., standard deviation, percentiles, equal interval) (figure 1MMT.1) and/or changing the spatial scale of the map, while still mapping the same phenomenon, can lead to different interpretations (the so-called modifiable areal unit problem, see introduction).

Cartograms are maps where the area is not preserved (figure 1MMT.2). Instead, regions are reproportioned relative to the magnitude of the data displayed (as opposed to their true physical size). For example, population size may be substituted for regional area, distorting the area of the map to convey the information.[2] Finally, population geographers have also consistently made use of *flow maps*, particularly to represent migration streams (flows) from one region to another.[3] Other uses include transportation flows, information exchange, and disease transmission. By changing the width of the lines, flow maps can be used to portray differences in the size of the flow, and directions of the flow are represented with arrows.

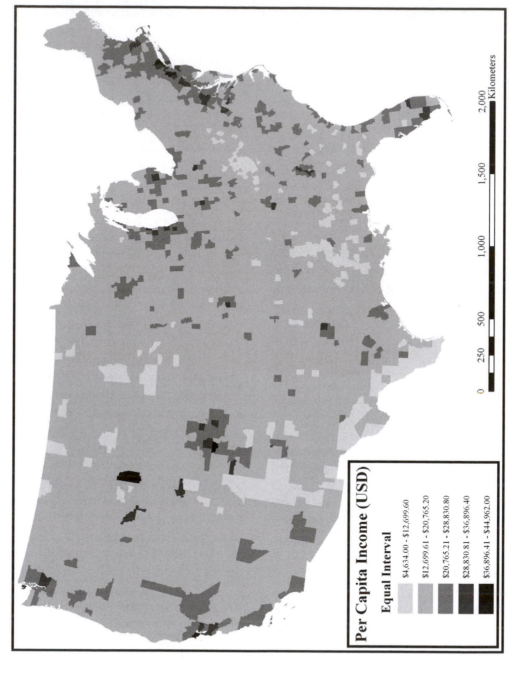

Figure 1MMT.1a

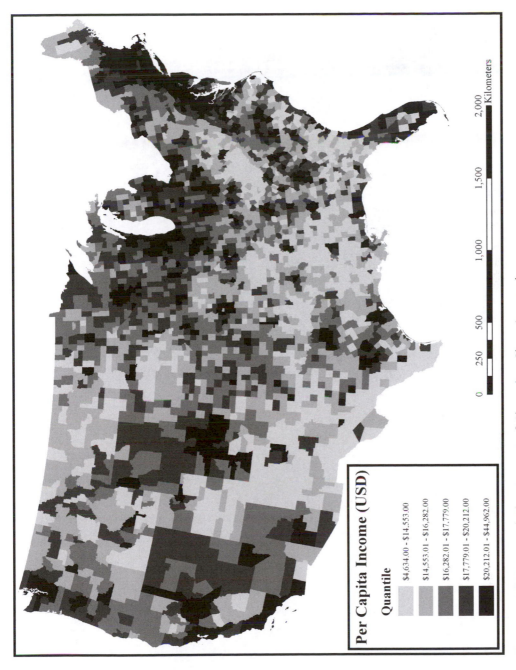

Per Capita Income (USD)

Quantile

- $4,634.00 - $14,553.00
- $14,553.01 - $16,282.00
- $16,282.01 - $17,779.00
- $17,779.01 - $20,212.00
- $20,212.01 - $44,962.00

0   250   500   1,000   1,500   2,000
Kilometers

Figures 1MMT.1a and 1b   Impact of Changing Class Interval.

These two maps show the impact of changing class intervals in a map projection. Both maps illustrate income by county (1999), with the first using class intervals based on equal intervals and the second based on quintiles.

Source: Author.

Figure 1MMT.2   Total Population as a Cartogram.

The size of each territory shows the relative proportion of the world's population living there.

Source: Copyright 2006, Social and Spatial Inequalities (SASI) Research Group (University of Sheffield) and Mark Newman (University of Michigan), www.worldmapper.org/copyright.html. Used with permission.

GIS AND MAPPING

Data display, storage, management, and manipulation have been assisted with the increasing availability of geographic information systems (GIS) over the past decade. Using digital maps and geographic information, GIS systems provide the capability to store, retrieve, display, and analyze geographic data. Most mapping and GIS packages, such as MapInfo and ESRI's popular Arc series of programs, provide the user with the quick and relatively automated ability to create and analyze maps. However, the caveat of "garbage in—garbage out" remains, as users must still consider how best to represent the data and which data to present. Changing the nature of the data to be presented, for example by replacing absolute population counts with proportional representation or a population rate, may alter the final product and its interpretation. Similarly, the seemingly mundane choice of color and data categories can result in misleading maps.[4] In addition, the imposition of boundaries between mapped units and variation in the size of the spatial units tends to create a somewhat artificial pattern. Indeed, there is a large geographical literature on the best way to represent data in graphical and map form.[5]

As an alternate to mapping, spatial analytical techniques such as kernel estimation, spatial moving averages, or kriging provide options for a smoother representation of the data that gets around issues associated with borders. Rather than limiting data representation to specific boundaries (such as census tracts or counties), which can result in a biased interpretation since it frequently appears that the value of interest suddenly changes at the boundary, these methods typically work by essentially averaging data over some defined geographic area, and can be found in many popular GIS and mapping programs, as well as more specialized spatial analysis programs such as R, S-Plus, CrimeStat, and GeoDa.[6] These programs are also able to perform more complex analyses that enable understanding and modeling of underlying geographical trends and testing for the presence of autocorrelation, or geographical correlation over space.

METHODS, MEASURES, AND TOOLS: POPULATION ESTIMATES AND PROJECTIONS

Population geographers and demographers are frequently called upon to provide population estimates or projections.[1] Although these two terms are frequently used interchangeably, they differ in important ways. For instance, a *population estimate* is a calculation of the size of a population for a year between census periods or for the current year. Estimates are frequently based on existing census numbers; components of population change such as migration, fertility, and mortality; and other information that reflects changes in population, which may be derived from employment information, postal location, or tax records. *Population projections* are calculations of population size for a future point in time.[2] Information on past, present, and future population size can be used to project the population. In both cases, the accuracy of estimation and projection tools is based on the rules and assumptions of the methods used.

POPULATION ESTIMATES

We can consider the estimation of a population between census periods, using the following

$$P_{t+x} = P_t + B_{t,t+x} - D_{t,t+x} + M_{t,t+x}$$

where P_{t+x} is the population to be estimated at time $t + x$, P_t is the beginning period population, $B_{t, t+x}$ is the number of births between t and $t + x$, D is the number of deaths, and M is population change due to migration (international migration and domestic migration if the projection is for a subnational scale) over the same period. In effect, this equation is simply a "residual method" seen elsewhere in this text—the difference in population size over a period of time reflects the demographic processes that occur. However, not all of this information may be available, and estimates may be required. For instance, as most governments do not collect emigration statistics, net international migration (total immigration minus total emigration) would not be available, and estimates of emigration would be required.

Alternatively, midyear population estimates may be made as a simple average between two known years

$$P_e = P_1 + \frac{n}{N} (P_2 - P_1)$$

where P_e is the estimated population size; P_1 and P_2 are the known beginning-of-period and end-of-period population sizes, respectively; n is the number of months from the P_1 census to the date of the estimate; and N is the number of months between the P_1 and P_2 censuses. This method assumes constant (linear) growth between the two census periods, and provided that the period between the two census intervals is relatively small, yields an acceptable population estimate.

A third technique is to apply a known (or estimated) rate of population growth to a population, such that

$$P_e = P_2 - r [(P_2 - P_1)/t]$$

where t represents the number of years between the censuses and r is the population growth rate, defined as follows (where ln refers to the natural logarithm).

$$r = [\ln(P_2 / P_1)] / t$$

While relatively simple, these methods are also problematic in their inherent assumption of linear population change. In fact, the assumption that population change is smooth is not supported within the literature, given that population mobility has frequently been tied to both short-term and long-term economic events. Moreover, the reliability of such estimates decreases (1) at smaller geographic scales, either because of less reliable data or because they are more subject to short-term shifts in population and (2) with longer periods between censuses.

POPULATION PROJECTIONS

Population projections use past and current census information to project future population size. Projections can be as simple as an extrapolation of current population trends into the future. That is, for example, if we know the population for several past census periods, we can roughly fit a line into the future to project the population. A similar approach is to assume that the current population growth rate can be applied to project the population forward, as follows.

$$P_{t+10} = P_1 + rP_1$$

It should be noted that the above equation assumes that the growth rate, r, is based on a ten-year period (i.e., $n = 10$), with the resulting projection ten years into the future. The projection period can be adjusted to fit other time frames. Nonlinear growth (i.e., exponential, where the population curves upward over time) can also be considered, such as follows.

$$P_{t+10} = P_1 (1+r)^n$$

A related projection technique is to use regression analysis. The advantage of this method is that multiple historical census figures can be used in the analysis, and the analyst can also pursue nonlinear representations of population growth.

While these methods may provide a useful and "rough-and-ready" short-term projection, they do not reference population processes, and are therefore subject to the same problems as discussed with population estimates, namely that the growth rate, r, is valid into the future.

Oftentimes, these methods are used to project populations for some total population, such as a country or state. They can also be applied to multiple subpopulations, which raise an interesting accounting issue. Suppose, for instance, that you have been requested to project the future populations of each state and that you know the overall national population. However, addition of each state population to find the national population would more than likely yield a national estimate that was different from the known estimate, meaning that the estimated state populations would need to be rescaled. This can be done through, for example, apportionment. In this case, the projected state populations can be multiplied by the known (current) state share of population. This is, however, a largely unsatisfactory measure, as it assumes that the proportional distribution of the population does not change over time.

Overall, these simple projection tools require limited information, yet can assist in projecting the total population of a region. They do, however, come with drawbacks. First, they do not distinguish the components of population change, such as fertility, mortality, and migration, separately. Second, information about the age and gender structure of a population is frequently required, and these tools generally do not provide this level of detail. Third, the methods presented above assume that past trends will continue into the future, although short-term and long-term changes to the economy and changing personal preferences can influence future population structures.

COHORT COMPONENT MODELS

As a partial response to the criticisms of the above projection methods, we can turn to cohort component models. These models typically allow age-sex disaggregation of the population, along with the consistent estimation of regional populations and the total population. Two principal concepts underlie the cohort component method. First, the population is typically divided into age and sex cohorts of like individuals. Second, the models focus upon components of change, with the population of each cohort subjected to fertility, mortality, and migration processes that advance the population and change its structure.

Assuming first a single-region cohort component model with no migration, the model can be defined using matrix notation as

$$p(t + n) = G^n p(t)$$

where p(t) is a column vector of a age-sex groups within the population at time t, p($t + n$) is the projected population at time $t + n$, and G is a "growth" matrix containing birth rates and survival probabilities obtained from vital statistics. Note that birth rates are associated only with the child-bearing age groups, and all rates are assumed to remain constant throughout the projection. Multiplication of G by p(t) projects the population forward in time, thus "aging" and "surviving" a population over time via extrapolation.

Multiregional cohort projection models use the cohort survival concept to age individuals from one age group to the next while extending the basic model by introducing interregional migration. In a two-region system, for example, each region is linked to each other via migration flows, such that out-migration from one region defines in-migration to the other. Like basic cohort projection models, multiregional population projection models typically involve determining the starting age-region distribution and age-specific regional schedules of mortality, fertility, and migration to which the multiregional population has been subjected to during the past period. Based upon the initial population, the projection procedure is identical to that described above, with fertility, mortality, and migration rates applied to the initial population and projected into the future.

While the matrix equation remains unchanged from that presented above, each of the matrices become increasingly complex as additional regions are added. For instance, population is subdivided into age groups, with each age group further subdivided by region. The structure of the growth matrix is also altered so that the age and location of individuals can be simultaneously modeled. As in the single-region model, the growth matrix is assumed to remain constant throughout the projection period. Commonly, the length of the projection period is equated with the width of the age group. That is, if the migration interval is five years (the interval used in the US, Canadian, and Australian censuses), the age group is defined by an interval of five years, as is the projection period. Therefore, the present number of ten- to fourteen-year-olds who are subjected to the appropriate rates defines the expected number of fifteen- to nineteen-year-olds in a population five years from now. Repeated multiplication of the matrix equation projects the population further into the future, so that projecting the population fifteen years into the future ($n = 3$) may be written as follows.

$$p(t + 5n) = G^3 p(t)$$

While these models are useful short-term projection devices, projections associated with longer time horizons are questionable given the assumptions inherent within the models. Most models assume, for instance, that (1) the probability of movement between regions does not change over time; (2) the population is homogeneous, with each individual governed by the same set of probabilities; (3) the probabilities apply to a fixed time; and (4) the *Markov property* holds, which assumes that the probability of migrating between two areas is dependent only upon the current location.

Clearly, most of these assumptions are unrealistic. First, the stationarity of migration rates over the life of the projection is unlikely, given that different groups (i.e., blacks and whites, immigrants and the native-born) will have differential migration probabilities. Moreover, migration probabilities should reflect shifting economic opportunities or amenities and the general aging of the population. Second, the Markov property assumes that the probability of migration is dependent only upon the current location. In other words, previous locations and behavior do not influence current migration decisions. While simplifying the modeling task, the Markov assumption is problematic given the high mobility of most individuals. The return migration literature,[3] for example, is well documented, with returns to a "home" region invoking the importance of prior migration experiences. Despite these problems, long-term projections utilizing this method offer insight as to where the population is headed, *if* present demographic rates are to hold over the longer term.

Chapter Two

Population Data

D ATA IS THE CORNERSTONE of demographic and population analyses. The existence of high-quality, publicly released data files enables much of this research, with the use of such data often accompanied by theoretical approaches commonly grounded in positivistic science, the goal of which is to verify (or falsify) empirical observations and to construct laws that can be generalized to a wide variety of models and theories. However, their use can also be problematic. In part, such data files are often considered incomplete. For example, they often miss details and the motivations for migration, immigration, and assimilation and instead rely upon empirically quantifiable notions of movement, acculturation, and statistical inference. Even the immigrant population is typically broadly defined and fails to distinguish between legal immigrants, illegal entrants, and refugees. Likewise, few data files detail the motivations for fertility choice. Perhaps not surprisingly, questions have arisen over the continued use of public data files and positivistic methods as a primary insight into population questions at the personal and societal levels.

Data differs in its content (what variables or constructs are included in the data), quality (how representative is it of the population), timeliness (what time period does it cover, or how related is it to specific events), coverage (geographic area) and availability (can the analyst access the data?). Given that each of these are important issues that can affect the analysis and interpretation of the data, it is useful to spend some time discussing alternate data sources. This chapter presents and discusses different types of data. It begins by differentiating between populations and samples before discussing both qualitative and quantitative data, their sources, issues of data quality, and the benefits and costs of each type of data. The "Focus" section examines the US census and the American Community Survey (ACS), and the "Methods, Measures, and Tools" section discusses working with data.

WHAT IS A POPULATION?

Before going too far, we should define what we mean by population, as it is a word that can be used to describe various concepts, with a biologist's definition differing from that of a population geographer, by whom it is usually used to define a group of people. So far in this text, the concept has been generally used to describe the population of the world, a country, a city, or some other geographic unit. A population could equally represent people in a class at school, the population of juniors on campus, or the entire campus population. Regardless, each population has some boundary that defines who is included in the population (and equally important, who is excluded from it) and/or a common, shared characteristic (i.e., students in the class), so that the definition may be as precise as possible by either including or excluding individuals from the population. If, for example, our population is that of New York, we also need to specify what we mean by "New York." Without a geographical reference, answers that include the state, New York City, or the New York metropolitan area would be equally correct, yet each gives a very different answer. We must also consider the time period we are looking at. Are we, for instance, interested in the population of New York in 1900 or 2000, or somewhere between these two dates? The inclusion of time in the definition can make population a dynamic or changing concept.

While the intent is to carefully define what we mean by population, it is often difficult or impractical to work with a complete population, particularly if we are dealing with something as large as the population of a country. The numbers may be too large, the logistics too great, or the price tag too outrageous to count everyone on our own. Imagine, for instance, trying to count everyone in New York or another metropolitan area, and to also get them to answer questions on age, marital status, family size, education, mobility, and so on at the same time! The US Census Bureau does this every ten years with its decennial census (see "Focus"), but it is a huge, massive, and costly undertaking.[1] The 2010 census, for example, is estimated to cost over $14 billion, or about $16 per person, making it the most expensive census ever![2] As an alternative, population geographers will frequently use *samples* to represent the population.

Samples may be representative of the population, such as the American Community Survey or the Public Use Microdata Sample (PUMS), which is a 1 or 5 percent sample of the population based on the census. Samples such as these accurately reflect the structure and composition (age, gender, income, education, etc.) of a population and can be inflated with the use of sample weights to yield the actual population size for a specific geography. Samples may also be non-representative or purposive in nature, such that the researcher includes individuals of particular interest, such as new immigrants, older migrants, or women from a particular ethnic group. In such cases, results cannot be generalized or transferred to a larger population, as they are often specific to the group that is studied,[3] but fill the particular role needed by the researcher.

TYPES OF DATA

Generally speaking, there are two broad classes of data. Primary data refers to data that is collected by the researcher. It is usually collected one time only, is likely confined to a particular geographical area, and is typically a relatively small sample reflecting a particular problem or issue. While primary data can be costly and time-consuming for the researcher to collect and produce, it is usually flexible in that the researcher can define the questions and content of the survey along with the sampling frame—or how individuals are selected—to suit the particular needs or research questions.

Secondary data reflect data that have been collected by an organization, government body, or someone else using predefined questions, sampling frame, and geographic area. This data has also been typically checked, verified, and "cleaned," so that it is ready for public use. Advantages of such data sets are their (often) national representation and the detailed, robust sampling methodology that is used to construct the sample, so that data users can be assured of the representativeness of the sample: that it accurately represents the population it is based on. Sources of secondary data include, but are not limited to, formal statistical agencies such as the US Census Bureau, Bureau of Labor Statistics, or other national or international statistical agencies, with statistical agencies such as Statistics Canada or the US Census Bureau offering a number of different data sources, including censuses, labor force surveys, and health surveys. In the United States, data files include the Census and Current Population Survey (CPS) and longitudinal files such as the Population Survey of Income Dynamics (PSID), the National Longitudinal Survey of Youth (NLSY), and the ACS, which has replaced the decennial census "long form."

Both primary and secondary data sources can include qualitative and quantitative data. Qualitative data consists of nonnumerical information and may be obtained through case studies, open-ended interviews, focus groups, participant observation, or diary methods. Participants may, for example, be asked for an oral history of their moves, including the reasons for moving and their destination choice and other related questions. Typically, these oral histories provide a rich understanding of the process in question but are also limited in terms of their ability to generalize findings beyond the sample or context of the analysis, given that they are often based on a small sample size. In contrast, quantitative data is numerical and includes counts, such as the number of people by age and gender in a specific area, measures of their educational attainment, place of residence and mobility data, and other socioeconomic or sociodemographic details. From these, rates, proportions, and other measures can be generated through statistical means to describe the population of interest.

DATA SOURCES

Geographers are often interested in such things as population structure and composition, transportation, population-environment issues, and population health. To understand, comment on, and offer solutions to these problems means that appropriate data is important. Where can population geographers turn to find the data and how "good" must data be to answer these questions? We can consider five main data sources: censuses, representative sample surveys, vital/civil registrations, indirect sources, and primary data that are collected by the analysts themselves.[4]

Census Data

The census—defined as the collection of demographic, economic, and social data pertaining to a particular time and country—is perhaps one of the best known and most used sources of population data. Counting or enumerating every individual in a population, the census offers a "snapshot" of a population at a particular time. In counting people, most censuses allocate them to their usual place of residence. These so-called de jure censuses differ from de facto censuses, which allocate people to their location at the time of enumeration. That is, if a person who works in Chicago, Illinois, but lives in Gary, Indiana were enumerated at work, they would be allocated to Chicago based on the de facto method but Gary based on the de jure method. De jure censuses are preferred as they provide a better indication of the permanent population in an area. In most cases, basic demographic and social characteristics of each person are also collected, including age, gender, marital status, household structure, educational attainment, and income. In addition, other household

characteristics may be collected, such as type of dwelling, occupation, and ethnic origin of respondents. In most cases, people are counted at their usual place
of residence.

The widespread use of census data and other public data is due in large
part to their validity and the degree of geographic, social, and economic detail
embedded in the files (figure 2.1). Moreover, the growth of data has corresponded to increasing computational abilities and a refinement and broadening
of the analytical tools used within population research, including the ability to
test hypotheses through inferential techniques and gain insight into the causes
and consequences of population movement. Not surprisingly, therefore, censuses represent a primary data source used by many population geographers. In
the United States, the census has been carried out every ten years since 1790
(in years ending in 0), while Canada collects its census every five years (in years
ending in 1 and 6). Both originated with the simple need to have a count of the
population, but evolved to collect information relating to a variety of population
characteristics. Most other nations also carry out censuses, although data quality and timing will vary.[5]

Representative Sample Surveys

Representative sample surveys are another source of population data, including
national, regional, or state/province representative sample surveys that collect
population information on individuals and/or households. A representative data
source allows the user to draw generalized conclusions. These surveys do not
have to focus exclusively on population topics to provide useful information.
For example, in addition to running the census program, Statistics Canada runs
a number of nationally representative data collection tools, including health,
immigration, and youth surveys. While not meant to be population counts,
these data sources provide background population characteristics, including
age, location, gender, income, educational attainment, and household structure, to name a few. Other representative data sources that are frequently referenced by population geographers include other data files from the US Census
Bureau, such as the ACS, which has been designed to replace the census long
form (see "Focus") and the CPS. The CPS is a monthly survey of the American
population and is the primary source of information on the labor force characteristics of the US population.

Vital Registrations

Vital registrations or civil registration systems record demographic events such
as births, deaths (including cause of death), marriages, divorces, and population movements and provide yet another source of demographic data. Mortality

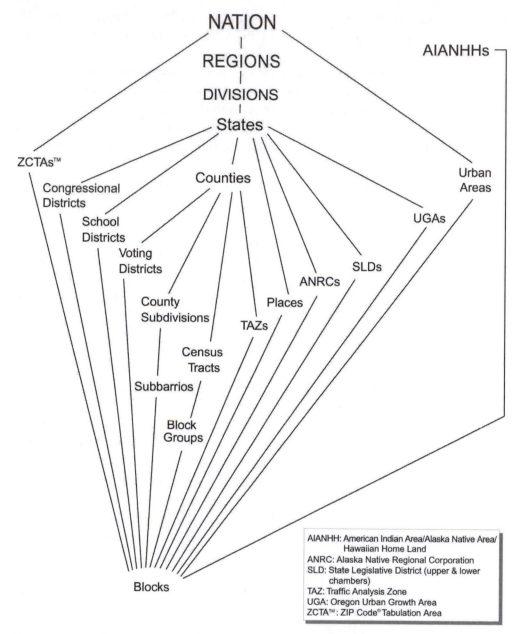

Figure 2.1   The Hierarchy of Census Geographic Areas.

Source: "Appendix A: Census 2000 Geographic Terms and Concepts," US Census Bureau, www.census.gov/ geo/www/tiger/glossry2.pdf.

statistics are, for example, used in population projections to calculate the probability of surviving into a future period of time, while information on cause of death can be used to protect the health of communities. Most countries have legal provisions within their constitutions to ensure that vital events are recorded, although the type of information that is registered will vary from country to country, with vital registration systems more expansive (i.e., capturing population mobility in addition to births and deaths) in several European countries.

Other Secondary Data Sources

Beyond the census and its related products, numerous other secondary data sources are available for use by population geographers. In the United States, for example, agencies such as departments of Health and Education and the Bureau of Labor Statistics (BLS) also commonly collect statistics that either directly or indirectly provide population data. The Internal Revenue Service (IRS) also publishes migration data based on the addresses of tax filers, which allows the mobility of the tax-paying public to be tracked from year to year.[6] Immigration statistics (including refugee and asylee numbers) can be sourced from the Department of Homeland Security, and comparative international data can be sourced from Integrated Public Use Microdata Series (IPUMS) International, the PRB, and various United Nations (UN) agencies.[7] In addition, other agencies or organizations, such as the World Health Organization (WHO), the UN, and country-specific statistical agencies, collect and disseminate population data, and the Center for International Earth Science Information Network (CIESIN) has interesting data applications, including a "census by satellite."[8]

Analysts may also turn to less conventional secondary data sources for population information. One such use of these sources is illustrated by Foulkes and Newbold (2008),[9] who turned to data from local school boards and utility companies to measure mobility in small rural communities. In this case, data from the US Census Bureau was dated or was not available at the scale of analysis (small rural villages) used in the study. School board data was drawn from the Illinois State Board of Education's School Report Card file, which provided mobility and poverty data for each school district and individual school in the state, from which mobility rates could be calculated based on movement of students in and out of the school district. In addition, and as a potentially more inclusive source capturing mobility across all households (as opposed to just those with children in the school system), sewage-billing records were used to provide additional insight into local mobility, with change in billing name associated with movement into or out of the community. Although the use of this data allowed an analysis of population mobility among a subgroup of people (rural poor migrants) that was otherwise missing from both the literature and from other data sources, it also illustrated the issues of using indirect sources, including data quality, comparability, replication, costs, and moral and ethical concerns.

Individualized Data Sets

In some cases, data from secondary sources is insufficient. Data may, for example, be outdated (as it was in the example above). Data may also miss, or lack sufficient numbers, for a particular population group or represent the wrong geographical scale. In each case, the researcher may be forced to construct her or his own data set(s). These "personalized" data sets offer a number of advantages, including enabling the researcher to select the sampling scheme, define the geographic scope and range of questions that are to be used, and include both qualitative and quantitative components in the research. Of course, there are also drawbacks to individual data sets. Most research questions or scripts will need to be vetted by institutional review boards, and researchers need to be aware of confidentiality and privacy issues. Although this is far from insurmountable, researchers need to ensure that quantitatively based samples will be sufficiently large or generalizable if they want to do statistical analysis or generalize to a larger population. Although the intent of qualitative studies is not to arrive at generalized conclusions, the collection, transcription, and coding of both quantitative and qualitative data can also be costly and time-consuming. The rewards, in terms of a data set that fits exactly the researcher's needs, can be large.

DATA QUALITY

Not all data sources are created equal, and they will differ in terms of their universality, quality, spatial scope, generalizability, validity, reliability, and replicability. In any data set, errors can be introduced in multiple ways, including the data collection process itself. For a census to be universal, everyone must be counted, but problems arise when some individuals or groups, such as the homeless, are difficult to count or refuse to be counted. For example, while there is always some undercount in any census, a post-census survey of the 1990 US census found that approximately four million people were missed. Populations were undercounted at different rates, with greater undercounting among the homeless, minority males in poverty, and Native Americans.[10] Underenumeration was particularly significant for cities. Apportionment of congressional seats and legislative redistricting was also affected by the undercount. Local governments demanded (and received) population recounts, as federal transfers were reduced given the underestimated population sizes.

Respondents may also introduce errors into the data, affecting its quality. In some cases, respondents may not answer a question or set of questions, with questions regarding income often poorly answered. In other cases, individuals may attempt to deceive or provide answers that they feel are socially appropriate rather than their own. Famous among respondent (mis)information is age, with many tending to provide a younger age than reality. Likewise, questions related to past events are subject to "recall bias," such that facts, dates, or events are not recalled with complete accuracy and are dependent upon memory. In fact, most any question may be subject to some respondent bias, and a large literature exists on how best to construct and implement a survey.[11] Common issues also include the incorrect recording or transcribing of information or incorrect phrasing of questions. There was much discussion, for example, over the phrasing of the "come to stay" question for immigrants in the 1990 US census, with the question variously interpreted to mean the person's first entry into the United States, when they received permanent residency, or ultimately when they received US citizenship.[12] For researchers interested in immigration and adjustment, the timing differences can have significant implications! Finally, statistical agencies themselves may alter data quality by suppressing data, particularly for small populations or small areas, where data may be suppressed to protect confidentiality. The ACS (see "Focus" section), for example, will only release data for small geographic areas based on five-year rolling averages. In comparison, data for larger units will be released yearly.

For a geographer, space and its definition are often key. For those wishing to compare phenomena across space, representative data sources or census files offer a pragmatic solution: to generate space through a custom survey is probably time- and cost-prohibitive! But, if the analyst is interested in a particular locale or space, especially those for which formal data is inadequate or not available, individual one-time surveys are often best. For instance, a researcher interested in neighborhoods may need to use census-defined census tracts to proxy the neighborhood.[13] But, given the spatial variability of census tracts, particularly in rural or less dense areas, and the variability with which people define their neighborhood, this definition may be wholly inadequate.

As such, and despite the availability of a broad variety of data sources, caveat emptor (buyer beware) applies. Analysts should be careful to note whether data sources are nationally (or regionally) representative. Similarly, do vital registration systems capture all the data? For instance, births and deaths (particularly infant deaths) may not be reported, and causes of death may be mislabeled, incorrect, or missing. In general, completeness of registration is fairly high in the developed world; some South American countries, including Argentina,

Chile, and Colombia; and some Asian countries, including China, Sri Lanka, South Korea, and Japan. However, vital registration systems in most sub-Saharan African countries do not adequately or completely collect information on vital events.

CONCLUSION

In recent years, the abundance of secondary data sources has enabled geographers and other social scientists to make important contributions to understanding the demographic trends that shape our societies. The widespread use and availability of census and other public data are due in large part to their validity and the degree of geographic, social, and economic detail embedded in the files. The growth of data has also corresponded to new computational abilities and a refinement and broadening of the analytical tools used within population research. Moreover, given the geographer's interest in space and spatial relationships, the use of such large data files is therefore somewhat pragmatic: generating "space" through other means, such as individual one-time surveys, is typically cost- (or time-) prohibitive, as the sample size either needs to be large to adequately represent a particular location and/or needs to be replicated across space to capture spatial differences. This has not, of course, stopped researchers from constructing their own data sets or relying on qualitative data to understand demographic processes. In fact, these data sources should be seen as complementary rather than competitive, allowing different approaches and insights into population processes.

FOCUS: CENSUS DATA AND THE ACS

THE CENSUS

Censuses serve as a tool to count the population and ascertain its basic makeup. Many nations conduct censuses (counts) of their populations as tools to allocate government seats, funding, or other resources. Mandated by the United States Constitution, the first US census was conducted in 1790, and has been collected every ten years since then. The information collected by the Census Bureau is then used to dis-tribute congressional seats and federal funds and to make decisions at every level of government.[1]

While the US census originated as a simple population count, it evolved over the years to include a variety of related population questions beyond age, gender, and address. In addition, a proportion of the population in the United States was frequently asked to complete the so-called census long form. Answered by approximately one in six people, the long form included detailed socioeconomic and socio-demographic questions, including schooling and education, income, housing type, citizenship, immigration status, ethnicity, and race of all respondents in the household. This data is typified by the Public Use Microdata Sample (PUMS), published by the US Census Bureau. PUMS files are large, representative samples (1 or 5 percent) of the US population based upon the decennial census.

The main advantage of working with a file like the PUMS is the detail embedded in the files and the ease of generating population statistics such as migration numbers, flows, and net migration rates at a variety of spatial scales. Another significant advantage is the size. The fact that the PUMS is representative of the entire US population enables generalizability, validity, reliability, and replicability of analyses. Analyses can, for example, be replicated across space and time, such that changes in the structure or makeup of a population can be observed and tracked over time. For geographers interested in population mobility and migration, the PUMS also included a question on place of residence five years ago. First appearing in the 1940 census, it provided a measure of the mobility of the US population by contrasting place of residence at the time of the census with place of residence five years earlier, allowing a window into the migration habits of the population. In addition, the census includes information on nativity (immigrant or nonimmigrant) and period of entry into the country, which enables analysis of the mobility and economic characteristics of the foreign-born population.

While data files such as the PUMS provide detailed snapshots of the total population, secondary data sources have their limits. Oftentimes, key assumptions regarding relationships, measures, or definitions within the data must be made in order for the analysis to proceed. Because of their nature, analyses of secondary data files are often constrained by the data contained within them. For example, although the US census asks about immigrant status, it does not include information on whether an immigrant is legal or illegal. Thus, secondary data files typically offer little flexibility in defining variables or constructs.[2] Second, much of the information collected by the decennial census is quickly outdated. In effect, the census provides a snapshot of the population at one point in time on census day, while missing changes to the population that happened in the intervening years. Third, although long-term census data is available, with census files dating to 1850 available from the Integrated Public Use Microdata Series USA (IPUMS-USA),[3] the data is not always comparable. If the researcher is interested in comparing populations across time, changes in variable definitions (i.e., the changing nomenclature for cities or occupation codes) or the introduction/re-phrasing/removal of questions to surveys complicates analyses.

THE AMERICAN COMMUNITY SURVEY

Given budget issues and congressional concerns with the invasiveness of questions in the census long form, the 2000 census was the last time the long form would be used.[4] The 2010 census will return to the more simple idea of a population count, collecting just name, age, sex, date of birth, race, ethnicity, relationship, and housing tenure. More detailed demographic information will be based on the ACS, which is perhaps the best known and one of the largest examples of a representative data source.[5] Meant to replace the information typically collected on the census long form, the ACS provides current and up-to-date population estimates, along with estimates of demographic, economic, social, and housing characteristics of the US population at various levels of geography.[6] While it is not designed to count the population, it does provide an estimate of what the population looks like each year through the use of statistical sampling, surveying approximately one in forty households each year, with addresses selected at random and representing other addresses in the community (figure 2F.1).

For large geographies such as states or large metropolitan areas, population estimates will be released on a yearly basis. Given the sample size involved, population estimates for smaller geographies will be based on rolling averages. For small areas with a population less than twenty thousand, population estimates will be based on five-year averages. Areas with a population of twenty thousand to sixty-five thousand will be based on three-year averages,[7] with these rolling averages updated yearly. Similarly, population characteristics may pose problems for the release of the data, and releases may be forced to the five-year cycle. For instance, in areas with small ethnic or racial groups, the numbers may be too small to release yearly.

The ACS provides a number of advantages over the census long form, with the most significant advantage being the timeliness of the data. For instance, ACS data will mean that population counts will be updated on a yearly basis for large metropolitan areas (up to five years for smaller metropolitan areas) rather than every ten years based on the census. In addition, migration will be measured through a question asking place of residence one year ago. This means that migration researchers will be able to accurately evaluate yearly migration data on an ongoing basis. In comparison, the census bases its migration question on place of residence five years prior to census day, meaning that the actual migration might have happened up to ten years before the data is released! Second, the ACS will allow more up-to-date information on the characteristics of the population relative to the demographic event. For instance, the census measured sociodemographic and socioeconomic information at census day, but might be five years beyond the migration event and therefore outdated. In contrast, migration events and demographic or economic characteristics will be more tightly matched in the ACS, so that the person moving for educational reasons will be more closely correlated with the migration event itself. Third, the ACS will eliminate the gap in migration data. That is, migration data based on census returns has only been available for the second half of the decade, so that migrations in the first five years of each decade are missed. With the ACS, migration will be tracked every year.

For the population geographer interested in migration, the ACS also poses significant new analytical questions and problems.[8] For instance, by comparing place of residence on census day and five years prior, the old long form provided a consistent definition and timeframe of migration. The ACS, however, compares place of residence on the day the form is completed relative to where the respondent lived a year earlier. In this way, the window for migration (one year) is significantly less than with the long form (five years), and the timing of the migration is variable from one respondent to the next. So, two respondents in the same community may complete the ACS at two very differnt times in the same calendar year, and the relative timing of their migrations could reflect vastly different economic opportunities. In addition, comparison of migration totals from the two sources will be problematic, since the number of migrants recorded over a five-year interval is considerably less than five times the one-year number[9] and the two totals cannot be easily reconciled.[10]

METHODS, MEASURES, AND TOOLS: WORKING WITH DATA

Good research should always be based on properly devised research questions that address gaps in the literature and are guided by appropriate theoretical foundations. At the same time, theoretical perspectives, methods, and data are also key to good research. While good data can help inform results, it does not guarantee "good" results. Likewise, researchers must use the appropriate methods to uncover what the data illustrates. Again, however, the choice of the research method or tool can alter results, even to the point of biasing outcomes and conclusions! In short, while we can use the analogy of "garbage in equals garbage out" (by substituting data/ methods for garbage), we could have good data (methods) but still get garbage results if we haven't used it properly or haven't used the appropriate method.

THEORETICAL PERSPECTIVES

Regardless of the type of question to be addressed, theory is critical to providing a context for interpreting results and defining methods. If we take the example of migration, each individual migrant has his or her own reasons for migration, ranging from poverty and employment opportunities to amenities and health, with explanations encapsulated in various migration theories.[1] For instance, the human capital theory describes migration as an individual choice, with migrants treated as rational actors and able to look at various options, including origin and destination, wage rates, job security, and so on, while also accounting for the costs of migration. Alternatively, the *structural* perspective defines movement based on the social, economic, and political structures that shape people's lives, so that migrations are often forced.[2]

COLLECTING AND OPERATIONALIZING THE DATA

Following the research statement, one of the first tasks is to collect the appropriate data, a task that can be as complex as the actual use of the data. If a researcher is interested in a fairly specific segment of the population, such as young adults who are just leaving college, data collection may simply involve turning to existing data sources such as the census, downloading the data, and then defining the appropriate sample (i.e., by age). While the census is an easy data source to turn to, gathering data for the census is a complex task in itself. For instance, the 2000 census provided employment for some 860,000 temporary workers, and was billed as "the largest peacetime mobilization of resources and personnel."[3] Preparations for the 2010 census began almost immediately after the 2000 census was completed. As early as 2003, the Census Bureau was field

Person 1

(Person 1 is the person living or staying here in whose name this house or apartment is owned, being bought, or rented. If there is no such person, start with the name of any adult living or staying here.)

1 **What is Person 1's name?**

Last Name *(Please print)*　　　First Name　　　MI

2 **How is this person related to Person 1?**

☒ Person 1

3 **What is Person 1's sex?** *Mark (X) ONE box.*

☐ Male　　☐ Female

4 **What is Person 1's age and what is Person 1's date of birth?**
Please report babies as age 0 when the child is less than 1 year old.
Print numbers in boxes.

Age (in years)　　　Month　Day　Year of birth

→ **NOTE: Please answer BOTH Question 5 about Hispanic origin and Question 6 about race. For this survey, Hispanic origins are not races.**

5 **Is Person 1 of Hispanic, Latino, or Spanish origin?**

☐ **No,** not of Hispanic, Latino, or Spanish origin
☐ Yes, Mexican, Mexican Am., Chicano
☐ Yes, Puerto Rican
☐ Yes, Cuban
☐ Yes, another Hispanic, Latino, or Spanish origin – *Print origin, for example, Argentinean, Colombian, Dominican, Nicaraguan, Salvadoran, Spaniard, and so on.* ↗

6 **What is Person 1's race?** *Mark (X) one or more boxes.*

☐ White
☐ Black, African Am., or Negro
☐ American Indian or Alaska Native — *Print name of enrolled or principal tribe.* ↗

☐ Asian Indian　☐ Japanese　☐ Native Hawaiian
☐ Chinese　☐ Korean　☐ Guamanian or Chamorro
☐ Filipino　☐ Vietnamese　☐ Samoan
☐ Other Asian – *Print race, for example, Hmong, Laotian, Thai, Pakistani, Cambodian, and so on.* ↗　☐ Other Pacific Islander – *Print race, for example, Fijian, Tongan, and so on.* ↗

☐ Some other race – *Print race.* ↗

Person 2

1 **What is Person 2's name?**

Last Name *(Please print)*　　　First Name　　　MI

2 **How is this person related to Person 1?** *Mark (X) ONE box.*

☐ Husband or wife　　☐ Son-in-law or daughter-in-law
☐ Biological son or daughter　　☐ Other relative
☐ Adopted son or daughter　　☐ Roomer or boarder
☐ Stepson or stepdaughter　　☐ Housemate or roommate
☐ Brother or sister　　☐ Unmarried partner
☐ Father or mother　　☐ Foster child
☐ Grandchild　　☐ Other nonrelative
☐ Parent-in-law

3 **What is Person 2's sex?** *Mark (X) ONE box.*

☐ Male　　☒ Female

4 **What is Person 2's age and what is Person 2's date of birth?**
Please report babies as age 0 when the child is less than 1 year old.
Print numbers in boxes.

Age (in years)　　　Month　Day　Year of birth

→ **NOTE: Please answer BOTH Question 5 about Hispanic origin and Question 6 about race. For this survey, Hispanic origins are not races.**

5 **Is Person 2 of Hispanic, Latino, or Spanish origin?**

☐ **No,** not of Hispanic, Latino, or Spanish origin
☐ Yes, Mexican, Mexican Am., Chicano
☐ Yes, Puerto Rican
☐ Yes, Cuban
☐ Yes, another Hispanic, Latino, or Spanish origin – *Print origin, for example, Argentinean, Colombian, Dominican, Nicaraguan, Salvadoran, Spaniard, and so on.* ↗

6 **What is Person 2's race?** *Mark (X) one or more boxes.*

☐ White
☐ Black, African Am., or Negro
☐ American Indian or Alaska Native — *Print name of enrolled or principal tribe.* ↗

☐ Asian Indian　☐ Japanese　☐ Native Hawaiian
☐ Chinese　☐ Korean　☐ Guamanian or Chamorro
☐ Filipino　☐ Vietnamese　☐ Samoan
☐ Other Asian – *Print race, for example, Hmong, Laotian, Thai, Pakistani, Cambodian, and so on.* ↗　☐ Other Pacific Islander – *Print race, for example, Fijian, Tongan, and so on.* ↗

☐ Some other race – *Print race.* ↗

Figure 2F.1a　The 2008 ACS Questionnaire.

Source: US Census Bureau.

Housing

Please answer the following questions about the house, apartment, or mobile home at the address on the mailing label.

1 **Which best describes this building?**
Include all apartments, flats, etc., even if vacant.

- ☐ A mobile home
- ☐ A one-family house detached from any other house
- ☐ A one-family house attached to one or more houses
- ☐ A building with 2 apartments
- ☐ A building with 3 or 4 apartments
- ☐ A building with 5 to 9 apartments
- ☐ A building with 10 to 19 apartments
- ☐ A building with 20 to 49 apartments
- ☐ A building with 50 or more apartments
- ☐ Boat, RV, van, etc.

2 **About when was this building first built?**

- ☐ 2000 or later – *Specify year*
- ☐ 1990 to 1999
- ☐ 1980 to 1989
- ☐ 1970 to 1979
- ☐ 1960 to 1969
- ☐ 1950 to 1959
- ☐ 1940 to 1949
- ☐ 1939 or earlier

3 **When did PERSON 1 (listed on page 2) move into this house, apartment, or mobile home?**

Month   Year

A *Answer questions 4 – 6 if this is a HOUSE OR A MOBILE HOME; otherwise, SKIP to question 7a.*

4 **How many acres is this house or mobile home on?**

- ☐ Less than 1 acre → *SKIP to question 6*
- ☐ 1 to 9.9 acres
- ☐ 10 or more acres

5 **IN THE PAST 12 MONTHS, what were the actual sales of all agricultural products from this property?**

- ☐ None
- ☐ $1 to $999
- ☐ $1,000 to $2,499
- ☐ $2,500 to $4,999
- ☐ $5,000 to $9,999
- ☐ $10,000 or more

6 **Is there a business (such as a store or barber shop) or a medical office on this property?**

- ☐ Yes
- ☐ No

7 **a. How many separate rooms are in this house, apartment, or mobile home?**
Rooms must be separated by built-in archways or walls that extend out at least 6 inches and go from floor to ceiling.

- *INCLUDE bedrooms, kitchens, etc.*
- *EXCLUDE bathrooms, porches, balconies, foyers, halls, or unfinished basements.*

Number of rooms

b. How many of these rooms are bedrooms?
Count as bedrooms those rooms you would list if this house, apartment, or mobile home were for sale or rent. If this is an efficiency/studio apartment, print "0".

Number of bedrooms

8 **Does this house, apartment, or mobile home have –**

	Yes	No
a. hot and cold running water?	☐	☐
b. a flush toilet?	☐	☐
c. a bathtub or shower?	☐	☐
d. a sink with a faucet?	☐	☐
e. a stove or range?	☐	☐
f. a refrigerator?	☐	☐
g. telephone service from which you can both make and receive calls? *Include cell phones.*	☐	☐

9 **How many automobiles, vans, and trucks of one-ton capacity or less are kept at home for use by members of this household?**

- ☐ None
- ☐ 1
- ☐ 2
- ☐ 3
- ☐ 4
- ☐ 5
- ☐ 6 or more

10 **Which FUEL is used MOST for heating this house, apartment, or mobile home?**

- ☐ Gas: from underground pipes serving the neighborhood
- ☐ Gas: bottled, tank, or LP
- ☐ Electricity
- ☐ Fuel oil, kerosene, etc.
- ☐ Coal or coke
- ☐ Wood
- ☐ Solar energy
- ☐ Other fuel
- ☐ No fuel used

Figure 2F.1b   The 2008 ACS Questionnaire.

Source: US Census Bureau.

testing questions via dress rehearsals, and by 2008 it had begun recruiting workers and updating address lists for the actual census.

For others, data must be collected through primary means such as surveys or interviews. If the latter, the sample must be identified and recruited (which individuals are asked to complete the survey and what is the sample structure—is it random? Snowball?, etc.)[4] and then asked to complete the interview, survey, or whatever data collection tool is being used. Typically, if the researcher wants results that are generalizable, then the sample must be random and representative of the population of interest. In other cases, the researcher may want to oversample particular communities or groups to ensure adequate information, while randomness may not be an issue in other cases. Collected data must then be entered or transcribed and checked for entry errors. If it is quantitative data, it should be also be checked for its representativeness of the population, which is usually done by comparing sample characteristics such as age and gender, along with such attributes as education and income, to known population values, such as those drawn from a census.

After this, we are nearly ready to start working with the data. So, how do we operationalize the data and what analytical methods are best? If we are examining population movement, how we define population movement is critical and depends on the research questions as well as the data. For instance, the international migration/immigration literature distinguishes *temporary immigrations*, such as short-term relocations; *transnationalism*; or *permanent immigration*. Likewise, the domestic migration literature also distinguishes between seasonal moves, such as the seasonal movement of "snow birds" between colder and warmer climates, and local moves (i.e., city), regional moves (i.e., county), or moves between states/provinces. Other issues, including the length of interval over which movement is captured (critical for looking at temporary migration); the size, shape, and characteristics of the receiving and sending regions; and the composition of the sample population, affect the analysis. As such, researchers must clearly define the population of interest.

METHODS

Research methods need to be defined, with researchers able to choose between a variety of different methods, selecting that which is best for their data. Qualitative data, for example, demand qualitative techniques, including the coding and interpretation of common themes or issues in the data,[5] with this analysis embedded within appropriate theoretical perspectives. For example, Strauss and Corbin suggest proceeding through open, axial, and selective coding.[6] Open and axial coding involve line-by-line coding of the data (microanalysis). During open coding, the data is examined and initial themes and concepts are generated. This process involves reading through each interview line by line looking for themes and concepts. Axial coding reexamines the themes and concepts identified within open coding by identifying their interrelationships (i.e., the networks and hierarchies that exist among and between them). Axial coding results in the development of an array of interrelationships between the various themes identified during open coding. In the final stage, selective coding is used to integrate and refine the categories and subcategories identified through open and axial coding. This requires the identification of central categories that represent the main theme of the research, which is defined as one that "has the ability to pull the other categories together to form an explanatory whole."[7] These central categories form the larger theoretical framework.

For the quantitative geographer, a series of tools are also available. Descriptive statistics, for example, including the calculation of means, standard deviations, or basic cross-tabulations, characterize the data and allow its exploration. Such descriptive analyses also provide a way to ensure that the sample is representative of the population of interest. While this stage is less crucial when using data files such as those from the US Census Bureau or Statistics Canada, which are representative of the population, it is key for researchers using data they have collected themselves. Following the initial description of the data, the analyst may turn to other methods and techniques, including inferential and multivariate statistics. Geographic information systems and spatial analytical techniques, including mapping of data, understanding geographic trends in the data, and searching for clustering or hot spots, are also widely used. All bring statistical significance to the analysis and allow a better understanding of the data. Many of these techniques are discussed elsewhere in this text.

Chapter Three

Population Distribution and Composition

THERE IS IMMENSE VARIATION in the distribution and composition of societies, whether measured by age, ethnicity, race, or where people live, with the composition of a population playing a major role in guiding decisions about the provision of government and other services. Not surprisingly, population geographers are frequently called upon to describe the related concepts of population distribution and composition. Population distribution refers to the geographic pattern of the location of a population, including its density and where it lives, whereas population composition refers to the characteristics of the population in a given area.[1] This chapter explores the related topics of population distribution and composition. Its "Focus" section looks at the changing face of the population of the United States, while the "Methods, Measures, and Tools" section introduces the concept of life tables, a mathematical way of describing the shape and structure of a population.

POPULATION DISTRIBUTION

At a global and even national scale, populations are distributed unevenly. Large parts of the globe, including the North and South poles and deserts, are sparsely populated, providing few options for their inhabitants in terms of livelihood and survival and harsh living conditions. Other areas, including agriculturally productive areas, are densely populated. Even in the United States, large parts of the interior plains are comparatively sparsely populated, with the population overwhelmingly located along the western and eastern seaboards and Gulf Coast.

Geographers have a number of tools at their disposal to describe the observed distribution of a population. The most common representation of a population is the population size for a given geographic area (such as the state of Illinois), or the proportion of a population living in an area (the proportion of the US population that lives in the state of Illinois). Importantly, we need to clearly identify the population and area that we are trying to describe (see chapter 2). Most commonly, the population will be contained within some political unit, such as a census tract, neighborhood, city, state, or nation, so that reliable and meaningful statistics are available and referenced to a particular point in time. We may also be interested in defining a particular subpopulation, such as the number of African Americans or immigrants in a particular geographic area. While important enough on its own, the simple count tells us little about its geographic distribution or its composition. For greater information, we turn to other measures.

Population Density

A common measure of population distribution is *population density*, an expression of the degree to which a population is clustered within a given area j, expressed as

$$D_j = P_j \, / \, A_j$$

where P_j is the population (count) in area j and A_j is the geographic area of interest, usually defined as miles or kilometers squared. Clearly, this measure is a rough guide to how dense a population is. If we were to calculate the population density for Canada, for instance, we would arrive at a density of 3.3 people per square kilometer, giving it one of the lowest population densities in the world. However, the density of Canada's population varies dramatically, with the majority of Canada's population living within approximately two hundred kilometers from the US border, while parts of Canada's largest city—Toronto—have population densities in excess of 1,000 per square kilometer.[2] As such, density is an incomplete measure of population distribution, and reflects a number of physical factors, such as the availability of resources and suitability of climate, as well as human factors, such as social and economic resources. Nevertheless, density is commonly used to compare population distribution across countries or regions. Applying this measure at the global scale reveals striking contrasts in the population density of the world's countries. Relative to Canada, the density of the United States is over ten times higher (32 people per square kilometer) (see Figure 3.1), China's population density is 139, and Hong Kong has a population density of 6,403 per square kilometer.[3]

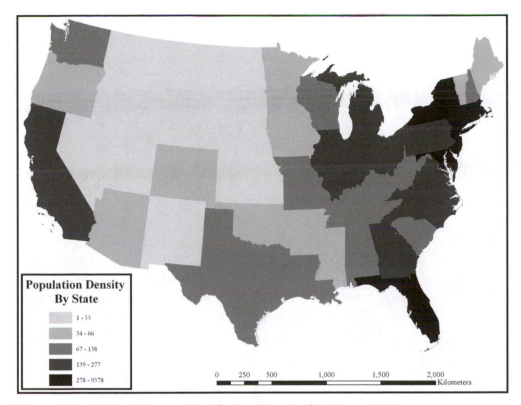

Figure 3.1   United States Population Density by State, 2000.

Readers can also see population density at the county scale at www.census.gov/population/ www/censusdata/2000maps.html.

Source: Data derived from the US Census Bureau.

Maps

In addition to measures of population density, maps are frequently used to represent the distribution of a population, including dot and choropleth maps (figure 3.2). Dot maps, for instance, may be used to represent the distribution of a population. Typically, one dot is equated with the location of one person or a group of people across space. Choropleth maps, like figure 3.1, may also be used, with regions such as states or counties shaded relative to their population density (or other population attribute). In both cases, choices of scale, symbols, and other design issues, as well as the actual placement of dots, are important considerations when constructing the map.[4]

POPULATION COMPOSITION

In addition to the distribution of a population, population geographers are interested in its composition or characteristics. For instance, the composition

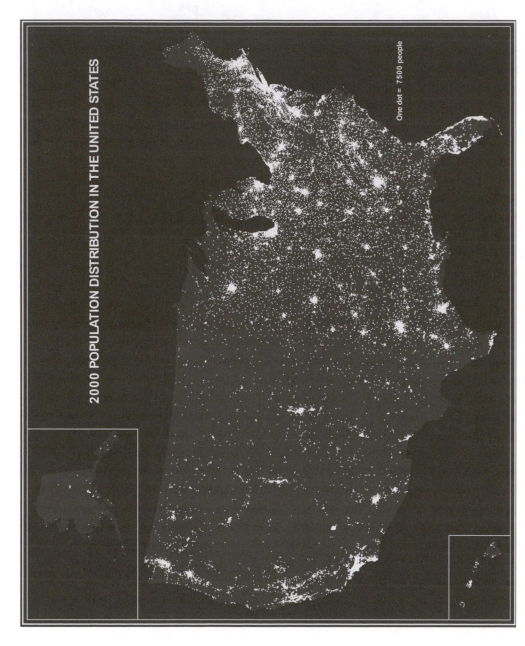

Figure 3.2.   2000 Population Distribution in the United States.
Source: US Census Bureau.

of the population in a given city will be different from that of its surrounding rural area. Likewise, the composition of a suburban population will likely differ from that of the inner city, or differ from suburb to suburb. For this reason, the composition of a population is intrinsically linked to its distribution, a feature that is dependent on geography.

Population Pyramids

Population pyramids provide the analyst with a way of describing the sex and age composition of a population. Expressed graphically, the age of the population is placed on the vertical axis and the share (or number) of the population along the horizontal axis, with males typically shown on the left and females on the right. Typically (although not exclusively), five-year age groups are used in their construction, with an open-ended age group (i.e., eighty-plus) for the oldest segment of the population.

Construction and observation of the pyramid reveals a number of features of a population. First, age pyramids are generally wider on the bottom than on the top, an outcome of increasing mortality with increasing age and a characteristic of above-replacement fertility. Second, the base of the pyramid is typically wider for males than it is for females, reflecting the sex ratio at birth (see below). Conversely, the upper portion of the pyramid favors females, reflecting differences in mortality and life expectancy between males and females, with females having greater life expectancies. Third, observation of population pyramids over a period of time can reveal changing population composition. For instance, observation of the population pyramid for the United States in 2005 reveals an age structure that is nearly pyramidal: increasing age is associated with a decreasing share of the population (figure 3.3a). The projected pyramid for 2025 suggests a more rectangular age structure (figure 3.3b), reflecting the aging of the baby boomers, increased life expectancy, and declining fertility levels. Together, these mean smaller numbers amongst the youngest age groups and an increasing proportion of elderly.

The shape of population pyramids may also reflect the impact of war or disease. In some parts of sub-Saharan Africa, HIV/AIDS has dramatically altered population pyramids due to declines in life expectancy and an increase in death rates. Consequently, the traditional population pyramid, with a wide base of young and tapering with increasing age, is being restructured and is better characterized as a population "chimney" in countries that have high HIV prevalence rates (figure 3.4). As AIDS "hollows out" the young adult population, it generates a base that is less broad with fewer young children. With fewer women reaching and surpassing their childbearing years and with women having fewer children, the most dramatic changes occur when young adults who were

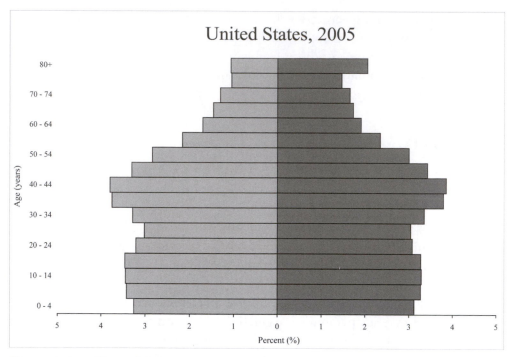

Figure 3.3a   United States Age Pyramid, 2005.

Source: Data derived from US Census Bureau.

infected in their adolescence die, substantially shrinking the adult population, particularly the population in their twenties and thirties.

Sex Ratios

The *sex ratio* of a population is defined as the number of males per 100 females. Values greater than 100 imply more males than females, with the opposite true for values less than 100. Typically, sex ratios at the national scale are somewhat less than 100. However, this obscures variations by age. At birth, males usually outnumber females, with a sex ratio of approximately 105 (105 boys for every 100 girls). This advantage is quickly lost with increasing age, as males have shorter life expectancies such that the sex ratio swings in favor of females in the older age groups and results in national sex ratios being less than 100. Based on the 2000 US census, the sex ratio for the young aged zero through fourteen was 104, and for those sixty-five and over was just 70.

Beyond natural biological effects that influence the sex ratio across age groups, five other effects may alter the sex ratio across space or over time. First, and occurring at smaller geographic scales, migration may have an important impact, particularly if males are more prone to migration than females. The net

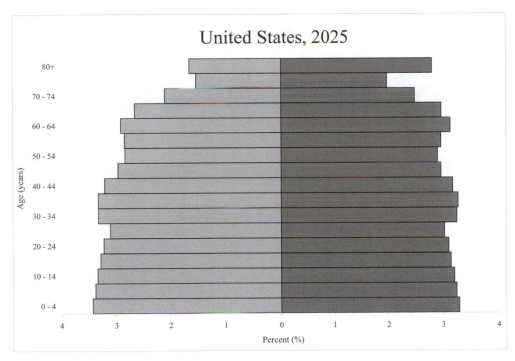

Figure 3.3b   United States Age Pyramid, 2025.

Source: Data derived from US Census Bureau.

effect may be to lower the adult sex ratio in sending regions (i.e., places men are migrating out of, leaving women behind) and to increase the ratio in the destination places. Resource and "boom" towns have often been associated with high sex ratios. Additionally, historic immigration patterns have also favored males, with men first establishing themselves in the host country before bringing a spouse and family over. Second, environmental effects may have an effect on sex ratios at birth. Although still poorly understood and debatable, exposure to environmental contaminants, including endocrine disruptors, which are found in a variety of chemicals; PCBs; and dioxins, may alter the live-birth sex ratio, or the ratio of boys to girls that survive childbirth.[5] Third, there may be genetic/biological reasons for variations in the sex ratio at birth. There is, for example, a greater possibility of male conception at the beginning and the end of the ovulation cycle (where the probability of spontaneous abortion is greatest).[6] Sex ratios have also been linked to mother's age, with older women more likely to have girls. As women delay marriage and childbearing, more females may be born.[7] Fourth, in societies that value male children but small family sizes, women may opt for ultrasounds to determine the sex of their children, practice infanticide if the child is female, or underreport female births. Reports of this practice are common from China, where the official one-

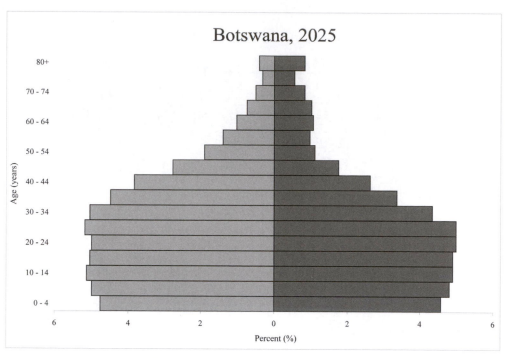

Figure 3.4   Projected Population Structure with AIDS, Botswana 2025: The AIDS "Chimney."

Source: US Census Bureau, IDB, 2008.

child policy restricts family sizes. In places, the sex ratio approaches 120, while the live-birth sex ratio is approximately 135.[8] It is interesting to note that the preference for male children among some Asian cultures has been transplanted to the United States, with the sex ratio increasing to 1.17 (rather than the usual 1.05) if the first child was a girl in families of Chinese, Korean, and Indian descent. If the first two children were boys, the ratio increased to approximately 1.5, indicating a much greater preference for boys.[9] Finally, sex ratios appear to vary by latitude, independent of cultural or economic factors.[10] Ratios in latitudes close to the equator were more equitable—50.7 percent boys in Africa—and were the highest in Europe and Asian countries (51.4 percent boys). Of all of these factors, however, identifying the contribution of any one single variable is extremely difficult.

Population (Median) Age

Population geographers and others are frequently asked to describe the age of a population. Is it young or old, and how best to describe this? As a measure of the average age of a population, *median age* (meaning half the population is younger and half is older) is commonly used. In 2000, the median age of the

US population was 35.3 years, the highest it had ever been. Between 1990 and 2000, the median age had increased by two-and-a-half years, reflecting the aging of baby boomers born between 1946 and 1964. By 2005, median age had continued to increase, reaching 36.4 years, and it is expected to continue to increase over the coming years, reaching 38 years by 2025.[11] California has one of the country's youngest populations, with a median age of 34.4 years. New York state, on the other hand, is relatively old, with a median age of 37.5 years. Many of the northeastern states have relatively older populations, with Maine having the oldest population (41.2 years). These older ages are reflective of the out-migration of younger age groups, while states in the South and West have generally younger populations given the in-migration of the young. Interestingly, Florida has a relatively old population (39.5 years), reflecting its role as a retirement destination.

Dependency Ratios

In addition to the median age of a population, we can identify the proportion that is young or old within a population, such as the proportion of a population that is dependent (typically aged fifteen years or less), the labor force–aged population (fifteen to sixty-four years), and the older population (aged sixty-five-plus). More specifically, *dependency ratios* capture the age distribution of the population relative to the labor force–aged population. Generally, the "dependent population," either aged zero to fifteen or sixty-five and over, are contrasted with individuals aged fifteen to sixty-four and who can "support" either young or old dependents. When there are more working-age adults relative to children and the old, the labor force age group has a lower dependency burden: fewer people to support with the same income and assets. Parents, for example, provide most of the financial support for their children, including housing, clothing, and education. At the same time, taxes paid by workers pay for programs and support health and social-welfare programs and education, with the young and old relatively dependent on these.

Three dependency ratios are commonly used. The first, the *young dependency ratio* (YDR), refers to the relative size of young dependents to the labor force population, defined as follows.

$$YDR = (P_{0-14} / P_{15-64})*100$$

Likewise, the *old dependency ratio* (ODR) is defined as follows.

$$ODR = (P_{65+} / P_{15-64})*100$$

The *total dependency ratio* (TDR) is defined as follows.

$$TDR = ((P_{0-14} + P_{65+}) / P_{15-64})*100$$

In all of these examples, P_{x-y} refers to the population aged x–y (i.e., zero through fourteen).

We can use the United States to illustrate this measure (see table 3.1). Between 1996 and 2025, the young dependency ratio is expected to stay relatively constant (approximately 0.30). Reflecting the slow aging of the US population and the aging of baby boomers into retirement, the old dependency ratio is expected to increase from 0.19 in 1996 to 0.29 by 2025. This means that while there were approximately four workers for each older person in 1996, this will drop to three workers by 2025, with potential implications for taxation and welfare support.

Despite their widespread use and intuitive meaning, the use of dependency ratios can be problematic, particularly when linked to policy. In part, the measure would be more reflective of economic reality if the young dependent age group was defined as zero through nineteen and the labor force as those aged twenty to sixty-four, given the reality that relatively few fifteen- to nineteen-year-olds are working full time in most developed countries. The definition for the old dependency ratio also implies, for example, that all people over age sixty-five are in some sense dependent on the population of working age, given the use of payroll taxes to support health and social-welfare programs. For this reason, changes in the old dependency ratio are assumed to have a greater effect on government spending and the economy. However, "dependency" does not suddenly change with age. In fact, there is a growing tendency for many youth to remain financially dependent on their parents for a longer period of time than was seen even in the 1980s.[12] It is not uncommon, for example, to find children in their twenties still living with parents and either active in the labor force or still in school. Similarly, many of those over sixty-five remain active in the labor force and make important economic contributions. Concurrently, there are individuals in the labor force age group that have withdrawn

Table 3.1. Dependency Ratios, United States, 1990–2025

Year	Young dependency ratio	Old dependency ratio	Total dependency ratio
1990	0.33	0.19	0.52
1996	0.33	0.19	0.53
2000	0.32	0.19	0.51
2005	0.31	0.19	0.49
2010	0.30	0.19	0.49
2015	0.31	0.22	0.53
2020	0.32	0.26	0.57
2025	0.32	0.29	0.61

Source: Based on data derived from the US Census Bureau.

from the labor force for reasons including health. For this reason, we must interpret dependency ratios with caution.[13]

CONCLUSION

The distribution and composition of a population often lies at the heart of describing a population, reflecting such things as its age and gender structure both visually and numerically with knowledge of its age structure and sex structure acting as building blocks in terms of understanding the population and the provision of services. Governments will, for instance, gauge the provision of services based on the age of the population, so that areas with a larger proportion of older adults will receive the necessary level of services. The rise of GIS and related spatial analysis techniques has also provided new venues for looking at the distribution of a population. Indeed, the popularity of GIS and new analytical tools has meant that more people understand why "geography matters" when it comes to population issues.[14]

Multiple processes, including fertility choices, migration, and mortality, can affect population structure and composition. Declines in mortality, for instance, increase the proportion of older adults and also shift the gender balance in favor of females. Fertility tends to have significant changes on a population's composition, with decreasing fertility associated with population aging. Migration will also redistribute a population and its characteristics, with the potential for significant short-term impacts, as it tends to be age- and sex-selective, typically selecting younger adults while favoring one gender over another in some situations. Thus, analysts need to be aware of the potential effects of these processes on a population, particularly if longer-run trends are desired. However, we save the discussion of these impacts for elsewhere in this book.

FOCUS: THE CHANGING FACE OF THE US POPULATION[1]

Over its history, the size, composition, and distribution of the US population has changed significantly. Historically, the distribution of the country's population followed western expansion and the annexation of new territory such as the Louisiana Purchase in 1803, the Mexican Cession in 1848, and the Texas Annexation in 1845. Exploration, land, resources, and new frontiers attracted new immigrants as well as Americans to settling in these new territories and slowly shifted the distribution of the population westward, a process which continues to this day. The westward drift of the US population has been captured through the use of population centroids,[2] which represent the geographic center of the population. Starting on the east coast in the late 1700s, it has slowly but consistently drifted west and south over time. By 1890, it was located in southeast Indiana, and moved west of the Mississippi by 1990 and into Phelps County, Missouri by 2000. The distribution of the US population can also be captured through population density. Historically, population density was just 1.8 persons per square kilometer in 1790, and 8.3 per square kilometer by 1900.[3] By 2000, the country's population density had increased to 31 people per square kilometer.[4] Washington, D.C., is the most densely populated area, with 3,621 per square kilometer. Wyoming is the least dense state in the continental United States, with just 1.96 persons per square kilometer.

The nation's changing population composition can be measured by shifts in its age profile, reflected in such measures as median age, population pyramids, and dependency ratios. Again based on the 2000 census, the median US age was 35.3 years,[5] up from 32.9 years in 1990. The jump in the median age largely reflects the aging of the baby boom cohort, although the aging of this cohort has not yet influenced the dependency ratios, with both the young and old dependency ratios relatively consistent between 1990 and 2000 (0.33 and 0.19 for the young and old, respectively). That is, for example, there are about five people in the labor force supporting each older adult. However, this is a significant departure from what it was in 1900, when the old dependency ratio was 0.07 (reflecting shorter life spans and higher fertility), while the young dependency ratio has consistently drifted downward as fertility has decreased.[6] As the baby boom cohort ages further into retirement, however, the old dependency ratio will start to increase. By 2030, the last of the baby boomers will have turned sixty-five, and nearly 20 percent of Americans will be over sixty-five, compared with just 13 percent today.[7]

Not surprisingly, the distribution of the nation's older population varies across the country.[8] Florida had the largest proportion (16.8 percent) of older (sixty-five and older) people in 2000 (median age equals 39.5 years), reflecting its attractiveness to retirees. States in the Great Plains and some northeastern states such as Rhode Island, Pennsylvania, and West Virginia also have comparatively large proportions of older people. In contrast, many of the western and southeastern states have relatively smaller proportions of the old. States with some of the youngest populations include Utah, Colorado, and Texas.

The changing ethnic and racial composition of the country perhaps reveals the most fundamental and far-reaching changes occurring in the nation. Originally shaped by historical immigration flows from western Europe and the slave trade, the composition of the United States was long defined by its white and black roots. This began to change in the 1960s with the liberalization of the country's immigration policies, which increased immigration flows from Asia and other "nontraditional" origin areas. The number of new entrants has also increased, totaling over one million new arrivals per year early in the new century. Over the 1990s, legal and illegal immigration flows from Latin America, and particularly Mexico, altered the country's ethnic composition, making ethnic and racial minorities the majority population (compared to non-Hispanic whites) in both California and Texas.

Based on the 2000 census, 11.1 percent of the country's population is foreign-born. Although this is less than historical standards (15 percent in 1910), the proportion of foreign-born could surpass the historical high by 2025, and may reach as high as 20 percent by 2050. The largest proportion (51.7 percent) is from Latin America, and

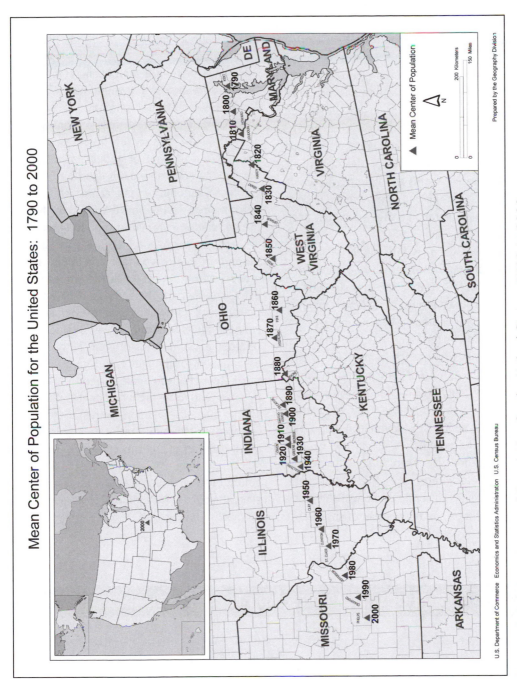

Mean Center of Population for the United States: 1790 to 2000

Figure 3F.1   Mean Center of Population for the United States: 1790 to 2000.

Source: US Census Bureau.

particularly Mexico. Asians represent 26.4 percent of the foreign-born, with major origin countries including China, India, and Pakistan. Europeans represent just 15.8 percent of all foreign-born in the country.[9] In comparison, Europeans represented 74.5 percent of all foreign-born in 1960.[10] The country's ethnic composition has also been altered far beyond the usual immigrant magnets of cities like New York or Los Angeles. Reflecting a changing distribution within the United States, recent arrivals have filtered across the country, so much so that suburban and rural America is dealing with immigration issues seemingly overnight.[11]

So significant is the impact of the foreign-born on the composition of the American population that the Census Bureau predicts that ethnic and racial minority groups will represent the majority of the population by the early 2040s. By that time, Americans identifying themselves as Hispanic, black, Asian, American Indian, Native Hawaiian, and Pacific Islander will outnumber non-Hispanic whites.[12] By 2050, non-Hispanic whites will represent just 46 percent of the population, down from 66 percent in 2008. The main reasons for this, as noted elsewhere, are the significantly higher levels of fertility amongst these minority groups and the number of immigrants

entering the United States. Individuals are also changing how they identify themselves, with more identifying themselves as multiracial. In short, the future US population will appear much more diverse than it currently does.

Finally, there are significant compositional differences between native-born Americans and the foreign-born. For instance, 79 percent of the foreign-born were aged eighteen to sixty-four in 2000, compared to 60 percent of natives. Similarly, only 10 percent of the foreign-born were eighteen years old or less, compared to 28 percent amongst the native-born. This gives the population pyramid of the foreign-born a shape similar to a football, with a small proportion in the younger and older age groups, and the majority in the labor force ages. In large part, this reflects immigration policy, with most immigrants arriving as younger adults. However, if we consider the US population in terms of ethnicity or race, as opposed to immigrant and native-born, the picture changes again. Given that fertility rates tend to be higher amongst minority groups than non-Hispanic whites, these differences are shaping the future ethnic and racial makeup of the United States. For instance, between 1990 and 2000, the population under eighteen had the largest gain since the 1950s, with minorities accounting for most of this growth.

METHODS, MEASURES, AND TOOLS: LIFE TABLES

Demographers often rely on life tables as a way of summarizing mortality and life expectancy within a population. Essentially, information contained in the tables represents the probability of surviving from one

age to another and the life expectancy for a person aged x. Table 3MMT.1 illustrates a basic life table for the United States (both sexes, 2006),[1] which can be interpreted as a summary of the mortality experiences of a cohort of individuals born at time t. The initial size of the cohort, l_o, known as the *radix*, is often set to one hundred thousand. Two assumptions are key to the life table. First, rates of age specific mortality will not change over the lifetime of members of the cohort. Second, as the cohort ages, individuals will die according to the specified death rates. The individual columns in the table are defined as follows.

$_hM_x$ the observed age-specific mortality for individuals age x to $x + h$

$_hq_z$ the probability that an individual aged x will die before reaching age $x + h$

l_x the number of individuals in the cohort surviving to age x

$_hd_x$ the number of individuals in the cohort dying between ages x and $x + h$

$_hL_x$ the number of person-years lived by the l_x individuals between ages x and $x + h$

T_x the cumulative number of person-years lived by the cohort beyond age x

e_x the life expectancy (in years) for the person surviving to age x

Each hypothetical cohort is subjected to an age-specific mortality rate ($_hM_x$), beginning from birth. For each age group, the value of q is derived from M, and then d is derived.

We start with the derivation of the age-specific death rates as follows.

$$_hM_x = {_hD_x} / {_hP_x}$$

The numerator, $_hD_x$, is the observed age-specific deaths. The denominator, $_hP_x$, is the observed age-specific population, which is typically defined as the midyear population.

These mortality rates can be used to define the probability of dying, $_hq_z$, which is defined as follows.

$$_hq_x = \frac{h_{l,}M_x {}_hP_x}{_hP_x + (h/2)_hM_x {}_hP_x}$$

This essentially indicates that the probability of not surviving to the next age group $x + h$ is related to the number of deaths in that cohort relative to those alive at age x, assuming, of course, that deaths are distributed equally across the time period. Using data from table 3MMT.1, the probability that an American aged forty does not survive to age forty-five is 0.01129.

Within each cohort, a given number of individuals ($_hd_x$) die, so that the given number of individuals reaching a particular age x is reduced as the cohorts age. The number of deaths can be determined as

$$_hd_x = l_x {}_hq_x$$

or the number of individuals reaching age x (l_x) multiplied by the probability of dying before age $x + h$. This also means that the number of individuals surviving until the beginning of the next age group ($x + h$) is equal to the following formula.

$$l_{x+h} = l_x - {}_hd_x$$

Returning to our example based on table 3MMT.1, the number of deaths ($_hd_x$) occurring in the forty to forty-five cohort is 1,090. Since 96,611 members survive to age forty, the number surviving to age forty-five is $96,611 - 1,090 = 95,521$.

The number of person-years lived by the cohort over h years is defined as follows.

$$L = \frac{h(l_x + l_{x+h})}{2}$$

That is, L_x is a function of the number of persons alive at the midpoint of the age group ($l_x + l_{x+h}$)/2 and the number of years in the

Table 3MMT.1.   Life Table: United States of America, 2006, Both Sexes

Age	$_hM_x$	$_hq_z$	l_x	$_hd_x$	$_hL_x$	T_x	e_x
< 1	0.00662	0.00658	100,000	658	99,408	7,800,885	78.0
1–4	0.00028	0.00112	99,342	111	397,101	7,701,477	77.5
5–9	0.00014	0.00070	99,231	59	495,981	7,304,3777	73.6
10–14	0.00017	0.00087	99,162	86	495,593	6,808,396	68.7
15–19	0.00063	0.00314	99,075	311	494,598	6,312,803	63.7
20–24	0.00094	0.00468	98,764	463	492,664	5,818,205	59.9
25–29	0.00094	0.00470	98,301	462	490,353	5,325,541	54.2
30–34	0.00108	0.00537	97,840	526	487,884	4,835,188	49.4
35–39	0.00145	0.00722	97,314	703	484,813	4,347,305	44.7
40–44	0.00227	0.01129	96,611	1,090	480,329	3,862,492	40.0
45–49	0.00344	0.01705	95,521	1,629	473,531	3,382,163	35.4
50–54	0.00509	0.02513	93,892	2,359	463,561	2,908,631	31.0
55–59	0.00719	0.03531	91,532	3,232	449,582	2,445,071	26.7
60–64	0.01116	0.05427	88,301	4,792	429,523	1,995,488	22.6
65–69	0.01670	0.08014	83,509	6,692	400,813	1,565,965	18.8
70–74	0.02611	0.12257	76,816	9,415	360,543	1,165,152	15.2
75–79	0.04088	0.18546	67,401	12,500	305,754	804,609	11.9
80–84	0.06624	0.28414	54,901	15,599	235,506	498,855	9.1
85–89	0.10640	0.42024	39,301	16,516	155,217	263,350	6.7
90–94	0.16970	0.56226	22,786	12,811	75,493	108,132	4.7
95–99	0.27059	0.69487	9,974	6,931	25,613	32,639	3.3
100 +	0.43319	1.00000	3,343	3,043	7,026	7,026	2.3

Source: WHO Statistical Information System (WHOSIS), www.who.int/whosis/database/life_tables/ life_tables.cfm (accessed 11 June 2008).

cohort, *h*, assuming that deaths are distributed equally over the age group. For the forty to forty-five cohort example, the number of person-years lived is 5 x (96,611 − 95,521)/2 = 480,330.

Next, the cumulative number of person-years lived by the cohort beyond age *x* (*T*ₓ) is found by adding $_hL_x$ from *x* to the last group,

$$_hT_x = \sum_{i-x}^{z} {_hL_i}$$

where *z* is the oldest cohort in the life table. The number of person-years remaining to be lived beyond age forty-five for the example cohort is 3,382,163.

Finally, the remaining life expectancy for

those individuals currently aged *x* (*e*ₓ), is calculated by dividing the number of person-years lived beyond age *x* by the number of persons reaching age *x*.

$$e_x = \frac{_hT_x}{l_x}$$

Therefore, the expectation of years to live for an American reaching age 45 is 35.4 years (3,382,163 / 95,521), equal to an expected age of 80.4.

There are three exceptions to the above noted calculations. First, deaths for infants are more likely to occur in the first half of the year than in the second. Consequently, children less than one year old are typically tabulated separately. One method to estimate this is defined as follows.

$$L_0 = \frac{l_0 + l_1}{2}$$

Following this, and since the age group zero to one has already been estimated, $h = 4$ should be used (rather than $h = 5$, assuming the age interval is equal to five years) for the calculation of L for the age group one to four.

Second, the last age group is open-ended. In this case, q is allowed to equal 1.0, since everyone reaching this age group must die in it.

$$_{\infty}d_z = l_z$$

Finally, the number of person-years lived by individuals in the oldest age group also needs to be adjusted. In this case, demographers assume that the age-specific mortality rates in this oldest age cohort are equal to those observed in some theoretical "stationary" population (m_z), which is an unchanging population arrived at by adding l_o births to the population each year. Given that $M_z = m_z$, we can derive as follows.

$$L_z = \frac{d_z}{M_z}$$

USE Of LIFE TABLES

Far from being a set of abstract calculations, life tables are commonly used within the insurance industry to set insurance premiums and are typically further disaggregated by age (i.e., single-year age groups) and gender, given survival differences between males and females (with females typically surviving longer). They can also be used to determine survival ratios. For example, the proportion of forty- to forty-five-year-old Americans who reach their forty-fifth birthday is defined as follows.

$$\frac{5l_{45}}{L_{40}} = \frac{5(95,531)}{480,329} = 0.9943$$

Chapter Four

Fertility

A T ITS MOST BASIC, population size and growth is determined by the combined effects of fertility, or the ability of a society to reproduce itself, and mortality, or death. Worldwide, large variations in fertility rates are observed, with some of the highest rates observed in sub-Saharan Africa and some of the lowest rates in Eastern Europe, where several countries are faced with population decline.[1] Clearly, there is a large variation in fertility behavior, with fertility determined by both biological and social components. This chapter begins with an examination of fertility patterns. It then discusses the determinants of population fertility and the evolution of fertility trends. The "Focus" section contrasts fertility rates in North America and Uganda, and the "Methods, Measures, and Tools" section explores the various measures of fertility.

FERTILITY PATTERNS

The past two hundred years have witnessed a tremendous change in fertility patterns across the globe. The question for us is what determines fertility rates, why have they changed (decreased) over time in some places and not in others, and why are they typically slow to change? The demographic transition theory has frequently been used as a template to mark the shift from high to low

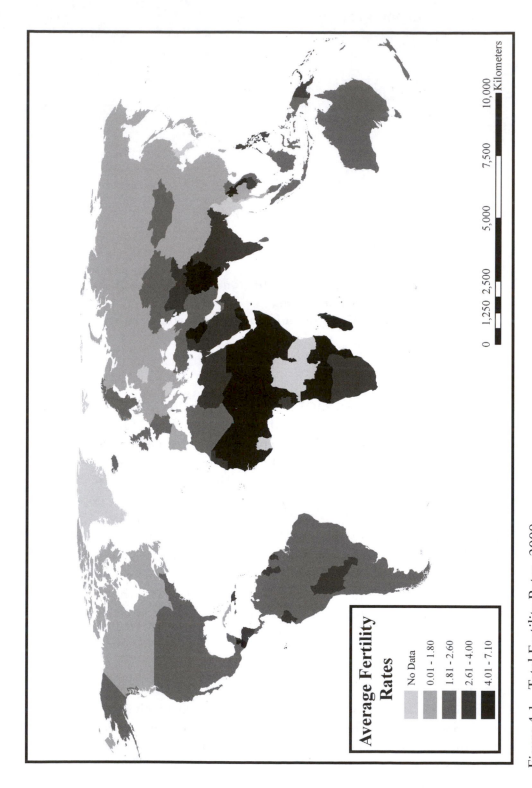

Figure 4.1   Total Fertility Rates, 2009.

Source: Derived from PRB.broadside

Average Fertility Rates

- No Data
- 0.01 – 1.80
- 1.81 – 2.60
- 2.61 – 4.00
- 4.01 – 7.10

0   1,250 2,500   5,000   7,500   10,000

Kilometers

mortality and fertility, along with the consequent population explosion as life expectancy and mortality rates are improved. This shift in fertility regimes occurred throughout much of North America and Europe in the nineteenth and early twentieth centuries. In North America, fertility rates had already declined to 3.5 by 1900, down from rates in excess of 5 in the first half of the 1800s.[2] The transition to modern fertility patterns, marked by stable and slow population growth, was essentially completed by the 1930s. In other countries, the transition occurred much later, with many developing countries not experiencing mortality declines until the 1950s, while others have yet to experience substantial declines in fertility. While providing a pattern of fertility decline, the demographic transition theory does not provide us with the reasons for fertility decline.

From the perspective of the developed world, one of the most important demographic events in recent history was the *baby boom*, which presented a departure from the long-term trend of declining fertility. Generally referring to those born between 1946 and 1964, it affected the United States, Canada, and other nations involved in World War II, although the demographic impacts tended to be greatest in North America. Although the baby boom was demographically important, with baby boom generation's numbers impacting the provision of education in the 1950s and 1960s, career and leisure pursuits as individuals entered the labor force, and now retirement, social welfare programs, and health care as the baby boom generation ages into retirement within the next decade,[3] it was a short-term phenomenon. Instead of representing a sea change in fertility behavior, it only temporarily boosted fertility levels. Over the longer term, fertility rates continued a decline that was first noticed decades earlier.

WHAT DETERMINES FERTILITY?

Characteristic of preindustrial societies, survival in prerevolutionary Russia was difficult. Life expectancy was just over thirty years. Infant death rates might have reached upwards of 30 percent of all live births, and 50 percent of all children died by the age of five. In response to such high death rates, families were large, with family structure reinforced by cultural practices, including early marriage before the age of twenty, and any form of birth control was a criminal offense.[4] To remain single was a disgrace, and divorce was a sin. Within forty years of the Russian Revolution, fertility rates had declined to levels comparable with most Western societies.

While social, economic, and environmental considerations demanded large families in prerevolutionary Russia, the Hutterites, a devoutly religious group found in the United States and Canada, value large families, with an average size of eleven children recorded in the early 1900s.[5] Even at its peak, the fertility of this group fell far below the biological maximum, defined by *fecundity*, or the physiological ability of individuals to have children. What are less evident are the social dimensions which work to keep fertility below its maximum level, including the roles of economic issues, the government, and other institutions in altering fertility behavior. Similarly, cultural values regarding family size and the social roles of men and women alter fertility and the timing of fertility reduction. In many African states, for example, women enter into sexual unions at younger ages and contraceptive use remains low, but families average six or seven children, far below the biological maximum. Cultural practices, including breast-feeding or abstinence from intercourse after birth and indigenous birth control techniques, help to keep fertility below its maximum.

We can look at the experiences of the Hutterites, Russia, and other countries in order to generalize the determinants of fertility. While "distal" and "proximate" determinants of fertility can be identified,[6] demographer John Bongaarts identifies four variables that explain nearly all the variation in fertility levels across populations.[7] These include the proportion married or in a sexual union, the proportion using contraceptives, the proportion of women who are infertile, and the incidence of abortion. First, in all societies, marriage has clearly been an institution that has promoted fertility. The longer a woman waits to enter a sexual union, the lower the fertility rate. Conversely, where women marry at a young age, fertility rates tend to be higher due to the increased exposure to risk of pregnancy and longer periods over which pregnancy could occur. Cultural values and practices relating to sexual activity, childbearing outside of marriage or union, and contraceptive use will have an impact upon fertility decisions as well. In the past, the age at entry into marriage and the age at entry into a sexual union were the same, but the increasing availability of modern birth control techniques and acceptance of premarital intercourse has meant that this is no longer the case. Celibacy and abstinence (either voluntary or involuntary [i.e., because of impotence]), along with frequency of intercourse within a union, will either eliminate or alter the risk of pregnancy.

Second, contraceptive use and abortion are the key determinants of fertility in most developed countries. The "reproductive revolution," signaled by the availability and development of modern and effective family-planning methods such as the birth control pill, made it easier to avoid pregnancy. Increased access to methods of birth control and the desire to limit family size helped fertility reductions, and, when they are used in developing countries, fertility decline has been much more rapid than the decline developed countries experienced during their fertility transition. Despite the reproductive revolution, contraceptive use varies dramatically over space and echoes variations in fertility levels. Among women who are in sexual unions and of reproductive age who use modern contraceptives in the United States and Canada, for example, the rate of modern contraceptive usage is approximately 70 percent.[8] Somewhat lower levels of use are observed in Europe, particularly in Eastern Europe where contraceptive use rates are approximately 44 percent, reflecting historically lower levels of contraceptive availability and acceptance and higher abortion rates.

In the developing world, contraceptive use lags behind usage rates found elsewhere, but family-planning programs have had a strong influence on fertility by raising the awareness of means or the need for contraception and control. Contraceptive use is lower in Asia, Latin America, and Africa as well, with less than 10 percent in some areas of the latter using modern birth control methods. Instead, the regulation of fertility largely lies with traditional methods (i.e., withdrawal or abstinence), and the low incidence of contraceptive use is attributed to religious beliefs or societal values. Various governments have also decried the use of birth control methods as an unwanted intrusion of lax Western morals, even in the face of the HIV/AIDS epidemic, with the risk of transmission reduced through condom use.[9] When and how birth control is practiced also varies. Women in developed countries tend to start using birth control in their late teens or early twenties to delay childbearing and, following the birth of a child, to achieve desired spacing. In the developing world, contraception use frequently starts *after* the desired family size is achieved.

Third, abortion is one of the most common forms of modern birth control in the world, and is assumed to be an important reason for low birth rates in much of the developed world.[10] Legal in much of the world, including Canada, the United States, much of Europe, China, India, and Russia, some of the highest reported rates of abortion are found in Eastern Europe and Central Asia, with an observed rate of approximately forty-five per one hundred in 2003 in the Russian Federation,[11] where access to abortion is easier than access to contraceptive devices.[12] China, a country that typically had high abortion rates, has seen rates decline in recent years, although anecdotal evidence suggests rates of illegal abortion are high.

Finally, the inability to conceive is associated with voluntary or involuntary fecundity. Breast-feeding, for instance, reduces (but does not eliminate) the likelihood of pregnancy for as long as twenty-one months following childbirth.[13] With modernization, breast-feeding has tended to decline, which may be of particular concern within the developing world where, in the absence of other birth control techniques, fertility may increase. Sterilization also provides a method for lowering fertility, although this is a more popular procedure in developed countries, where it is generally used to prevent further pregnancies after a desired family size has been achieved.

Together, these four variables explain nearly all variations in fertility, with the importance of each determinant depending on the cultural, economic, health, and social factors within a population. In many African societies, babies are breastfed until age two or three, and women may be expected to abstain from intercourse for up to two years after birth, both of which increase spacing between births. Although Bongaarts provides insight into the key determinants of fertility, the question remains as to what determines the social forces that mold fertility choices. Why, for instance, would marriage be delayed? Why would contraceptive use increase? How do the cultural values attached to children change?

To answer these questions, we must turn to theories of fertility transition over time and space.[14] These may be roughly distinguished by microeconomic interpretations, characterized by Easterlin's "supply and demand" framework,[15] and the "diffusion-innovation" perspective, proposed by a number of authors.[16] Both frameworks find their roots within the demographic transition theory (chapter 1), which ascribes declines in fertility to societal changes related to industrialization and urbanization. In the face of declining mortality and improved economic opportunities, the demographic transition theory implies that people will eventually realize that more children will survive into their reproductive years than can be afforded, resulting in a decline in fertility that preceded modern birth control methods. Urbanization and industrialization therefore set the stage for declines in fertility, such as in pre–twentieth century Europe and North America, creating a way of life that made it more expensive to raise children.[17] Rather than using children to augment household income, children were to be "invested" in through such means as educational opportunities.

The linkages among urbanization, industrialization, and fertility (see also chapter 9) within the demographic transition theory were, however, criticized, especially within the context of the developing world, where the correlation between development and fertility is weak. Several countries in Asia (i.e., Bangladesh) and Latin America (i.e., Haiti) remain poor and underdeveloped and have low levels of urbanization, but are also experiencing fertility decline. In other words, development and economic security is not a sufficient condition to cause fertility to decrease. Building upon the demographic transition theory are the neoclassical theories of fertility decline. Easterlin's classic supply-demand framework defines fertility choice as the outcome of a rational calculation of the costs and benefits associated with fertility behavior, contextualized relative to cultural and household expectations. Families try to maintain a balance between the potential supply of children and the demand for surviving children. Where death rates are high, high fertility ensures the survival of some of the children to an economically active age, and there is no incentive to control fertility. The response to high mortality reflects children as a source of security and labor, a preference for a son, or a desire to "replenish" the population. In effect, children may be likened to pension plans, contributing to production and income within the household or the care of elders, making large families a necessity and an investment in future security.

If, on the other hand, supply exceeds demand, fertility regulation becomes important. The decision to control fertility is then based upon the financial and social costs of raising a child, as more children are being produced and surviving into their reproductive years. Casting fertility behavior as an economic choice means that children are, in many ways, seen as luxury items and subject to both time and investment. Investment is represented by the *direct costs* of education, clothing, food, and so forth as well as *opportunity costs*, representing foregone investments and purchases of other consumer goods. Parents are then faced with a trade-off between quality and quantity. In the developed world, quality is emphasized, with resources concentrated on a relatively small number of children. Children in the developed world are not expected to contribute to the economic well-being of the household, or to support parents in their old age. Instead, they represent large direct costs associated with education, clothing, and food, along with indirect or opportunity costs of having children at a time when the same dollar value could be spent on other consumer goods and demands for leisure time.

Criticism of neoclassical determinants of fertility behavior has led social scientists to link changes in fertility behavior to the diffusion of ideas across space.[18] As with any process, diffusion of social norms or new ideas varies spatially, with the timing of the fertility transition hinging upon the diffusion of social norms and new ideas, including birth control techniques. In the past, the preference for small families diffused out of urban areas, from high- to low-income groups, and from country to country. Although important, diffusion is not a spatially smooth process. For instance, poor or inadequate transportation or communication infrastructure, especially evident in rural, agricultural, and poor regions of the world, creates barriers that alter or slow the diffusion of new ideas or norms. Religious ideology remains a persuasive force, limiting the success of family-planning programs and the promotion of birth control methods. Cultural practices may likewise preclude the use of contraceptive devices, such as the condom, which is viewed as interference during sexual intercourse in some cultures.

The uptake of new ideas or norms also depends upon the individual. If new ideas such as birth control are to be accepted, individuals must feel that they exert some power or control over life events.[19] In societies where women lack control and power, fertility rates tend to remain high. The key, therefore, is to produce greater equity between males and females, which is accomplished vis-à-vis improvements in educational attainment, occupational status, or income opportunities. Improved education status and paid employment have reduced fertility, with a near-universal relationship between improved educational levels among women and decreased fertility. Women with better levels of education also tend to have a higher uptake of family planning, tend to wait longer between pregnancies, and stop childbearing at an earlier age than those who are less educated. Even a secondary-level education has been associated with a one-third to one-half reduction in the number of children born relative to women with no education.[20]

There is an even stronger relationship between women's education and child health, with higher educational attainment linked to healthier and better-nourished children, which in itself promotes a reduction in fertility. Although the exact relationship is unclear, completion of education may delay entry into marriage and expands employment options, suggesting that women delay fertility in order to earn an income. Employment also exposes women to new ideas, behaviors, and influences outside of the family. However, gender equity in employment is vital: if employment does not translate to power and does not enable women to make decisions regarding health care, contraception, the timing of children, and so forth, then declines in fertility are unlikely to occur.[21]

FERTILITY LEVELS: TOO HIGH OR TOO LOW?

When discussing fertility levels, we tend to focus on the fertility rate and the idea of "replacement fertility." After all, this gives us the sense of whether or not a population is able to replace itself over time. Demographers refer to a TFR of 2.1 as replacement fertility or the number of children needed to exactly replace their parents' generation, accounting for premature death. Yet, these averages tend to hide regional variations in fertility rates, such as the difference in fertility between Hispanics and white non-Hispanics in the United States, or between the French-speaking Quebecois and the larger Canadian population. Moreover, the replacement level is not necessarily consistent: in the developing world, the TFR required for replacement ranges from 2.5 to 3.3 because of higher mortality rates.[22] It is, incidentally, worth noting that there is relatively little separating population growth from population decline. Taking a TFR of 2.1 as replacement fertility, fertility rates in excess of 2.1 will result in population growth. Conversely, rates less than replacement will result in population decline! Both sides of replacement fertility also bring their own troubles.

Implications of High Fertility

By this point, the implications of high fertility should be fairly self-evident. Fertility rates in excess of the replacement level mean an increasing population, and it is certain that the world's population will continue to grow for the foreseeable future. Continued population growth poses deep problems for many nations, particularly where governments are fiscally strained, state institutions are weak, and health and educational systems are poor. In some cases, the strain of population growth is already showing as governments are unable to maintain investment in public infrastructure, including health care and education. In many cases, high population growth erodes economic growth, deepens poverty, and counters other achievements in social sectors.[23] Population growth and, ultimately, the absolute size of the population will continue to pose challenges to societies and their governments as they deal with growing scarcities of land and water, raising the potential for conflict.

Implications of Declining Fertility

While birth rates remain high in much of the world, an increasing number of countries are dealing with below-replacement fertility.[24] Low birth rates and a slowing or decreasing population growth rate have their own set of problems. Although the anticipated consequences of an aging society are still unclear, the PRB concluded that low fertility is a serious problem, having more disadvantages than advantages and making it a politically unsustainable position.[25] From a demographic perspective, low fertility results in an increasing proportion of elderly. In Canada, the elderly population (aged sixty-five-plus) represented just 7.8 percent of the population in 1951, growing to 14 percent in 2009. Current projections place it at approximately 20 percent by 2026, altering the age distribution of the population from its typical pyramidal shape, dominated by a young population, to a rectangular one, characterized by a proportionately larger elderly population.[26] Although having the highest TFR in the Western world, the United States has seen similar increases in its share of the elderly population, representing just 4.1 percent of the population in 1900, 13 percent in 2009, and projected to grow to nearly 20 percent by 2030.[27] In Europe, the elderly already represent greater than 15 percent of the population in several countries, including Sweden (18 percent), the United Kingdom (16 percent), and Belgium (17 percent), with continued growth ensured.

Economists have tended to assume that the marketplace will be able to react to population change. If children are scarce, they will become more valuable, and the system will correct itself, either by finding substitutes for children (unlikely!) or by placing greater value upon children, achieved through various incentive programs. Yet, the recession of 2008–2009 suggested that this was not the case, with economic opportunities the real driver of fertility. While the full effects of the recession on fertility will not be observed until 2010 or later, it appeared that many families were postponing having children as the recession built and fear of losing jobs or income grew. Moreover, some analysts were wondering if the recession would create a new mindset that it was either work or family, not both.[28] It is also unclear what the economic effects of low or negative population growth would be.[29] Ester Boserup, a Danish economist, promoted the idea that population growth triggered economic development.[30] Over the long run, countries with growing populations would be more likely to post strong economic growth than a stationary or declining population. It has generally been assumed, for example, that population growth provides an economic stimulus: the growing population needs services and goods, with their purchases driving economic growth. Conversely, declining population growth rates imply slower economic growth with individuals buying less and saving more, a notion that most developed societies have adopted. Although simplistic, we can draw an analogy with the housing market—given declining population and a shrinking market, why would individuals invest in a home knowing that there will be fewer buyers (and therefore lower prices) in coming years? Similarly, the economic recession of 2009 was deepened, in large part, by a reluctance of individuals to buy in the face of soaring unemployment.

With an aging population, the costs of providing services to it will be carried by a smaller labor force. The negative economic impacts associated with low or negative population growth may be associated with greater inequalities within society. There is little doubt that countries with an aging population will face an increased burden of supporting the elderly, placing pressure on social-welfare programs. Countries with low fertility rates will have a smaller labor force with which to support the elderly population and may face severe labor shortages that threaten the economic livelihood or stability of the country.[31] The changing age structure of the population therefore raises questions regarding the provision of income security for the aged, housing, transportation, and other services, highlighted by recent debates regarding the crisis (and reform) of Social Security in the United States. Health care provision is of particular concern, since the elderly, and particularly those older than seventy-five, consume a disproportionate share of medical services. Concurrently, the welfare of children may suffer as funds are diverted to meet the needs of the elderly population.

The largest negative consequences of low or negative population growth may, in fact, be political rather than economic.[32] Internally, countries may face a "graying of politics," as political and economic concerns increasingly represent those of older generations at the expense of the young. Internationally, a shrinking population has been associated with demographic marginalization. A "population implosion" may infringe upon the very essence of nationality, with governments fearing that a declining population will threaten the ability of a country to defend itself. Even national identity is at stake, with national influence dependent upon the vitality and size of a population.

Overall, the negative economic impacts of an aging population are expected to be minimal. Instead, an aging population may be associated with higher savings rates, greater expertise, less unemployment, and higher innovation, although educational costs for retraining and continuing education of an older labor force are likely to increase. Likewise, low or negative population growth should not influence rates of technological change, consumption, or investment, although the distribution of these impacts across regions or age groups is unlikely to be equal, as is the case with the consumption of medical care.[33]

AFRICA'S FERTILITY TRANSITION?

Since the 1950s and the beginning of the population explosion in the developing world, demographers and governments alike have searched for indications that the characteristic high fertility levels found in the developing world would decrease. While fertility rates have declined as expected in most instances, they have stalled in others, such that population growth will continue for the next few decades, fueled by population momentum associated with the young age structure, increased life expectancies, and above-replacement fertility. The multidimensional factors associated with fertility decline, which are further complicated by national and international policies, make it difficult to ascertain whether all countries will complete some form of fertility transition. Pressure within segments of China's population to have more than the allotted one child shows a continuing desire to have larger families, and the problems associated with a rapidly aging population may force the government to relax its fertility policy. Fertility rates continue to remain above replacement in many other regions. Despite early successes in reducing fertility in Bangladesh, which saw fertility rates drop from over 6.0 children per woman in the early 1970s to 2.5 in 2009, fertility rates have remained relatively unchanged over the past twenty years. Similarly, Egypt's birth rate has remained equal to or greater than 3.0 since 1993, and it is uncertain whether it will be further reduced.[34]

After observing fertility transitions in Asia and Latin America, all eyes have focused upon Africa, where fertility rates remain stubbornly high, and most African nations (notably in sub-Saharan Africa) have made little progress toward the fertility transition.[35] In short, much of Africa is still waiting for the fertility transition. Africa is arguably faced with the most pressing fertility concerns: some fifty years after mortality levels were dramatically reduced in the developing world, Africa's TFR remains high at 4.8, while sub-Saharan Africa still has fertility rates well in excess of 5.0. Fertility rates this high, corresponding to an annual increase of 2.5 percent, enable the population to grow rapidly. While population growth is expected to slow and there is emerging evidence that fertility rates will ultimately decline, the population of Africa will, under current conditions, double by 2050. In sub-Saharan Africa, only South Africa, Zimbabwe, Kenya, and Namibia would appear to have entered a period of transition in fertility behavior, which could be characterized by higher contraceptive use, longer life expectancies, and a declining fertility rate, although HIV/AIDS threatens this success. Fertility reduction remains a distant goal for the majority of sub-Saharan countries.

Although most observers expect fertility rates to ultimately decline in African states, the question remains as to when large-scale reductions will occur, how far rates will drop, and how long it will take to achieve significant reductions. Like explanations for fertility decline, the answers to these questions are also multidimensional. First, although contraceptive use is increasing, it is used more for control of the spacing of children[36] or after desired family size is achieved, rather than as a form of fertility control to limit family size. Just 23 percent of married women use some form of modern birth control in many African nations, which compares with 69 percent in North America. Based on a study in three French-speaking West African countries, there was a high level of awareness of contraceptives, but use of contraceptives was low amongst married women and higher among unmarried women who were sexually active.[37]

Second, childhood mortality remains high in many African nations. As we have already noted, mortality rates have decreased within Africa, but perhaps not sufficiently to initiate fertility decline. The general rule is that life expectancy at birth must be greater than fifty years for fertility levels to decrease. This has only been recently achieved in some African states, while in others (particularly sub-Saharan states), life expectancy hovers near or remains below the fifty-year mark. Third, the HIV/AIDS crisis may reverse gains in life expectancy (see discussion of the demographic implications of HIV/AIDS in chapter 5). Although there is no evidence that fertility choices will be affected, declines in life expectancy have already been noted. It has been estimated that life expectancies in Zimbabwe are now twenty-one years lower than they would have been without AIDS.[38] Fourth, gender equity is a distant goal in many societies. Women remain marginalized, literacy rates remain low, and rapid population growth and economic crises in the 1980s and 1990s prevented many countries from expanding educational opportunities to meet the growing population. Too frequently, the consequence is poor reproductive health. Health care systems are also casualties of high rates of population growth and stagnant economies that have limited development, modernization, and investment in basic health care services. Many systems are poorly funded or in ruin, preventing access to the most basic of health services at times when both mother and child are in need.

In the past, policy options have offered little hope of reducing fertility levels in Africa,[39] evidenced by the experiences of the United Nations and other international groups that have worked since the 1950s to address population growth issues. This is not to imply that progress in reducing fertility has not been (or is not) possible, merely that the implementation of successful family-planning programs is challenging, recognizing that there are particular needs to target the underprivileged and those in rural areas through the provision of family planning, the encouragement of gender equality, education, and economic development. In general, countries that have invested in health and family planning have slower population growth and greater economic development than those countries that have not made such investments. Many African governments have recognized the intimate link between population and development, and have promoted programs that would reduce fertility levels, but have frequently lacked the financial ability to fully implement programs. Alternatively, they have not sufficiently involved all stakeholders, including religious leaders and men that would work to ensure success by altering social, political, and economic forces influencing fertility choices that prove slow to change. Ensuring that fertility rates are reduced in Africa will provide an ongoing challenge.

WOMEN'S REPRODUCTIVE HEALTH

Underlying many fertility decisions, and ultimately their outcome, is women's reproductive health, which includes safe motherhood, HIV/AIDS, adolescent reproductive health, and family planning. Clearly, these are not mutually exclusive concerns, although they are more often than not developing world concerns. Maternal mortality, for example, is greatest in sub-Saharan Africa (920 maternal deaths per 100,000 live births), with many countries experiencing rates in excess of 1,000. In comparison, maternal mortality is only 6 in Canada, 17 in the United States, and 12 in western Europe.[40] Morbidity associated with poor reproductive outcomes is also significant.[41]

Not surprisingly, maternal mortality is associated with the absence of good medical care before, during, and after delivery. For instance, a majority of births in sub-Saharan Africa are not attended by skilled health personnel, and antenatal care is frequently lacking and sought out only when there is a complaint.[42] Equally problematic, there is frequently a lack of awareness about the importance of, and need for, medical care during pregnancy. Maternal mortality is compounded by gender roles and social and economic conditions within individual societies. For example, cost and accessibility of reproductive health care providers may limit use, particularly in rural areas where trained providers are few, access to information is either limited or difficult, and the population simply lacks the funds for appropriate care.[43] Similarly, while women may prefer to seek female health care providers, few may be available and husbands may be the ones who decide whether to seek care. As a consequence, males must also be included in reproductive health discussions. Complications from illegal and unsafe abortions are also a major cause of maternal death or morbidity, and one that is common in areas where access to safe abortion is limited or illegal. In Nicaragua, complications from unsafe abortions have been identified as one of the leading causes of hospitalization among women, and upward of 8 percent of maternal deaths may be linked to complications associated with unsafe abortions.[44]

Adolescents are perhaps at greatest risk for negative reproductive health outcomes, given their potential exposure to sexually transmitted diseases, unintended pregnancies, and complications from pregnancy and childbirth.[45] Worldwide, more adolescent girls die from pregnancy-related causes than any other cause, and maternal mortality is four times as high for women younger than seventeen years. In part, their poor reproductive health reflects an inability to address adolescent reproductive needs and early marriage, and lack of knowledge or experience in terms of family planning. Female genital cutting, or the removal of all or part of a young girl's external genitalia, remains a major reproductive health issue in some African and Middle Eastern countries, and can lead to infertility and other health complications.

In large part, improvements in female reproductive health reflect increased access to trained health care providers and education, including family planning, which contributes to both maternal and infant health by reducing the number of unintended pregnancies. As noted earlier in this chapter, the use of contraceptive devices varies widely. There is, however, a relationship between family-planning programs and the practice of some form of family planning, whether that is contraception use or some other method to limit and space pregnancies. In Iran, which introduced family-planning programs in the 1980s, 56 percent of married women practice modern family planning. Correspondingly, rates tend to be lower in countries with newer or more limited family-planning programs. At the same time, unmet need for contraceptive devices—which includes such diverse issues as fear of contraception's side effects, disapproval by husband or family, religious objections, and difficulties in obtaining contraceptives—limits the success of family-planning programs. Unmet needs are typically highest amongst poor and uneducated women.[46]

CONCLUSION

While generally declining, fertility rates vary at the global and local scales. Although low fertility is implicitly desired, resulting in slower or negative population growth, there is little agreement on what constitutes a desirable rate of population growth. Is it sufficient to simply replace the current generation? Can societies with below-replacement fertility, such as many European countries, survive politically and grow economically? What are the political, economic, and social implications of below-replacement fertility? In such countries, governments may actively promote fertility through pronatalist policies, typically by providing financial incentives to couples. Yet, how can governments speak of needing to increase fertility when there is an abundance of it elsewhere that could be used to augment growth in the developed world through immigration? Elsewhere, countries with rapid population growth will attempt to reduce fertility and slow population growth, with China's experiment at fertility control being the most widely known (see chapter 10, "Focus").

FOCUS: CONTRASTING FERTILITY RATES AND CHOICES IN NORTH AMERICA AND UGANDA

When we compare the fertility choices and rates between the developed and developing world, large differences in both are typically exposed.[1] These contrasts can be highlighted by looking at two cases—North America and Uganda.

THE NORTH AMERICAN EXPERIENCE

While fertility rates over the past century have fluctuated, they have generally declined. In 1900, the fertility rate was approximately 3.5. As the nation moved into the depression of the 1930s and World War II, fertility rates dropped. Post–World War II, this picture changed dramatically with the baby boom. In the United States, the TFR peaked at 3.58 in 1957, up from 2.19 immediately after the war. By the mid-1960s, fertility rates had once again dropped to levels similar to those observed prior to the baby boom, with fertility rates continuing to drift slowly downward. By the 1970s, the TFR stood at approximately 1.7. After the 1970s, fertility moved upwards slightly toward 2.0 children per woman in the 1980s and 1990s, and reached 2.1 in 2001, giving the United States one of the highest total fertility rates in the developed world. Most re-

cently, birth rates in the United States fell, leading some to speculate that the recession of 2008/2009 was to blame, echoing similar fluctuations in fertility associated with economic cycles.[2]

The United States and Canada share a similar demographic profile and history, with Canada also experiencing declining fertility from 1900 through the Depression and wars, followed by the postwar baby boom. In Canada, the TFR reached a slightly higher level (3.9) and peaked slightly later (1959) before dropping below the replacement level of 2.1 by 1972. Surprisingly, the decline was led by the French-speaking province of Quebec, where the role of the Catholic church in society was assumed to ensure that fertility rates would remain higher than those observed elsewhere in Canada. In more recent years, Canada's fertility experience has diverged from that of the United States. As of 2009, its fertility rate was 1.6, much lower than that observed in the United States. Despite sharing similar social changes, such as reduced marriage rates, increased average ages for marriage, and increased educational levels, Canada's fertility experience has tended to follow more closely that of Europe.[3] The important difference may lie in Canada's immigrant population, which given immigration policy, tends to be highly educated, implying lower levels of fertility.

In both the United States and Canada, the baby boom reflected the pent-up demand for children following World War II and the Depression, along with rising incomes and expectations and earlier marriages. Likewise, the drop in fertility in both countries was associated with several factors.[4] First, couples were increasingly delaying marriage as women placed greater emphasis on education and the development of their own careers over development of families. This was also closely related to income potential: higher education meant increasing income opportunities. Consequently, staying at home to raise a family meant income foregone. Second, the 1960s marked the sexual revolution and the increased availability and acceptance of contraception, and particularly the contraceptive pill. Together, these made planning and spacing of pregnancies easier, or ensured that a pregnancy would not occur altogether. Third, an economic interpretation has also been applied to explain declining fertility, given the "demographic squeeze" due to the baby boom generation. As these children aged first into school, then postsecondary education, and finally the labor market, male wages fell at the same time as more women entered the market, in part to compensate for declining wages and as an expression of their own career interests and educational attainment. As a result, marriage and families were postponed.

As already noted, US fertility is higher than most developed countries, and is even higher than some countries in the developing world. Various reasons for this difference have been put forward.[5] In large part, its relatively high fertility rate has been attributed to its ethnic diversity, with minority groups having higher fertility than native-born white Americans.[6] For instance, the TFR for non-Hispanic whites is 1.9. In contrast, Asian Americans had a TFR of 2.0, blacks 2.1, and the TFR was 3.2 amongst Hispanics. For Hispanics, fertility rates are likely higher for reasons including lower educational attainment and cultures and religions that promote larger families. Although fertility rates amongst foreign-born Hispanics are much higher than amongst their native-born counterparts, Hispanic fertility rates are likely to decline toward those of native-born Americans over successive generations.[7] Second, differences in the cost of childbearing have been suggested: generally higher costs for housing and other commodities in Europe, for example, increase the costs of raising a family, and therefore result in lower fertility levels.

THE UGANDAN EXPERIENCE

Having one of the highest levels of fertility in Africa (the 2009 TFR was 6.7) and a rapidly growing population, Uganda presents a strikingly different picture, reflecting its stage in the demographic transition. Over the past fifty years, the fertility rate changed little, and actually increased slightly during the 1970s and 1980s.[8] As a consequence, the country's population is young, with a stunning 49 percent below the age of fifteen. This young population has yet to move into its reproductive years, meaning that Uganda's population is projected to grow to 51.8 million by 2025, up from 30.7 million in 2009,[9] and fertility rates are expected to remain high.[10]

In large part, Uganda's high fertility reflects a continuation of social trends and the need for large families in order to diversify income opportunities and help the household. In short, fertility has not yet adjusted to increased life expectancy and reduced mortality within the population. War and political and economic turmoil have also helped to ensure that fertility remains high. At the same time, the PRB reports a huge unmet demand for contraception, suggesting that there is a desire to decrease fertility levels by either avoiding pregnancy or through better spacing of pregnancies.[11] That is, there is a demand for contraception, but it is not readily available or affordable. Indeed, only 24 percent of married women aged fifteen to forty-nine use some method of birth control, while only 18 percent use a modern method. The PRB, however, estimates that some 35 percent of married women in the same fifteen to forty-nine age group would prefer to use contraception, but cannot access it. In addition, unmet needs may reflect a lack of awareness of modern contraception techniques, social and cultural constraints that limit a woman's ability to control birth decisions, and fears of side effects or that use of birth control could be seen as a sign of promiscuity.[12]

METHODS, MEASURES, AND TOOLS: MEASURING FERTILITY

The basic notion of measuring fertility is understanding how the size of a population can be determined by birth choices. The fertility of a population is commonly measured in various ways, the most common of which are presented here. Fertility measures are broadly divided into two types. Period data refers to a particular time period (i.e., calendar year or some other period of time) and is essentially a cross section or snapshot of fertility at a particular point in time. Conversely, cohort measures follow a group of women over time, describing how their fertility choices and behavior vary over the period. Data used to measure fertility are drawn from a variety of sources. Commonly, governments will collect birth data and compile it along with other so-called "vital" statistics. While comparing fertility is facilitated by age standardization, it can also be complicated due to variations in the quality and quantity of collected data: the better the data, the more accurate the conclusion.

In 2006, a total of 4,265,555 births were registered in the United States. The crude birth rate was 14.2, and the total fertility rate was 2.1.[1] Although we have discussed the meaning of the TFR, how else can we measure fertility? Perhaps the most basic measure of fertility is the *crude birth rate* (CBR), defined by

$$CBR = 1,000\left(\frac{B}{P}\right)$$

where B is the number of annual births and P is the midyear population at risk of giving birth (i.e., women in their reproductive years). While simple to calculate and providing a quick measure of the contribution of fertility to population change, the crude birth rate does not account for the age and sex structure of a population, and therefore does not allow comparison across populations or regions. That is, women from regions with the same crude birth rate may in fact have very different propensities to have children. Consequently, the *age-specific fertility rate* (ASFR, $_hF_x$) is commonly used, and defined as

$$_hF_x = 1,000\left(\frac{_hB_x}{_hP_x^f}\right)$$

where $_hB_x$ is the number of live births to women aged x to $x + h$ during the year, and $_hP_x^f$ is the midyear population of females aged x to $x + h$, and h is the width of the cohort, typically defined as five years and corresponding to population data that is commonly available in data files such as the census.

The TFR measures the expected total number of children that a woman will have over her reproductive career, assuming (1) survival at least through the childbearing ages and (2) that children will be born according to the age-specific rates as women age. This measure is commonly used in describing fertility patterns and in comparing the rates of fertility across different regions and is a better measure of fertility than the crude birth rate because it is independent of the age structure of the population. It is defined by the following formula.

$$TFR = h \sum_x {}_hF_x$$

The TFR is calculated by summing all of the age-specific fertility rates (F_x) over all reproductive age groups and then multiplying the result by the width of the age group used (h).

While the TFR can be used to gauge whether a population is growing or declining due to fertility, the *gross reproduction rate* (GRR) provides the expected number of female children a woman will have, relative to age-specific rates and assuming survival through the reproductive years. In this way, the GRR provides an alternate measure of whether a population is replacing itself and is defined by multiplying the TFR by the percentage of births that are female. GRR values close to 1.0 represent one female exactly re-

placing herself, so the population growth rate will be equal to 0. Values less than 1.0 indicate that the next generation of women will not replace themselves, while the current generation will more than replace themselves if the GRR is greater than 1.0.

Finally, the *net reproduction rate* (NRR) is a more precise indicator of whether a population will grow or decline over time by accounting for the fact that not all females will survive to childbearing ages, which is an underlying assumption of the GRR. The NRR defines the number of daughters born to a woman if she were subject to prevailing age-specific fertility and mortality rates in the given year. The NRR is defined as the following formula.

$$NRR = \frac{w}{l_0} \sum_x {}_hF_x {}_hL_x$$

In essence, this is the gross reproduction rate multiplied by the proportion of female babies surviving to the midpoint of the age interval, which can be derived from a life table. If the calculated NRR is equal to 1.0, each generation of women is exactly replacing itself. If it is greater than 1.0, the population will grow, while a value less than 1 is the converse (shrinking), and 0 indicates that the current generation will not be replaced.

Cohort measures of fertility include *completed fertility*, which measures the total number of births to a cohort of women. Alternatively, *fertility intentions* provide an estimate of the number of children a woman intends to have over her reproductive years. However, fertility intentions can be altered by changing preferences or economic situations, which may increase or decrease the number of desired children.

Chapter Five

Mortality

THE DECLINE IN MORTALITY RATES from their historically high levels initiated the demographic transition. In much of Europe and North America, declines in mortality were apparent shortly after the onset of the Industrial Revolution. These improvements to human survival and longer life spans resulted in rapid population growth, aided by modernization and advances in sanitation and nutrition, with Europe's population more than doubling between 1800 and 1900.[1] By the first half of the twentieth century, developed countries had completed their mortality transition, characterized by long life expectancies, low infant death rates, and slow population growth rates. In the developing world, the initiation of mortality declines in the postwar era during the second half of the twentieth century brought rapid population growth. Here, the pace of mortality decline tended to be much more rapid than that experienced in the developed world, assisted by the importation of modern medicines, health care, immunizations, and improved nutrition and sanitation.

This chapter explores mortality differences and the related subject of morbidity, or illness within populations. It begins by discussing the mortality transition, or the decline in mortality rates, and the epidemiological transition. It then explores differences in the rates and causes of mortality between black and white Americans and increasing mortality in Russia. The chapter also discusses the significance of IPDs and their reemergence before focusing on HIV/AIDS and its impact on population mortality. The "Focus" section contrasts the mortality experiences of the United States, Zimbabwe, and Mexico, and the "Measures, Methods, and Tools" section defines the common measures of mortality.

MORTALITY TRANSITIONS

For much of human history, the average person could probably expect to live only twenty to thirty years. Infant mortality rates were high, and approximately half of all deaths occurred before age five, usually associated with poor nutrition or infanticide. With advances in agriculture and the domestication of animals, humans were able to establish year-round settlements. Infectious diseases such as bubonic plague found a new home in human settlements and became the prevalent cause of death, as denser populations and relatively poor sanitation allowed infectious diseases to thrive. Trade between settlements transported illness and disease across space.[2] The nineteenth and twentieth centuries saw improvements in housing, sanitation, and nutrition, allowing mortality to decrease and life expectancy in Europe and North America to increase to forty years.

The poor health standards and living conditions observed in American, Canadian, and British cities during the Industrial Revolution gave rise to new public health initiatives. This intervention was spearheaded by the elite not out of goodness but out of fear that their own health and, perhaps more importantly, their profits, hinged upon the conditions of the working poor.[3] Although infectious diseases, including tuberculosis, bronchitis, pneumonia, influenza, and measles, remained the main cause of death, their incidence declined with environmental improvements, such as improved living conditions, and occurred long before medical intervention was widely available.[4] However, some diseases, such as diphtheria, did not respond to societal improvements, declining only when large-scale immunization programs began. In fact, it wasn't until the 1950s that a decline in mortality, particularly amongst the older population, could be associated with the application of low-cost public health programs. Since then, improvements to life expectancy within developed countries have generally been attributed to advances in medical and biological sciences as opposed to general economic improvements or public health. The mortality transition also results in a shift in the ages when the majority of deaths occur. In countries at the beginning of the transition, younger age groups are at greater risk of dying, since children are particularly susceptible to many infectious diseases. Even now, approximately 40 percent of deaths in the developing world occur among children less than five years old. In the developed world, most deaths occur among the elderly, with less than 2 percent of deaths occurring among those less than twenty years old.

Despite improvements in indicators such as life expectancy or infant mortality within the past fifty years, widespread variations remain, even in the developed world (figure 5.1). As of 2009, life expectancy in the developed world averaged seventy-seven years, being slightly longer for women (eighty-one) than men (seventy-four). In the developing world (excluding China), life expectancies are lower, averaging sixty-seven and sixty-three years from birth among women and men, respectively.[5] Improvements have been slower in sub-Saharan Africa than in any other region,[6] with life expectancies in sub-Saharan Africa just fifty-one years, compared to seventy-eight years in North America, seventy-three years in Latin America, and sixty-nine years in Asia. At eighty deaths per one thousand births, infant mortality rates are similarly higher in sub-Saharan Africa. In comparison, infant mortality rates are only six per one thousand in the developed world.

Omran's Epidemiological Transition

Abdel Omran's epidemiological transition provides a useful framework for looking at these temporal trends in mortality,[7] echoing the decline in mortality set out in the demographic transition theory. However, Omran's theory asserts that

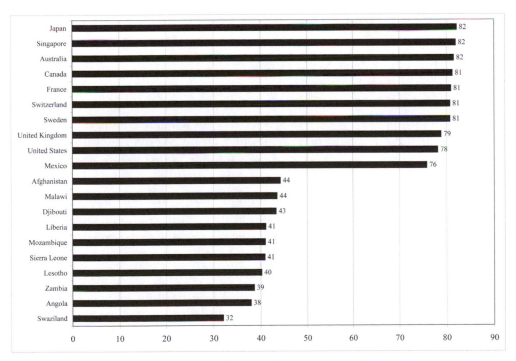

Figure 5.1   Life Expectancy in Selected Countries, 2009.
Source: PRB.

modernization not only brings about reductions in overall mortality levels and the timing of death, but also results in a shift in the major causes of death from infectious and contagious diseases to chronic, degenerative disorders. As recently as the mid-eighteenth century, tuberculosis, cholera, diarrhea, and pneumonia-influenza were the leading causes of death throughout the world. Through much of the latter half of the twentieth century, resources were marshaled to control infectious and parasitic diseases. By the late 1990s, only pneumonia and influenza remained among the top ten causes of premature death within the developed world. Instead, chronic non-communicable and degenerative diseases such as cancer, diabetes, liver, cardiovascular, or neurological diseases have replaced infectious diseases as the leading cause of death in the developed world. As the incidences of disease and premature death were reduced, individuals were able to enjoy longer life expectancies.

Countries occupy different stages in this transition and progress through it at different rates. Unlike in the developed world, where socioeconomic improvements resulted in declining mortality over a span of decades, most developing countries have moved quickly through the epidemiological transition, directly benefiting from the transfer of public health knowledge and medical technology and medicines from the developed world. This has meant that the developing world has experienced a much more rapid decline in mortality levels than that experienced in the developed world.

DIFFERENCES IN MORTALITY

The past one hundred years have seen remarkable improvements in life expectancy and infant mortality. Reductions were particularly dramatic in developing countries when countries gained the ability to treat or eradicate infectious diseases such as malaria, smallpox, and yellow fever and where improvements in basic health status had immediate effects. Despite improvements in indicators such as life expectancy or infant mortality, mortality rates vary across the globe and by age, sex, sociodemographic status, race, ethnicity, and location, with the developed world characterized by lower death rates than elsewhere. Yet, in summarizing worldwide variations in mortality measures, we tend to make two assumptions. First, we assume that health indicators will constantly improve. We have come to expect improvements in life expectancy as medical science continues to make discoveries and as the population is increasingly taught to make positive lifestyle choices (i.e., maintaining physical fitness or not smoking) that will extend or protect life. Second, we generally assume that poor indicators of health are only found in the developing world. In other words, we assume that the Western, developed world has the advantage of an accessible and developed health system that ensures population health. Yet, neither of these assumptions is correct, as the following two examples illustrate. These health and mortality differentials are particularly problematic, not because they represent populations that require large-scale intervention and have little access to health care, but for the exact opposite reasons. That is, in the presence of a large health care infrastructure, poor mortality experiences within segments of the population seem to be a paradox, yet they are common.

Race and Ethnicity: The Case of the United States

Americans have access to some of the best health care in the world, and their health care system consumes a significantly higher proportion of America's gross domestic product (GDP) than other developed countries.[8] A casual observer might, therefore, expect the United States to have the lowest infant mortality rate or the highest life expectancy. In fact, with a 2005 infant mortality rate of 6.86[9] and a life expectancy of seventy-eight years from birth, health indicators within the United States are rather poor by Western standards. In some cases, health indicators are more akin to those found in the developing world than the developed world, with the US infant mortality rate higher than that found in twenty-eight countries, including Cuba and Hungary, placing American indicators closer to the bottom of the developed world's list than the top.

In large part, the poor performance of American mortality indicators reflects the poor health status and mortality conditions of its minority populations,[10] with large differences by race and ethnicity.[11] Non-Hispanic black, American Indian, Alaska Native, and Puerto Rican women have the highest rates of infant mortality, while Asian and Pacific Islanders, Central and South Americans, Mexicans, and Cubans have the lowest.[12] Disparities are particularly noticeable between African Americans and whites. The 2005 IMR for non-Hispanic whites was 5.76. In comparison, the IMR for non-Hispanic blacks was 13.63. For Puerto Ricans, it was 8.3. In part, increases in preterm birth and preterm-related causes of death are major factors associated with the high IMR in the country.

Similarly, despite dramatic improvements in life expectancies since 1900 (from approximately 33 years to 73.2 years in 2005), black life expectancies remain shorter than those of white Americans, who average 78.3 years of life,[13] with the gap in life expectancy between blacks and whites growing over the past fifty years.[14] African American mortality rates are higher than those observed within the white population at every age except the very oldest, and African Americans have higher rates of death relative to whites from almost every major cause, especially for heart disease, cancer, HIV/AIDS, and homicide. The increased risk of death is magnified among young African American males, where homicide is the leading cause of death, while white men are more likely to die in accidents (table 5.1). Young blacks are also several times more likely to die from AIDS than whites.

Smaller geographic scales show these same racial disparities. Infant mortality rates amongst blacks are more than two times those observed amongst whites, with some of the highest rates observed in the Southern states.[15] Within the state of Illinois, the 2004 IMR (7.2) was worse than the national average. This value, however, reflects a white (2004) IMR of just 5.9, and an IMR of 15.5 among African Americans,[16] a rate that is higher than Sri Lanka (11)! At an even smaller geographic scale, the 2002 IMR within the City of Chicago was 14.8 among African Americans, but just 5.1 among whites.

While the disparities in mortality experiences of black and white Americans are startling, they reflect the continued marginalization of blacks within American society, measured by inequalities in education, economic status, or occupation. Despite improvements in their overall economic and social status from the 1930s onward and legislation that has reduced the social and economic gulf between the two groups, the gap remains substantial. For instance, median household income in 2006 was $48,201, yet for blacks, the median income was only $31,969.[17] Minority children suffer disproportionately from economic deprivation, with the proportion of children in poverty among blacks approximately three times that of white children in 2006.[18] Differences in mortality by race remain even after comparing individuals with similar levels of income and education.

The prevalence of poor mortality outcomes is also linked to the structure of the American health care system. The lower socioeconomic position of blacks makes the affordability of private medical insurance less likely. While public health programs such as Medicare or Medicaid are available for the poor or elderly, these programs are limited and means-tested. For the remainder, it has become too expensive to pay for private health insurance, and an estimated 47 million Americans had no insurance in 2006.[19] Amongst blacks, over 20 percent did not have health insurance, compared to 14.5 percent amongst whites, and rates of noninsurance for black children were double those observed for white children in 2006. Regardless of race, lack of health insurance typically means that individuals forgo medical treatment, rely upon social service agencies for assistance, or utilize emergency room services, where the cost of medical attention is significantly greater.

Concurrently, the health system provides fewer services and clinics in poor areas.[20] Physicians, clinics, and institutions locate in areas with higher financial returns, and inner-city areas have fewer services. The number of public hospitals that provided care for the poor declined from 1,778 in 1980 to 1,197 in 1999, victims of hospital closures, acquisitions, or mergers.[21] Inner-city areas

Table 5.1. Leading Causes of Death: Black and White Males Aged 25–34 in the United States, 2006

	Black males			White males		
Rank	Cause of death[a]	Number	Rate	Cause of death	Number	Rate
—	All causes	6,684	252.3	All causes	20,581	127.0
1	Assault (homicide)	2,163	81.6	Accidents (unintentional injuries)	8,180	50.5
2	Accidents (unintentional injuries)	1,333	50.3	Intentional self-harm (suicide)	3,526	21.8
3	Diseases of the heart	597	22.5	Assault (homicide)	1,501	9.3
4	HIV disease	508	19.2	Diseases of the heart	1,431	8.8
5	Intentional self-harm (suicide)	429	16.2	Malignant neoplasms	1,401	8.6
6	Malignant neoplasms	265	10.0	HIV disease	392	2.4
7	Diabetes mellitus	104	3.9	Diabetes mellitus	227	1.4
8	Cerebrovascular diseases	77	2.9	Cerebrovascular diseases	198	1.2
9	Anemias	71	2.7	Congenital malformations, deformations, and chromosomal abnormalities	189	1.2
10	Chronic lower respiratory diseases	66	2.5	Chronic liver disease and cirrhosis	182	1.1
—	All other causes	1,071	40.4	All other causes	3,357	20.7

Source: United States, *National Vital Statistics Report* 56, no. 5 (2007).

[a] Based on International Classification of Diseases, Tenth Revision.

have difficulty in recruiting doctors and frequently depend upon federal programs such as the National Health Services Corps, created in 1970 to provide basic care to inner-city neighborhoods. Not surprisingly, therefore, where people live matters in terms of health, reflective of the "context-composition" discussion found within the health geography literature.[22] African Americans are, for instance, more likely to live in areas that have poor or limited health care services, and are therefore more likely to experience poor health.[23]

Mortality in Russia: Reductions in Mortality Improvements

Despite the mortality transition and its expected improvements, it is not necessarily a one-way street. That is, mortality can, in some cases, increase, reversing decades of improvement, with Russia providing an example.[24] As recently as 1900, Russian life expectancy was only slightly greater than thirty years, reduced by infant mortality rates that most likely reached three hundred per one thousand and a child mortality rate of up to 50 percent.[25] Within a relatively short period of time, the former Soviet Union had successfully reduced mortality and increased life expectancy within its population, with rates in the early 1960s comparable to those found in the United States and elsewhere in the developed world. Despite these dramatic improvements in health in the postrevolutionary period, the Soviet Union could not keep pace with the West with respect to basic health outcomes from the 1960s onward. As life expectancy and infant mortality continued to improve in the West, they deteriorated in the former Soviet Union. By the 1990s, observers of Russia's demographic system noted that male life expectancy had dropped from sixty-five years in 1987 to fifty-seven in 1994. Similarly, female life expectancy dropped by more than three years to an average of seventy-one years.[26] Although there is some disagreement about what caused the declines in mortality, most placed this decline within the context of the breakup of the Soviet Union in 1989 and the corresponding economic and social turmoil, along with inadequate health services, lack of prescription medicine, alcohol abuse, and high smoking prevalence.

Russia's mortality experiences run counter to typical expectations, demonstrating that mortality decline and the epidemiological transition are not unidirectional. While the exact causes of the deterioration of health outcomes are unknown and debated, they reflect a much longer process dating back over thirty years to the Soviet era. Infant mortality in the Soviet Union was always relatively high, but research in the 1970s by Davis and Feshbach noted infant mortality rates had started to diverge from Western experiences.[27] While infant mortality rates continued to decline in the West, rates in the former Soviet Union stabilized at approximately twenty-five, and then increased to over thirty by the mid-1970s. At about the same time, the Soviet Union stopped publishing detailed mortality statistics, a point that speaks for itself.[28] Davis and Feshbach attribute the increase in the infant mortality rate to social, economic, and medical reasons, including increased smoking and drinking among mothers, poor maternal nutrition and health, inadequate health care during pregnancy, and unsanitary conditions in hospitals. They also noticed strong regional differences in mortality, with the rise in infant mortality led by Central Asian republics, including Uzbekistan and Kazakhstan, along with the Caucasian republics of Georgia and Armenia.

The declining life expectancy among Russian men in the 1990s was not new either, but instead reflected longer-term trends, with Soviet indices worsening relative to the West as early as the 1970s. After a temporary improvement in life expectancies in the 1980s, which was attributed to an aggressive anti-alcohol campaign under then-president Mikhail Gorbachev, the gap between the Soviet Union and the West continued to grow through the 1990s. As with infant mortality, a portion of the widening gap was the result of increasing life expectancy in the West. But the gap also reflected deeper institutional problems within the Soviet Union itself, including inadequate health services and the general neglect of the Soviet and Russian health care system. Alcohol abuse and high rates of cardiovascular disease and injury also contributed to declining life expectancy.

Although male life expectancy had rebounded to sixty-six years by 2001, it dipped again in subsequent years, and was just sixty-one years in 2009. Russia's infant mortality rate has continued to drop, moving from sixteen in 2001 to nine in 2009. Still, it remains to be seen whether these measures will improve in the near future. The democratically nascent Russia continues to grapple with economic and social reform, and its health care system remains in a state of crisis. Russia must first catch up to the levels of infant mortality and life expectancy that were observed in the 1960s before approaching Western levels. In the meantime, political uncertainty and stalled economic reforms mean that its health institutions remain underfunded and social and economic conditions remain poor, neither of which is conducive for improvements to life expectancy.

INFECTIOUS AND PARASITIC DISEASES (IPDs)

Infectious and parasitic diseases encompass a range of diseases, including cholera, HIV/AIDS, and tuberculosis, to name a few. With the advent and widespread use of powerful antibiotics in the mid-twentieth century, science and the medical community thought that many IPDs were controllable, and ultimately could be eliminated as serious causes of death. The control of measles, mumps, polio, and other common childhood diseases further solidified the impression that modern medicine would overcome diseases that had been a scourge to humans for centuries.

In the postwar era, huge financial resources were committed to the eradication of infectious and parasitic diseases. Most notable among these programs was the eradication of smallpox, an infectious disease that had mortality rates in excess of thirty percent and was the leading cause of death in Europe in the 1800s. Its successful defeat in the 1970s through a global immunization program seemed to confirm that infectious diseases could be controlled through large-scale public health initiatives. Another major program targeted malaria, a health problem that has plagued humanity throughout history. The drainage of swamps and the control of mosquitoes, the "vectors" that carry malaria, through the application of the pesticide dichlorodiphenyltrichloroethane (DDT), resulted in dramatic reductions in the number of new cases.

The (Re)emergence of Infectious and Parasitic Diseases

Successes, such as the eradication of smallpox, proved to be temporary, and the past two decades have seen a reemergence of IPDs as major threats to societal health.[29] After 1963, commitment to malaria programs waned and the disease returned, worse than before. Long-term use of DDT had given birth to DDT-resistant mosquitoes, not to mention DDT's own deadly legacy linked to cancer and environmental effects. Concurrently, inadequate treatment regimes, poor drug supplies, and the misuse of drugs contributed to the rise of drug-resistant malaria.[30] Despite worldwide attempts to control malaria, the disease is as prevalent today as it was at the start of the campaign.[31] Similarly, and despite the success of inoculation programs, many children remain at risk for other infectious diseases, and IPDs remain the leading cause of death in the developing world. Measles remains one of the five leading causes of death in children under five years.[32] Although the prevalence of measles has been reduced remarkably within the past five years, it continues to account for a large number of preventable deaths (an estimated 197,000 deaths worldwide in 2007, including 177,000 deaths among children).[33] Worldwide, IPDs represent upwards of 54 percent of all deaths among children, while over 60 percent of deaths in Africa can be attributed to IPDs.

The reemergence of malaria should have served as a warning that complacency in the fight against infectious diseases was not an option and indicated that diseases could emerge or reemerge as the causal microbe evolved into a more infectious form or as new pathways to infection appeared. The rise of new IPDs, including Ebola, a usually deadly disease for which there is no known cure; multidrug-resistant tuberculosis, malaria, and meningitis; and new forms of cholera, has further shaken our complacency in science's ability to control infectious disease.

A variety of factors have been responsible for the reemergence of IPDs. One reason that infectious diseases cause a larger percentage of deaths in areas such as sub-Saharan Africa is purely demographic. The proportion of the population surviving into older ages, where the risk of death from chronic degenerative diseases is greater, is small in many parts of the developing world. Instead, young populations, widespread poverty, malnutrition, and inadequate public health care systems contribute to the high death toll, even though a majority of existing IPDs can be prevented through immunization, safe drinking water, proper food storage, safe-sex practices, and personal hygiene. Changes to the natural environment have also contributed to IPDs' reemergence. Human-induced changes can cause genetic changes in organisms or the vectors that transmit diseases (e.g., as in the case of DDT-resistant mosquitoes). Further, the misuse of antibiotics has contributed to the rise of drug-resistant forms of malaria and tuberculosis, and HIV/AIDS has resulted in an increase in tuberculosis and pneumonia. Agricultural practices affect the environment within which microbes live and spread, and social, economic, and political conditions have facilitated their return and spread. Population movement has long been an important avenue for the spread of disease. Historically, the bubonic plague was brought to Europe from Asia, and European explorers brought smallpox to North America and Oceania, decimating the indigenous populations, who had no resistance to the disease. Settlement and urbanization have concentrated populations and allowed the sustained presence of diseases that were formerly epidemic in small areas or for short periods. Cholera, nearly nonexistent in rural areas, quickly rose to epidemic proportions with urbanization as people were brought together and the risk of contagion was escalated in crowded and unsanitary conditions. Today, rapid urbanization in the developing world repeats this process as migrants settle in crowded and inadequate conditions.

The twenty-first century brings with it new challenges in the control of IPDs. For instance, the surge in IPDs has been due to a breakdown in the provision of public health, with civil strife a prime cause, as it disrupts the distribution of needed drugs and food. Rapid population growth and urbanization have meant that governments have not been able to provide adequate or basic health care or infrastructure such as clean water. Perhaps more worrisome is the speed and ease of transference of disease. The rapidity of movement across countries through jet travel poses additional challenges to the control of IPDs, with airplanes offering a highly effective means of transportation for disease, with the potential to spread illness and disease across the world in a matter of hours.

Additionally, there are an increasing number of cases in which individuals or societies reject immunization. In North America and elsewhere in the developed world, rejection may be based upon religious grounds and/or (unfounded) fears that immunization is linked to increased incidence of childhood autism.[34] Elsewhere, the failure to immunize and thus protect children from preventable IPDs is based on religious grounds. In Nigeria, for example, the government in the northern state of Kano stopped immunizing children against polio in 2004 amidst fears and claims by religious leaders that the vaccine made girls infertile.[35] Polio is a disease that is spread through human feces and can result in paralysis in one in two hundred people. Instead of hoping to eradicate polio, the World Health Organization was fighting to contain the virus, which had spread quickly to countries including Sudan, Benin, Botswana, Chad, Ghana, Togo, the Ivory Coast, Cameroon, and the Central African Republic. In these cases, the spread of the virus was likely due to the relatively porous borders in the region, while air travel has likely resulted in its spread to countries including Afghanistan, Indonesia, Egypt, Niger, Nigeria, and Pakistan.

HIV/AIDS

The human immunodeficiency virus (HIV), the virus that causes AIDS (acquired immunodeficiency syndrome), has altered mortality patterns and life expectancies globally, and perhaps best summarizes the potential for the emergence of new infectious diseases and their devastating effects. Although new research has pushed back the biological origins of the disease to between 1884 and 1924,[36] with evidence of HIV found in tissue samples from 1959,[37] it only attracted attention in 1981 when it was identified among gay men in the United States. Commonly thought to have emerged somewhere in central Africa and present-day Congo, the scientific community is still at a loss to explain exactly where it came from, although the most plausible theory is that the virus somehow moved from monkeys into humans, perhaps through hunting or religious or cultural ceremonies. With little interaction and population mobility, it potentially survived for decades within the human population, albeit at very low levels and within a spatially confined area. Civil war in the Congo in the early 1960s likely facilitated its movement into the larger population, carried by soldiers and aided by refugee movements and famine. It would emerge as a major public health concern and a leading cause of death throughout the world within a generation.

HIV/AIDS has resulted in an epidemic that is far more extensive than was initially forecasted. In 2007, 2.7 million were newly infected with the virus, 2 million people worldwide died of AIDS, and 33 million people were living with HIV/AIDS. Most HIV cases (95 percent) are found in the developing world, where the scale of the epidemic has profound economic, social, demographic, and political implications. It is just as important, however, to realize that the epidemic is far from over, with the Centers for Disease Control and Prevention (CDC) reporting in 2008 that HIV/AIDS was spreading faster in the United States than had been thought, with over 56,000 people newly infected with HIV. African Americans were disproportionately more likely to be infected, with black women nearly fifteen times as likely to be infected as white women and Hispanic women four times as likely to be infected as white women. At the same time, black men are six times more likely to be infected than white men, and approximately three times more likely than Hispanic men.[38]

Spatial Variations in HIV/AIDS in Africa

The challenges posed by HIV/AIDS vary from place to place, but are perhaps felt most acutely within sub-Saharan Africa, where AIDS remains the leading cause of death (table 5.2). In 2007, the region recorded an adult (aged fifteen to forty-nine) infection rate of 5.0 percent, with 22.5 million infected. Sub-Saharan Africa represents over 67 percent of the world's cases.[39] Although infection rates are high in the region, the prevalence of HIV/AIDS is unequal, meaning it is inaccurate to speak of a single, African epidemic. While initially centered in the countries of central and eastern Africa, the epidemic has exploded in southern Africa, while prevalence rates remain steady at five percent or less in many West African states, and East Africa has seen some modest declines in HIV prevalence among pregnant women in urban areas (figure 5.2).[40]

The epidemic peaks in southern Africa, where 26.1 percent of all adults (aged fifteen to forty-nine) in Swaziland are infected, and 23.9 percent of adults in Botswana are infected. Growing from just 1 percent in the early 1990s, the prevalence rate in South Africa is now 18.1 percent among adults, giving the country the dubious distinction of having more people infected with HIV than any other country. National adult HIV prevalence also exceeded 15 percent in Lesotho, Namibia, Zambia, and Zimbabwe.

These spatial variations in HIV/AIDS prevalence are likely rooted in a complex web of behavioral, social, and biological factors that interact with the continent's varied economic, social, and political systems.[41] The exact reasons for the spatial variation remain unclear, however, and a number of theories have been advanced.[42] One possibility lies in the patterns of sexual activity or networking within sub-Saharan Africa that promote heterosexual infection. Premarital and extramarital intercourse, age at first intercourse, number of partners, polygamy, the low status of women, wife inheritance, and use/frequency of contact with prostitutes have been implicated as practices that increase the risk of infection. While there are elements of truth to the networking theory, it is important to place it within the proper social, cultural, and

Table 5.2. Regional HIV/AIDS Statistics and Features, 2008

Region	Epidemic started	People living with HIV/AIDS	New infections, 2007	Adult prevalence rate[a] (%)	% of HIV positive adults who are women	Main mode(s) of transmission[b]
Sub-Saharan Africa	Late 70s–Early 80s	22 million	1.9 million	5.0	57	Hetero
North Africa and Middle East	Late 80s	380,000	40,000	0.3	48	Hetero IDU
South and Southeast Asia	Late 80s	4.2 million	330,000	0.3	28	Hetero IDU
East Asia	Late 80s	740,000	52,000	0.1	22	IDU Hetero MSM
Latin America	Late 70s–Early 80s	1.7 million	140,000	0.5	35	MSM IDU
Caribbean	Late 70s–Early 80s	230,000	20,000	1.1	49	Hetero Hetero MSM

Table 5.2.   (Continued)

Region	Epidemic started	People living With HIV/AIDS	New infections, 2007	Adult prevalence rate[a] (%)	% of HIV positive adults who are women	Main mode(s) of transmission[b]
Eastern Europe and Central Asia	Early 90s	1.5 million	110,000	0.8	34	IDU
Western and Central Europe	Late 70s Early 80s	730,000	27,000	0.3	26	MSM IDU
North America	Late 70s–Early 80s	1.2 million	54,000	0.6	25	MSM Hetero IDU
Oceania	Late 70s–Early 80s	74,000	13,000	0.4	20	MSM
Total		33 million	2.7 million	0.8	48	

Source: Based on data derived from the United Nations Program on HIV/AIDS (UNAIDS), www.unaids.org.

[a] The percentage of adults (fifteen to forty-nine years of age) living with HIV/AIDS in 2008.

[b] Hetero (heterosexual transmission), IDU (transmission through injecting drug use), and MSM (sexual transmission among men who have sex with men).

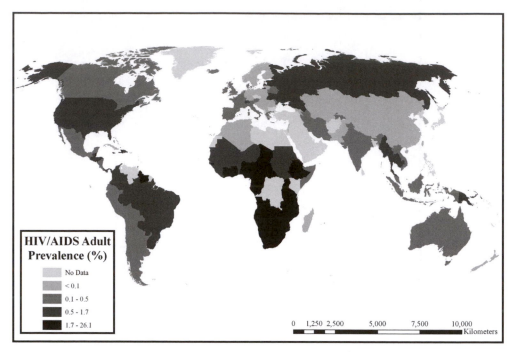

Figure 5.2   HIV Prevalence Rates, 2007.

Source: Data derived from UNAIDS, www.unaids.org.

political context of sub-Saharan Africa, rather than creating an ethnocentric version that portrays African societies as sexually promiscuous.[43] A second theory relates to the increased prevalence of other sexually transmitted diseases in sub-Saharan Africa, with sexually transmitted diseases resulting in lesions to the skin, allowing easier infection. A third suggests that the presence of other infections such as malaria or tuberculosis can increase the amount of HIV in the blood, thereby increasing the ability to infect a partner.

While there are successful models for controlling HIV/AIDS within the African continent and reductions in prevalence rates have been noted, many sub-Saharan countries were slow to adopt HIV/AIDS-awareness programs or to simply recognize the existence of the virus. The discussion of sex or sexuality was taboo in many societies, and HIV/AIDS carried a stigma that governments and individuals alike tried to avoid, denying it as a problem and failing to invest in public education. Countries lost time in introducing measures to contain HIV because the disease and its significance were not fully understood, or governments denied that it was occurring. The Kenyan government, along with other governments in the region, denied that AIDS existed in the early and mid-1980s and rejected condom use. As recently as 1999, the South African president Thabo Mbeki questioned whether HIV causes AIDS.[44] For years afterward, the country lagged the world in dealing with HIV/AIDS by not providing antiretroviral medicines to its population, with one study estimating that the government could have prevented the premature deaths of some 365,000 people if it had provided the necessary drugs.[45] Although South Africa slowly recognized the significance of the disease and moved to provide AIDS drugs to its population, progress was slow. Economic disparities, poor health systems, and drug shortages further hamper HIV/AIDS control.[46] In many countries, access to condoms, anti-AIDS drugs, and health care facilities were (or still are) limited for economic, political, or cultural reasons, and many countries continue to lack sufficient screening facilities, drugs, and health care workers. Throughout the developing world, only a small proportion of pregnant women are given drugs that would prevent the transmission of the virus to their child, meaning that approximately nine hundred children are born each day with the AIDS virus.[47] Many unknowingly carry the virus and infect others, with one estimate suggesting that upward of 90 percent of the infected population are unknowing carriers.[48]

Demographic, Economic, and Social Implications of the AIDS Crisis in Africa

Sub-Saharan Africa is a region coping with the cumulative impact of HIV/AIDS, where the disease has probably lasted longer than elsewhere in the developing world since it is thought to have originated there. Here, HIV threatens to destroy decades of progress measured by health and economic indicators, as well as generating personal suffering and hardship. In 2007, it was estimated that 1.7 million sub-Saharans were newly infected with HIV, although this represents a significant drop from 3.8 million new infections in 2000.

Demographic Effects

The most obvious effect of the HIV/AIDS epidemic is the increase in mortality rates.[49] Already high relative to the developed world, mortality rates have risen higher in countries that are affected by AIDS than they would have without AIDS. In South Africa, for example, mortality is projected to climb from 16 per one thousand (in 2005) to 25 per thousand in 2025, before declining somewhat by 2050 (figure 5.3).[50] In countries with high HIV prevalence, life expectancy at birth has also fallen. In southern Africa, average life expectancy at birth is estimated to have declined to 1950 levels, or approximately 50 years. In Zimbabwe, AIDS is expected to reduce life expectancy (from birth) from its 1997 level of 51 years to 39 years in 2010, with further reductions expected by 2025. As of 2009, life expectancy at birth was only 40 years.[51] Without HIV/AIDS, it is estimated that life expectancy would increase to 69.5 years within the next ten

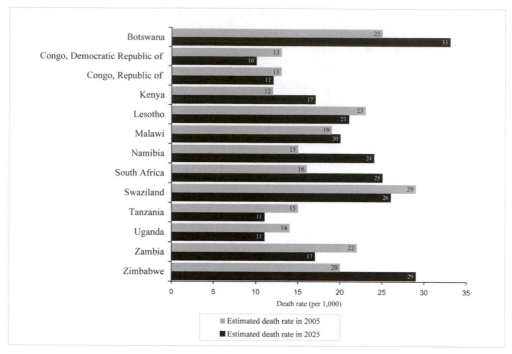

Figure 5.3   Estimated Death Rates in Selected African Countries: 2005 and 2025.

Source: Data derived from IDB, www.census.gov/ipc/www/idb/.

years. For children born in some countries, including Lesotho and Zambia, life expectancies are also below 40 years. In South Africa, fifteen-year-olds have a greater than 50 percent chance of dying from HIV-related causes.[52]

Given higher mortality rates, the AIDS epidemic can also alter population growth rates. Projections by the US Census Bureau, for example, suggest that several African countries, including Botswana, South Africa, and Zimbabwe, will experience negative rates of natural increase by 2025. Several other sub-Saharan countries will see their growth rates approach zero within the next twenty-five years, declines that are far faster than would be expected without AIDS, and significantly different from 2005 rates (figure 5.4).

AIDS deaths are premature deaths, and consequently alter the age structure of the population as well as life expectancy. We would typically expect to see increasing life expectancy associated with improvements to diet and health. AIDS, however, changes the equation. Turning once again to those countries hardest hit by HIV/AIDS, life expectancy is likely to decline in multiple countries before recovering somewhat by 2025 (figure 5.5). In Botswana, for instance, life expectancies peaked at approximately sixty-four years in the early 1990s before declining to less than forty-seven years in 2000–2005. Conse-

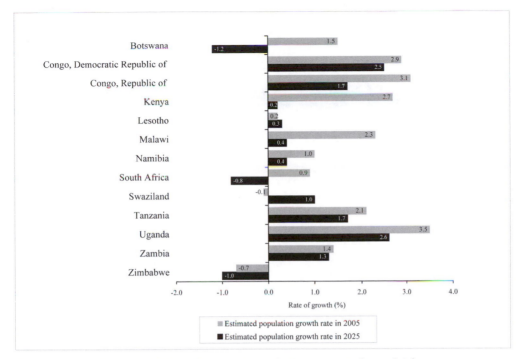

Figure 5.4   Estimated Population Growth Rates in Selected African Countries: 2005 and 2025.

Source: Data derived from IDB, www.census.gov/ipc/www/idb.

quently, the traditional population pyramid, with a wide base of young and tapering with increasing age, is being restructured and characterized as a population "chimney" in countries that have high HIV prevalence rates, as AIDS "hollows out" the young adult population, generating a base that is less broad and with fewer young children. With fewer women reaching and surpassing their childbearing years and with women having fewer children, the most dramatic changes occur when young adults who were infected in their adolescence die, substantially shrinking the adult population, particularly those in their twenties and thirties.

Social Implications

The effect of HIV/AIDS reaches into almost every corner of daily life and affects individuals, family units, and societies. In countries worst affected by the epidemic, HIV occurs against a backdrop of deteriorating public services, poor employment, and poverty, all of which work to reduce coping ability. Existing evidence suggests that households bear a large part of the burden, with differences in the ability to cope based upon wealth and income.[53] In poor

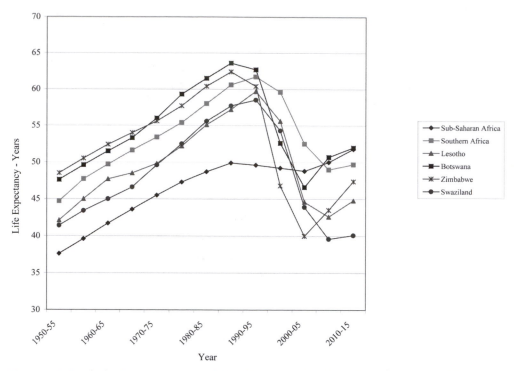

Figure 5.5   Life Expectancy and the Impact of HIV/AIDS in Selected Regions and Countries: 1950/1955–2010/2015.

Source: Data derived from Population Division of the Department of Economic and Social Affairs of the United Nations Secretariat, *World Population Prospects: The 2006 Revision*, esa.un.org/unpp.

households, the death of an adult member reduces money for food, with poor households receiving little financial help from family and friends. Many other households are unable to cope with the death of a family member or the burden of care that is associated with either sickness or death. Socially, fear and shame are still frequently associated with the disease, hindering prevention and care while potentially exposing others to the virus. Death of just one parent also disrupts life and economic abilities. Even if they are not infected, the responsibility for care of children lies with women. With widows lacking property and inheritance rights in many African countries, the epidemic compounds the burden placed upon AIDS widows, who are faced with the loss of their economic livelihood. Oftentimes, children are left with a future that only reflects what the streets can offer.

Although AIDS tends to kill proportionately more young or middle-aged persons who were infected in adolescence, its effect on the very young is startling, and has created a cohort of AIDS orphans. In sub-Saharan Africa, it is estimated that nearly twelve million children are AIDS orphans.[54] Orphaned children face a variety of social and economic challenges. Economically, the large number of orphans increases the burden of communities and governments to provide food, shelter, health care, or schooling. Young orphans are rarely able to cope with agricultural tasks, leading to crop failure and the death of livestock. Socially, AIDS orphans may be burdened by the psychological damage of seeing a parent die. Immediately relevant is the question of who raises the orphaned child. Grandparents or extended family members are frequently called upon to raise him or her, but this occurs at the same time that they had expected to have a reduced role in the family. Instead, they are forced into the parenting role once again, including the need to provide economic security. However, the increased number of orphans has altered the ability and willingness of families and communities to help, and the task threatens to outstrip the capacity of the extended-family system. For those lacking an extended family, street gangs provide an alternate "family," but one that exposes them to violence and anti-social behavior, as well as sexually transmitted infections (STIs) or HIV as they exchange sex for food and money. Although the number of orphans is large, this represents only a portion of the children who are affected by HIV. Millions more are living with parents who are ill, becoming primary caregivers for their parents or siblings.[55] Like orphans, they are more likely to drop out of school, more likely to suffer from malnutrition, and may be compelled to work.

Economic Implications

HIV/AIDS also threatens the economic stability of countries through a variety of routes by straining already fragile health care systems, decreasing the quality and quantity of labor, reducing economic output, and decreasing the amount of disposable income. The epidemic has increased the demand for health care, along with the costs of providing care and drugs and maintaining and improving infrastructure. In order to deal with the epidemic, countries have generally placed a larger share of domestic spending on HIV/AIDS, but this tends to draw expenditures away from other needs. Training and the staffing of health centers pose additional hardships, particularly because of AIDS-related illnesses or the death of health care workers from AIDS. Concurrently, non-AIDS patients are frequently crowded out of health care facilities, and tuberculosis is emerging as the leading cause of death among those infected with HIV.[56]

From an educational standpoint, the epidemic threatens the coverage and quality of education. As teachers die from AIDS, African countries will be faced with a teacher shortage, class sizes are likely to increase, and governments are faced with the costs of training replacement teachers over the longer term. Failure to do so or to meet the demand for teachers will result in a population that lacks the skills needed to fully participate within the economy. Moreover, education may not be reaching those who need it the most. This includes orphaned children, who may be forced to drop out of school to earn a wage or work on the family farm or because they can no longer afford school fees. In turn, there is an increased likelihood of infection, with Joint United Nations Programme on HIV/AIDS (UNAIDS) studies demonstrating that those with lower levels of education were more likely to engage in casual, unprotected sex.[57] On a larger scale, HIV/AIDS is stripping the ability of sub-Saharan countries to build for the future, robbing them of the ability to generate and supply what Homer-Dixon calls "ingenuity," and threatening their very survival.[58]

The impact of AIDS is also felt within the labor force, where it reduces the number of workers and degrades the quality or productivity of work at the same time that it undermines education and the ability of the system to provide the needed skills. Responsible for a large burden of sickness, HIV/AIDS leads to increased absenteeism from work, medical costs, and higher costs for training of new workers. Faced with high prevalence rates and lower productivity, companies may outsource their labor requirements. Alternatively, companies may reduce their investment in areas with high HIV prevalence. Either way, the cost of caring for sick workers is shifted from the company to households or governments and undermines the economic security of workers.

While it is difficult to measure the economic impact of HIV/AIDS, there is growing evidence that as HIV prevalence increases, the growth of national income, measured by GDP, falls.[59] Among countries with prevalence rates greater than 20 percent, GDP growth may be reduced by as much as 2 percent per year. In South Africa, UNAIDS estimates that the overall economic growth in the coming decade may be 0.3 to 0.4 percent per year lower than it would be without AIDS. What this means is that household income will be reduced at the same time that countries spend more on the care of AIDS patients or orphans, and AIDS will alter the distribution of income, with the number of households in poverty expected to increase while poor households will see a drop in income. In South Africa and Zambia, it is estimated that household income is reduced by 60 to 80 percent in AIDS-affected households, most of which were already poor households, due to coping with AIDS-related illnesses. While the large pool of unemployed may replace unskilled workers, the impact of HIV/AIDS on the education of future workers will likely mean a shortage of skilled workers. Investment, which promotes long-term economic growth, will suffer as money is diverted into health care expenditures.

CONCLUSION: THE FUTURE OF MORTALITY

Changes to the mortality experiences of populations were one of the most significant events of the twentieth century. Unlike the previous century, the twenty-first century will likely see less dramatic changes to life expectancy within the developed world. Similarly, the developing world will likely see some change, although the degree of change and direction is unclear. It is, in fact, likely that life expectancy will *decrease* in parts of the developing world as infectious diseases, including HIV/AIDS, continue to take their toll. As we look ahead over the coming decades, five nonexclusive issues relating to the mortality and morbidity experiences of populations can be raised, including the implications associated with aging societies, the threats to mortality gains posed by urbanization, the renewed threat of infectious and parasitic diseases, and the provision of health services and other programs to improve population health.

First, the twentieth century has witnessed remarkable improvements in life expectancy, with a concurrent increase in life expectancy after age sixty-five. Advances in medical technology have meant that an increasing number are surviving into old age, but it is amongst the "old elderly," variously referred to as those greater than seventy-five, eighty, or even eighty-five years, that the largest increases in morbidity (sickness) are observed. Therefore, are improvements to life expectancy a double-edged sword? For example, what are the implications of aging Western societies in terms of increased morbidity, service provision, and support of a growing elderly population? Has this increase come at the expense of an increasing number of years of morbidity? Readers can consult PRB's online discussion (http://discuss.prb.org/content/interview/detail/3581/).

Second, emerging health concerns may place many urban residents at a disadvantage with respect to mortality experiences in the near future. Urban health advantages hide the huge disparity between the urban poor and their wealthy counterparts, particularly in the developing world, where mortality experiences are frequently far worse in poor urban areas as compared to rural areas.[60] In one study in Bangladesh, for example, infant death rates varied from 95 to 152 per 1000 in urban areas, higher than both middle-class urban areas (32) and rural Bangladesh.[61] Continued in-migration from rural areas and increasing population density may push mortality and morbidity higher in urban areas. Many cities in the developing world have also grown faster than their infrastructure, leaving large proportions of their populations without adequate and safe water or sanitation, allowing diseases associated with poverty to increase in urban areas. Given these trends, the traditional advantage of urban areas is likely to be diminished in the future.

Third, infectious and parasitic diseases remain a threat to health. In the developed world, there is a need for action to avoid epidemics associated with the importation of disease. Despite safety nets that are designed to prevent diseases from entry, such as the health screening of immigrants, the system is not foolproof, and infectious diseases can spread quickly, as witnessed by the rapid and global spread of the swine flu virus (H1N1) in 2009. Systems and procedures must be in place if epidemics are to be avoided. The developing world faces its own set of problems. Among these, the poor living conditions associated with rapid urbanization and poverty in many developing-world cities create an ideal breeding ground for disease. Throughout 2008 and 2009, Zimbabwe faced a cholera epidemic, a preventable water-borne bacterial illness that causes severe diarrhea, vomiting, and dehydration and can lead to death in a matter of days if not treated. Attributed to the collapse of its health system and the breakdown of its water treatment system following years of economic crisis and government mismanagement, it was estimated that at least 3,623 people died in a six-month span, and over 76,000 were infected.[62] All of these deaths were preventable.

Fourth, some commentators have openly wondered if increasing obesity levels that are widely observed in the United States and elsewhere will ultimately mean that the current generation of youth will actually have shorter life spans than their parents. With obesity closely linked to increased cardiovascular disease, diabetes, and other health complications, this remains a real possibility.

Finally, improvements in life expectancy and infant mortality can hardly be removed from the provision of health care and related services. While some authors[63] have called for a medically driven response to the problems of IPDs and other health threats via the development of new vaccines, antibiotics, and improved laboratories, these methods carry a high price and may be years in research and development, and their applicability in the developing world is limited if drug companies do not make the drugs available. If expensive medical programs and intervention cannot provide the assurance of basic population health, other directions must instead be pursued. As a starting point, improvements to life expectancy must be achieved through a renewed commitment to public health programs and basic health care, providing a frontline defense against IPDs, maternal health problems, and other health concerns.

The provision of basic health care to meet the needs of the population is only one piece of the health puzzle, being insufficient on its own to ameliorate or remove inequalities in morbidity or mortality. Instead, it is increasingly realized that the broader determinants of health, including education, sanitation and nutrition, lifestyle options (i.e., smoking, drinking, and drug use behavior), housing conditions, and personal power, impact directly upon health and mortality experiences.[64] Despite the importance of these factors and their contribution to health, governments have been relatively slow to address disparities.[65] Clearly, however, investments in public infrastructure to provide clean drinking water, sanitation, appropriate housing, public education, or other programs, let alone the provision of basic health care services within the developing world, are limited. While needed, such a broad response to health conditions and mortality experiences is likely to be constrained by budgets and inadequate resources. Attempts at broad responses are further constrained by population growth and political agendas that shape economic assistance, with growth frequently slowing the attainment of these goals in low-income countries and creating a young population that places large demands upon costly educational, social, and health services. Solutions will not come easily or inexpensively.

FOCUS: MORTALITY DIFFERENCES—THE UNITED STATES, MEXICO, AND ZIMBABWE

Although we all must die, differences in mortality rates are found in numerous places and for different reasons. The mortality transition can be illustrated by a comparison of mortality data across countries. In this case, we will contrast Mexico, Zimbabwe, and the United States. Graphing the age-specific death rates of males and females (figure 5F.1), the observed J-shaped function is a characteristic that is found in all countries and populations. The standard age pattern is characterized by differences between males and females and by death rates that are comparatively high in the first year of life, decline through childhood and adolescence, and then increase into old age. Among women, lower death rates are shown from birth onwards. This sex differential is typically greatest for young adults, with the death rates of fifteen- to twenty-four-year-old males approximately three times that of females in the same age group, a difference that is largely attributed to the increased risk of HIV/AIDS, suicide,

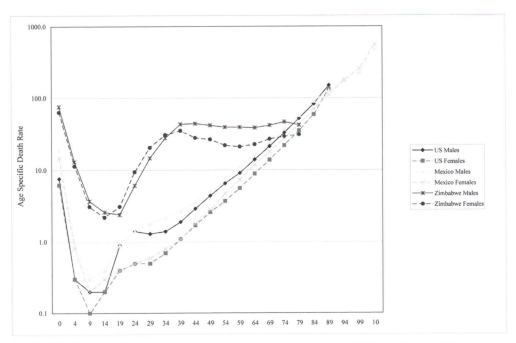

Figure 5F.1   Age-Specific Death Rates, US, Mexico, and Zimbabwe, 2005.

Source: Data derived from WHO, www.who.int/countries/en/#M.

accidents, or homicides among young males. Moreover, despite overall gains in life expectancy over the past thirty years, fifteen- to twenty-four-year-old males have actually experienced increasing mortality,[1] even though most deaths in this group are preventable.

Across all the ages, observed mortality rates in Zimbabwe exceed those found in Mexico or the United States, while the United States has a slight advantage (in terms of lower mortality rates) over Mexico. Differences in cause-specific mortality regimes are illustrated in table 5F.1. Values in this table represent the age-standardized death rates (per 100,000) by cause, with age standardization enabling comparison of the importance of death rates across countries while accounting for different population structures. With the lowest all-cause age-standardized death rate (543.5), the United States has clearly passed through the epidemiological transition. Major causes of death include cancers, including breast, colon, and lung cancers, as well as heart or cerebrovascular diseases and road traffic accidents.

With a high all-cause death rate (1,950) and HIV/AIDS as the leading cause of death, Zimbabwe represents a counterexample to that of the United States, and has yet to enter the mortality transition. Reflective of many countries in the developing world, infectious and parasitic diseases including diarrhea, tuberculosis, and measles rank within the top ten causes of death. A lack of health care providers, impoverished health care systems, and war are responsible for the high mortality rates. Clearly, many of these causes of death are easily preventable. In many ways, after years of economic erosion and the decimation of its health care system, Zimbabwe is worse off as compared to other developing countries.

Mexico is in the midst of its mortality transition: mortality rates have fallen over the past four decades, but the age-specific death rate remains higher than observed in the United States. Missing are infectious or parasitic diseases. Instead, mortality is increasingly characterized by the growth of noncommunicable diseases such as heart and cerebrovascular diseases, diabetes, and high blood pressure and accident rates. However, socioeconomic inequalities in Mexican society have led to inequities in access to basic health services. The poorer southern states have the highest disease prevalence and mortality rates for preventable causes and have the highest concentration of rural and indigenous populations.

While death rates give a quick illustration of an individual's risk of dying, demographers typically prefer the complementary measures of life expectancy (the average duration of life beyond age x) or the IMR (the number of deaths of infants less than one year of age divided by the number of births). Both measures provide descriptions of the mortality experiences of a population and a society's quality of life. In 2009, the US IMR was 6.6, and individuals could expect to live seventy-eight years. In Zimbabwe, the IMR was 60, and individuals could expect to live forty-one years from birth. Finally, the IMR in Mexico was 19, with a life expectancy of seventy-five.

Table 5F.1. Top Ten All Ages Causes of Death: United States, Mexico, and Zimbabwe, 2002

	# (thousands)	%	ASDR[a]
United States			
All causes	2,420	100	543.5
Ischemic heart disease	514	21	105.8
Cerebrovascular disease	163	7	31.9
Trachea, bronchus, lung cancers	157	7	39.0
Chronic obstructive pulmonary disease	128	5	27.2
Alzheimer's and other dementias	93	4	15.4
Diabetes mellitus	76	3	17.5
Colon and rectum cancers	64	3	14.8
Lower respiratory infections	59	3	11.3
Breast cancer	45	2	11.2
Road traffic accidents	45	2	15.0
Mexico			
All causes	469	100	646.1
Diabetes mellitus	55	12	86.8
Ischemic heart disease	52	11	81.6
Cerebrovascular disease	26	6	41.7
Perinatal conditions	26	6	21.6
Chronic obstructive pulmonary disease	24	5	26.8
Cirrhosis of the liver	16	3	35.7
Lower respiratory infection	15	3	19.4
Congenital anomalies	12	3	10.5
Road traffic accidents	12	3	13.2
Hypertensive heart disease	10	2	16.7
Zimbabwe			
All causes	270	100	3,314.8
HIV/AIDS	180	67	1,950.2
Lower respiratory infections	10	4	138.2
Tuberculosis	7	3	84.4
Perinatal conditions	6	2	30.3
Cerebrovascular disease	6	2	119.4
Diarrheal diseases	6	2	42.0
Ischemic heart disease	5	2	110.4
Protein-energy malnutrition	3	1	16.3
War	2	1	33.8
Measles	2	1	11.5

Source: Based on World Health Organization (WHO) data, www.who.int/countries/en/.
[a] Age-specific death rate.

In 2005, a total of 2,448,017 deaths were registered in the United States, translating to a crude death rate of 825.9 deaths per 100,000 and an age-adjusted death rate of 798.8 deaths per 100,000.[1] What do these different measures mean and which is a better representation of mortality in a society? As with fertility, a number of different measures may be used to describe mortality. As before, the quantity and quality of information available determine the detail and accuracy of mortality measures, with data compiled as vital statistics measures. The simplest measure, largely given the limited information required and the ease of calculation, is the *crude death rate* (CDR):

$$CDR = \left(\frac{D}{P}\right) * 1{,}000$$

where D is the total number of deaths recorded in a year, and P is the population at risk of dying. Typically, the midyear population is used for the denominator.

Like the crude birth rate, however, the main problem is that it does not take account of the age and sex structure of a population in the likelihood of death. This means that a comparison of the CDR across countries is problematic given different age distributions and variations in mortality between genders. Therefore, if we were to contrast two equal-sized populations, but with one having a larger proportion of older individuals, its crude death rate would be higher, but is not necessarily indicative of a greater risk of death.

We therefore turn to the *age-specific death rate* (ASDR), which accounts for age and sex composition of the population:

$$ASDR = \left(\frac{D_{t,t+5}}{P_{t,t+5}}\right) * 100{,}000$$

The ASDR measures the number of deaths for people in a specific age group (usually measured in five-year age groups, t to $t + 5$) divided by the average number of people in that same age group. This measure assumes that death is recorded by age and gender and that accurate knowledge of the population by age and gender is also known.

Measures of infant mortality are also commonly used to describe death rates in the first years of life. Given that a large number of deaths within the first year of life are directly associated with childbirth, the infant mortality rate (IMR) is defined as:

$$IMR = \left(\frac{D}{B}\right) * 1{,}000$$

or the number of deaths to infants aged less than one year relative to 1,000 live births. As discussed elsewhere in this book, there is considerable variation in infant mortality throughout the world. A comparable measure defines mortality within the first five years of life. Known as the *child mortality rate* (CMR), it reflects the impact of undernourishment, war, or early childhood disease, and is defined as the number of deaths to children under five relative to the population aged five and less that is at risk of dying. Even now, approximately 40 percent of deaths in the developing world occur among children less than five years old.

The *standardized mortality rate* (SMR) is the ratio of the number of deaths observed in a specified population to the number that would be expected if that population had the same mortality rate as the standard population, where the standard population is arbitrarily chosen (i.e., a specific region or time period). The SMR is often used to compare outcomes in two or more groups.

The *cause-specific death rate* is the rate of death from specific causes, such as cancer, heart attack, or stroke. Like the measures presented so far, cause-specific death rates would contrast the number of deaths due to a particular outcome (i.e., lung cancer) relative to the population at risk of dying, and should also be adjusted for age and gender differences. However, accuracy can be a problem in some situations, particularly where cause of death is not accurately recorded or determined.

Finally, we may sometimes express mortality differences in terms of *life expectancy*, or the average number of years beyond age *x* an individual can expect to live under current mortality levels. Life expectancy is usually referenced from birth, but as we saw in the discussion of life tables in chapter 3, it can be expressed from any age. *Life span* also refers to the longest period over which a person may live.

Chapter Six

Internal Migration

THE UNITED STATES, Australia, New Zealand, and Canada display among some of the highest levels of population mobility observed in the world. In each of these countries, around one in every six people change their place of residence every year, almost double the rate of movement typically observed in many European countries. This high mobility has been attributed to a variety of factors, including peripatetic traditions inherited from immigrant forebears, the relatively open nature of land, and the housing markets in these countries. Historically, internal movement was related to the opening of new frontiers (i.e., the westward expansion of Canada and the United States) or the discovery of gold and the ensuing gold rushes. More recently, population movement is associated with economic conditions; the attraction of amenities, as in the American Sun Belt; and employment opportunities.

Of all the demographic processes, it is perhaps migration and immigration (covered in the next chapter) that have gained the most attention from geographers. In large part, this likely reflects the intrinsic nature of population movement: by moving from an origin to a destination, space is involved, and we can ask questions about the motivation for migration, the impact migration has on sending and receiving regions, who moves, and so forth. At the same time, measuring and defining the movement of population is much trickier than measuring fertility or mortality, given issues associated with both space and time that are discussed below. The following chapter explores migration by focusing on its definition and measurement and alternate theories of migration. The "Focus" section considers contemporary internal migration in the United States, and the "Methods, Measures, and Tools" section discusses the various measures of migration.

DEFINING MIGRATION

As with fertility and mortality, researchers attempt to quantify and measure the movement of a population. However, the statistical representation of migration is somewhat more problematic: mortality, for example, is a given and measurable event. Likewise, fertility is measurable. Population mobility is somewhat trickier. When, for example, has an individual migrated? Is it when they purchase a new house down the street or across the country? Likewise, does the relocation need to be permanent, or can it be a temporary one? If temporary, how long should the absence be?

To define migration events, we need to consider the impact of our definition of space (i.e., boundaries and size) and the time interval over which migration is measured and differentiate between migrants and migrations before we can quantify movements. We start by distinguishing between the number of migrants and the number of migrations. The number of migrants refers to the number of individuals who have made one or more migrations during a specified interval, while the number of migrations counts the total number of recorded movements. This distinction is important, as some individuals will move more than once during a specific time interval, so the number of migrations is typically greater than the number of migrants.[1]

Geography and Migration

Simply defined, migration involves a change of usual residence by a person, family, or household. However, this definition does not account for spatial scale (i.e., the distance of the move), making it useful to distinguish the type of move by geographical scale. *Residential mobility* typically refers to short-distance (within city or labor market) residential relocations. These moves are often associated with changing housing preferences and needs and do not necessarily involve changing jobs. *Internal migration* generally involves a permanent relocation crossing an internal political boundary (i.e., state boundaries) that results in the migrant changing labor markets.[2] Finally, *international migration* involves moves that cross international borders and is typically highly restricted. These broad distinctions have dominated migration research for the past four decades.

Similarly, the size, shape, and characteristics of the spatial units that migration occurs in or across will influence the number of observed migrants. That is, use of alternate spatial units, such as counties, states, or regions, will alter the count of migrants (along with the reason for migration). In general, the larger the spatial unit, the fewer migrants will be counted moving in or out of that region. For this reason, we see fewer individuals making long-distance migrations as compared to local, residential moves. For instance, based on the 2000 census, 11.6 million people moved between the four census regions (Northeast, Midwest, South, and West), including a net in-migration to the West, which gained 12,048 individuals.[3] During the same 1995-2000 interval, over 22 million moved between states. An even larger number made more local moves, with 65.4 million moving within the same county, and another 25.3 million moving between counties but within the same state.[4] The state of California, meanwhile, lost over 755,000 individuals during the same period. Likewise, what is comparatively a long-distance migration from northern California to southern California would not be counted as a between-state (interstate) migration. The same distance migration on the East Coast would cross multiple state lines.

Time and Migration

The timing and duration of a migration is also an integral part of its definition. Over what interval of time should migration be measured? *Seasonal or temporary* migrations, for instance, are short-term relocations, such as moves made by students or seasonal workers, but both the US and Canadian censuses only identify migrants as individuals who have changed their usual place of residence. Time intervals that are too short risk capturing short-term, temporary relocations, including students moving to attend university or relocations associated with short-term work reassignments or vacations. While important and worthy of study in their own right, these temporary moves add noise and confusion to the system when a person is interested in permanent relocations. Conversely, too long of a time interval will end up missing migrants, particularly those who migrate and then either "return" to their origin region or make a second, "onward" migration to a different destination.[5]

Many geographers and migration researchers (at least in the United States, Canada, Australia, and western Europe) rely on the census to define migrations and migrants, while population geographers in Scandinavian countries are more likely to use the registration systems that track individuals and households over time. Since 1940, the US census has, for example, asked respondents their usual place of residence on census day and place of residence five years prior.[6] Together, these two points in time enable the analyst to define a migrant. That is, if the respondent indicated one location on census day and a different one five years prior, and these two locations are different counties, then the person is defined as a migrant. In many ways, this five-year migration question has become the "standard" way of defining migration, and other countries, including Canada and Australia, use similar metrics to define population migration.[7]

While the five-year migration question may be standard, it is inexact. For instance, by virtue of its definition, it measures a single move, say between 1995 and 2000, and therefore misses multiple moves over the period. With Americans some of the most mobile people in the world, making on average ten migrations over their lifetimes, the timing of moves may be significant. Specifically, the five-year migration question may miss return (i.e., migrations that return an individual to some defined starting point) and onward (subsequent migrations to a destination other than the origin) migrations.[8] In short, the five-year migration question tends to underestimate migration flows within a population. The census also misses moves in the first five years of the decade (i.e., 1990–1995 for the 2000 census), a problem if significant events might have altered migration choices and numbers.

Although most migration studies typically rely on census data that is collected based on a change in residential location within a five-year interval, an additional consideration when calculating migration measures is the length of the period over which they are measured. For instance, assuming we are using census data that measures migration over a five-year period (as the US census did before the ACS was introduced), the number of migrants recorded over a five-year interval is considerably less than five times the one-year number.[9] Moreover, we can't simply multiply the number of migrants captured in a one-year window by five, meaning that the reconciliation of one- and five-year data is not straightforward. Finally, the move to record mobility and migrations through the new ACS will raise new questions and issues with respect to the measurement and definition of mobility, since the ACS measures migration over a one-year time interval and compares place of residence on the day the form is completed relative to where the respondent lived a year earlier (see "Focus," chapter 2).

WHY DO PEOPLE MIGRATE?

While population geographers are interested in the counts, flows, and directions of migrants, they are also interested in asking why people migrate. After all, migration is a fundamentally social or economic phenomenon, and the reasons for migration will vary from person to person, household to household, and over time and across geographic regions, meaning that the reasons for a local move will likely differ from the reasons for longer, interstate relocations.[10]

Some will move, for example, for a new job or in the hope of a new job and others will move for housing issues, while yet others will move for amenity-, health-, or care-related reasons.

We can get a sense of the reasons for migration from table 6.1. Based on the 2006–2007 CPS, the most important reason for moving was the desire for a new or better home/apartment, representing over one-third of all moves in the year. Cheaper housing was the second most important reason (18.5 percent), followed by the desire for a better neighborhood or less crime (12.8 percent). Other reasons, including moves associated with health needs or relocation for education, were proportionately less important. Clearly, however, age is also closely associated with reasons for migration. Among the young, aged twenty to twenty-four, nearly 17 percent of all moves were associated with attending or leaving college. For the old, health reasons were much more important motivators (21.8 percent). Most surveys do not ask, however, why individuals (or households) migrate. Thus, it is frequently left to the analyst to infer the reasons why individuals migrate. Information relating to the origin and destination of a migrant can, for example, be combined with other information from census or other data files, including age, gender, employment status, marital status, and so on, along with broader measures such as labor-market effects or amenities. When information is combined with multivariate methods, we can infer reasons for population movement.

This is still incomplete, and migration must be contextualized or viewed relative to a migration theory that allows us to interpret or understand the motivations for migration. The current "state of the art" of migration theory actually represents more than a century of analysis, with much of the basis for modern migration theory stemming from the work of Ravenstein,[11] who provided the

Table 6.1.   Reasons for Move by Age (%): 2006–2007

Reason for move	Total	20–24	30–44	65+
Wanted new or better home/apartment	36.6	31.9	40.1	22.9
Wanted better neighborhood/less crime	12.8	10.3	14.0	9.8
Wanted cheaper housing	18.5	18.9	18.1	13.2
Other housing reason	15.8	12.2	16.3	22.3
To attend or leave college	4.5	16.9	1.4	—
Change of climate	0.9	0.5	0.6	4.2
Health reasons	3.2	1.2	2.4	21.8
Natural disaster	1.1	0.3	1.3	2.7
Other reason	6.8	7.7	5.8	3.1

Source: Data derived from US Census Bureau, Current Population Survey (CPS), *Geographical Mobility, 2006–2007*.

first insights into its determinants. Premised on individuals' desire to better themselves, Ravenstein described the spatial, population, and economic determinants of migration. Among the more important generalizations, Ravenstein concluded that migration occurred in a "stepwise" manner (i.e., movement from farm to hamlet, hamlet to village, village to town, with moves continuing into progressively larger centers), that each migration stream tended to have a compensating counterstream, that the majority of migrations are short-distance, and that the major cause of migration was economic. These often-quoted generalizations have stood the test of time and have formed the basis of scientific discussion and theoretical development over the years.

Everet Lee advanced and updated Ravenstein's ideas,[12] creating a framework for migration analysis that involves the "pull" effects of the destination, the "push" effects of the origin, intervening opportunities, and personal characteristics. For example, high unemployment rates in the origin would constitute a "push" factor and high wages in the destination would "pull" (attract) migrants. Between each potential origin and destination was a set of intervening opportunities, the most important being distance. These intervening opportunities could, for example, direct the migrant to another destination or decrease the likelihood of migration by imposing costs to the move. Finally, a set of personal factors, such as age, level of education, marital status, and occupation, were allowed to influence migration. Like Ravenstein's work, Lee's conceptualization of migration has informed and generated much empirical work.

Wilbur Zelinsky hypothesized the "mobility transition."[13] Similar to the demographic transition, Zelinsky argued that the patterns of internal migration in a country would shift over time as the country developed. In the earliest stages of development, rural-to-rural movements, including frontier expansion, would predominate. Later, and with industrialization, rural-to-urban movements would prevail, as individuals moved to cities in search of employment. Finally, urban-to-urban movements would dominate as the economic system matured.

While the migration theories put forward by Ravenstein, Zelinsky, Lee, and others have shaped migration research, more formal theories have been advanced and developed within economics, sociology, and geography. Naturally, the emphases of these disciplines have differed, with economists tending to emphasize the economic influences upon migration, sociologists interested in the validity of economic rationality and individual behavior, and geographers focusing upon the role of space.

THEORIES OF INTERNAL MIGRATION

Despite the regularities and correlations observed in migration flows, and the occasional expressed reason for migration, students of migration need a more theoretical understanding of migration flows. Because of the diversity of the migration literature, it is convenient to differentiate between *macroadjustment* theories and *microbehavioral* theories of migration, a distinction that conditions the way that migration is modeled with respect to the wider operations of housing, labor markets, and social relations. Macro theory, on the one hand, has typically been concerned with the analysis and explanation of flows, focusing upon the relationship between migrations and objectively defined macroeconomic variables, such as wages or employment. Microbehavioral theory, on the other hand, has focused upon broad topics, including human capital explanations of migration, residential mobility, and return and onward flows, while also considering influences that prompt migration and the choice of a destination.

Macroeconomic Theories of Migration

Interregional migration was initially viewed as a response to wage differentials, formally expressed by the so-called macroadjustment model.[14] Drawing upon neoclassical economics, the macroadjustment model argued that labor migrates in response to interregional wage differentials, moving from low- to high-wage regions.[15] As it does, labor supply will decrease in low-wage areas due to out-migration, forcing wages to rise. On the other hand, increasing labor supply in high-wage regions will force wage rates to be lowered until wage rates are equal across space. Empirical results have confirmed that individuals are more likely to choose destinations with higher wage rates.[16]

The macroadjustment model has, however, been subject to a number of criticisms. Foremost amongst these is the assumption that labor will move from low- to high-wage regions, allowing wage levels to equalize across the system. This assumes, of course, that there are no barriers to migration. However, perfect mobility is rare. At its simplest, distance is still a barrier to movement, imposing the physical costs of movement along with potential psychological costs associated with, for example, family separation. Market conditions such as worker recognition and accreditation requirements, and social-welfare programs, including unemployment insurance, may prevent migration (or, at a minimum, delay the need to migrate). At the same time, incomplete information on the part of potential migrants (i.e., not knowing all possible alternatives) and "stickiness" in the labor and wage market (i.e., associated with labor unions or minimum-wage requirements), complicate or impede the free movement of individuals.[17]

Second, while wages are undoubtedly important in motivating migration, it is unclear whether regional wage levels move toward equilibrium through migration. That is, the persistent regional income disparities in highly mobile countries such as the United States suggest that the consequences of migration have little to do with the regional equalization rates prescribed in the macroadjustment model. Other market effects—such as the role of labor unions or minimum-wage laws—likely keep wages stable. Several studies have challenged the assumption that migration is an equilibrating process, finding that migration instead leads to increased social and economic polarization, more reflective of a process of cumulative causation.[18]

Third, the existence of other variables and personal factors, which have been observed to have significant effects upon the migration decision, suggests that the macroadjustment model is too simplistic in its reliance upon wages. By way of an example, an important variable missing from the macroadjustment model is unemployment, a problem underscored by experiences during the Depression of the 1930s. During this time, positive net migration to rural areas was observed despite the fact that wage rates in urban areas remained considerably higher than those in rural areas, a situation that the wage-differential approach could not explain. The population movements during this time were, however, due to the severe unemployment in urban areas, suggesting the effect of unemployment upon migration decisions. When applied to the current migration system, higher unemployment in a region should generate higher levels of out-migration, while in-migration should be negatively related to unemployment levels.[19]

Finally, the operationalization of the macroadjustment model has typically relied upon the use of either net migration flows (the number of in-migrants minus the number of out-migrants from a region) or the net migration rate (obtained by dividing the volume of net migration by the population of that region). However, the use of net migrants (or rates) is problematic, since there are no "net migrants" in the real world.[20] Moreover, net migration rates are not appropriately defined, relying on a denominator that does not express the population "at risk" of migrating. This misspecification confounds movement propensities with relative population stock levels, hides regularities in the age pattern of mobility, and leads to misspecified explanatory variables. Consequently, models based upon the macroadjustment framework should rely upon gross migration streams or rates (i.e., number of in- or out-migrants or migration rates based upon an appropriately specified at-risk population).

Expanding Macroeconomic Theory

In overcoming these problems, macro theory has been expanded to include a variety of effects hypothesized to influence migration.[21] Environmental considerations are, for example, important in the migration decision, evidenced by the growth of Sun Belt states in postindustrial America. Amenities such as a warm climate or scenic areas offering recreational outlets such as skiing and hiking have become increasingly important in explaining the attraction of the American and Canadian West coasts (i.e., California, Washington, Oregon, British

Columbia) and interior states such as Arizona and Colorado. All of these areas reflect the increasing desire by an affluent population to reside in these areas, the ability of employers to locate in these areas, and the increasing ease of communication and transportation that has "shrunk" distance.

Linguistic, ethnic, and racial differences have also been recognized for their role in generating and directing internal migration flows. In Canada, for example, there is a well-known dichotomy between the migration propensities of French and English Canadians, with French Canadians less likely to out-migrate from Quebec (Canada's French-speaking province) and more likely to return to it than their English-speaking counterparts. In the United States, race has long been observed to influence migration patterns, with African Americans having different internal migration patterns than their white counterparts.[22]

Microbehavioral Approaches

Microbehavioral approaches to migration differ in three important ways from the macro models discussed above. First, micro theoretical approaches represent an alternative view of migration and the decision-making process, typically replacing economic rationality with satisficing behavior, such that individuals evaluate only a subset of the possible alternatives. Second, the microtheoretic tradition has focused on the migration sequences and decisions of individuals using data from residential histories, publicly released census files, or longitudinal data sets, while macro approaches have commonly (although not exclusively) focused upon aggregate migration data. Third, micro theories have typically distinguished between the decision to move, the destination choice, and the interrelation between the change of residence and other changes in the status of the migrant (i.e., socioeconomic mobility or housing).

Empirically, micro approaches offer two additional advantages. First, they allow the specification of migration measures for individuals with particular characteristics (i.e., the out-migration of the unemployed) that tend to be less misleading than similar measures based upon aggregate data (i.e., the out-migration rate from a high-unemployment area). For example, it is easier to reveal the push effect of unemployment using behavioral models than the macroadjustment model. Second, in assessing the effect of a key factor (i.e., level of education) on migration behavior, micro approaches offer greater flexibility in controlling for the effects of other factors (i.e., ethnic background, age) and therefore typically yield less biased results.

The Human Capital Theory of Migration

At the interregional scale, the human capital theory defines migration as an investment in human capital,[23] or changes to the stock of skills and knowledge embodied in an individual, whereby the costs of migration are balanced against future expected returns measured by lifetime earnings. That is, if benefits exceed costs, then the individual will migrate, with the individual choosing to migrate to the location that offers the greatest returns. Both benefits and costs could be monetary (i.e., the dollar cost of moving) or psychic (i.e., the psychological costs of moving away from family and friends). Consequently, human capital theory offers several advantages over the wage-differential approach. Importantly, it does not cast migration as a purely economic decision. While economics and income opportunities figure prominently in the decision to move, other nonwage effects are brought to bear upon the decision. Second, it offers a concise explanation of why migration rates are observed to decline with age, acknowledging that the psychic costs of migration tend to increase with age. Moreover, younger individuals have longer periods within which to capture the benefits (expected income) of migration than their older counterparts. Third, spatial dimensions are incorporated within the theory, with the cost of moving related to distance. Finally, the model both reflects a microeconomic approach and can be aggregated to look at migration flows by sections of the population.

Although human capital theory provides a number of theoretical advantages over macroadjustment theories and has been widely applied and expanded within migration research, it too is not without its shortcomings. First, it assumes perfect information, both on the part of the potential migrant as well as on the part of the modeler, both of which are unrealistic expectations. Instead, information acquisition is associated with costs (i.e., time and effort to collect) and is variable over space, meaning it is variable in its quality and quantity from one individual to another. Second, the theory assumes that the migrant (or modeler) can estimate lifetime earnings at alternate destinations, a task that is difficult regardless of the perspective. This difficulty has commonly led to the replacement of lifetime earnings by current income, decreasing the model's attractiveness and applicability.

The Job-Search Model of Migration

As an alternative microapproach, the job-search model captures the movement of labor across space,[24] distinguishing between *speculative migrations*, which are undertaken in the hope of finding suitable employment at the destination, and *contracted migrations*, which are undertaken after having secured employment. For job searchers, potential returns are typically greatest in urban labor markets, underscoring the continued population movement into large metropolitan areas (immigration or movement "up the urban hierarchy" from smaller to larger urban areas). Contract migration may be the more common form of movement, particularly over longer distances, minimizing the risks of migration through the securing of employment beforehand.

Residential Mobility and Life-Cycle Theory

The application of microbehavioral models to residential mobility was largely driven by a lack of specificity derived from aggregate analyses, with one of the central theoretical issues underpinning residential mobility theory reflecting the distinction between the decision to move and destination choice. In this context, mobility allows residential needs to be adjusted in response to changing life-cycle needs or other requirements. Rossi's "life-cycle" theory[25] proposed that life-cycle changes, such as leaving the parental home for education or first job, marriage, the growth of the family, and declining health, would drive residential relocation decisions through changing housing requirements (typically space), with each change in the life-cycle "stage" prompting relocation. The search process is undertaken once the decision to move has been made, and reflects needs, social aspirations, income, and the role of institutions, including real-estate agents and banks. At small spatial scales, therefore, migration interacts with the housing career of the migrants.[26] In addition, characteristics of the household (i.e., age, sex, marital status, household status), individual housing units (i.e., size, structure, availability), and wider characteristics of the origin and destination areas (i.e., neighborhood structure, ethnic/racial structure, housing availability) were hypothesized to influence relocation decisions.

Yet, life-cycle theory can not account for all residential moves. Several authors have argued that large proportions (perhaps up to 25 percent) of residential moves are "forced" rather than "voluntary."[27] Further limiting the decisions of individuals or households are the constraints imposed by a variety of institutional forces, including the effects of racism or discrimination, tenure choice, housing supply, and the role of specific agents (such as real-estate agents), who may limit housing options as they steer potential buyers to (or away from) particular locations. For the poor, residential options may be particularly constrained, with the poor having fewer options in terms of location, the availability or quality of housing stock, and its cost. Life-cycle theory is also less relevant in North American society, where "traditional" nuclear households are becoming less common. Instead, alternative family arrangements, including single-parent families, dual-income households, alternative lifestyle households, "empty nesters," or singles are increasingly dominating the social makeup of societies (composing greater than 50 percent of all households), with each group having its own housing needs and preferences. We can no longer assume a homogenous population.

Behavioral theory and models have also been applied to the analysis of elderly migration. Although the distinction between the decision to move and destination choice remains, the factors driving the migration process generally differ from what has been considered in the above theories. The reason is simple: most elderly have quit the labor market and are thus less sensitive to the changes in the market than others. Consequently, the decision to migrate is strongly influenced by a set of personal resources, such as health and income.[28] Older individuals who are healthier are more likely to move to high-amenity areas, while even older individuals (aged seventy-five-plus) are more dependent and may move to seek help either from family members or institutions. Likewise, the destination pattern of elderly migrants is quantitatively different from that of the general population, focusing upon high-amenity areas like British Columbia in Canada and Florida or Arizona in the United States.[29] For assistance-seeking migrants, the search space is generally more limited than that of the general population, constrained by the location of family or other assistance providers such as nursing or chronic-care homes.

Alternative Models

Discontent with traditional economic-based theories and the continued reliance upon census products or other published data has led to calls to revise existing approaches to migration in terms of theory, models, and data sources.[30] McHugh notes, for instance, that migration is about people, their connections to multiple places, and "people living in the moment while looking backward from where they came from and forward to an uncertain future" (1997, 15).[31] Over the past decade, there have been increasing calls (and action) for a richer examination of the spatial and temporal aspects of migration than has commonly been achieved. The census, for example, represents a snapshot of the population at a specific point in time, and yet we assert some connectivity between space, time, and individuals based on a few questions relating to mobility. Place of residence at two points in time does not capture the complexity of migration, the nature of which is emerging (for example) in the new transnational migration literature[32] or in McHugh's work[33] associated with seasonal snowbirds in Arizona.

The reconceptualization of migration has meant that it is not seen as just an economic event performed by economically rational individuals but as an event that is "culturally produced, culturally expressed and cultural in effect."[34] As such, chronic mobility may, for example, reflect dwindling place ties, rootlessness, or a sense of adventure, rather than economic rationality. Migration also reflects past, current, and future states of affairs, such as current income, employment status, and family situation or anticipated changes in employment, income, or health. Yet these concepts are frequently missing from much of the migration literature. The true reason for migration may therefore lie buried within the migration event, being invisible to the researcher relying on cross-sectional or longitudinal data and econometric tools. This reconceptualization is seen in numerous areas associated with migration research. Alejandro Portes and his colleagues,[35] for instance, have pursued ethnographic studies of immigrant communities and their adjustment in US society. The literature on transnational migration has also approached migration issues through ethnographic and survey techniques.

MIGRANT SELECTIVITY AND MIGRANT CHARACTERISTICS

Despite the high mobility rates observed in the United States and other countries, not everyone moves. In fact, migration is highly selective, meaning that different individuals, defined by their sociodemographic or socioeconomic characteristics, will be more or less likely to migrate over their life spans. Consequently, migration rates will differ by personal characteristics such as age, race, income, housing tenure, education, and marital status. Perhaps the most important determinant of migration is age, with the young consistently more likely to migrate than older individuals, an outcome observed regardless of location, time, or geographic scale (figure 6.1). The likelihood of migration is somewhat more complicated than this. For instance, the very young (typically defined as less than fifteen years old) are considered to be "tied" migrants, following their parents as they relocate. Even still, the very young (and their parents) are more likely to migrate as compared to families with young teenagers, reflecting both their parents' declining likelihood to relocate as well as parental desire to minimize disruptions to school and friend networks as their children grow.

Migration rates increase dramatically as individuals age into the late teens and through the twenties. Close to one-third of twenty- to twenty-nine-year-olds move each year, reflecting movements out of the parental home into their own residences, moves to or from college, or moves related to employment. Following this, migration rates generally decline toward retirement as it becomes more difficult and costly to relocate (both physically and emotionally) as families grow and as individuals and families have built up a network of friends and other assets, such as a house or property, in their locations. Oftentimes we see a small increase in migration rates around retirement, reflecting the desire to be closer to amenities, while final late-life migrations are often associated with health issues, bringing individuals closer to family for care or into institutions. Many of the reasons for changing migration propensities by age can be attributed to *life-cycle changes*, notions made popular by Rossi.[36]

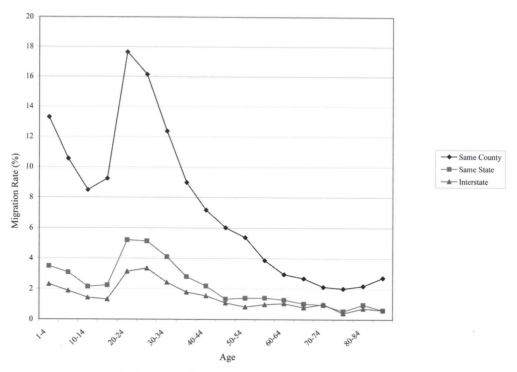

Figure 6.1   Age Schedule of Migration (percent): United States, 2006–2007.

Source: Data derived from US Census Bureau, Current Population Survey, "Geographical Mobility, 2006 to 2007."

Sjaastad's[37] human capital theory also helps to explain differing migration rates by age, with young adults having a longer career time to recoup the costs of moving than older individuals.

Beyond age and life-cycle events, other factors are also closely and consistently associated with migration selectivity (table 6.2). We observe, for instance, that more educated individuals are more likely to migrate, based on the reasoning that they are better able to collect, synthesize, and interpret information on alternate locations. Likewise, the better educated may have more options open to them and are therefore more likely to engage in longer-distance migrations. Levels of long-distance migration also tend to increase as income or occupational status increases, and renters are more likely to migrate as compared to home owners, particularly over short distances, such as within-county moves.

We can also identify demographic factors, including gender, marital status, and the presence of children, as correlates of migrant selectivity. In most developed countries, men and women have virtually the same rates of migration, reflecting gender equality. In many developing nations and in terms of international migration, however, men frequently have higher rates of migration as they move in search of employment, while women remain at home to care for

Table 6.2. Migration Rates (%) by Selected Demographic Characteristics:
United States, 2006–2007

	Migrant	Same county	Same state	Interstate
Educational status (age 25 +)				
Not a high school graduate	12.5	8.8	2.1	1.0
High school graduate	10.5	7.2	2.0	1.2
Some college	11.2	7.1	2.4	1.5
Bachelor's degree	11.1	6.2	2.5	1.9
Professional or graduate degree	10.3	5.2	2.1	2.3
Marital status (age 14 +)				
Married, spouse present	8.8	5.3	1.8	1.4
Married, spouse absent	23.2	14.4	2.6	3.3
Divorced/separated/widowed	13.2	9.1	2.5	0.8
Never married	18.4	12.2	3.5	2.1
Home tenure				
Owner	4.1	1.4	0.3	0.7
Renter	20.1	5.4	1.0	2.4

Source: Data derived from US Census Bureau, CPS, *Geographical Mobility, 2006–2007*.

family. Typically, individuals who are single (and also younger) are more likely to migrate, especially over longer distances, as they are not "tied" to others in the same household. Married couples, on the other hand, are often less likely to migrate, as relocation is often associated with career disruption for at least one of the partners.[38] In a similar way, families with dependent children are less likely to relocate, given disruptions to school and social networks.

THE MIGRATION PROCESS

Migration and relocation can represent a response to multiple factors that do not affect everyone in the same way, witnessed by migrant selectivity of, for example, young adults. Still left unanswered is what generates the desire to move? Conceptually, we can think of the process as having at least three steps, with the first representing the decision to migrate, the second the decision of where to migrate to (destination), and the third being the decision to actually migrate. Of course, these processes could be occurring simultaneously. Alternatively, only the destination search is important, such as for those whose jobs have been relocated. However, for modeling and theoretical reasons, the literature often distinguishes between the three steps.

Given our earlier distinction between types of moves (i.e., residential mobility versus internal migration), the motivations for these types of migrations will also differ. Residential mobility, for example, is closely allied with changes in the demand for housing services. For example, disparities between housing needs and expectations, such as the need for more room as a family grows or downsizing as household units shrink, may give rise to "residential stress." Beyond some threshold, residential stress exceeds inertia (the forces keeping an individual or family in place), and the search for a new residence begins.[39]

Clearly, life-cycle theory could not account for all residential moves, with a large proportion (perhaps up to 25 percent) of residential moves "forced" rather than "voluntary."[40] Further limiting the decisions of individuals or households are the constraints imposed by a variety of institutional forces, including racism or discrimination, tenure choice (own or rent), housing supply (number, cost, and type of housing), and the role of specific agents (such as real-estate agents), all of which may limit housing options. Residential options may be particularly constrained among the poor and groups that are discriminated against, with both having fewer options in terms of location, the availability or quality of housing stock, and housing cost. In housing markets that are heavily controlled by local or national agencies, on the other hand, there are likely to be significant differences both in the operation of housing markets and in terms of residential choice. Individuals or households in such situations may have few residential options, decreasing the likelihood of movement. For longer moves, the decision to move is often based on economic conditions—poor job prospects and high unemployment in the origin may, for instance, trigger a migration. Amenities, particularly for older individuals, may also be important, as households migrate to escape colder climates.

The search process is undertaken once the decision to move has been made. For longer-distance migrations, individuals will search locations that may offer more amenities or better income and employment opportunities. At the same time, all moves involve a local scale, or the neighborhood location where the household ultimately settles. At this local scale, the search process reflects needs, economic opportunities, social aspirations, income, and the role of institutions, including real-estate agents and banks. At small spatial scales, therefore, migration interacts with the housing career of the migrants.[41] In addition, characteristics of the household (i.e., age, sex, marital status, household status), individual housing units (i.e., size, structure, availability), and wider characteristics of the origin and destination areas (i.e., neighborhood structure, ethnic/racial structure, housing availability) influence destination choice. Finally, the actual decision to move is made. In some cases, the search process may not reveal a suitable destination or option, and the move is called off. In many other cases, the economic, housing, social, or lifestyle benefits are greater than the costs, and the move is made.

CONCLUSION

Despite different migration theories, most researchers agree that individuals or households migrate to improve their situation, with the various migration theories stressing different aspects (i.e., economic, social, environmental) of this commonality. In reality, much of the literature has actually tended to augment the distinction between micro and macro approaches, a problem that may, in part, be due to the different perspectives that the various disciplines bring to the table. The strong disciplinary focus has remained, although there has been considerable cross-disciplinary fertilization in recent years, as well as a greater embrace of qualitative methods in considering population issues. Despite the profusion of migration research, relatively few dramatic theoretical advances have been recorded in the past two decades. Instead, greater emphasis has been placed upon a more analytic/policy-oriented approach, meaning that many of the theoretical (or methodological) additions have built upon existing theories. Consequently, theoretical development in the past two decades has been incremental in nature. By and large, the availability of data (i.e., new longitudinal files and increased accessibility to public-use files such as the Public Use Microdata Sample) has been more important in influencing empirical and theoretical research over this period. For example, theoretical advancements associated with return migration, whereby an individual returns to an earlier region of residence, related to life cycle or employment have been enabled by improved data availability.[42]

FOCUS: CONTEMPORARY INTERNAL POPULATION MOVEMENT IN THE UNITED STATES

The US population has long been regarded as one of the most mobile populations in the developed world. In large part, the willingness to move and relocate over long distances, both for short-term periods as well as permanent relocations, is arguably entrenched in the US psyche, associated first with frontier expansion and exploration, then movement into urban areas, and more recently movement to rural and semirural locations. To a large extent, population movement in the United States followed the stages of Zelinsky's mobility transition theory, echoing the nation's historical and economic development. The opening of the American West, for example, prompted large-scale relocation from the eastern seaboard. Later, the Great Depression of the

1930s was associated with movement out of the American plains and westward into California. Resource discovery and development, such as California's gold rush and the development of the oil industry in Texas, spurred further population movement. Over the past three decades, the bulk of population movement has been between urban areas and from central cities to the suburbs.

Knowledge of population movement was aided by the introduction on the 1940 census of a migration question asking respondents where they lived five years ago. Since World War II, population movement has been dominated by four large themes. First, preferences for warmer climates and amenities prompted movement to the Sun Belt. At the same time, changing economic conditions, characterized by the decline of American manufacturing in the northeast United States and the emergence of the so-called Rust Belt and the coincident rise of industry in the South, prompted population movement into the Sun Belt. Second, rural areas continued to lose population, especially in the rural Midwest, upper Great Plains, and the Mississippi Delta.[1] Third, suburbanization, or the movement from towns and cities to the rural-urban fringe, gathered momentum immediately after the war, prompted interest in short-distance migrations, and had far-reaching impacts on the structure of American cities. Fourth, "counterurbanization" emerged during the 1970s, signaling a shift in net migration toward nonmetropolitan areas, movement that was in stark contrast to the long-standing movement up the urban hierarchy and toward larger metropolitan areas. While this appeared to decrease in importance in the 1980s, urban-to-rural movements reappeared in the 1990s and 2000s.

Evidence from the 1990s and the early to mid-2000s showed a general continuation of these long-standing migration patterns. Other consistent patterns were also apparent. For instance, the Northeast and Midwest continued to lose population through the millennium, and migrants continued to move to the southern states, a process that had started with deindustrialization.[2] Similarly, many of the country's largest cities experienced net out-migration, again reflecting a decades-long pattern. However, populations in the largest metropolitan areas were reinforced by immigration, such as in the cases of New York and Chicago.[3]

There were also, however, significant changes in the mobility patterns of Americans. Overall, migration and mobility rates declined (see figure 6F.1), a phenomenon partially associated with population aging (older individuals are less likely to migrate than younger individuals). At a regional scale, the pace of out-migration from northeastern and midwestern states declined somewhat between 2000 and 2004 as compared to rates observed in the 1990s, although the Northeast still lost 281,000 over 2006–2007. The South continued to be the primary destination for migrants, with a net in-migration of 307,000 over 2006–2007 (table 6F.1), although the pace of this movement also declined, and only the Atlantic states, such as Florida, were important destinations, reflecting the movement of retirees.

Beyond these large-scale movements, migration has reshaped America's features in other ways. While this book has yet to tackle immigration, the internal migration of immigrants in the United States has resulted in spatial assimilation or the reduction in differences in residential patterns across groups.[4] While spatial assimilation occurs over time, with new immigrants generally more segregated than those who have been resident in the country for a longer period, segregation levels are greater for foreign-born black immigrants than they are for Asian, white, and Hispanic immigrants, and poorer immigrants tend to be more segregated as well.

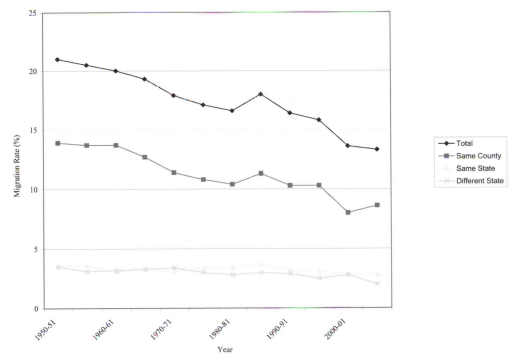

Figure 6F.1   Mobility Rates by Type of Movement: United States, 1950/
1951–2005/2006.

Source: Data derived from the US Census Bureau, based on Current Population Survey data.

Table 6F.1.   Interregional Migration Flows (in Thousands): United States,
2006–2007

Destination in 2007	Region of residence in 2006				
	Northeast	Midwest	South	West	Total
Northeast	−281	65	194	54	313
Midwest	92	60	265	231	588
South	401	315	307	316	1,032
West	101	148	266	−86	515
Total	594	528	725	601	2,448

Note: Bold cells represent net gain/loss for the period. Over the 2006–2007 period, approximately 2,448,000 Americans relocated.
Source: Data derived from the US Census Bureau based on CPS data.

The country's population is also being redistributed across the metropolitan hierarchy. Plane noted that the largest "mega-metropolitan" areas (populations greater than 2,500,000) gained from other large metropolitan areas, while they lost population to the very bottom of the urban-rural hierarchy, namely "micropolitan" (metropolitan places with populations between 10,000 and 49,999 in addition to being associated with an urban core) and nonurban counties.[5] In large part, the movement down the urban hierarchy and toward smaller urban areas or even some selected rural areas represents the continuation of the counterurbanization trend first noted in the 1970s, along with location preferences, amenities, and population aging.

Not all rural areas benefited from this migration, with many losing population through the 1990s and early 2000s. Despite the above discussion of movement down the urban hierarchy, it is important to realize that the growth of these rural and micropolitan areas is selective. For remote rural America, including much of the Great Plains and the rural Midwest, population loss associated with migration has essentially continued unabated since the Depression. Population loss in these rural areas can be attributed to the loss of employment, lack of services such as schooling, poverty, and in some cases a lack of amenities such as warmer winters or recreational opportunities.[6] At the same time, net in-migration has benefited other rural areas, and in particular those either closer to urban areas or those that have amenities, as advances in telecommunications and transportation have enabled preferences for living in smaller areas that are close to urban areas.[7] For instance, migrants from large cities such as Los Angeles, New York, Chicago, and San Francisco have increasingly relocated to counties more than forty miles away from the city core, bypassing suburban areas that are closer to the center and the inner city.[8]

Although young adults in their twenties remain the most mobile segment of the population as they move for education- or employment-related reasons, the penchant for mobility amongst Americans seems to be declining. Long-term analysis shows that the frequency of longer distance moves (anything across county lines) has declined over the past forty years.[9] In large part, this reflects increased female participation in the labor force, which decreases the ability to make long-distance moves amongst households. In addition, the aging of the population decreases mobility rates as well, with older individuals and households less likely to migrate long distances.

It is unclear whether these migration patterns—and particularly the preference for moving further and further from the city center—will be sustained into the near-term future in light of rapid increases in the price of oil and gas in the later part of the 2000s. The *New York Times* suggested that the increasing cost of fuel threatened to slow migration away from cities.[10] While an excess housing supply and the credit crunch of 2008 compounded the problem and make it difficult to identify the exact reason for housing price changes and differences, housing prices beyond the urban core fell in value faster than those within. However, anecdotal evidence suggested that the rising cost of energy is the primary reason home prices have fallen, particularly in the outer suburbs. The outcome may be increased preference for inner-city locations, the exact opposite of what had happened for the preceding decades.

Measuring migration is not necessarily straightforward, and the migration researcher must account for time and space when counting migrations. Nevertheless, a number of tools or measures are available that allow us to quantify migration flows. Between 1995 and 2000,[1] some 22 million people moved between states, or more than seven percent of the nation's population. Of these, about 1.4 million people moved into California. During the same period, over 2.2 million people moved out of the state, meaning a net population loss through migration of 755,536 and a gross migration of nearly 3.7 million. When expressed as a rate (per one thousand), California's in-migration rate was 47.1, its out-migration rate was 71.7, and the resulting net migration rate was -24.6, meaning that it lost 24.6 people through migration for every one thousand individuals living there in 1995. Nationally, the in- and out-migration rates were 45.7 for the period.

MIGRATION PROPENSITY

A basic measure of migration is the *migration propensity* (p_{ij}), which shows the relative proportion of the population beginning the period in one region (*i*) who are found in other regions by the end of the period, defined as

$$p_{ij} = \frac{m_{ij}}{P_i}$$

where P_i is the population of the origin (starting) region at time $t-1$ (i.e., the beginning of the census interval), and m_{ij} is the number of migrants moving from *i* to each destination *j*.

GROSS MIGRATION FLOWS AND RATES

Oftentimes, population geographers are interested in the propensities of a population to leave (enter) a particular destination (origin) regardless of where they migrate to or from. When relying on the census, migrants and migrations are defined based on place of residence at the start of the census interval (five years prior to census day) and compared with place of residence at the time of the census. Once defined, the number of out-migrants leaving an origin (O_i), the number of in-migrants entering a destination (I_j), or the number moving between two points (M_{ij}) can be counted. For instance, the number of out-migrants from region *i* (O_i) can be defined as the following formula.

$$O_i = \sum_{i \neq j} m_{ij}$$

In the same way, gross in-migration to region *i* (I_i) is determined by adding up all its in-migration flows.

While the number of migrants may be instructive, it can also be misleading. Large regions, such as states like Texas or California, will both produce a large number of migrants given their population size and also attract a large number of migrants, while smaller regions or states will experience the opposite. Migration rates are therefore typically constructed based upon the population *at risk* of migrating. For instance, the *out-migration rate* (OR_i) from region *i* is defined as

$$OR_i = (O_i \ / \ P_i) * 1000$$

where O_i is the number of out-migrants from region *i*, and P_i is the population of region *i*.

Similarly, the *in-migration rate* (IR_j) to region *j* is defined as

$$IR_j = (I_j \ / \ P_j) * 1000$$

where I_j is the number of in-migrants to region j and P_j is the population of region j. Strictly speaking, this specification does not accurately capture the population at risk of migrating to region j. Instead, it defines the at-risk population as the population of the destination region.[2] But if they are already residing in j, they can't in-migrate to j! A more precise definition of the in-migration rate would be

$$IR_j = (I_j \,/ \sum_{j \neq k} P_k)*1000$$

where the denominator represents the population of the entire system excepting region j.

Net Migration Flows and Rates

Frequently, population geographers will want to know the overall effect of migration on a region's population. Did it, for example, grow or decline (and by how many) due to migration over a period? This can be determined by *net migration* (N_i), which is defined as the difference between the number of in-migrants and the number of out-migrants to/from region i.

$$N_i = I_i - O_i$$

The *net migration rate* is defined similarly as the difference between the in- and out-migration rates. While useful for ascertaining overall population effects, the use of net migration in most cases is problematic, as it essentially represents a constructed figure and not an actual migrant.[3] As such, it is not commonly used when modeling migration.

MIGRATION EFFECTIVENESS

Migration researchers may also be interested in the relative proportion of arriving and departing migrants. *Migration effectiveness*[4] (E_i) is defined as the ratio between net migration (in-migration − out-migration) and gross migration (in-migration + out-migration) flows.

$$E_i = 100 \left(\frac{I_i - O_i}{I_i + O_i} \right)$$

E_i tells the percentage of "turnover" that results in population change and does not depend on the population size of the region in question. Large values (as opposed to those close to zero) are defined as more "effective," in that migration flows are more one-way. A related measure is *stream effectiveness*, which captures movement between two particular regions.

$$e_{ij} = 100 \left(\frac{m_{ij} - m_{ji}}{m_{ij} + m_{ji}} \right)$$

Chapter Seven

International Migration Flows

Immigrants and Transnational Migrants

MIGRATION HAS BECOME increasingly important as a vehicle for population change, with three dominant themes, namely internal and rural-to-urban migration, international labor migration (legal and illegal), and refugee flows. Out of all the possible population movements, international migration perhaps generates the greatest political, economic, and demographic interest owing to the large numbers of individuals that cross international borders.[1] In 2005 alone, it was estimated that there were 191 million international migrants, or 3 percent of the world's population. Of these, 120 million immigrated to developed countries, representing a doubling of flows between 1985 and 2005.[2] The balance of yearly international flows are between developing countries.[3]

Fundamentally, immigration is an economic process motivated by a combination of "push" factors in the origin, including poor employment prospects, large populations, and low wages. The major sending regions are defined by Asia, North Africa, and Latin America, while both the developing world and developed world are important destinations. This chapter explores the theories and drivers of international migration along with concepts of transnational migrants before considering policy and illegal immigration in the context of the United States. The "Focus" section explores the so-called "gap" in US immigration policy, and the "Methods, Measures, and Tools" section discusses how international flows may be measured.

MAJOR INTERNATIONAL FLOWS

In the past, immigration was an important component of nation building in the United States, Canada, Australia, and New Zealand, and indeed remains a "myth" within many of these countries. The enduring and near-mythical status attained by places like Ellis Island in New York, Canada's Pier 21 in Halifax, or Australia's settlement by exconvicts are important components of each nation's development and psyche. Countries have also encouraged labor recruitment through programs such as the Bracero Program, which recruited Mexican laborers for work in the United States, or Germany's "guest-worker" program, which was created to supply German industry with low-cost labor. In both cases, the respective governments found that these temporary migrations institutionalized and encouraged long-term and permanent migrations, with businesses continuing to be dependent on immigrant workers.

We can make broad distinctions in international flows between developed-world countries, between the developing and developed world, and between developing-world countries. Of these three sets of flows, flows between developed countries tend to be dominated by professionals: those that are able to move with relative ease between countries and whose skills are in demand in the destination countries. Flows between developed countries account for relatively few international movements given immigration policies in receiving countries that impose restrictions on international moves. International migration from the developing to the developed world is also tightly controlled, with importing countries often placing a yearly limit on the number of entrants and a preference on highly skilled or educated entrants, as well as allowing entry under humanitarian or family reunification guidelines. Principal receiving countries include the United States, Canada, Australia, western Europe, Scandinavia, and Russia,[4] where higher wages and increased opportunities serve as immigrant "pulls," while sending countries include a long list of origins. In the United States, over 1.052 million immigrants received permanent residency in 2007,[5] with major immigrant origins including China (76,655), Columbia (33,187), Cuba (29,104), the Dominican Republic (28,024), El Salvador (21,127), and Guatemala (17,908). International movement between developing countries is a third major flow. Although somewhat less restrictive, movement between countries in the developing world is still often controlled by the receiving country, with most flows characterized by laborers.

THEORIES OF IMMIGRATION

As articulated by Douglas Massey and colleagues, immigration is a complex demographic and economic process,[6] with a number of theories advanced to explain international migration. We can typically distinguish between those factors that initiate international migration and those that perpetuate immigration. Notwithstanding the diversity of these theories, no single theoretical viewpoint captures all the nuances of international population movements. In part, this is because national policies have created and influenced immigration flows, either intentionally or unintentionally. Consequently, immigration must be set within the broader context of national policies that promote or impede it.

Similar to internal migration, *neoclassical economic theory* focuses on macro-level factors such as employment opportunities.[7] Essentially, this theory argues that international migration occurs because of imbalances in the supply and demand for labor, with the theory arguing that wages will be higher in countries experiencing a growing economy and scarcity of labor as compared to slower-growth economies. Because of the difference in wage rates, individuals will immigrate in search of higher wages. Doing so will increase the labor pool in the high-wage country, and as supply increases, wages will drop. For immigrant-sending countries, the decrease in the pool of labor will push wages up. Ultimately, the theory argues that wages will equalize between the two countries as the labor pools are changed. Similar to the faults noted in the discussion of internal migration, international migration is not free, but restricted by immigration law and policy. For sending countries, the absolute size of the change in the labor market due to emigration is small, with no apparent impact on wages for those remaining.

The *New Economics of Migration Theory* expands the discussion of macro determinants of migration to include such things as the volatility of local agricultural markets, access to credit, and remittances.[8] In this case, emigration is the result of household decision making, with emigration allowing diversification of income sources. That is, international migration reflects family choice to spread the risks of migration. Oftentimes, the family will pay the travel expenses of the migrant in exchange for the migrant sending money home, diversifying income sources for the family.

The *dual-labor market theory* argues that international migration is determined by the labor needs of economies in the destination cities or countries, focusing on shortages in the labor markets of receiving countries and high- and low-status positions, with immigrants frequently filling low-status (and low-income) job positions.[9] The theory argues that the employment market can be subdivided into two sectors: the primary sector, which employs the highly educated and supports them with high wages, and the secondary labor market, which is characterized by low wages, unstable working conditions, and limited advancement. Frequently, secondary-sector positions are filled by the young or racial and ethnic minority groups. However, with slowing fertility rates and legislation that has created greater equity in the workplace for all groups, shortages have emerged, which are filled by immigrants from the developing world.

The *world systems theory* suggests that the main cause of emigration is globalization. With globalization, the world has divided into a set of developed and developing countries, with developing countries dependent on the developed world for investment and economic growth. The search for land, materials, and labor as developed countries invest in the developing world results in changes to production and pushes the unskilled out of jobs and off the land in the developing world, forcing international migration. The theory also proposes that flows will tend to be country-specific, with the developing world sending immigrants to the developed-world countries with whom they have the greatest contact, often the outcome of colonial ties.

Theories that discuss the perpetuation of international migrations include *social network theory*. Social network theory focuses on individual decisions, linking immigrants with family, friends, and the larger immigrant community between the origin and destination countries. In this way, continued immigration is promoted, as individuals in the destination are able to relay information back home regarding job opportunities while also providing links to accommodation and a broader community within which to interact. By doing so, the linkages and immigrant organizations decrease the costs of immigration (both physical and psychological) and increase the potential success of international migration.

Myrdal's *cumulative causation theory* argues that immigration alters the social context in which individual immigration decisions are made and makes further international migrations more likely.[10] In the destination, the entry of immigrants into particular occupations may reinforce the demand for other immigrants to fill similar jobs. More generally, immigrants send income and knowledge of job opportunities and housing home, perpetuating immigrant flows from an origin to a destination. Income remittances in particular are important. Remittances act as an income stream for the sending family and may further encourage international migration to increase and diversify income sources.

Finally, *institutional theory* suggests that ongoing international migration is the result of informal and illegal migration and organizations that facilitate or promote migration. Various institutions or groups may facilitate international migration by providing services, including securing housing or jobs. Illegal immigration may also be promoted as organizations smuggle people across borders.

THE IMPACTS OF IMMIGRATION

The United States has long defined itself as being a nation of immigrants, with immigrants arriving in search of economic opportunity, political or religious freedom, or to reunite with their families. Despite the long history of immigration, public attention has increasingly focused on the size, origins, and implications of large-scale immigration.[11] Over the past fifty years, polling has charted increasing opposition to immigrants within the United States. Ongoing and emerging debates reflect associated concerns: How will immigrants assimilate or incorporate themselves within the host society? How will the larger society be changed?

Discussions of the costs and benefits of immigration reflect a long-running debate found within most countries that receive a large number of immigrants, with answers cutting across economic, social, fiscal, and demographic perspectives.[12] Undoubtedly, public awareness is higher in those locations that are primary magnets for immigrants, including California, New York, Illinois, Florida, and New Jersey. But concerns with the impacts and number of immigrants are not limited to these areas. Recent reports, including the 2000 US census and the ACS, indicate that the foreign-born are increasingly found in areas that have not been traditional destinations for immigrants.[13] States such as Iowa that could hardly be described as immigrant magnets are now counting larger foreign-born populations where the new arrivals frequently fill low-paying or unskilled positions, and their presence forces communities to deal with issues of immigration and assimilation that had previously been unheard of in small-town America.

Economic Impacts

Economically, the bulk of evidence indicates that immigration has a rather minimal but positive impact on economic well-being.[14] Immigration most directly benefits the immigrants themselves, making them financially better off in their host country relative to their origin, even though they tend to earn less on average than the native-born in their host country and are predominately found in low-paying, low-skilled positions within the workforce. Domestically, immigrants increase the supply of labor, boost production and demand for goods, and have commonly been regarded as a potent short-term policy tool, allowing skill shortages in the labor force to be alleviated quickly. Although the economy as a whole may gain, immigration may also create losers, including the less skilled native-born, who may compete directly with immigrants in the job market and who may see wages fall. Again, however, the available evidence suggests that immigration has only a small negative impact upon the wage and labor opportunities of the native-born. In the formal sector, minimum-wage laws, unions, and low unemployment rates have ensured "wage stickiness," although workers in the informal economy or in regions that receive large numbers of immigrants may be somewhat more disadvantaged.

Fiscally, the debate on whether immigrants pay more in taxes than they receive in benefits is contentious and complex. In an analysis of the impacts of immigration on US society, the National Research Council (NRC)[15] found that immigrant-headed households make small positive contributions to federal tax revenues.[16] At the state and local levels, the picture is less clear, with net fiscal burdens reported in immigrant-receiving states such as New Jersey and California. In other words, the NRC calculated that immigrants receive more in services than they pay in taxes in these two states. However, the increased burden is explained by the fact that both states are important immigrant destinations with large numbers of immigrants. In turn, immigrant households tend to have a greater number of school-age children and therefore receive more transfers. Likewise, immigrant households tend to have lower incomes and less property, so they consequently pay lower taxes. Over generations, however, descendents of immigrants may contribute far more in taxes than their parents received. Fiscal burdens may be particularly acute at the local scale. In Phoenix, Arizona, the burgeoning Hispanic population, many of whom are believed to be illegal, has exerted pressures on institutions such as local school boards, hospitals, and libraries, even as their presence has been acknowledged to sustain the state economy.[17] If the state or federal government does not reimburse local costs, the burden would fall to local taxpayers, a situation in which it is easy to imagine increased calls for immigration control.

Long-term projections of the fiscal costs and benefits of immigration reveal that they balance over the lifetime of immigrant residency. Immigrants, like the native-born, pose greater burdens during childhood and old age, owing to the costs of education and health care. During their labor force years, they tend to make a net fiscal contribution. Fiscal burden also varies by origin and education, with European and North American immigrants making a net fiscal contribution. On the other hand, immigrants from Central and South America create a fiscal burden owing to lower incomes, lower levels of education, and more school-age children than other households. Importantly, it must be realized that education and service provision to the poorly educated or low-income native-born pose similar fiscal burdens. In other words, the question of fiscal burden is not just an "immigrant" issue.

Of course, the discussion so far has focused on the economic impacts for receiving countries. But what about those countries that send immigrants? As an outcome of globalization, international migration provides the labor, with workers pushed out of their home countries by a lack of economic opportunities and pulled by opportunities elsewhere. As an economic lifeline, money is often sent home to family and used for consumption and new housing. These remittances have grown in economic importance, with international migrants sending home an estimated $318 billion in 2007. India ($27 billion), China ($26 billion), Mexico ($25 billion), and the Philippines ($17 billion) are the leading beneficiaries of these capital flows.[18] Unofficially, the dollar value is probably much larger when money is sent home directly with family or friends or through unregulated transfer agents. In relative terms, small countries benefit the most, with some increasing their national incomes by more than 20 percent. Egypt, for example, receives more from money sent home from its migrant laborers than it does from ships transiting the Suez Canal.[19] The United States is the largest remittance source (estimated at $42 billion being sent out of the country in 2006), with the balance of the developed world, along with oil-producing countries, the other main sources for these remittances.

Demographic Impacts

Demographically, immigration has frequently been touted as a cure to an aging population. As noted earlier, most developed countries have entered a period of below-replacement fertility. Economic development associated with urbanization, industrialization, economic uncertainty, and the welfare state has translated into a reduced need or desire for children. The result is an increasing proportion of elderly and a decreasing share of the population aged fifteen years and younger. In effect, we are seeing a fundamental change in the age distribution of the population away from the traditional "pyramidal" structure, with a large share of the population concentrated in the younger age groups, toward a "rectangular" age structure with a more even distribution of the population across ages (see discussion of population pyramids in chapter 3). In response, immigration could be used to offset the demographic implications of an aging population if young immigrants were targeted as the most desirable entrants.

Clearly, immigration has a profound impact on the demographic structure of the United States, with immigration a significant contributor in the country's population growth, which is expected to total 438 million by 2050.[20] Moreover, the relatively high fertility levels in the United States reflect higher fertility among minority groups, particularly Hispanics.[21] Most studies, including those of the NRC, have found that immigration merely postpones or alleviates the onset of an aging population, although it is likely that immigration has allowed the United States to maintain relatively high fertility levels. In part, family reunification offsets the desired demographic effects as young adults sponsor their parents. Moreover, the dynamics of demographic change now underway within the developed world imply that the population will continue to statistically age in the coming decades.

The most visible impact of immigration will be changes to the cultural, racial, or ethnic composition of receiving countries as immigrants account for an increasing share of population, issues that most developed countries are already grappling with. Between 1990 and 2000, about one-third of the growth of population in the United States was due to immigration, with the number of foreign-born exceeding 31 million. Over the longer term, the share of non-Hispanic whites is projected to decline from 67 percent to 47 percent by 2050, while the shares of Hispanics and Asians will grow, reflecting both immigration and higher fertility levels within these groups.[22] Socially, opposition to immigration has frequently focused on the perceived cultural and racial differences between immigrants and the native-born, but this raises debates associated with whether the receiving country has one culture or many. In Europe or Canada, the answer to this question is simple but reflects near-polar ends of the spectrum. Most European states see their borders encompassing a single nationality, hence the concern with increasing numbers of foreigners and their "dilution" of national identity. Canada, on the other hand, is a multicultural society, an agenda that has been fostered and actively promoted by the federal government for the past thirty years. In the United States, the answer is less clear but no less important. The unified vision of the "melting pot" contrasts with the reality of immigration. Immigration to the United States may have altered impressions of culture, but it does not necessarily suppress the cultural identity of immigrants, making the United States a de facto multicultural society as well. Even among groups that have been long-term residents of the United States, such as Germans or Scandinavians, their cultural heritage is embraced, and the identity of these groups has left lingering impressions upon the cultural and economic landscape.[23]

IMMIGRATION POLICY

The demographic realities of low fertility and an aging population mean that European countries are faced with a labor force crisis. Given the difficulties and limitations associated with fertility policies as discussed in chapter 4, increased immigration may be the only option for meeting Europe's employment requirements, but it is fraught with political, social, and cultural problems. Increased nativism in Europe and the United States, along with the emergence of anti-immigrant violence and right-wing political parties that have cultivated a fear of foreigners, serve as a warning bell. In response, Europe has moved to limit immigration, but attempts to restrict it have often led to increased "backdoor" immigration through family reunification policies, illegal immigration, or seasonal-worker admission. The failure to control immigration means that European societies must be prepared to transform themselves into immigrant destinations, something that most states are unwilling to do at this time. In part, doing so raises questions regarding the integration of immigrants into the social, economic, and political structures of the host nations. The problem for all of these states is that they must define who "belongs" within their borders. In Europe, immigration has not provided a foundation as it has in North America, and the cultural shift involved in moving from labor exporter to labor importer is huge. Consequently, immigration debates are part of the much broader debate of national identity that pervades the economic, social, political, and cultural aspects of a society.

Traditional countries of immigration, such as the United States, Canada, and Australia, cannot sit idle and hope that the emergent storms over immigration and national identity will pass them by. Fueled by shifts in immigration sources, policies, and rights in the past three decades, welfare reform in the late 1990s, California's Proposition 187 (barring immigrants from various social and medical services), Arizona's Proposition 200 (barring illegal immigrants from voting or seeking public assistance), cases of increased nativism, illegal immigration control, and the Balkanization debate provided evidence of the potential for public concern with legal and illegal immigration alike. Up until the 1960s, immigration to the United States and Canada was shaped by white Anglo-Saxon images of society. Liberalization of immigration policies during the 1960s broadened the scope of immigration, but injected new racial and ethnic tensions into the debate, even as they were defined as white versus black differences. But such debates cannot be cast in a "black versus white" or an "us versus them" context. In both Canada and the United States, there is a growing population that identifies with a mixed racial or ethnic heritage, and intermarriage between racial or ethnic groups is increasing. In the 2000 US census, for example, Americans could choose to identify themselves by more than one race, and responses pointed to an increasingly diverse population. Selling immigration's humanitarian dimension is an alternative option, albeit one that is unlikely to meet with widespread success.

The recent history of European immigration policies and the pressure of domestic and international changes suggest that there is relatively little room for states to maneuver immigration policy. Countries might pursue economic development in origin countries, a policy that the European Union is pursuing in North Africa and which is roughly equivalent to the maquiladoras that line the Mexico–US border. Over the short term, however, the economic restructuring generated by such policies may actually increase immigration as redundant workers search for employment. As a second option, states are increasingly reliant upon the removal of political rights among immigrants, flying in the face of decades of advances. Most nations, including France, Germany, and the United States, are now advancing a mix of agendas that remove or reduce access to welfare services, including education and health care; reduce employment options; and reduce programs meant to block the integration of immigrants and discourage permanent settlement. Recent policy shifts in the United States highlight this trend. In order to regain control of its borders, the United States has moved to restrict access and, in doing so, has realized that this requires a rollback of civil and human rights for noncitizens. Legislation, including welfare reform and California's Proposition 187 (see later in this chapter), either removed or proposed to remove rights and protections given to US immigrants. An additional example is the policy of interdicting Haitian immigrants on the ocean to prevent them from reaching the United States and initiating the refugee process.[24]

Removal of the right to work is particularly problematic. Unless the right to work is withdrawn, curtailing the rights of immigrants is unlikely to reduce immigration, since there is little evidence that demonstrates that the provision of social services is an important reason for movement. Instead, employment and income are the main determinants: As long as countries demand low-cost labor, immigration will continue. As the native-born shun low-paying, manual-labor positions, there is a demand for inexpensive and illegal labor. Moreover, removing the right to work is hardly a deterrent, given the role of the underground economy and illegal immigration in the developed world. It is estimated, for example, that 50 to 80 percent of US farm workers are illegal immigrants, with an annual entry of an estimated 150,000 illegal immigrants into the United States.[25]

Given the experiences of the United States and other countries, closing the doors to immigrants is unlikely to stem the flow given the strength of pull and push factors in both origin and destination areas. Realizing that state control over immigration is limited and incomplete, labor unions have, in the past, voiced *support* for more open and moderate immigration policies.[26] Fearing that immigrants would compete with the native-born for employment and reduce wages, unions have traditionally sought to limit immigrant numbers, making the current involvement of unions in the immigration debate a seemingly strange bedfellow. In recent years, however, unions in Europe and America have supported liberalized immigration policies and courted immigrant workers as a way of protecting workers and labor standards for all. In the United States, the American Federation of Labor and Congress of Industrial Organizations (AFL-CIO) withdrew their support for employer sanctions and called for an amnesty of illegal immigrants in February 2000, a call that was repeated in the spring of 2009 as discussions moved forward on President Obama's proposed revamping of US immigration law.[27] Similarly, one proposal that would benefit the agricultural sector would increase the number of seasonal workers in the United States from forty thousand to two hundred and fifty thousand per year, a measure that has been supported by some unions since these workers would be represented by unions.[28] In Los Angeles, unions have focused their organization efforts on immigrant workers, allowing them to add members faster than anywhere else in the United States.[29] Promoting moderate labor immigration is seen as one way to protect workers, ensure a safe work environment, reduce illegal immigration, and maintain union strength at a time of dwindling membership.

A Short History of US Immigration Policy

For much of the first century of its existence, US immigration was largely unrestricted, and it wasn't until 1875 that the Supreme Court ruled that the federal government had authority over immigration.[30] Over subsequent years, the number of immigrants entering the country gradually increased, reaching a peak in the decade immediately before World War I (figure 7.1) While both the Depression of the 1930s and World War II reduced the number of immigrants entering the country on a yearly basis, numbers increased in the postwar era, surpassing one million entrants in the early 1990s as well as after 2000.

In large part, the variations in immigrant numbers over the years represent both changing economic conditions and changing immigration policy. The years between 1875 and 1920 witnessed the increasing regulation of entry into the United States, with regulations excluding those with criminal records, diseases, or unacceptable moral standards; anarchists; and particular groups based on origin or nationality. The 1882 Chinese Exclusion Act represented the first of several acts that restricted Asian immigration, with the Japanese excluded in 1907 and all Asians excluded in 1917. During the 1920s, national quotas were established that favored northern and western Europeans in an effort to maintain the racial and ethnic mixture in the United States. The Emergency Immigration Act of 1921 was the first to place quantitative restrictions on immigration, with annual immigration from a country limited to 3 percent of the number of foreign-born from that country that resided in the United States in 1910, when northern and western Europeans dominated the country. In effect, the law shifted immigrant origins away from regions that were not favored, including southern and eastern Europe, emphasizing instead an Anglo-Saxon immigration agenda. Interestingly, the quotas did not place restrictions on immigrants from the Western Hemisphere. Canadians were seen as no different from the existing American population stock, and immigration from Cen-

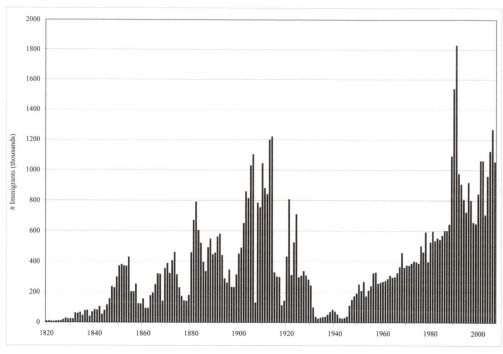

Figure 7.1   Persons Obtaining Legal Permanent Resident Status: 1820–2005.

Source: Based on 2007 *Yearbook of Immigration Statistics*, Office of Immigration Statistics.

tral and South America was not deemed a problem. In subsequent years, quotas were made increasingly tight, altering either the percentage or pushing back the base year, further reducing the number of immigrants allowed entry. But when restrictions were imposed on immigration, illegal immigrants were created. In response, Congress established the US Border Patrol in 1924, charged initially with apprehending illegal entrants.

The blatantly racist restrictions within American immigration policy were not removed until 1952 with the passage of the Immigration and Nationality Act. The act introduced a preference system for those with needed skills. For the first time, limits were placed on the number of immigrants from the Western Hemisphere and a preference system was set in place, with priority given to family members of American citizens and permanent residents as well as those with needed job skills. The quota system was finally lifted in the 1965 revisions to the Immigration and Nationality Act and was replaced with hemispheric limits, having a significant impact upon the nature of American society. Although it was unintended, the family preference category dramatically shifted immigration away from traditional origins such as Europe toward new origins in Central and South America and Asia. Prior to 1965, Europeans represented the majority of immigrants arriving in the United States, but this group represented just 11.5 percent in 2007. Instead, approximately 41 percent of all immigrants were from the Americas by 2007, with Mexico representing the single largest origin (13.6 percent).[31] Totaling 34 percent of all immigrant arrivals, Asians were the second-largest group. Minor adjustments were made to the Immigration and Nationality Act through the 1970s and 1980s, a period marked by an increasing awareness of the scope of illegal immigration, with the Immigration Act of 1990 being the last major revision. Although family reunification remained a significant component, the act increased the number of immigrants admitted on a yearly basis and expanded the number of visas given on economic grounds to 140,000 per fiscal year (tables 7.1 and 7.2).[32]

In framing US immigration policy, US legislators have attempted to balance competing economic, social, and humanitarian goals. It is, for example, argued that a large illegal immigrant workforce is not beneficial for the United States. But competing interests have led to policy gridlock, a fragmented policy agenda, and unanticipated consequences, resulting in an emerging gap between the *goals* of national immigration policy and the *results* of those policies.[33] In her analysis of US immigration, Kitty Calavita argues that historical and current policies are best summarized as a triad of opposites between employers and workers, between an economy that needs unskilled workers and the political class that is unwilling to confront the conflicts this creates, and between human rights and border control.[34]

Illegal Immigration

Most developed countries have instituted restrictions and barriers to immigration and recast immigration as a national security issue. But, if a country tries to close the door to immigration, will it succeed? Experiences from Europe and the United States, including the 1986 Immigration Reform and Control Act (IRCA) and recent clampdowns on illegal border crossings, suggest not. In fact, restricting legal immigration may only serve to increase illegal immigration or other backdoor immigration through family reunification programs, illegal immigration, or seasonal-worker admission.

Beyond policy, enforcement also bears upon the presence and number of illegals within the country. Given the robust economic conditions and low unemployment rates of the late 1990s, reports suggested that the then–Immigration and Naturalization Service (INS) was no longer pursuing or prosecuting illegal aliens once inside the United States. Since 9/11, concerns with terrorism have led the Department of Homeland Security to focus on restrictions to entry into the United States and to increasingly crack down on illegal residents in the country through a series of high-profile raids on businesses.[35] The Immigration and Customs Enforcement (ICE) branch of Homeland Security highlights their successes on the Internet.[36]

Table 7.1. Class of Admission of Legal Immigrants to the United States, Fiscal Years 2006–2008

	2006		2007		2008	
	Number	%	Number	%	Number	%
Total, all immigrants	**1,266,129**		**1,052,415**		**1,107,126**	
New arrivals	446,881	35.3	431,368	41.0	466,558	42.1
Adjustments	819,248	64.7	621,047	59.0	640,568	57.9
Preference immigrants	**381,310**	**30.1**	**357,076**	**33.9**	**394,272**	**35.6**
Family-sponsored immigrants	**222,229**	**17.6**	**194,900**	**18.5**	**227,761**	**20.8**
Unmarried sons/daughters of US citizens	25,432	2.0	22,858	2.2	26,173	2.4
Spouses of alien residents	112,051	8.8	86,151	8.2	103,456	9.3
Married sons/daughters of US citizens	21,491	1.7	20,611	2.0	29,373	2.7
Siblings of US citizens	63,255	5.0	65,280	6.2	68,859	6.2
Employment-based immigrants	**159,081**	**12.6**	**162,176**	**15.4**	**166,511**	**15.0**
Priority workers	36,960	2.9	26,697	2.5	36,678	3.3
Professionals with advanced degrees	21,911	1.7	44,162	4.2	70,046	6.3
Skilled workers, professionals, other workers	89,922	7.1	85,030	8.1	48,903	4.4
Special immigrants	9,539	0.8	5,481	0.5	9,524	0.9
Employment creation	749	0.0	806	0.0	1,360	0.1
Diversity	**44,471**	**3.5**	**42,127**	**4.0**	**41,761**	**3.8**
Immediate relatives of US citizens	**580,348**	**45.8**	**494,920**	**47.0**	**488,483**	**44.0**
Spouses	339,843	26.8	274,358	26.1	265,671	24.0
Children	120,064	9.5	103,828	9.9	101,342	9.2
Parents	120,441	9.5	116,734	11.1	121,470	11.0
Refugees	**99,609**	**7.9**	**54,942**	**5.2**	**90,030**	**8.1**
Asylees	**116,845**	**9.2**	**81,183**	**7.7**	**76,362**	**6.7**
Other immigrants	**43,546**	**3.4**	**22,167**	**2.1**	**16,218**	**1.5**

Source: 2008 Yearbook of Immigration Statistics.

Table 7.2. Immigrants Admitted to the United States by Selected Country of Birth, Top Ten Origins, Fiscal Years 2006–2008

Rank	2006			2007			2008		
	Country	Number	%	Country	Number	%	Country	Number	%
–	All Countries	1,266,127	100.0	All Countries	1,052,415	100.0	All Countries	1,107,126	100.0
1	Mexico	173,749	13.7	Mexico	148,640	14.1	Mexico	189,989	17.2
2	China	87,307	6.9	China	76,655	7.3	China	80,271	7.3
3	Philippines	74,606	5.9	Philippines	72,596	6.9	India	63,352	5.7
4	India	61,369	4.8	India	65,353	6.2	Philippines	54,030	4.9
5	Cuba	45,614	3.6	Columbia	33,187	3.2	Cuba	49,500	4.5
6	Columbia	43,144	3.4	Haiti	30,405	2.9	Dominican Rep.	31,879	2.9
7	Dominican Rep.	38,068	3.0	Cuba	29,104	2.8	Vietnam	31,497	2.8
8	El Salvador	31,782	2.5	Vietnam	28,691	2.7	Columbia	30,213	2.8
9	Vietnam	30,691	2.4	Dominican Rep.	28,024	2.7	Korea	26,666	2.4
10	Jamaica	24,976	2.0	Korea	22,405	2.1	Haiti	26,007	2.3

Source: 2008 Yearbook of Immigration Statistics.

Figure 7.2   Caution: A Roadside Sign in San Diego.
This sign warns motorists on busy Interstate 5 of the potential for people, including women and children, to be on the highway, posted in response to illegal immigrants' entering the United States in this area and escaping custody.
Source: Author's photo.

Policy Responses to Illegal Immigration

Ultimately, the imbalance between policy goals and realities may engender greater hostility toward immigrants, placing increased pressure on the government to restrict immigration. In 1986, for example, 1,615,854 illegal aliens were apprehended along the US–Mexico border, and aliens were brazenly entering the country by running directly past immigration agents at border crossings (figure 7.2). Such images provoked fears that the United States had lost control of its borders, and calls for tighter restrictions intensified.

Searching for ways to control immigration and responding to public concerns, legislators moved to restrict immigrant access to welfare and social benefits (seen in California's Proposition 187, Arizona's Proposition 200, and welfare reform in 1996) and to make entry more difficult, exemplified by increased border patrol measures. California's Proposition 187,[37] which was designed to remove public funding from all illegal immigrants, polarized immigration viewpoints within the state and pushed local immigration concerns into the national and international spotlight.[38] Propelled by the real and perceived costs posed by illegal immigrants, including welfare (ab)use, criminal activities, and employment costs, California lawmakers attempted to curb the tide of illegal immigration into the state and encourage some illegal immigrants who were already resident to leave. Proposition 187 was designed to exclude illegal immigrants from schools and colleges, deny nonemergency health care to illegal aliens, require the police to verify the legal immigrant status of all people arrested, and require teachers and health care workers to report illegal aliens to the INS. While its provisions did not affect legal immigrants within the state, it nonetheless created an atmosphere in which all people of color, both legal and illegal, became suspect. Internationally, both Mexico and El Salvador expressed concern with Proposition 187, citing human rights violations. More realistically, both were likely concerned with the potential negative economic effects associated with a large number of returning workers.

Passed by public vote in November 1994 with 59 percent of the vote, Proposition 187 received broad-based support throughout the state and revealed the depth of frustration among California's voters with illegal immigration. Shortly afterward, a federal court ruled Proposition 187 to be unconstitutional, citing the fact that immigration was a federal, not state, matter and that federal law requires free public education to all children. The widespread support for Proposition 187 had considerable ethnic and spatial variation, stressing the complexity of the immigration debate and providing insight into public reaction to immigration and anti-immigrant sentiments.[39] Ethnic divisions in voting patterns followed expected divisions, with 63 percent of white non-Hispanics voting in support of the proposition. Greater support was found among middle- or upper-income white and Republican voters, expressing a simple anti-immigrant sentiment. African Americans and Asians were moderately likely to support the measure, voting 56 and 57 percent in favor, respectively, while only 31 percent of Hispanics supported Proposition 187. Analysis of the vote at the local scale shows additional variations, with greater support among Hispanic neighborhoods with higher socioeconomic status, suggesting a desire to control illegal immigration and mirroring white, non-Hispanic sentiments. Even in inner-city Hispanic communities, there was a surprising degree of support for the measure.

William Clark, a professor of geography at the University of California, suggested that voter response to Proposition 187 could not be defined simply as nativist or racist reactions, but instead reflected local responses to immigration. Recalling the findings of the NRC, Californians were forced to deal with the real and perceived consequences of immigration locally, where potentially significant (and costly) fiscal effects were more likely to occur.[40] Thus, Proposition 187 may simply have been a reaction to high immigration levels in the late 1980s, local fiscal implications, and the recession of 1990–1991, which seemingly increased the cost of service provision by the state and local governments. Clark also suggested that the voting behavior placed California's concerns at odds with the national role of the United States as a receiver of immigrants, along with businesses' desire for low-cost labor.[41] A darker implication is raised by George Sanchez, who argued that Proposition 187 presented immigrants as scapegoats for California's economic problems in the early 1990s.[42]

California is not alone in its concern over illegal immigrants and their fiscal consequences. Arizona is also a frontline state and is also wrestling with a growing illegal population. In response, the electorate passed Proposition 200 in the 2004 elections, barring illegal immigrants from voting or seeking public assistance for state and local benefits that were not federally mandated. Although lawmakers had attempted to avoid the problems associated with California's Proposition 187, Proposition 200 still faces court challenges.[43] Even municipalities are enacting restrictionist immigration policies.[44] Prince William County, a suburb of Washington, D.C., has enacted laws similar to propositions 187 or 200 that aim to limit immigration in the face of large demographic change, including the denial of benefits to individuals who can't prove residency and requiring police to check the immigration status of people who are arrested.

Revisions to welfare in 1996 placed immigration concerns within a national forum. Officially known as The Personal Responsibility and Work Reconciliation Act, the act fundamentally altered welfare provision in the United States by cutting money to welfare programs, giving states greater control over spending, and enacting work and duration restrictions to programs. Although its impact upon the native-born was just as significant, welfare reform directly targeted immigrants and their use of programs. Revisions barred most legal immigrants from receiving Supplemental Security Income (SSI) and food stamps, two programs where immigrants received proportionately more benefits than the native-born.[45] At the time, it was estimated that upwards of five hundred thousand aliens lost their eligibility for SSI. An additional one million were estimated to lose their eligibility to receive food stamps. Aliens legally admitted to the United States after August 22, 1996 (the date revisions took effect) were also barred from federal means-tested programs during their first five years of residency. States were also eligible to bar qualified aliens from receiving Temporary Assistance for Needy Families (TANF),[46] Medicaid, and Title XX social services that funded, among other programs, childcare and elderly services. Although objecting to provisions restricting eligibility for public benefits, President Clinton signed the bill. In subsequent years, several directives and new bills worked to soften the impact of the restrictions upon immigrants, and many state governments provided additional funding to services.

Perhaps the greatest impact on the number of illegal entrants to the United

States has not been policy and enforcement tools, but the global recession, which started in late 2007. Growth of the illegal population in the United States (and other countries) slowed with the start of the recession, and evidence suggested that the number of illegal immigrants entering the United States dropped dramatically as the recession took hold.[47] Concurrently, illegal residents already in the United States tended to "stay put," preferring to ride the recession out by searching for employment in the United States for two broad reasons. First, while the recession severely reduced employment options in the United States, it was also affecting opportunities in their origin countries. Second, individuals would likely not want to risk the dangers of future border crossings given increased border security and the likelihood of apprehension.

The US Border Patrol

Ultimately, the "first line of defense" against illegal entry falls to the US Border Patrol, which works within the Citizenship and Immigration Services (USCIS) to detect and prevent the smuggling or entry of illegal aliens into the United States. In response to increasing concerns with the numbers of illegal immigrants entering the country, the Border Patrol increased the scope of its operations beginning in 1994 along the southern border with Mexico, the primary entry point from Central and South America. A series of operations, including Operation Gatekeeper in San Diego, Operation Hold-the-Line in El Paso, and Operation Safeguard in Tucson, were meant to control the border in each of these areas by cutting off avenues of illegal entry (figure 7.3). Most operations included a variety of interventions, such as new fencing and use of new technology including infrared scopes, underground sensors, and computer tracking of illegal entrants to deter illegal entry. By USCIS measures, these programs have been highly successful, reducing the number of apprehensions from over 450,000 in 1994, to 284,000 apprehensions in 1997, to 111,515 in 2003 within the San Diego sector alone.[48] Programs in other sectors reported similar "successes" (table 7.3). While total apprehensions appeared to dip in 2003, they climbed again to over 1.2 million for 2004, 2005, and 2006, suggesting that the desire of individuals to enter the United States illegally had not decreased, despite increased border security.

The reality is that these programs may be somewhat less effective than advertised. While reducing the number of crossing attempts at key locations such as San Diego or El Paso, the deterrence effect of increased surveillance and capture has diverted the streams of illegal aliens to areas that have not received the same degree of attention from the Border Patrol.[49] Operation Hold-the-Line at El Paso, Texas, for instance, succeeded in reducing local border crossings (i.e., local domestic workers who traveled short distances), but failed to deter long-

Figure 7.3   The US–Mexico Border.
The fence separating the United States and Mexico in San Diego. Would-be illegal immigrants are on the Mexico side, waiting for nightfall, when they will attempt to enter the United States.

Source: Author's photo.

distance, illegal labor migration. Instead, crossings were diverted to Arizona or elsewhere along the border, where the number of apprehensions increased.[50] The problem is also indirectly seen in the Border Safety Initiative (BSI), a binational program initiated in 1998 between the United States and Mexico. With increasing risk of apprehension in traditionally high-traffic areas, illegal entry has shifted to hazardous areas such as deserts or mountains, where the number of deaths among illegal entrants rose from 44 in 1999 to 207 in 2005.[51] Meant to reduce injuries and fatalities along the southwest border, one of the primary aims of the BSI has been public education with respect to the risks associated with illegal crossings, especially as illegals who are little prepared for the hardships of these locations are forced to cross in remote areas.

In placing additional resources along the border and proposing other policies aimed at controlling illegal immigration, the US government was effectively recasting the immigration debate as a national security issue. These concerns have become dominant themes within the immigration debate. Following the terrorist attacks of September 11, 2001, the potential threat to national security by immigration was further solidified as immigration and border issues were consolidated under the Department of Homeland Security. At the same time, a

Table 7.3. Yearly Border Patrol Apprehensions, Fiscal Years 2002–2008

Border Patrol Sector	2002	2003	2004	2005	2006	2007	2008
All Southwest	929,809	905,065	1,139,282	1,171,428	1,072,018	858,722	705,022
San Diego, CA	100,681	111,515	138,608	126,909	142,122	152,459	162,392
El Centro, CA	108,273	92,099	74,467	55,726	61,469	55,881	40,962
Yuma, CA	42,654	56,638	98,060	138,438	118,537	37,994	8,363
Tucson, AZ	333,648	347,263	491,771	439,090	392,104	378,323	317,709
El Paso, TX	94,154	88,816	104,399	122,689	122,261	75,464	30,310
Marfa, TX	11,392	10,319	10,530	10,536	7,517	5,537	5,390
Del Rio, TX	66,985	50,145	53,794	68,510	42,634	22,919	20,761
Laredo, TX	82,095	70,521	74,706	75,342	74,843	56,715	43,659
Rio Grande Valley, TX	89,927	77,749	92,947	134,188	110,531	73,430	75,476
All Other Sectors	25,501	26,492	21,113	17,680	17,118	18,065	18,818
Blaine, WA	1,732	1,308	1,354	1,001	809	749	951
Buffalo, NY	1,102	564	671	400	1,517	2,190	3,338
Detroit, MI	1,511	2,345	1,912	1,792	1,282	902	961
Grand Forks, ND	1,369	1,223	1,225	754	517	500	542
Havre, MT	1,463	1,406	986	949	567	486	427
Houlton, ME	432	292	263	233	175	95	81
Livermore, CA	4,371	3,565	1,850	117	—	—	—
Miami, FL	5,143	5,931	4,602	7,243	6,032	7,121	6,020
New Orleans, LA	4,665	5,151	2,889	1,358	3,054	4,018	4,303
Ramey, PR	835	1,688	1,813	1,619	1,436	548	572
Spokane, WA	1,142	992	847	279	185	337	340
Swanton, VT	1,736	1,955	2,701	1,935	1,544	1,119	1,283
Total	1,062,270	1,046,422	1,264,232	1,291,142	1,206,457	960,756	791,568

Source: 2008 Yearbook of Immigration Statistics.

coherent and sustainable solution to illegal immigration remains elusive, with the number of illegal immigrants in the United States estimated to be 11.8 million as of 2007.[52]

TRANSNATIONAL MIGRANTS

Although international migration for economic reasons is well-entrenched, a relatively new form of international movement is reflected in transnationalism.[53] Transnationalism can be broadly defined as a process by which immigrants create and maintain social, economic, and political relations through activities linking the origin and destination. This type of international movement highlights the complexity of international migrations and makes transnational migrants inherently different from other immigrants in that while they settle and become incorporated into their new place of residence they simultaneously maintain connections through a variety of social, economic, or political linkages outside the host country and most likely their country of origin. At the international scale, transnational migrants, such as businesspeople who work in one country while their partners and children live in another country, are increasingly common, reflecting economic and personal needs. Oftentimes, residency is determined by life-cycle stage, with transnationals often choosing to live in one country for economic opportunity during prime working years and residing elsewhere for educational purposes or retirement.[54] More generally, transnational migrants tend to be skilled workers. So-called "astronaut families," where either one or both parents reside primarily in one country while their children remain in another, can be considered a distinctive form of transnationalism.[55] In both cases, their relative transience between countries makes it difficult to arrive at reliable estimates of the true magnitude of transnationalism.

CONCLUSION

Both forms of international migration—legal and illegal—are the major determinants of population distribution between countries. Countries are slowly awakening to the realization that immigration policy is truly problematic. Whichever way they turn—either to restrict immigration or to promote particular components of immigration—is not guaranteed to achieve the desired results. Attempts to decrease immigrant flows have proven largely unsuccessful in the face of economic restructuring and globalization. Increasing immigration is problematic in its own way, threatening ethnic, racial, or social instability, while creating a cadre of low-paid workers that would reduce wages and compete for positions with the native-born. Opening the doors may represent a slippery slope that governments would not be able to back away from, with immigration further spiraling beyond their control. Both measures carry the risk of mixed messages that condone immigration on the one hand while reducing it on the other. Ultimately, the future shape of immigration policy is unclear.

FOCUS: THE "IMMIGRATION GAP"

Over the past hundred years, most governments have attempted to control the movement of populations into and out of their countries, and state governments wrote and rewrote immigration law throughout the later half of the 1900s to reflect emerging economic and demographic needs as well as the reality of the civil rights movement. The United States (and other developed countries) tightly control who enters through various measures including numeric limits on the number of entrants per year and skill qualifications. While many policies appeared to succeed at first, states have found it increasingly difficult to control immigration since the 1980s, with large amounts of illegal immigration. For instance, the number of illegal residents in the United States is estimated to be 11.8 million as of 2007,[1] with as many as 800,000 people entering the country illegally each year, despite the increased attention to border security since 9/11.[2]

Despite their best attempts to impose tighter entry restrictions and other controls,[3] labor-importing states are faced with an immigration control crisis, defined by Wayne Cornelius and his colleagues as the "gap" between immigration control policies and their outcomes. While governments desire to control immigration, the reality is that they have less confidence in their ability to control immigration now than fifteen to twenty years ago. The gap between immigration policy and reality is aided and abetted by three concurrent factors.[4]

First, various domestic factors have limited the state's ability to control its borders. For example, programs such as Germany's guest worker program or the Bracero Program in the United States were meant to be short-term, with workers cycling in and out of the country as needed. The very existence of such programs, however, legitimized and concretized the movement of workers across international borders, connected regions, and created pathways for future immigrants by spreading information about jobs and receiving areas. Existing immigrant communities within the receiving regions have served as anchors for new arrivals, cushioning the stress of relocation. When states have attempted to restrict immigration, these networks maintain flows through illegal immigration and family reunification. Likewise, policies meant to close the border have created permanent residents from temporary workers. Concerned with labor shortages, employers maintained their existing pool of immigrant workers. Workers, on the other hand, feared that they would not be able to return should they leave their host countries. Instead, they remained. Both France and Germany have, at different points in time, declared their borders closed to further immigration, only to see the number of foreign-born increase through family reunification clauses or other "backdoor" immigration routes, including illegal immigration. Similarly, US domestic policies have failed to deter illegal immigration. Nowhere is this inability of policy to deter illegal immigration better illustrated than through the Immigration Reform and Control Act of 1986 (IRCA), which sought exemptions for California's agricultural growers to continue to use undocumented workers at the same time that other employers were required to verify the employment eligibility of workers.

Second, a number of factors from outside the state have contributed to the gap between policy and reality, including globalization and economic restructuring. Globalization opens economies to greater trade and capital flows and increases demands for cheap labor within industrialized countries. Stopping or controlling immigration becomes increasingly hard because of the underlying demand for inexpensive labor. With globalization, employers have shown an increasing insensitivity toward economic fluctuations. That is, employer demand for cheap labor remains strong even in conditions of relatively high unemployment, and employers have been successful in recruiting workers and co-opting state policies for their benefit. Concurrently, population growth and economic restructuring within

labor exporting countries promote economic and social disparities and create a ready pool of labor that encourages emigration. A second exogenous factor is that advances in communications and transportation technology are increasingly accessible to immigrants, aiding the expansion of international migration networks and sustained immigration flows.

Third, the rise of liberalism and the extension of human rights to foreigners within developed countries have further legitimized their position within host countries, hampering state efforts to control immigration. Policies aimed at protecting rights have helped immigrants get into countries (e.g., asylum) as well as remain within the host country. Canada, for instance, has had problems in the administration of its refugee policy,[5] and Germany's generous asylum policies were seen as a quick and easy way to gain entry. Although some of the rights acquired by the foreign-born in the 1960s and 1970s have been lost through new legislation, they remain a barrier to immigration control.

METHODS, MEASURES, AND TOOLS: COUNTING IMMIGRANTS, ILLEGAL IMMIGRANTS, AND EMIGRANTS

Many of the measures that were introduced in the previous chapter to measure and quantify internal migration can also be used to quantify immigration. Typically, international movements are simply identified by the number of people moving from a country (emigrants), into a country (immigrants), net immigrants (the difference between immigrants and emigrants), or the number moving between two specific countries. We can also speak of the *immigration rate*

(usually defined as the number of immigrants relative to the population of the receiving country), *emigration rate* (the number of emigrants relative to the population of the sending country), and so forth. Given security and national policy concerns, governments in the developed world have a good count of *legal* immigration into a country at any one point in time, along with information such as the origin country, year of arrival, demographic measures of the immigrant (i.e., age, education, family structure), and immigrant type (such as whether they are refugees, or are entering the country to be reunified with a family member, to go to school, or to work).

The problem, however, is that while most countries, and particularly those in the developed world, keep track of the number of immigrants entering the country for permanent residency, relatively little is known about the number of illegal immigrants and the number of emigrants from a country, such is the task of trying to count these individuals, often under very difficult conditions.

COUNTING EMIGRANTS

Estimating the number of emigrants from a country represents the complexity of the task: Which individuals are truly leaving the country? What is the duration that they need to be away and/or the reason they emigrated before being defined as emigrants? The number of emigrants is frequently estimated based on a "residual" method, which defines the number of emigrants as the residual after accounting for the total population resident in a country on census day along with births, deaths, and immigration over a particular interval of time. Very simply, the number of emigrants over the period between t and h can be defined as the following formula.

Emigrants $(t, t + h)$ = total population $(t−h)$ + births $(t, t + h)$ + immigrants $(t, t + h)$ − deaths $(t, t + h)$

In other words, the known number of immigrants and births over a period $t + h$ is added to the enumerated population at some point in the past (t) minus deaths over the same period.

More complex estimates of the number of emigrants can also be made. Statistics

Canada, for example, provides quarterly estimates of the country's population, a component of which is an estimation of the number of emigrants. These estimates are based on a number of sources, including data from the Office of Immigration Statistics, the US Department of Homeland Security (DHS), and Canadian social welfare programs. The first two sources are used to estimate emigration to the United States, while Canadian social welfare data provides an estimate of emigration to other countries (a major destination for Canadian emigrants) based on withdrawals from the program. Still, a number of further adjustments need to be made, given that there are typically delays in reporting and receiving data files, and that not everyone is covered by the social welfare data that is used.

COUNTING ILLEGAL IMMIGRANTS

Given that the total number of illegal immigrants in the United States is assumed to be greater than ten million, with impacts on service provision and labor supply and policies, the federal government is keen to have a robust estimate of their numbers. Arriving at firm estimates of the number of illegal immigrants is, however, difficult, given the reluctance of illegal immigrants to answer surveys and identify themselves, fearful that they may be deported. In the United States, Jeffrey Passel has used a variation of the residual method noted above to estimate the number of illegal immigrants.[1] First, the legally resident foreign-born population is estimated based on admissions from the DHS as well as data on refugees admitted and asylum granted. After allowing for legal temporary migrants and for legal immigrants missed in the census or CPS, an estimate of the illegal population is derived by subtracting the estimated legal population from the census or CPS figure for the total foreign-born population. This initial estimate of the number of unauthorized migrants counted is then inflated for omissions. In a similar way, estimates based on the US experience suggest that greater than 30 percent of new immigrant adults granted residence in 1996 had previously illegally entered the United States, with some of these working illegally during their stay in the country.[2] While it is reassuring to see that these entrants ultimately legalized their status, it also highlights the "immigration gap" discussed elsewhere in this chapter.

Chapter Eight

Refugees and Internally Displaced Persons

RATHER THAN FOCUSING upon the individual generators of refugees and displaced persons and how or why they were generated, this chapter focuses upon the implications and options of displaced populations. The chapter begins by exploring the alternatives available to deal with refugee populations, including their return to the country of nationality, settlement in the country of asylum, or resettlement to a third country. The chapter then considers the internally displaced population, the most rapidly growing segment of displaced peoples. It concludes with a discussion of emerging issues and trends with respect to the displaced population. The "Focus" section looks at US refugee policy, and the "Methods, Measures, and Tools" section considers how refugees and internally displaced persons (IDPs) are counted.

DEFINING REFUGEES

As a subset of migration flows, refugees and displaced persons represent a growing population. Defined by the 1951 United Nation Convention Relating to the Status of Refugees and the 1967 Protocol Relating to the Status of Refugees,[1] refugees (and asylees)[2] are persons outside of their country who are unable to return owing to fear of persecution for reasons of race, religion, nationality, or membership of a particular social group or political opinion.[3] In 2007, more than sixty countries produced uprooted populations. According to the UNHCR,[4] the leading coordinator and protector of refugees, estimates placed the total number of refugees at approximately 9.6 million in 2007 (see table 8.1), along with asylees, internally displaced persons, and other individuals of concern.[5] Major refugee-generating countries included Afghanistan, the Sudan, Burundi, Democratic Republic of the Congo, former Palestine, Somalia, Angola, Vietnam, and Iraq.

Despite the legal definition within UN documents, who is or is not a refugee has significant implications with respect to the degree of support and protection an individual receives along with the priority given to the long-term resolution of his or her status. The fundamental right that refugee status confers is that refugees will not be returned to their country of origin against their will. Legally, this is known as non-refoulement, and nations that ratify the Convention and Protocol are obligated not to expel individuals without due process.

Table 8.1.   Refugees and Internally Displaced Persons by Major Source Countries, 2007

Internally displaced persons			Sources of refugees		
Rank	Country	Number	Rank	Country	Number
1	Colombia	3,000,000	1	Iraq	2,279,247
2	Iraq	2,385,865	2	Afghanistan	1,909,911
3	Dem. Rep. of the Congo	1,317,879	3	Sudan	523,032
4	Sudan	1,250,000	4	Somalia	455,357
5	Uganda	1,235,990	5	Burundi	385,727
6	Somalia	1,000,000	6	Dem. Rep. of the Congo	375,727
7	Cote d'Ivoire	709,048	7	Burundi	355,000
8	Azerbaijan	685,586	8	Occupied Palestine	335,219
9	Sri Lanka	459,567	9	Vietnam	327,776
10	Serbia	226,350	10	Turkey	221,939
11	Georgia	273,193	11	Eritrea	208,743
12	Cent. African Rep.	197,000	12	Myanmar	191,256
13	Chad	178,918	13	Angola	186,155
14	Afghanistan	153,718	14	Serbia	165,572
15	Bosnia & Herzegovina	130,984	15	China	149,095
16	Russian Federation	189,274	16	Sri Lanka	134,948
17	Yemen	77,000	17	Bhutan	108,098
18	Lebanon	70,000	18	Croatia	100,423
19	Myanmar	67,290	19	Central African Rep.	98,104
20	Timor-Leste	62,625	20	Russian Federation	92,856

Source: UNHCR, 2007 Statistical Yearbook, Table 2, www.unhcr.org (accessed 17 November 2008).

Defining individuals as refugees also obligates the host country to provide medical care, schooling, and basic civil rights that are enjoyed by other legal immigrants. In cases of large-scale refugee flows, the international community or agencies such as the UNHCR may fill gaps in the care of refugees.

Given the economic and political obligations associated with refugees, governments may dispute refugee claims to avoid these responsibilities.[6] The United States and other countries do not, for example, accord refugee status to so-called environmental refugees (individuals who are physically displaced from their homes and livelihoods by the effects of climate change) or to economic refugees. In both cases, these restrictions are largely out of fear within the developed world that this would open a floodgate of refugees into a system that is already strained by the existing number of political refugees. In essence, for example, recognizing economic refugees would legalize Mexican immigration into the United States, as entrants would simply need to claim economic refugee status to gain legal entry. Proving the legitimacy of a refugee claim is difficult, especially when clouded by ideological, social, or economic concerns. The United States, for example, has been accused of having a double standard. With its acceptance of Mariel Cubans in the early 1980s, most of whom did not meet the international definition of refugee status, the US government was accused of altering its definition of political refugees for political expediency. At roughly the same time, it denied entry to Haitians who claimed political asylum, with the government defining them as voluntary and economic migrants, even with evidence of political persecution by the Haitian government. Likewise, the question of what defines "fear" may not, for example, be a sharply defined fear of individual persecution. Instead, it may be fear of being caught in the cross fire, which has little to do with individual traits. This is not meant to belittle the fear of the individual, since this fear is no less real. Consequently, the definition of refugee generally extends beyond persecuted individuals to whole groups of people fleeing danger.

With the end of the Cold War between the East and West, the nature of conflict has changed from large-scale confrontations backed by superpowers to smaller, internal struggles. Old alliances have been disrupted and totalitarian regimes that had kept the social order have been toppled. The former Yugoslavia is a case in point as Serbian leadership struggled to maintain control of Yugoslavia in the face of unilateral declarations of independence by Slovenia and Croatia in 1991. Later, in its wars in Bosnia and Kosovo, it would attempt to carve out a "greater Serbia." In the process, an estimated 863,000 refugees were generated during the Bosnian conflict in the early 1990s, and an additional 900,000 were generated in Kosovo in 1999. Similar situations have occurred in regions of the former Soviet Union, including conflict in the Russian Republics of Georgia and Chechnya, while thousands of Afghan refugees fled the country to neighboring Pakistan to avoid conflict between pro- and anti-Taliban forces. The country remained the second-largest generator of refugees in 2007. In Africa, decades of political turmoil following the end of the colonial era continue to generate a seemingly endless list of conflicts and refugees, including Sudan, Burundi, Eritrea, Angola, and the Democratic Republic of the Congo.

ALTERNATIVES FOR REFUGEES: NO EASY WAY HOME

Once refugees are outside their home country, the international community is faced with three broad alternatives in assisting the refugee population, including voluntary repatriation, settlement in the country of first asylum, or resettlement in a third country.[7] Of these, voluntary return to the home country is the ideal solution, particularly for the refugee. It is perhaps also the most difficult of the three alternatives, since a minimum requirement for return is the resolution of the problem that created the refugee flows in the first place. Additional material and financial support for the refugees may also be needed until they can reestablish their livelihoods after their return. Despite its difficulties, voluntary repatriations have succeeded, the most recent being the ongoing return of Afghanis in the post-Taliban era. However, their return and continued security have depended heavily upon assistance from nongovernmental organizations such as the Red Cross, donations and support from other nations, and the continued presence of security forces.

Permanent settlement outside of the home country, typically referred to as country of first asylum, is a poor second alternative. But, it is also frequently the only practical one. The welcome that a country extends to refugees depends upon a complex set of considerations, including economic strength, political stability of the host government, and compatibility of refugees with the host society. Given that many countries of first asylum are in the developing world, most have difficulties meeting the needs of refugees. Even provision of basic needs including water, sanitation, food, and shelter, may prove difficult given poor infrastructure or the lack of financial resources to deal with the refugee population. By necessity, host governments are forced to put their native-born populations first. Any attempts to do otherwise may increase tensions between the native-born populations and the refugees. As such, most countries rely heavily on organizations such as the Red Cross or UNHCR to provide assistance in meeting the basic needs of the refugees in the short term.

Support of refugees is not necessarily a short-term effort. Over the longer term, refugee populations may continue to require external support and they may or may not be fully incorporated into their host countries, a problem that is exemplified by Palestinians.[8] Spread throughout Jordan, Lebanon, and Syria, along with the West Bank and Gaza Strip in Israel, Palestinians became refugees when they fled Israel in 1948 (when the state of Israel was established) or later during the 1967 Six-Day War between Israel and its neighbors. The United Nations, through its Relief and Works Agency (UNRWA), provides education, health, and relief and social services to Palestinians. With the exception of Jordan, where more than half of the population is Palestinian, the admission and integration of Palestinians by other Arab countries have been less than enthusiastic, largely out of fear by the host governments that removal of the refugee label would destroy chances of recreating a Palestinian state.

In other cases, the presence of refugees may inflame tensions between countries or ethnic groups. In Lebanon, the delicate balance between Muslims and Christians has prevented Palestinian refugees from naturalization for fear that the political balance would be upset. In other cases, fighters or militia members often use refugee camps as a base, promoting instability within the refugee camp as well as externally to the camp, as in the case of Rwandan refugee camps in Zaire. These refugee camps became the base for rebel Hutu fighters, who conducted border raids into Tutsi-dominated Rwanda during that country's conflict in the 1990s.[9] Complicating matters, soldiers, who were often guilty of genocide within Rwanda at the start of the crisis, frequently controlled food and other supplies within the camps, and the UNHCR was accused of feeding and protecting those accused of genocide. Their safety within the refugee camps was hardly guaranteed. Later, in the face of a relatively powerless UNHCR, the predominately Hutu refugees became the target of Tutsi rebels within Zaire, who would eventually overthrow the Zairian government of Mobutu Sese Seko and establish the Democratic Republic of Congo, furthering the bloodshed.

Racially or ethnically heterogeneous societies face further pressures, where an influx of refugees may upset the existing delicate balance between groups. In the 1999 Kosovo conflict, for example, approximately one million ethnic Albanians sought refuge in the neighboring countries of Albania, Macedonia, and Montenegro.[10] In an already politically unstable region, the sheer number of refugees endangered the political stability of Kosovo's neighbors and threatened to embroil the region in a larger civil war.[11] Albania, for example, is the poorest country within Europe, with a weak political system that was already reeling from internal conflict and anarchy following the collapse of its government in 1997. Refugees were arriving in a remote and economically undeveloped part of the country, and its financial and economic ability to cope with the influx was limited.[12] In Macedonia, where ethnic Albanians represented 25 percent of the population, it was feared that a large influx of Kosovar Albanians, estimated at 239,000, would radicalize Macedonian nationalism and Albanian separatism, upsetting the existing ethnic balance and increasing the likelihood of an expanded regional war. These were not minimal concerns. With an estimated ethnic Albanian population of 506,000, the Macedonian Albanian population was inflated by approximately 50 percent. Since Macedonia's emergence as an independent state in 1992, internal conflict between ethnic Albanians and Macedonians (Slavs) had threatened the state's existence on numerous occasions. Although most refugees eventually returned to Kosovo and the conflict did not expand during 1999, this fear seemed to come to fruition in the spring of 2001 as Kosovar Albanians fought with Macedonian security forces for control of the Albanian-dominated areas in Macedonia.

The strain associated with Kosovar refugees was felt elsewhere in western Europe.[13] Although Germany, France, and Italy were all concerned with the number and location of refugees, Germany was perhaps the most vocal, openly expressing its belief that refugees should stay in the Balkans and out of northern or western Europe. This clearly meant that poor neighboring states would have to deal with refugees, but it also demonstrated the ability of the Kosovo conflict to destabilize and politically charge the European continent. However, the fear of western European countries also reflects European concerns with state identity and the influx of foreigners discussed in the previous chapter, with European countries becoming increasingly concerned with the social, economic, and political implications of large numbers of foreigners.

Symbolized in the late 1970s by Indochinese boat people and in the late 1990s by Kosovor Albanians, resettlement to a third country such as Canada, the United States, or Australia is long-term but the only option for many.[14] According to the UNHCR, some 75,300 refugees were resettled in 2007 globally, with the major countries of resettlement including the United States, which accepted approximately 48,300 individuals. Canada, Australia, and Sweden were also major resettlement regions (resettling 11,200, 9,600, and 1,800 refugees in 2007, respectively), but the total number of refugees resettled within any one year is small relative to the total number of refugees. Although there was a dramatic fall in the number of new refugees, some 1.5 million individuals were newly registered as refugees in 2006–2007 alone, relocating from countries including Liberia, the Democratic Republic of Congo, Burundi, Somalia, and the Central African Republic.[15] In other words, less than 1 percent of the refugee population was relocated to a third country in 2007. Remaining refugees were far less fortunate, experiencing life in desolate refugee camps, threatened by violence, and frequently marginalized by the host society. Even among those who are resettled, however, life is not easy. Refugees must adjust to their host country and frequently suffer from depression or posttraumatic stress disorder in the months immediately after arrival.

In contrast to those who legally immigrate for economic opportunities or family reunification, refugees are often the least successful of all entrants, frequently entering the host country with a poor or variable set of skills relative to other legal immigrants. Over a longer term, as has been the case with Cuban Marielitos or Southeast Asian refugees, most refugees become legal, permanent residents within their host countries. Although technically no longer labeled as refugees, this raises interesting questions and possibilities. Do, for example, former refugees attain similar benchmarks or levels of adjustment in the host country relative to legal immigrants or other refugees? In what direction do they assimilate? What is the time frame for assimilation and adjustment to the host country?

Existing evidence suggests that refugees continue to have divergent experiences after arrival, reflecting differences including the endowed human capital that refugees bring with them and their period of arrival (i.e., economic conditions in the resettlement country or whether they were among the first to flee, a group typically characterized by higher socioeconomic status). By definition, the refugee population is characterized by a broader diversity of human capital (i.e., skills or education) than the immigrant population, who typically self-select themselves into the immigration process (i.e., the better educated or those with more skills are more likely to immigrate) and who are screened by the host country. Among refugees, the endowed human capital or skills that these groups bring with them will influence the adjustment process, allowing the possibility of more rapid socioeconomic advancement among those with higher skills. Among Southeast Asian refugees, for example, differences in the adaptation of Sino-Vietnamese and ethnic Vietnamese refugees have been noted,[16] with the Vietnamese tending to be more economically integrated than other Southeast Asian refugees despite similar lengths of residency within the United States.[17] An emerging Vietnamese business class contrasts with other Southeast Asian refugees, best reflected by the Laotian population, who have lower rates of business ownership and are more likely to be dependent upon public assistance programs and on minimum-wage labor.[18]

Yet, the process of adjustment into the host society is something that is only partially dependent upon the abilities and experiences that refugees bring with them.[19] Instead, broader issues contextualize their opportunities and relative success or failure within the host country. Refugees often lack the networks and ties in the destination that can help with locating jobs or accommodations, making them more likely to require state assistance during the transition period. This poses a fiscal burden to the host country. In recent decades, government policies have played a key role in the admittance of refugees, with public assistance available to refugees that is not available to other legal immigrants. But, the availability of public aid may interact with other characteristics that potentially lead to different outcomes. Dependence upon government or other sources for assistance may prove beneficial or slow refugees' adaptation into the host society.[20] National or ethnic origin and the level of public and private reception also influence the postarrival success of refugee groups. Hungarians have successfully adapted to the United States and Canada, but their success was dependent not only on their skills, but also on the fact that they were white and fleeing a Communist country at the height of the Cold War. Although Mariel Cubans have fared relatively well, assisted by an already economically and politically strong Cuban community, differences between "white" and "black" Cubans have been noted.[21] Even recent arrivals are forced to conform to American expectations (and stereotypes) of race and its consequences for social mixing, residential location, and employment opportunities. Together, this is suggestive of a complex and unequal process that transforms "refugees" into "immigrants" and ultimately naturalized citizens of the host country.

INTERNALLY DISPLACED PERSONS

The growing number of conflicts and the evolving political landscape have also increased the number of refugees and IDPs. Unlike refugees, IDPs are unable to leave their country of nationality and typically cannot avail themselves upon international agencies for protection and assistance. Many are trapped in war zones, unable to cross international borders into safer areas. It is estimated that 13.7 million individuals were internally displaced in 2007,[22] the fallout of civil strife and ethnic unrest or disasters, and found in countries including Sudan, Colombia, Democratic Republic of the Congo, Iraq, Chad, Bosnia, Afghanistan, Lebanon and Georgia. In Sudan alone, two decades of war between the Islamic government of the north and the Christian south has produced over 1.2 million displaced individuals.[23] Because IDPs tend to fall through the cracks of international recognition and assistance, the United Nations has engaged the debate on who should be responsible for their care, a difficult situation given the importance associated with state sovereignty.

Internally displaced persons are often faced with an insecure future. They may be confronted with an ongoing internal conflict or without a safe place to stay, and domestic governments may view them as enemies of the state or as enemy sympathizers. Internally displaced persons are not protected by international refugee laws and have little access to international assistance, typically falling between the cracks of current humanitarian laws. In part, this reflects Western interests and the ability of certain conflicts to "grab the headlines," including conflicts that threaten the national security of developed countries or are defined as "interesting." In other cases, there is only indifference toward long-running disputes. Three of the world's most protracted conflicts—Sudan, Angola, and Colombia—are largely internal conflicts that are largely ignored by the Western media.

The failure to protect internally displaced persons is much more than just an awareness of the events but reflects the current viewpoint that state sovereignty is sacrosanct, making it extremely difficult to work with a displaced population in the country that was responsible for its displacement. Can the United Nations and international law, for instance, override issues of state sovereignty to provide humanitarian assistance? This issue was grappled with in both Bosnia and Kosovo during the 1990s, but no long-term resolution was made. Although assistance was ultimately provided in these cases, many other low-profile or long-term crises, such as the conflict in the Darfur district of Sudan, do not have this benefit. Instead, donor money or assistance is directed toward visible refugee crises. Nongovernmental organizations and other aid groups have had some success, but still reach only a small segment of the total displaced population. The UNHCR has increasingly become involved by assisting IDPs, but still deals with only a small proportion of the total displaced population, and it will only intervene when asked by the UN Secretary General and given consent by the state or parties involved.

Changing political circumstances, independent and sovereign states versus a rebel army, and control of territory complicate the provision of assistance. In response to the growing numbers of internally displaced persons, the United Nations has established a set of guiding principles to protect displaced populations.[24] These guiding principles call for the protection of a person's basic rights, outline the responsibilities of the state, and provide the individual with the right to leave a state. Although ignored by most governments with displaced populations, the principles have gained some acceptance, paving the way for increased involvement by organizations such as the UNHCR and the United States Committee for Refugees and Immigrants (USCRI).

THE FUTURE OF REFUGEES AND IDPs

With an increasing world population, conflict will become increasingly common, spurred by ideology, land, and the control of resources, ultimately leading to greater population displacement (see discussion, for example, in chapter 11). Widespread poverty also provides a fertile breeding ground for tensions that can erupt in violence. Together, the ongoing potential for political instability means that it is unlikely that the total number of displaced persons (refugees, asylees, and IDPs) will decrease soon. In response to increasing the relatively unrestricted flow of asylum seekers, countries will increasingly move to close their borders at a time when greater access is needed. In the United States, Canada, and other countries of resettlement, the overseas admission of refugees has traditionally been built upon a humanitarian basis. Given the events of September 11, 2001, however, receiving countries such as Canada or the United States revisited domestic refugee policies, restricting refugee admissions and tightening the screening process of refugee claimants. Over the short term, this meant a decrease in the number of refugee admissions to both countries, although refugee numbers increased in the following years.

In Europe, the asylum crisis in the 1990s led to a streamlining and harmonization of procedures and policies across the European Union, reflecting an increasing reluctance to offer refugee status. The reduction of benefits given to asylees, the imposition of a narrow definition of UN Convention refugees, and binding third-country policies have ultimately led to a partial closing of the doors. While the European Union has mounted a response to asylum seekers that maintains the spirit of the 1951 UN Convention, each country wants to take as few refugees as possible while attempting to shift the problem elsewhere. The variable and low recognition of refugee claims (i.e., confirming that a person is indeed a refugee under UNHCR guidelines) raises troubling questions, pointing to different standards of treatment for those seeking refugee status, and could further erode public support for refugees. Rather than being viewed with compassion, public opinion could perceive all asylum applicants as abusers of the system. For instance, the UNHCR notes:

> the recognition rate for Iraqi asylum-seekers in Greece shows zero while in Germany roughly two thirds of Iraqis were recognized as refugees. In the United Kingdom, on the other hand, only 15 per cent of all substantive decisions related to Iraqi asylum claims resulted in refugee status.[25]

New measures to screen refugees (and immigrants) and tighten asylum laws were also introduced following the September 11 terrorist attacks in the United States. In an effort to increase border security, both Canada and the United States have moved to harmonize immigration and refugee requirements by implementing the Safe Third Country Agreement on January 1, 2005. Under this agreement, certain asylum seekers in Canada and the United States are required to make their refugee claim in the country where they were last present, meaning that asylum seekers arriving in Canada at the land border from the United States will not be eligible to have their refugee claim determined in Canada. Similarly, the agreement allows the United States to return to Canada asylum seekers attempting to enter the United States from Canada.[26] However, critics argue that the law is more about security, that it will lead to increased illegal entry, and will decrease the flow of legitimate refugees. Statistics would tend to bear this argument out. Before the implementation of the Canada-US agreement, approximately twelve thousand to thirteen thousand refugees to Canada came through the United States annually.[27] Over the first three months of 2005, the number of individuals seeking asylum in Canada had fallen by as much as 40 percent compared to the same period a year before.[28] Similar safe third country asylum laws have been implemented in Europe. Yet, there is no clear consensus on what constitutes a "safe" country. Should countries such as Romania be declared "safe" when their democracies are young and still fragile?

If Europe, Canada, and the United States are unable to implement generous asylum practices, how can poorer countries be expected to allow large numbers of refugees entry? Many smaller states have refused to acknowledge refugees, fearful of the economic, political, and social implications of doing so. At the height of the Kosovo crisis, Macedonia closed its doors to refugees and physically removed others. In short, in backing away from refugee resettlement, the developed world is setting a dangerous and shortsighted precedent, one that the developing world has simply followed. Instead, governments have increasingly relied upon aid organizations and nongovernmental organizations (NGOs) to safeguard the rights of refugees and IDPs. It is incumbent upon the richer, developed world to do more, rather than providing their fair share of assistance. The challenge lies in states finding the balance between protecting their own interests and allowing for the legitimate claims of refugees, something that is difficult in itself.

The reluctance of developing countries to accept refugees must be partially attributed to the failure of the developed world to accept greater numbers of refugees, along with a hesitancy to become involved in humanitarian issues. Fears associated with a large influx of asylum seekers have host countries concerned with the control of their national borders, as they have grown fearful of the economic, political, and social instability that frequently accompanies large refugee flows. Compassion for refugee claimants has turned to fatigue, underlain by a feeling that refugees are simply abusing the system. The difficulty of distinguishing bona fide refugees from economic, voluntary migrants, superimposed upon national political, social, and economic concerns, clouds the picture. Refugee flows have therefore been redefined as a national security threat to the receiving country, with many countries looking to impose greater restrictions on asylum seekers and tighter refugee policies that include detention and interdiction.

Attempts to restrict asylum may, of course, be only partially successful. Like the attempts to restrict legal immigration discussed in the previous chapter, closing the doors to refugee movements may only serve to increase illegal entry. Already, European governments have a poor record of removing individuals who were not granted asylum. Instead, they slip into the underground economy. Refugees may also increasingly turn to smugglers as a means of reaching safety. Reports of refugees trying to get into England via the Channel Tunnel (smuggling themselves onto trucks or under trains and risking death by crushing, electrocution, or exposure) or travel by sea to Canada and the United States in boats that are barely ocean-worthy point to the desperation of these people. Once reaching a safe haven, their ordeal is hardly over, with most struggling for years in poor working conditions to repay smugglers under threats of violence to themselves or family members. Others are lured into prostitution. One estimate placed human smuggling as a $7 billion (US) annual business linked to the arms trade, drugs, prostitution, and child abuse.[29] Most governments in the developed world are trying to address problems associated with human smuggling, a growing phenomenon that preys upon the impoverished and desperate in the developing world. Both Canada and the United States are considering new legislation to slow the flow, including stiff penalties and life in prison for traffickers. But these policies also victimize the victims. Policies allowing detention mean that many would-be asylees are held for months pending a refugee hearing.

Closing the doors to refugee movements may also simply shift the refugee problem to one of dealing with an internally displaced population. If settlement in a second or third country is barred, then the number of internally displaced people must increase. So, while it may appear that the number of refugees has decreased (as the evidence to date would suggest), individuals are simply redefined as internally displaced. Their lack of protection under international law and lack of access to resources magnify the problem.

The forced displacement of individuals is not only the result of political instability, but can perpetuate instability as well. As is the cases of Kosovar Albanians in Albania and Macedonia or Palestinian refugees in Lebanon and other Arab countries, the presence of refugees may upset the political and ethnic balance within a state or strain a state's abilities to meet the obligations of a refugee population. Radicalism caused by population imbalances may result in members calling for the separation of the state or increased nationalism that further oppresses the minority group. In Israel, the peace process is complicated by Palestinian and Jewish demographics. The Palestinian population, which at 3.7 million is the world's largest refugee population, is characterized by high fertility in contrast to the relatively low rates of fertility and population growth among Israeli Jews.[30] The scattered Palestinian population and their right to return complicates the peace process. Israel opposes the Palestinians' return because of the democratic implications, while the existing infrastructure in Gaza and the West Bank would be heavily taxed if Palestinian refugees were to return.

CONCLUSION

Given ongoing political, ethnic, and religious conflicts across the globe, refugees and IDPs will remain a fixture of international population movements. The prospect of climate change may add a new refugee—the environmental refugee, or individuals who have been physically displaced from their homes and livelihoods by the effects of climate change. Changing precipitation patterns and increased drought in already arid areas, rising sea levels that inundate low coastal areas and islands, and increased frequency of severe weather may generate tens of thousands of these environmental refugees.[31] The Fourth Assessment Report of the Intergovernmental Panel on Climate Change (IPCC) predicted the displacement of hundreds of millions of people due to climate change by 2080,[32] and the United Nations Food and Agricultural Organization predicts that 135 million people are at risk of displacement due to desertification in Africa alone.[33] While the term is widely used, their formal legal status is undecided, and governments do not officially recognize them. Despite this, there is widespread informal recognition of these individuals.

FOCUS: THE UNITED STATES: WELCOMING REFUGEES?

Although relocation of refugees to a third country is a difficult and less-than-ideal option, the United States has a long history of admitting refugees for permanent resettlement,[1] including the resettlement of European refugees in the immediate post–World War II years, along with Hungarian refugees in 1956.[2] From over 200,000 refugee admissions in 1980, the number admitted on a yearly basis has declined over the last three decades (figure 8F.1), with a noticeable drop immediately after the 9/11 terrorist attacks. In 2001, for instance, nearly 69,000 refugees were admitted, a number which dropped to less than 27,000 the following year. These shifts reflected increased screening of applications, a decrease in the number of applications for refugee status, and a decreased approval rate, dropping from a 77 percent approval in 2000 to just 49 percent in 2001. By 2002, approval rates had increased to 60 percent, although the approved ceiling of 70,000 was not approached. Since then, the number of refugees admitted has climbed slightly, with the United States resettling 48,300 refugees in 2007, more than all other countries combined. Refugee admissions rebounded within a few years, averaging greater than 40,000 between 2005 and 2007, and increasing to over 60,000 in 2008 (table 8F.1).

Despite this, the evolution of US refugee policy was relatively slow, with ad hoc policies for refugee admission often adopted throughout much of the postwar era. The admission of Hungarian refugees came at the height of the Cold War, and the United States viewed the admission of this group as a foreign-policy tool to control Communism. Later, the absorption of some 132,000 Cuban refugees by the United

Table 8F.1.   US Refugee Arrivals by Top Ten Origins: Fiscal Years 2006–2008

Rank	2006 Country	2006 Number	2006 %	2007 Country	2007 Number	2007 %	2008 Country	2008 Number	2008 %
—	All Countries	41,150	100.0	All Countries	48,217	100.0	All countries	60,108	100.0
1	Somalia	10,357	25.2	Burma	13,896	28.8	Burma	18,139	30.0
2	Russia	6,003	14.6	Somalia	6,969	14.5	Iraq	13,823	23.0
3	Cuba	3,143	7.6	Iran	5,481	11.4	Bhutan	5,320	8.9
4	Vietnam	3,039	7.4	Burundi	4,545	9.4	Iran	5,270	8.8
5	Iran	2,792	6.8	Cuba	2,922	6.1	Cuba	4,117	6.8
6	Ukraine	2,483	6.0	Russia	1,773	3.7	Burundi	2,889	4.8
7	Liberia	2,402	5.8	Iraq	1,608	3.3	Somalia	2,523	4.2
8	Sudan	1,848	4.5	Liberia	1,606	3.3	Vietnam	1,112	1.9
9	Burma	1,621	3.9	Ukraine	1,605	3.3	Ukraine	1,022	1.7
10	Ethiopia	1,271	3.1	Vietnam	1,500	3.1	Liberia	922	1.5
11	Other	6,200	15.1	Other	6,312	13.1	Other	4,971	8.3

Source: 2008 Yearbook of Immigration Statistics.

States following the Cuban Revolution in 1959 reflected the same foreign-policy agenda.

In fact, it was not until the 1960s that refugee legislation was codified in the United States.[3] The 1965 Immigration and Nationality Act formalized US refugee policy by establishing that 6 percent of all immigrants (the so-called seventh preference category) could enter as refugees *if* they satisfied certain conditions. These included (1) departure from a Communist country or the Middle East; (2) that their departure was caused by fear of persecution on account of race, religion, or opinion; (3) that they had departed in flight; and (4) that they were unwilling or unable to return. In essence, the United States had adopted the United Nations definition of a refugee, but attached geographical and ideological caveats. It finally recognized the United Nations convention in 1968, but did not amend its immigration and refugee statutes to reflect its new obligations.

Only in 1980 did the United States pass the Refugee Act and fully ratify the UN convention, regularizing refugee admissions and institutionalizing resettlement assistance. Still, the act failed to change the political considerations underlying refugee admission and selection, and the refugee system remains highly politicized even now. Each year, the president and Congress determine the number of authorized admissions (the 2007 ceiling was seventy thousand) broken down by major origin region. The president and Congress also define who is of special humanitarian concern to the United States. This definition may be manipulated to bar entry to those from

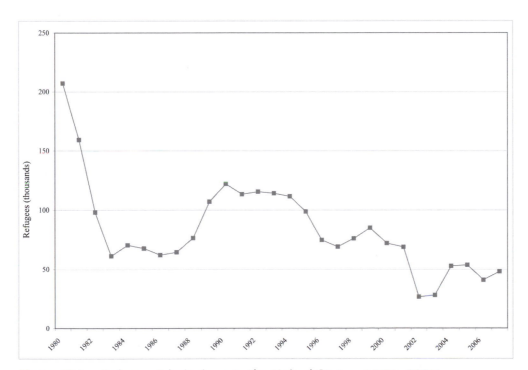

Figure 8F.1   Refugee Admissions to the United States, 1980–2007.
The impact of tightened security restrictions immediately post-9/11 is noticeable.
Source: Department of Homeland Security, *2007 Yearbook of Immigration Statistics.*

countries friendly to the United States, even in the face of observed persecution, as has been the case with Haitian entrants. Some critics have gone as far as suggesting that refugee flows from the former Soviet Union and its satellite states were more about family reunification in the 1990s than they were about the immigrants being true refugees. At the same time, needy refugees in Africa were overlooked, although there has been improvement in recent years.[4] Out of the 48,300 refugees admitted in 2007, approximately one-third sourced from Africa, including Somalia, Sudan, Ethiopia, and Liberia (table 8F.1). This proportion declined in 2008, with the largest proportion (74.5 percent) sourcing from Asia.[5]

While the United States accepted refugees specifically chosen for resettlement in the post–World War II era, it did not deal with large numbers of asylum seekers until the last two decades of the twentieth century, forcing reform of the refugee systems. In the United States, the 1980 Refugee Act provided a statutory asylum policy. Importantly, the asylum provision did not establish a limit on the number of aliens who could apply or be granted asylum in a year, meaning that any alien who arrives in the United States could request asylum, allowing the individual to remain within the country until the review is completed and entitling him or her to benefits.

The number of asylee cases is relatively small, with nearly 23,000 admissions in 2008. Major origins include China, Columbia, and Haiti (table 8F.2). Asylum cases are heard before an asylum officer who determines the validity of the claim.[6] Like the resettlement of refugees, political considerations appear to influence the granting of asylum, emphasizing control of the border rather than protection of individual rights, even though State Department involvement in asylum cases was supposedly reduced in

the 1990 revisions to the Refugee Act,[7] with regional variations in approval rates remaining in 1998. On average, 23 percent of asylum cases were approved in 2008. Not surprisingly, there was large regional variation in the rates of approval, and rates of approval were well below average in many Central American countries.[8] For example, out of all initial asylum applications, the 2008 approval rate was just 3 percent for Guatemala. In contrast, approval rates were generally higher among many Asian, North African, and Eastern European states. Refusal of asylum could result in detention and deportation.

US law also provides for a number of "refugee-like" situations, giving the government and president latitude for allowing entry or residency in a number of situations, but also underscoring the differential and ambiguous responses by the government to Haitian and Cuban entrants. Haitians, most of whom arrived by sea and claimed political asylum, were defined by the government as economic migrants searching for a way to leave the poorest country in the Western Hemisphere.[9] Yet, despite ample evidence of persecution by the Haitian government, the US government refused entry to most Haitians so as not to undermine the Haitian regime. Fearing a large and uncontrollable influx of Haitian refugees should the door appear to be opened, the US government has also vigorously pursued a policy of interdiction on the high seas, with detainees returned to Haiti. Differentiating between political and economic refugees is often difficult, and the situation is compounded when ideological considerations cloud definitions.

Arriving shortly after the 1980 Refugee Act was signed, the Mariel Cubans had a decidedly different reception, and only a minority met the conventional requirements of asylum.[10] Rather than processing the Ma-

Table 8F.2. US Asylees by Country of Nationality: Fiscal Years 2006–2008

Country	2006	2007	2008
China	5,575	6,361	5,459
Colombia	2,968	2,180	1,646
Haiti	2,998	1,660	532
Venezuela	1,363	1,170	1,057
Ethiopia	775	846	899
Indonesia	742	777	533
Iraq	366	685	423
Guatemala	637	681	281
El Salvador	596	569	493
Cameroon	587	505	443
All others	9,600	9,836	11,164
Total	26,207	25,270	22,930

Source: 2008 Yearbook of Immigration Statistics.

rielitos under the new system, the US government bypassed the Refugee Act and "paroled" Cubans directly into the United States. Eventually, the government regularized their status, allowing them to become immigrants in 1986.[11] The United States has also used a number of devices, including extended voluntary departure (EVD) and temporary protected status (TPS), to grant "safe haven" to groups in the United States in situations where a return to their country of nationality would be dangerous owing to political or other reasons, including natural disasters. The TPS statute provides aliens with employment authorization, but does not convey residency status.[12] Decisions to provide these measures have typically been based upon humanitarian grounds, and have been extended to the Chinese following the Tiananmen Square massacre in 1989 and to Hondurans and Salvadorans following the devastating earthquakes in those countries in the late 1990s.

The United States has moved to tighten its refugee and asylees process and insulate itself from becoming the primary destination for asylum applicants. The 1980 Refugee Act did not limit the number of aliens who could apply for or be granted asylum in any year, making it an unknown quantity in immigration. Although the United States has long used measures such as interdiction and detention to deter the arrival of asylum seekers, the Illegal Immigration Reform and Immigrant Responsibility Act of 1996 directly responded to the perceived abuse of the asylum system.[13] Persons entering the United States without documentation or with false identification were subject to immediate detention and could be deported. If asylum was requested, a screening process determined the credibility of their claim and whether the full asylum process should be initiated. Nor has the act been without its critics. With critics pointing to the policy of interdiction and detainment, the system has been accused of mistreating those it is meant to protect.

While receiving countries such as the United States will know the number of refugees that enter the country in any given year, counting the displaced population is an inexact science, and one that needs to be refined.[1] The UNHCR and the US Committee for Refugees and Immigrants (USCRI) figures illustrate this problem, with the UNHCR estimating the refugee population at some 9.6 million, while the USCRI estimate is 14 million. The UNHCR, for instance, counts "persons of concern" or refugees, asylum seekers, returned refugees, internally displaced persons, and stateless persons.[2] It does not count the over four million Palestinian refugees who fall under the mandate of the United Nations Relief and Works Agency for Palestine Refugees in the Near East (UNRWA). On the other hand, the USCRI counts include individuals recognized as refugees as well as asylum seekers and others who have more general forms of protection.[3]

Estimating the size of the refugee and displaced populations is difficult for several reasons. First, not all countries apply the same definition of who a refugee is, even if they have signed the 1951 Convention Relating to the Status of Refugees. In particular, many developed countries have made the asylum procedure increasingly complex, or individuals may apply for asylum in several countries to increase their chance of gaining entry. Either way, it is difficult to count the number of cases. Similarly, statistics are often hampered by the conditions and events generating flows, with differences in the quality and regularity of data. Further, refugees may not stop in designated camps, but may filter into the larger population. Counting internally displaced individuals can be even more complex, as the UNHCR and other aid organizations may have no or limited access to populations inside a country. Mobility or transience of this population increases the difficulty, particularly during war or conflict situations.

Yet demographic data and estimates of the size of the displaced population are relied upon by aid organizations to determine the amount and type of food, shelter, or other assistance needed. Detailed estimates of the age and sex distribution of the population would provide detailed information relating to the need, for example, for immunization or prenatal care.

Chapter Nine

Urbanization

ACCOMPANYING THE WORLD'S population growth has been the explosion in the size and number of urban areas. As of 2009, approximately 50 percent of the world's population lived in urban areas. While the developing world lags the developed world in the proportion urbanized (44 percent to 75 percent, respectively, and only 27 percent urbanized in the least developed countries; see figure 9.1), the urban population in the developing world is expected to grow rapidly in the coming decades, with upwards of 61 percent of the world's population living in urban areas by 2030.[1] In addition to the proportion of a population that lives in urban areas, we can also speak of the rate of urbanization, or how quickly urbanization is occurring. Based on data from 2000, the rate of urbanization in the developed world was just 0.83 percent, reflecting the already highly urbanized population and the relatively small share living in a rural area. In the developing world, the rate of urbanization was 3.5 percent. Placing urban growth in another perspective, the number of cities in the developing world with populations in excess of one million will jump from 345 in 2000 to 480 by 2015, with the growth of urban areas driven by natural increase,[2] net rural-to-urban migration, and urban reclassification as cities are redefined from smaller units. This chapter explores concepts of urbanization, including its definition, growth and change in urban centers, and how cities can plan for growth. The "Focus" section considers how urban growth can be planned for, and the "Methods, Measures, and Tools" section explores alternate definitions of urbanism.

DEFINING URBAN AND URBANIZATION

Simply speaking, we can define urban as any place that is nonrural, while urbanization is the process that transforms a population from rural to urban. In essence, urbanization represents a fundamental reorganization of human society, moving it away from a rural, agrarian-based society to one based around nonagricultural activities. While this definition of urban is a somewhat facile and fuzzy one, it implies the spatial concentration of a population that is organized around nonagricultural production. What we are really speaking of, however, are places where the population size exceeds some defined threshold and/or density (see this chapter's "Methods, Measures, and Tools" discussion of how urban areas are defined). More specifically, we can think of urbanization as a form of social and political organization. Definitions of what constitutes urban typically also include the notion that urban areas are centers of technological change and innovation and have a spatial concentration of power and economic activity.

A BRIEF HISTORY OF URBANIZATION

Although cities have now existed for thousands of years, the form, function, and characteristics of early cities differ dramatically from our modern cities. The following provides a brief discussion of the evolution of cities.

Early Cities through the Middle Ages

We can trace urbanization back to the emergence of early settlements associated with agriculture. While far from urban as we would define it (and perhaps better defined as "protourban"), early urbanization dates from 3500–3000 BC in the so-called Fertile Crescent of modern-day Iraq and Iran and the valleys of the Tigris and Euphrates rivers, where food surpluses and production allowed settlement in villages and increased population densities. By 2500 BC, cities had appeared in the Indus Valley and China (approximately 1800 BC). By modern standards, these early cities were relatively small, both numerically and proportionately. Ancient Rome, for instance, has been estimated to be home to about 500,000, but other cities, such as Athens, would most likely have been much smaller. In both cases, the majority of people likely lived as subsistence farmers in the countryside.

While a combination of events and processes likely generated city growth in ancient societies, three broad explanations for the emergence of these early urban areas have been put forward. First, *surplus theory* argues that cities arose after agricultural surpluses appeared. Locations that allowed agricultural production and irrigation—such as the Indus Valley or the Fertile Crescent—contributed to agricultural surpluses, which in turn freed labor from the land and allowed it to specialize in other tasks, including governance, manufacturing, or religion. These nonagricultural workers grouped together, forming the first cities. Second, *the city as a public good* suggests that urban growth is the outcome of religion or some other government service, such as security, that resulted in people grouping together. Many cities in the ancient world were organized in such a way to express the role of a god (or gods) and to project the image of a controlling religion on daily life. Similarly, cities could develop for security or military purposes, where the security of a population becomes a public good provided by the government. In essence, therefore, cities evolved as fortress and refuges. Third, *the city as center for exchange and trade* defines the emergence of cities as centers of trade. In this case, cities developed first, with rural development occurring later as a consequence of city growth and to feed the city population. Regardless of the actual origin, early cities likely would have relied upon in-migration to sustain their population, as deaths likely exceeded births. They also relied on a large population living outside of the city to feed the city's population and to provide residents with goods. Many of the early cities collapsed due to wars, disease, or the collapse of empires, with their populations returning to their rural roots.

The Medieval City

Early in the medieval period, cities and towns were nearly nonexistent. Instead, early medieval Europe was mainly composed of feudal kingdoms, although a few small towns existed as university centers or served defensive and/or administrative needs. The majority of the population lived in rural areas and engaged in subsistence agricultural production, and cities grew slowly. Emergent trading of food and other basic commodities established towns as merchant capitalist centers, although the proportion of the total urbanized population remained small, as did the towns themselves. Between the fifteenth and seventeenth centuries, merchant capitalism grew and transformed the basic function of cities to one of commerce. Urban development was further spurred by the scientific revolution and the beginnings of colonial exploration, which exploited colonial possessions and transferred riches to European centers, enabling cities that controlled trade to grow the fastest. European exploration and colonization of new lands, including Africa and the Americas, cemented the role of cities as places of commerce, trade, and political power. Ultimately, European colonialism would give rise to further urbanization in the world's peripheral regions, transferring Europe's urban patterns around the globe. These new cities were either associated with existing settlements, such as Delhi and Mexico City, or in new locations that served the needs of the colonial powers for administration or defensive positions. Such cities included Mumbai, Hong Kong, and Nairobi.

The Industrial Revolution and the Modern Era

Despite the growth of merchant capitalism, cities were still small. For example, the share of England's population that lived in London is thought to have increased by only eight percentage points (from 2 to 10 percent) between 1600 and 1800, yet London was the largest city in Europe in 1800 with a population of just slightly less than one million.[3] It was only with the Industrial Revolution and the growth of the British Empire that London experienced rapid population growth. Other estimates suggest that as recently as 1800, less than 5 percent of the world's population lived in urban areas. This would change quickly as the Industrial Revolution came to dominate and drive settlement patterns, first in Europe and then throughout the world. As economies slowly transformed, with increasing production inside the city, cities started to dominate their hinterlands, strengthening their economic and political position.

Starting in the United Kingdom in the late 1700s, the Industrial Revolution had tremendous implications for human settlement patterns, the outcome of critical changes in methods of production, the reduction of the labor force required for agriculture through mechanization, the implementation of industrial methods, and the expansion of trade. With the Industrial Revolution, agricultural production was increasingly mechanized, meaning that fewer people were required to work the land. Instead, employment opportunities in manufacturing, which were typically located in urban areas, led to the emergence of the first modern cities in England. Industry, and the Industrial Revolution, was largely dependent on cities for transport, labor, and infrastructure, and new opportunities and wages drew migrants into cities. Even with changing production and industrialization, however, cities continued to grow at a relatively slow rate. The majority of the population continued to live in rural areas, and mortality in the new cities remained high, meaning cities were not yet able to sustain their growth through natural increase.

As industrialization spread outward from the United Kingdom, so did the concept of cities. But it was not until the nineteenth century that modern urbanization really took off. Increasing industrialization created demand for labor in urban areas, and declining mortality rates allowed populations to grow quickly. Even in the United States, the process of urbanization was slow until 1820, when just 7 percent of the American population lived in urban areas, before accelerating through the rest of the nineteenth century. Rates of urbanization slowed again during the Depression of the 1930s and World War II before increasing in the 1950s and onward. Worldwide, cities continued to grow as they cemented their economic base as centers of commerce and trade, enabled by a large supply of labor for growing manufacturing and production. At the same time that their economic power grew, so did their political power, enabling control over larger populations and areas.

The economic and political roles of cities continue today, but in different ways. Early on, cities provided jobs in the new manufacturing industries, and laborers who were no longer needed in rural areas took on these roles. The industrial base of cities in the United Kingdom, including Glasgow, Manchester, Birmingham, and Sheffield, grew as industry required more and more workers. In large part, the concentration of both industry and workers created efficiencies of scale, reducing costs and increasing profits for manufacturing, and the large pool of labor in cities made it easy for employers to find workers.

In today's postindustrial and globalized world, the role and function of cities continues to change and evolve, while they remain centers and magnets for population settlement. In the developing world, cities combine both industrialization and commercial activities. In the developed world, most cities have lost their traditional industrial base and have transitioned to service economies, providing diverse employment opportunities in banking and finance, health care, and the knowledge economy. Increasingly, these cities are also seen as centers of culture and arts and home to the so-called creative class,[4] which has become a rallying point for city growth and promotion. In both the developed and developing world, cities offer consumption and social opportunities that are not available elsewhere, while providing economies of scale and agglomeration economies[5] that support their continued economic development and attract in-migrants. Cities also offer agglomeration economies, resulting from the geographic concentration of economic activities in general or specific industrial economies. These benefits are facilitated by such things as the transfer of knowledge across industries, the sharing of public goods and infrastructure, better labor matching between workers and employees, diversified employment opportunities, and the development of related suppliers and buyers. In short, cities continue to attract and retain people because of their "bright lights."

THE GROWTH OF MODERN CITIES

Modern cities have three main growth mechanisms: natural increase (the excess of births over deaths), net in-migration, and international migration. Throughout much of the history of urban areas, urban populations experienced higher mortality than their rural counterparts, with dense populations and limited sanitation facilitating the spread of diseases such as cholera or the plague, while the excess labor in rural areas meant that cities relied upon in-migration to sustain their population. More recently, death rates have been lower in cities than in rural areas, owing to the availability of clean water, sanitation, and health care provision. Consequently, urban growth has been fueled by in-migration and large natural increases amongst the urban population, echoing the demographic transition theory, particularly in the developing world, where birth rates remain high.

Like today, in-migrants were drawn to early cities for jobs. As early as 1889, Ravenstein noticed movement out of rural areas and into cities (see also chapters 6 and 7).[6] Movement "up the urban hierarchy" has therefore promoted city growth. Writing in 1885 in regards to the United Kingdom, Ravenstein commented that:

> the great body of our migrants only proceed a short distance. . . . It is the natural outcome of this movement of migration that . . . [t]he inhabitants of the country immediately surrounding a town of rapid growth, flock into it; the gaps thus left in the rural population are filled up by migrants from more remote districts, until the attractive force of one of our rapidly growing cities makes its influence felt, step by step, to the remote corner of the kingdom.[7]

In other words, movement was "stepwise" up the hierarchy into progressively larger centers, promoting the growth of the largest cities.

Zelinsky's hypothesis of mobility transition[8] updates much of Ravenstein's theories of migration and adds new dimensions in line with more recent population mobility. From the perspective of urban growth and change, Zelinsky argues that internal migration patterns will shift according to a country's economic development. Rural-to-urban migration will, for example, be associated with industrialization. Later, as economies and their urban systems develop, migration will shift to be dominated primarily by urban-to-urban migration, with movement up the hierarchy into larger urban centers. Ultimately, in most developed countries, migration will shift to movements down the urban hierarchy and into smaller urban areas or rural areas.

While seemingly exclusive events, there is also much overlap between natural increase, internal migration, and international migration in promoting urban growth. Likewise, immigration directly adds to the population count of some of the largest urban areas, such as New York, Chicago, or Los Angeles. In fact, many of the largest cities in the United States, including New York, Chicago, and Los Angeles, rely almost exclusively on immigration to sustain and grow their populations, as large parts of the population have migrated out of the city toward suburban or peri-urban locations. Immigrants, on the other hand, are attracted to urban areas. Moreover, the presence of ethnic enclaves and communities, particularly in main immigrant-receiving cities such as New York, Los Angeles, or London, reinforce this attraction while aiding the economic, social, and cultural integration of new arrivals. Likewise, domestic, internal migration remains an important component of the growth or decline of urban areas. As already noted, historically higher mortality levels in cities meant that they relied upon movement from rural to urban areas to sustain their populations as excess labor moved to cities in search of employment.

The Current State of Urbanization

Perhaps the most significant moment in the history of urbanization occurred in 2008, when it was estimated that half of the world's population lived in urban areas. Considering that less than 30 percent lived in an urban area just fifty years earlier, the growth of the world's urban population in such a short period of time is impressive. Yet, world regions differ greatly in their levels of urbanization, with the following discussion offering broad observations of the state of urbanization between the developed and developing world.

The Developed World

The developed world is essentially fully urbanized, with very low rates of urbanization (0.83 percent). If we were to apply Zelinsky's mobility transition theory, the United States and many other developed countries would have largely passed through it. Long gone are the days of frontier or rural-to-urban movement. Although the developed world is already highly urbanized, urban areas continue to transform and grow, characterized by three broad trends. First, consistent with Zelinsky's mobility hypothesis, *urban-to-urban migration* is the primary force, shifting the population between urban areas, rather than from rural to urban areas, meaning that migration between urban areas is the most significant source of population change.

Second, the 1970s revealed a very different pattern of population movement, with nonmetropolitan areas growing at the expense of metropolitan areas. In essence, the phenomenon of *counterurbanization*—or the decline in growth rates of some of the largest urban centers and increased growth rates of rural, nonmetropolitan areas—runs counter to decades of both rural-to-urban population movements and suburbanization. Shifting employment, amenities, and retirement contributed to this population movement, with counterurbanization first observed in the 1970s and again in the late 1990s. Observed in multiple developed countries, it led some to speculate that this was a new, postmodern dimension of the mobility transition.

Third, most developed countries experienced some degree of *decentralization*, or the movement of people and jobs away from central cities toward suburbs and peri-urban areas, or those areas at the urban-rural fringe. Attributed to numerous social, political, and economic factors, including racial tensions,

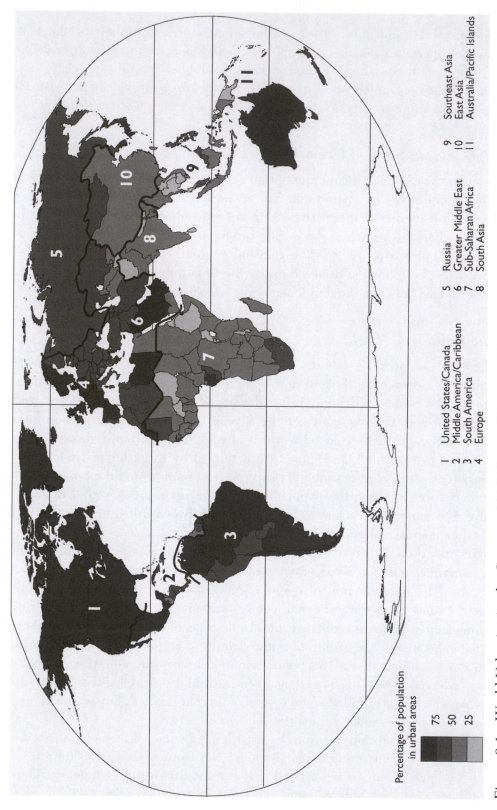

Percentage of population
in urban areas

75
50
25

1   United States/Canada
2   Middle America/Caribbean
3   South America
4   Europe

5   Russia
6   Greater Middle East
7   Sub-Saharan Africa
8   South Asia

9   Southeast Asia
10   East Asia
11   Australia/Pacific Islands

Figure 9.1   World Urbanization by Country, 2005. *Source*: Brunn et al., 2008, *Cities of the World*, figure 1.3. Reproduced with permission.

better education and recreational facilities, improved highways (accessibility), and lower home costs, decentralization has made most cities less dense but more spread out. While low gas prices and long-distance commuting have enabled decentralization, the new reality of higher gas prices may alter location choices, with residential patterns returning to greater population densities and closer to employment locations.

The Developing World

While the proportion of the population living in urban areas in the developing world is much less than in the developed world, the process of urbanization is rapidly reshaping urban areas' appearance. As in the developed world, urbanization trends in the developing world can be summarized by four main points. First, urban areas in the developing world will see *continued rapid growth*. The large and rapidly growing populations of many developing countries mean that there is large potential for continued urban growth, both in terms of people moving into cities (in-migration) as well as natural growth (the excess of births over deaths) of cities.

Second, *population concentration* will continue, with the population of developing countries increasingly concentrated in large cities of one million or more residents. At the same time, megacities of ten million or more will become increasingly important and numerous as migrants are attracted to these large cities in search of employment and opportunities.

Third, the developed world will be home to a *diversity of urban areas*. That is, urbanization and urban change in the developing world defies broad generalizations. In more developed regions and in Latin America and the Caribbean, over 70 percent of the population is urban, whereas in Africa and Asia, less than 40 percent of the population is urban. India, for example, which has some of the world's largest cities, is still just 29 percent urbanized, and China's pace of urbanization is rapid as it moves toward a market economy. With approximately 30 percent of its population living in urban areas in 1985, China's urban growth has been spectacular. Although constrained for years by its Hukou system, which restricted internal migration in China (see chapter 10), China's rate of urbanization has skyrocketed, with 46 percent living in urban areas by 2009. Recognizing the urban demand, China has also moved to establish over two hundred new cities. Elsewhere in Asia, in countries including Bangladesh, India, and Pakistan, cities are faced with almost unparalleled challenges. In India, for example, the population is approximately 70 percent rural, yet by 2030 the urban population of India is expected to exceed 600 million (India is currently home to a population over one billion). Although these countries are less urbanized than some African countries (India, for example, is only 29 percent urbanized, and Bangladesh was 25 percent urbanized in 2009), they already contain many of the world's largest urban agglomerations. Many African cities lack investment, and countries are dominated by a large "primate" city, or a city that is disproportionately larger than other cities within the urban hierarchy, rather than a network of cities.

Fourth, characterized by poor infrastructure and faced with an influx of people from rural areas, urbanization in much of the developing world has led to unplanned settlements and squatter settlements, growing regional inequities, insufficient urban infrastructure, poor health, and the degradation of resources. Rapid urbanization has often meant that governments have not been able to provide adequate or basic health care or infrastructure such as clean water, and mortality rates are frequently far worse in poor urban as compared to rural areas.[9] In one study in Bangladesh, for example, infant death rates varied from 95 to 152 per 1,000 in urban areas, higher than both middle-class urban areas (32 per 1,000) and rural Bangladesh.[10] Continued in-migration from rural areas and increasing population density may push mortality and morbidity higher in urban areas.

Megapolitan Cities

Megapolitan cities reflect the growth or merging of different cities into one large city or network of cities, such that divisions between urban areas are seamless. In the United States, this is characterized by the Boston–New York–Philadelphia–Baltimore–Washington urban area (the so-called BosNYWash region). Other megapolitan areas include the Midwest's Chicago–Gary–Milwaukee area, Southern California's Los Angeles–San Diego area, and northern California's San Francisco–San Jose–Sacramento region.[11] As of 2003, megapolitan areas in the United States represented more than two-thirds of total US population—nearly 200 million people—but contained less than a fifth of the land area in the lower forty-eight states.[12] Although the use of the megapolitan term, at least in the US case, does not fit with any urban definitions currently used by the US Census Bureau (see discussion in chapter 8's "Methods, Measures, and Tools"), these megapolitan areas cover a vast but integrated area connected by transportation networks, commuting flows, and some shared history.

Beyond the geographic reality that these cities are proximate to each other, the megapolitan concept realizes that

> modern cities are better reviewed not in isolation, as centers of a restricted area only, but rather as parts of "city-systems," as participants in urban networks revolving in widening orbits.[13]

Therefore, it is increasingly argued that the economic role of one city extends far beyond its metropolitan boundaries, extending to potentially influence world

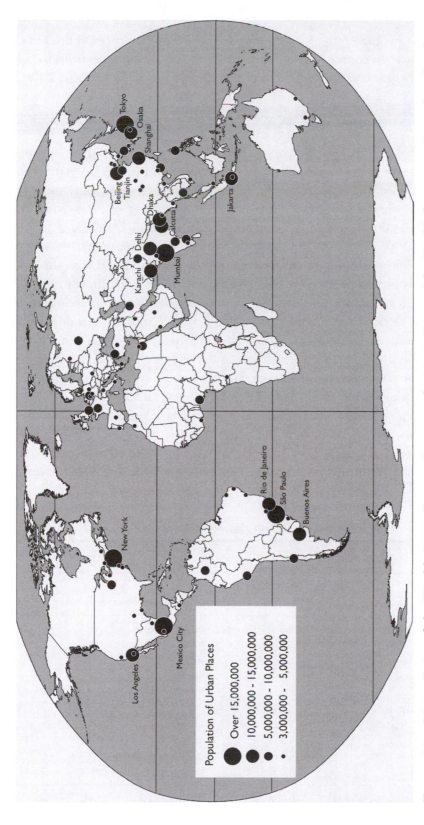

Figure 9.2   Major Cities of the World, 2005. *Source:* Brunn et al., 2008, *Cities of the World*, figure 1.1. Reproduced with permission.

affairs. Few would argue, for example, that the New York region does not influence the world economy, given its core financial sector, a realization that was particularly dramatic in the financial meltdown and credit crisis of 2008.

Megacities

Despite the fact that 50 percent of the world's population lives in an urban area, most are living in small towns or villages, and just 37 percent reside in cities of at least one million people. Although home to a relatively small proportion of the world's population (8 percent), the number of *megacities*, or cities with populations in excess of ten million, has grown from eight in 1985 to twenty in 2008, with the number projected to grow to at least twenty-two by 2015. The largest cities in the world are growing rapidly in size, and increasingly, many are found in the developing world (table 9.1). Indeed, in 1950 the three largest cities were in developed countries, with New York being the largest city in the world with a population of about twelve million. London and Tokyo were close behind, and Paris, Moscow, and Chicago were also in the top ten. By 2005, both Tokyo (35.2 million) and New York–Newark (18.7 million) remained in the list of top ten cities, but the remaining top ten megacities were located in the developing world. Three of these ten-million-plus cities are in India: Delhi, Kolkata (Calcutta), and Mumbai (see figure 9.2). The growth of these megacities is related to the same reasons and processes we saw with urbanization, including their economic attraction or the prospects of jobs and employment. Additionally, a rapidly expanding population base, driven by in-

Table 9.1.   The Ten Largest Urban Agglomerations: 1950 and 2015

1950		2015	
Agglomeration	Population (millions)	Agglomeration	Population (millions)
New York–Newark, USA	12.338	Tokyo, Japan	35.494
Tokyo, Japan	11.275	Mumbai, India	21.869
London, UK	8.361	Mexico City, Mexico	21.568
Shanghai, China	6.066	São Paulo, Brazil	20.535
Paris, France	5.424	New York–Newark, USA	19.876
Moscow, Russian Fed.	5.356	Delhi, India	18.604
Buenos Aires, Argentina	5.098	Shanghai, China	17.225
Chicago	4.999	Kolkata, India	16.980
Kolkata, India	4.513	Dhaka, Bangladesh	16.842
Beijing, China	4.331	Jakarta, Indonesia	16.822

Source: *United Nations World Urbanization Prospects: The 2005 Revision.*

migration from rural areas and smaller settlements, along with higher rates of natural increase, ensures their growth.

While there is, as of yet, no apparent limit to the size of cities before they produce more negative externalities and costs than benefits, and we can point to the ability of cities such as New York, London, or Tokyo to function, these cities are in the developed world. The majority of the new megacities will be in the developing world, and it is unknown whether the cities themselves or the states will be able to provide sufficient infrastructure and employment opportunities for the burgeoning urban population. More likely, the new megacities will be characterized by high levels of poverty, poor living conditions, inequality, poor health, and few employment opportunities.

IMPLICATIONS OF URBAN GROWTH

In the developing world, urban migrants are typically from rural areas, driven by the large gap in the standard of living along with poor rural conditions caused by environmental degradation and a skewed distribution of resources favoring the elite. With rural-to-urban migration fueling much of the growth of urban areas in the developing world, governments may not be able to cope with rapid population growth and the provision of services, including health care and education,[14] irrespective of the size of the city. Conflict is a possible outcome. For example, with poverty remaining one of the most pressing issues in urban areas, migration could breed economic frustration given insufficient employment opportunities and unfulfilled expectations. Perhaps as many as 42 percent (if not more) of the world's urban population can currently be classified as living below the poverty level, with urban poverty increasing in much of the developing world. In 1970, for example, urban areas contained just 36 percent of Latin America's poor. By 1990, the proportion had jumped to 60 percent. By 2025, the World Bank estimates that the majority of the world's population will be living in poverty.[15] Migrants may also have problems adjusting to urban areas. Seeking entry into groups for support and friendship in their new surroundings, they could easily be recruited into groups that espouse violence. Since many of the migrants are young men, generating a much larger demand for education and jobs, they are easily mobilized for political ends.

CONCLUSION

With the urban population expected to grow dramatically in the coming decades, the implications associated with the growth of large urban areas are enormous. Problems, including poverty, pollution, crime, class tensions, and transportation, will be on a scale never before seen. The situation is frequently worse in cities that have been strained by rapid population growth, little investment, and government ineptitude.[16] Infrastructure systems, such as water, roads, or electricity, have decayed as governments have been unable to keep up with the demand posed by continued in-migration from rural areas and smaller centers. The magnitude of urban growth in the developing world has generated an intense and ongoing debate about whether the developing world can accommodate the anticipated growth of cities and whether there is a potential for conflict in areas with few resources and slow economic growth.[17] Optimists claim good governance, proper management, and investment can overcome population constraints, although these are often missing in the developing world. Others are more concerned. Higher mortality, low standards of living, the poor living environment, depletion of resources, and increasing poverty and inequality are symptomatic of urban problems, all of which could weaken the state.

FOCUS: PLANNING FOR GROWTH

The growth of urban areas has often meant the construction of new infrastructure on the peripheries of cities (urban sprawl). While expensive in its own way, with sprawl straining the resources of cities and taxpayers alike, this has also meant the abandonment of older, inner-city areas. Sprawl, for instance, increases the need to drive while decreasing open space. Sprawl also means that tax money subsidizes new developments through the provision of water and sewer lines, schools, and police and fire protection, costs which are not fully offset by the taxes paid by the new users. Consequently, the continued growth of urban areas, and particularly large urban areas or megapolitan areas in the developed world, has increased the recognition of the need for planning to deal with the adverse effects of population growth, including urban sprawl, traffic gridlock, and the loss of agricultural areas.

Recent discussions of how best to plan urban growth in North America are frequently presented as "smart growth" policies.[1] With the intention of creating sustainable communities, smart growth aims to preserve open space while allowing for population growth through better transportation and increased population density by making efficient use of land and resources. Smart growth policies include ten planning principles, such as increased walkability, mixed-income communities, mixed land uses (i.e., residential and commercial), and compact neighborhoods. Emphasizing infill development and increased population, smart growth is, in part, meant to recreate the self-contained neighborhood of pre–World War II towns and cities, where the downtown, housing, schools, and employment are within walking distance. But it is also far more than just a modern spin on our image of small-town life, recognizing that community building happens on different scales. At the regional scale, smart growth addresses the issues of urban expansion, public transportation, farmland preservation, and environmental protection. At the local, neighborhood scale, smart growth addresses the issues of livability, community character, transportation, and housing choices.

In short, smart growth aims to reduce urban sprawl, manage growth, create livable communities, promote economic growth, and protect the environment. While there can be little argument over the need for "smart growth" (as opposed to the potential opposite), there is clearly a range of policy options and ultimately outcomes that result from these guiding principles. That is, developers, planners, politicians, and government agencies are able to interpret the principles as they see fit or select only components of the smart growth agenda. Nonetheless, the principles have also been widely implemented and have gained increased attention, with the following discussion outlining two examples.

URBAN GROWTH BOUNDARIES: PORTLAND, OREGON

Urban growth boundaries (UGBs) represent one way of delimiting where an urban area stops and a rural area starts. The primary reason for UGBs is to reduce sprawl and to conserve farmland and open space, both of which are achieved by limiting development to a specific region. Cities that have adopted UGBs include Seattle, Washington; Boulder, Colorado; Lancaster County, Pennsylvania; and Minneapolis/St. Paul, Minnesota. Portland, Oregon, is perhaps the best-known example of UGBs, and is frequently cited for its success in controlling urban sprawl through the implementation of UGBs in the early 1970s through the use of a mix of redevelopment, transportation, and land-

use policies. As early as 1973,[2] the Oregon legislature adopted land-use planning laws, requiring each city and county in the state to have a long-range plan addressing population growth, with perhaps the most significant component being the identification of UGBs. While boundaries were not meant to be static, their expansion was based on need. Planning documents also called for the protection of natural resources.

Like the rest of the state, the city of Portland needed to identify its urban growth boundary, a process that involved Washington, Multnomah, and Clackamas counties, twenty-four cities, and more than sixty special service districts. At the same time, it needed to provide for future population and industrial growth. Once defined, the boundary protected rural areas from population sprawl. Inside the urban growth boundary, land is used for housing, business, roads, parks, and other urban needs or systems. Urban development within the growth boundary has effectively resulted in the more efficient use of urban land through housing infill (i.e., developing vacant lots), increased density (i.e., increasing the housing density on a given lot), redevelopment of the downtown core, and increased public transportation.

GREENBELTS: SOUTHERN ONTARIO'S GREATER GOLDEN HORSESHOE AREA

With a population expected to exceed twelve million by 2031 and as an economically important region, the Ontario provincial government recognized the need for "big picture" planning for the Greater Golden Horseshoe (GGH). The GGH represents an area that includes the Toronto metropolitan area, stretching west through Hamilton to Niagara Falls, east to include Oshawa, and north toward the city of Barrie.

The need for planning was recognized in the related Greenbelt Plan and Places to Grow legislative pieces (Government of Ontario, 2005, 2006).[3,4]

The greenbelt legislation created an agriculturally protected area around Toronto, while providing for a diverse range of economic and social activities associated with rural communities, agriculture, tourism, recreation, and resource uses. The greenbelt also protected environmentally sensitive areas in the province. Concurrently, Places to Grow provided a strategy to "maximize benefits of growth," allowing communities to grow in a "complete" way by offering a mix of places to live, work, shop, and play. The plans identify where urbanization should and should *not* occur by directing growth to existing urban areas through intensification and by providing permanent protection to portions of the agricultural land encircling Toronto. Development was redirected from the urban edge to existing urban areas, with new suburbs required to be built at densities that could support and create complete "live/work" areas. Finally, through focusing of growth within existing urban areas, the legislation facilitated increased use of public transit over the private car.

IMPLICATIONS

While the need for planning to overcome issues of population growth and urban sprawl is straightforward, the reality of implementation is far different. Not surprisingly, smart growth seems to mean different things to different people, meaning there is often disagreement between various interest groups as to what it comprises. On the one hand, public agencies, including numerous municipal jurisdictions and local government agencies such as education

districts, park and recreation districts, water districts, and other agencies, each represent their own interests. On the other hand, private groups, including land developers, construction, and the real estate industry, represent another set of needs and issues, meaning that bringing these diverse groups together and reaching a consensus on planning issues is difficult and time-consuming.

Both the Portland, Oregon, and Ontario examples include elements of smart growth policies. Regardless of whether smart growth policies, defined urban growth boundaries, or the provision of greenbelt space or other planning tools are used, there are both positive and negative implications. Urban growth boundaries and greenbelt policies have, for example, increased population density (or are designed to increase density) and created mixed-use or mixed-income housing, arguably creating more friendly and vibrant communities. This is perhaps most apparent in city centers, where older, rundown centers have been revitalized as centers for housing, shopping, and business. Reductions in automobile dependence, pollution, and traffic levels have also been attributed to their introduction, particularly when public transit is promoted as a viable alternative.

On the other hand, the success of these policies in curbing urban sprawl is difficult to measure because it is not known what a city would have looked like without it—how would the city of Portland of today differ if UGBs had not been created? In many cases, development simply "leapfrogs" the boundary or greenbelt, increasing development pressure on communities outside of the greenbelt or UGB and creating urban sprawl beyond the boundaries. In Ontario, developers were already looking at locations beyond the greenbelt for new housing development even before the greenbelt legislation had been passed. In Portland, research concludes that the UGB has not slowed the pace of suburbanization or reduced automobile use.[5] In addition, significant urban development has occurred in neighboring counties, suggesting that Portland's UGB has simply diverted growth outside of Portland itself. Detractors have also voiced concern with the increased population density while noting the inflation of housing prices inside the UGB, given that land is essentially rationed and the housing supply is limited as population densities increase. Low-income households may be doubly disadvantaged, resulting in increased rental costs or increased commuting costs as they are priced out of the local housing market.[6]

METHODS, MEASURES, AND TOOLS: DEFINING "URBAN" ACROSS COUNTRIES

While the concept of an urban area is relatively straightforward, its definition is not, with different governments using different definitions of what constitutes "urban."[1] Definitions range from population centers of one hundred or more dwellings, to only the population living in national and provincial capitals, to statistical definitions based on minimum population thresholds and/or population densities. In Australia, urban areas are defined as population clusters of one thousand or more people and with a density of two hundred or more persons per square kilometer. In Italy, urban areas are defined as having populations in excess of ten thousand, while other European countries define urbanized areas on the basis of urban-type land use. Statistics Canada defines urban areas (UA) as population concentrations of one thousand people with a density of at least four hundred persons per square kilometer based on past census counts. All territory outside of a UA is considered rural. Statistics Canada also distinguishes urban areas based on population size. For example, census areas (CAs) are urban areas where the population count of the urban core is at least ten thousand. In addition, census metropolitan areas (CMAs) are those urban areas consisting of one or more adjacent municipalities situated around a major urban core. A CMA must have a total population of at least one hundred thousand, of which fifty thousand or more live in the urban core, and CMAs include cities such as Toronto, Vancouver, and Calgary. At the time of the 2006 census, Statistics Canada recognized twenty-seven CMAs. In less developed countries, various combinations of land use and population density are applied, as well as requirements that a majority of the population is not engaged in agriculture and/or fishing.

For the 2000 census, the US Census Bureau defined an urban area as the population located within an urbanized area (UA) or an urban cluster (UC), where UA and UC boundaries are defined to encompass densely settled territory, which consists of:[2]

- core census block groups or blocks that have a population density of at least one thousand people per square mile and
- surrounding census blocks that have an overall density of at least five hundred people per square mile.

It further distinguished urban areas based on population size between metropolitan and micropolitan statistical areas (metro and micro areas), which are geographic entities used for statistical reporting. A metro area contains a core urban area of fifty thousand or more population, and a micro area contains an urban core of at least ten thousand (but less than fifty thousand) population. Each metro or micro area consists of one or more counties and includes the counties containing the core urban area as well as any adjacent counties that have a high degree of social and economic integration (as measured by commuting to work) with the urban core.

Beyond distinctions of urban and rural, the US Census Bureau recognizes that American development patterns vary by spatial scale, and has thus created a scale of cities. Defined by the Office of Management and Budget (OMB), the term core-based statistical area (CBSA) refers to both metropolitan and micropolitan statistical areas. Metropolitan statistical areas must have at least one urbanized area of fifty thousand or more inhabitants. Micropolitan areas must have at least one urban cluster with a population between ten thousand and fifty thousand. In both cases, the largest city is designated the "principal city."

The various ways to define an urban area raises two important points. First, the various definitions make comparisons of urbanization levels across countries difficult. Consequently, the Population Reference Bureau uses the percentage of the total population living in areas defined as urban by that country in its annual *World Population Data Sheet* in order to provide comparability. Second, the different urban definitions highlight the fact that urbanization is a relative phenomenon: in countries that are sparsely settled or have small populations, the threshold for defining an urban area is typically smaller, while densely populated countries use alternate definitions.

Chapter Ten

Population Policies

GOVERNMENTS AROUND THE WORLD have expressed an interest in (and oftentimes need for) controlling the size, distribution, and composition of their populations. Some governments may approach population policy from the need of reducing fertility levels, while others will wish to increase fertility levels. Other countries attempt to control the quantity and quality of immigrants entering the country, or control the "quality" of immigrants by legislating selective immigration policies. Most developed countries already employ various population policies, albeit in various forms and to various degrees of success. For governments that wish to control populations through policy,[1] policy levers can be used to target death rates, fertility rates, internal migration, and immigration. A fifth dimension—economic policies—may also have implications for population structure and size. Immigration, internal migration, and fertility policies offer the most direct policy levers for governments to pursue population policy. Rather than death policies, governments focus instead on health and health care provision and healthy aging, with the intent of enabling older individuals to lead more active and productive lives for a longer period of time before requiring care or institutionalization. As a general rule, life expectancies in the developed world have increased over the decades, reflecting these policies.

This chapter explores population policy options, stressing both their success and failures. In particular, it looks at fertility policy, immigration policy, and internal migration policies. The "Focus" section highlights China's controversial one-child policy, and the "Methods, Measures, and Tools" section evaluates the success of population policies.

IMMIGRATION POLICY

Immigration can produce significant long-term population growth even in countries where fertility rates are equal to or have dropped below replacement level.[2] In the United States, approximately 60 percent of the nation's population growth is due to natural increase (the difference between births and deaths), while immigration accounts for the remaining 40 percent. However, immigration plays a much larger role in population growth when the children of immigrants are accounted for, particularly in the United States, where the large Hispanic immigrant population tends to have fertility rates significantly higher than native-born Americans. Indeed, projections indicate that immigrants and their children will account for 87 percent of the nation's population growth between 2005 and 2050, changing the ethnic and racial composition of the country.[3] In Canada, immigration already accounts for over 50 percent of the nation's population growth, and it is predicted to be the sole source of population growth by mid-century.[4] However, immigrant fertility rates in Canada are more or less equivalent to those of the broader population as compared to the United States, meaning that Canada (and other developed countries that receive large numbers of immigrants) does not reap as much of a second generation as the United States does.

Given that fertility levels in the developed world are expected to remain low, and that there is also relatively little change expected in terms of mortality rates, immigration becomes the central component of population change, and immigration policy is the de facto population policy in Canada, the United States, and many other developed countries. Of the potential policy options, immigration policy provides an almost immediate and direct impact on a population through such actions as defining the number of immigrants allowed entrance in any given year, the source countries for immigrants, and immigrants' qualifications.

In particular, immigration has a large impact on the size of the working labor force, an important fact for economists and demographers alike as they look to who will pay for social-welfare programs in the future as the working population declines. In the United States, immigration, and high fertility levels amongst immigrants, is a significant contributor of population growth. Canada has also used immigration to directly increase its population, with immigration accounting for approximately 70 percent of labor force growth. Canadian policy has targeted "economic" or "skilled" immigrants over the past decades, who bring with them specific tools needed within the Canadian economy. In Europe, the region has not been seen in the past as a major destination for immigrants (although short-term work programs are the exception), and current immigration numbers are insufficient to reverse population decline, while further increases in immigration levels may result in ethnic confrontation.[5] Governments choosing to increase immigration levels do so with greater risk, and several countries, including France and Germany, have witnessed anti-immigrant demonstrations in recent years. Most European countries have imposed strict immigration policies, and some have actively encouraged their foreign-born populations to leave.

Although immigration can be used to support a nation's demographic and economic growth, it can be a very poor tool for defining population policy. Newly elected governments may, for example, change immigration targets in response to various needs, whether these are a tightening of immigration flows in response to economic downturns or concern over national security issues, such as those visible as a result of the terrorist attacks in New York City in September 2001. Likewise, despite targeted numbers, the actual number of immigrants entering a country in a given year may exceed (or miss) the targeted number, while illegal immigration provides another route into a country.

Immigration policies have also exposed the difference between desired and actual outcomes—the so-called immigration "gap" that was presented in chapter 7. The United States is faced with a large gap between the realities of controlling immigration and politics, caught between the desire by employers for cheap labor and US-born workers whose livelihoods are threatened. These contradictions inherent in US policy can be observed in the Bracero program (1942–1964) of contract labor importation, which legitimized migrations between Mexico and the United States. In legitimizing immigration, it created long-term connections between the two countries and essentially condoned illegal immigration. The 1986 Immigration Reform and Control Act (IRCA) further exemplified these contradictions. Meant to solve the problem of illegal immigration, employer sanctions were put in place for those who hired undocumented workers. At the same time, IRCA immediately provided exemptions for California's agricultural growers to continue to use undocumented workers under the Special Agricultural Workers (SAW) program. Immigration control was further undermined when IRCA failed to require employers to check the veracity of legal documents. IRCA also provided amnesty for illegal aliens, allowing them to apply for legal status if they had been resident in the United States prior to January 1, 1982. While nearly three million immigrants were legalized, the amnesty program did not meet its goal of reducing illegal immigration over the long run. Instead, apprehensions of illegals entering the country skyrocketed within three years, and it was clear that others were rushing to fill the need for illegal labor. Subsequent studies demonstrated that the law did not provide a substantial deterrent to illegal immigration.[6]

Some two decades after IRCA, the US government continues to debate immigration reform.[7] The Fair and Secure Immigration Reform proposal, tabled in January 2004 by former president Bush, proposed turning illegal workers into guest workers, with incentives to return home at the end of the employment certificate. A corresponding Democratic bill would have allowed illegal workers to become legal immigrants, while the Agricultural Job Opportunity, Benefits, and Security Act (AgJOBS) bill debated in congress in spring 2005 would have applied only to agricultural workers, allowing workers meeting specific criteria to apply for temporary legal status. Early discussion around President Obama's push for immigration reform has also included pathways to legalize illegal immigrants while restricting the number of temporary workers to what is required by the US economy, measures that are endorsed by major labor unions.[8] The common denominators linking Obama's proposals with earlier reform attempts are the creation of additional networks that link immigrants within the US and Mexican labor markets and additional illegal entry.

INTERNAL MIGRATION

In most countries in the developed world, internal population mobility is unconstrained. Indeed, the United States, Australia, Canada, and other countries are liberal democracies that permit and often encourage the free movement of their populations, with individuals free to migrate in search of economic advantage or other personal choices and settle in the location of their choice. The exceptions have included the forced relocation of First Nations groups onto nontraditional reserves as the country expanded and European settlers expropriated the land for their own use or the relocation of communities faced with natural disaster. In some developing countries, however, internal migration is either enforced or restricted through government policies. Indonesia's transmigration policy, for example, was a long-standing government program that relocated Indonesians from the island of Java to less populated areas by offering economic and land incentives. But the forced relocation also sparked violent confrontations between Christians and Muslims in 2000 and 2001, two groups that had long-term settlement patterns that were largely exclusive of each other but that were forced together through government relocation policies.[9] On the other hand, China followed a path that could be described as restrained urbanization. Fearing an influx of rural peasants to its largest cities, China vigorously attempted to control internal migration through the Hukou system, which conferred "citizenship" to the locality of the mother. Citizenship conferred specific local benefits—access to health care, free public education, legal housing, and better access to jobs—that noncitizens were not eligible for. Under the system, individuals were broadly categorized as rural or urban workers. A worker seeking to move from the country to urban areas to take up nonagricultural work would have to apply through the relevant bureaucracies, and the number of workers allowed to migrate was tightly controlled.

Persons could change their citizenship one of three ways. First, permanent relocations were sanctioned through legal citizenship changes. Between the early 1980s and late 1990s, China authorized some 18 million citizenship changes a year, most of which involved rural-to-urban relocations. Second, individuals could temporarily relocate by holding a "visa," although it did not confer citizenship benefits in the temporary location. Third, individuals could migrate illegally, but were then unable to access local services such as health care and were subject to deportation back to their region of citizenship. Despite the risks and the lack of access to services, it is estimated that tens of thousands illegally migrated to China's urban areas in search of jobs.

Although restrictions on internal migration limited the growth of China's largest cities,[10] they did not succeed at curbing rural-to-urban migration. Instead, corruption and economic necessity drove "illegal" internal migration, despite a degree of social control that is unknown in most societies. Moreover, migrants were not necessarily the poorest of urban residents, and policies that restrict rural-to-urban migration are typically ineffective and hurt the poor.[11] Restraints imposed on population movement have also contributed to increasing social and economic inequality and the development of urban slums in China's cities, with migrants often living in dorms or urban villages characterized by poor living conditions. Since the late 1990s, the Hukou system has slowly been relaxed as China has reformed its economy, encouraging rural-to-urban migration and ensuring legal employment for migrants. Even still, access to some services is still restricted and based on citizenship, with ongoing concerns that the system has tempered China's economic growth.

FERTILITY POLICIES

Fertility Reduction: Antinatalist Policies

As we have already seen, fertility levels vary dramatically across the globe, ranging from very low fertility in much of the developed world and in particular Europe to very high fertility in portions of the developing world, including sub-Saharan Africa. While these differences partially reflect a developed world/

developing world divide, this is only part of the picture. Many countries in the developing world already have comparatively low fertility rates. While China's low fertility rate (1.6) has been artificially engineered through state control (see "Focus" section), fertility rates in other countries, such as South Korea or Taiwan, have declined largely on their own and beyond the scope of government intervention.

Fertility choices are generally perceived to be a personal, private affair. Indeed, the United Nations has affirmed the right of couples to determine the number and spacing of children. Despite this, most governments are, at least indirectly, interested in fertility rates, as these are harbingers of long-term population growth or decline, and many countries attempt to influence fertility decisions. For example, in countries where governments deem fertility too high, such as India, programs encourage lower fertility rates through family-planning programs that educate men and women on the benefits of smaller families and increase accessibility to and use of contraceptive devices. More stringent fertility programs, including China's one-child policy, have also been implemented in order to reduce fertility.

Although reductions in fertility have occurred, many governments, including Saudi Arabia, India, Sri Lanka, Pakistan, Niger, and Peru, still view their population growth rate as being too high. There has been growing recognition since the 1980s of the need to control population growth within developing countries, despite the complexity of trying to do so. In response, programs to reduce population growth rates by controlling fertility behavior have been enacted, ranging from laissez-faire to invasive. In the former case, India had initially hoped that generally improving economic prospects would ultimately lead to lower fertility levels, although changes to fertility behavior were not noted. Economic incentives to reduce the number of children or emphasize quality-of-life aspects associated with fewer children have also been promoted, but with limited effect.

More coercive and invasive programs have included sterilization. With mounting frustration over the failure of family-planning programs and economic development policies to bring about a decline in fertility, the Indian government instituted an enforced sterilization program in 1976. Officially, there was no coercion to participate in the program, but the fact that government employees needed to produce two candidates for sterilization, wide-scale bribery, and a series of disincentives, including the denial of licenses, essentially meant that sterilization was indeed forced upon the population. Although some twenty-two million individuals were sterilized, most were older males who had already achieved their desired family size, meaning that the program was once again ineffective in reducing total fertility.

Somewhere between these two extremes lies the provision of family-planning programs. The uptake of such programs can often depend on the willingness of a population to use such services or its government to provide family-planning services to reduce fertility. The added benefit of such programs has been to educate individuals of the risk of sexually transmitted diseases, including HIV/AIDS. Although contraceptive use is increasing worldwide, in the developing world it is used more for control of the spacing of children or after desired family size is achieved, rather than to limit family size. In addition, only 23 percent of married women in their reproductive years use some form of modern birth control in many African nations, which compares with 69 percent in North America. Oftentimes, however, the use of contraception is discouraged by political, cultural, or religious beliefs. In other cases, condom use could jeopardize relationships, implying potential contact with HIV or engagement in sexually risky behavior. Not surprisingly, therefore, fertility reduction programs have met with varying levels of success and have reflected the outcome of changing societal beliefs rather than the outcome of a specific program more often than not.

Fertility Promotion: Pronatalist Policies

While many countries are faced with overpopulation and rapid population growth, a handful of countries are faced with the opposite problem, too few births, an outcome of the long-term trend toward lower fertility rates. Beginning in the 1970s, TFR fell below replacement levels (2.1) in many industrialized countries. Lower fertility rates have meant slowing population growth in some countries, such as Canada and Australia, while in other countries, including Ukraine, Russia, Germany, and Hungary, population decline has already started, meaning that deaths outnumber births. The elderly already represent greater than 15 percent of the population in several European countries, including Sweden (18 percent), the United Kingdom (16 percent), and Belgium (17 percent), with continued growth of the older adult population ensured. Europe's population will no longer increase naturally after 2015, with population growth instead coming from immigration. Assuming immigration remains at its current level, Europe's population will start to shrink by the middle of the century, a situation that is echoed in Canada. Although having the highest TFR in the Western world, the United States has seen increases in its share of the elderly population too, growing from just 4.1 percent of the population in 1900 to 12.4 percent in 2000 and projected to grow to nearly 20 percent by 2030.[12] Even in China, where the government has long been concerned with rapid population growth, concerns have turned to an aging population and its support. Anxiety over a declining population, an expanding elderly population, and a smaller labor force that is expected to support the elderly has prompted concerns regarding the survival of social programs and a loss of economic and/or political power, and has led governments to explore ways in which fertility may be promoted. In both cases, other policies, such as access to legal abortion, child tax credits, or day-care services, indirectly influence fertility behavior.

Within most Western nations, the decline in birth rates below replacement levels has been linked to deep societal and economic changes.[13] Promotion of gender equity has meant that women have become increasingly educated and more likely to participate in the labor force. Increased employment and career aspirations have provided greater financial autonomy, contributing to declines in fertility as women seek careers outside their homes. Rising consumer aspirations further reinforce the opportunity costs of children, even as fears of unemployment, downsizing, and the uncertain future of the welfare state temper future economic prospects. Together, these effects have prompted many to either delay childbirth or to reduce the desired family size, challenging many long-held assumptions about the timing of marriage and children.

Though it is seemingly paradoxical, low birth rates and a slowing or decreasing population growth rate have their own set of problems. Although the consequences of an aging society are still unclear, many commentators have concluded that low fertility is a serious problem, having more disadvantages than advantages, making it a politically unsustainable position.[14] Fearful of "demographic suicide" and the economic implications of an aging population, many countries have adopted pronatalist policies intended to either promote fertility directly or ease the opportunity costs of children, with the hope that fertility rates will increase. Faced with slowing or declining population growth rates since the 1970s, Eastern European countries have the longest history of pronatalist policies.[15] Policies typically addressed the issue through a combination of financial incentives and restriction to contraception and abortion services. Meant to ease the opportunity costs of children, financial benefits commonly include paid maternity and paternity leave, free or reduced-cost childcare, and tax breaks for large families. Most of these programs are not advertised as fertility policy by explicitly targeting a desired number of children. Instead, policies are presented as antipoverty, prowoman, or profamily measures and are meant to influence socioeconomic conditions related to fertility decisions. Some countries, such as France and Australia, pay women for children. In France, the government pays women some $1,500 per month for each additional child. In Australia, falling fertility rates (TFR reached a low of 1.73 in 2001) prompted the government to pay families who have children a $3,000 bonus. Since then, the TFR has increased to 2.0 (2009), although critics suggest that it either represents a change in the timing of fertility (but no real increase in the number of desired children) or the "echo" of a large early 1970s cohort that are just now having children.[16]

ECONOMIC POLICY AS POPULATION POLICIES

National or regional economic policies often have a population component or impact on population policies along with population structure. In the United States, policymakers and business leaders are concerned with the slowing growth of the labor force as baby boomers age, with growth slowing from 2.6 percent growth per year during the 1970s as baby boomers entered the labor force, to 1.7 percent per year in the 1980s, to 1.1 percent in the 1990s. Over the coming decades, growth in the labor force is projected to be just 0.6 percent. Additionally, there are concerns that as baby boomers retire labor productivity will drop as more experienced workers are replaced by people with fewer years on the job.

Fearful of aging populations, declining labor force size and experience, and the support of their older populations, many governments in the developed world have moved to adjust labor force participation rates. For instance, governments have abolished mandatory retirement ages, have reduced or delayed retirement benefits, and/or now actively encourage labor force participation amongst the old. For instance, with the delay of Social Security benefits to age sixty-seven (from sixty-five) and the abolishment of mandatory retirement in the United States, labor force participation for those over fifty-five has increased since 1995. Other countries have enacted similar legislation and observed similar results. The hope is that the older population—individuals that society has typically defined as "retired"—will remain active in the labor force and largely self-supportive, while also paying into tax and pension funds. While the number that elect to delay retirement from the typical age of sixty-five (or earlier) remains small, the proportion is growing, with many baby boomers expecting to remain employed beyond the typical retirement age.[17]

Other programs, including those that promote gender equity or reading and literacy amongst women, are also closely associated with changing fertility preferences, with increased educational opportunities for women linked to lower fertility. Clearly, health care provision is also an economic policy. In general, countries that have invested in health and family planning have slower population growth rates and greater economic development than those countries that have not made such investments. However, health care systems are also casualties of high rates of population growth and stagnant economies that have limited development, modernization, and investment in basic health care services. Many systems are poorly funded or in ruin, preventing access to the most basic of health services.

THE ROLE OF THE INTERNATIONAL COMMUNITY: CONFLICTING MESSAGES

Early Efforts: 1950s–1970s

Although we like to think that reproductive choices are personal, states and their governments will often take either an active or accidental role in promoting fertility. Growing concern within developed countries with rapid population growth in the post–World War II era prompted international institutions and governments to try to influence fertility policies.[18] At first, the developing world was slow to respond to programs promoting fertility reduction, arguing instead that economic development was the best contraceptive. Population policies were also viewed as an infringement upon state sovereignty from former colonial or imperial powers. With stagnating economies, high child mortality, and an increasing realization that women wanted to limit their own fertility, governments in the developing world increasingly warmed to the idea that population growth should be slowed. The United Nations became the driving force through its sponsorship of the first meeting on global population in 1954. Other UN organizations, including the WHO and the United Nations Children's Fund (UNICEF), have incorporated reproductive health into their programs and under the auspices of the UNFPA.

The US government has taken a more independent approach, preferring to direct its money through its own Agency for International Development (USAID), reflecting its own concerns and policy goals.[19] Largely driven by security concerns that saw rapid population growth as a threat to US security via trade, political conflict, immigration, or damage to the environment, USAID has been the largest single donor to family-planning programs. Initially, programs emphasized family-planning practices or specific demographic targets but grew by the 1970s to provide contraceptive information and related health services to support child and maternal health. Critics have long argued that the programs were too narrowly focused, failing to respect religious beliefs or making insufficient investments in social and economic opportunities. Most notably, abortion opponents criticized US involvement in family-planning programs because of their belief that family-planning programs promote abortion. In fact, US law has prohibited the use of such funds to pay for abortion services since the 1970s.

Shifting Priorities: 1980s–present

The 1980s saw a significant shift in US population policy under the Reagan administration. Supported by economic optimists, including Julian Simon, who argued that world population growth was "good," the administration declared at the 1984 International Conference on Population in Mexico City that population growth actually had a *neutral* effect upon economic development. Reflecting its connections with the religious right, the Reagan administration also opposed the use of funds for abortion services, withdrawing all financial support from any organization that provided such services even when using their own money to provide legal abortions. At the same time the United States was reversing its position on population growth, developing countries had largely stepped back from their earlier opposition to family-planning programs. Instead, the benefits of small families and the need to slow population growth were promoted. Despite US opposition, the 1984 conference ultimately supported family-planning initiatives and urged governments to make such services available.

After taking office in 1993, the Clinton administration waived funding restrictions set in place by the previous Republican administrations and increased funding to family-planning programs. Eight years later, the Bush-Cheney administration reinstated restrictions to family-planning programs within days of taking office,[20] returning to restrictions imposed at the time of the Mexico City conference, while President Obama reversed the restrictions again.[21]

The so-called "global gag rule" that was enforced during the Bush administration denied US funding to private overseas organizations if they used other (non-US) monies to provide abortion services or if they lobby for changes to the abortion law in their own country.[22] Unfortunately, such restrictions actually undermined the success of family-planning programs. Ultimately, the global gag rule undermined family planning's objective of preventing unwanted pregnancies and improving maternal and child health. In fact, the ubiquity of abortion suggests that there is a large unmet need for family-planning programs that can prevent the use of abortion services by providing counseling or other options.[23] In cases where legal abortion is not an alternative, women may choose illegal abortions, increasing the risk of death or injury when faced with an unwanted pregnancy. Family-planning programs can also reduce fertility levels by helping with birth spacing, improving the odds of survival of mother and child, preventing unsafe abortions, and reducing the incidence of sexually transmitted diseases, including HIV. Studies have clearly shown that as use of family-planning methods increases, abortion rates decrease, and that increased funding of family-planning programs reduces abortion.[24]

Leading up to the fifth UN conference on population, held in Cairo in 1994, discussions once again centered on the relationship between population growth and development. Despite the success of family-planning programs in the developing world, critics of these programs viewed them as an invasion of personal liberties. Instead, it was argued that family-planning programs should be better integrated into a broader view of health, and that women's well-being should be of paramount importance. Responding to the critics, the conference redefined views of population growth and how to address it, linking population growth to sustainable development. Rather than focusing primarily on national interests, the conference promoted investment in human development, particularly the status of women. Family planning was to be integrated into a broader health agenda, including pre- and postnatal care, sexually transmitted diseases, and cancer screening. Infant, child, and maternal mortality and the alleviation of poverty were to be targeted, and universal access to family-planning services and primary school education and increased access by girls and women to higher education were promoted. However, abortion was not promoted as a method of family planning, clearly recognizing the legal, moral, and religious viewpoints on abortion within different countries.

Reviews of the 1994 conference were mixed. Many countries had articulated and implemented new population policies along with reproductive health programs. However, funding shortfalls by donor countries, including the United States and other developed countries, limited the reach and effectiveness of programs. The success of the Cairo conference must also be evaluated within the context of broader health reforms and economic liberalization. Many developing countries had already started to change their policies and institutions, promoting a broader health agenda that incorporated reproductive health and gender equity. For example, the World Health Organization's Health for All by 2000 (HFA 2000) program was an early promoter of societal health.[25] Initiated in 1977, HFA 2000 emphasized the promotion and protection of health realized through the provision of primary health care that stressed comprehensive basic services for all rather than sophisticated curative medical care for a few. Primary health care thus became WHO's basic strategy for health improvement, notable for its concern with factors supporting health, including water supplies, sanitation, education, and food supply, along with programs promoting child and maternal health and family planning. A particular emphasis was placed upon the health and education of children, adolescents, and women within the developing world. There is increasing recognition that childhood health is linked to health in later life. Consequently, improving early-childhood nutrition and greater access to immunizations, better hygiene, improved education opportunities, and safe water supplies have been promoted. Among women, for whom gender differences are often reinforced by societal or cultural norms, programs have targeted equity issues, working to narrow gaps in literacy, education, and income opportunities.

CONCLUSION

Population policy is clouded by a multitude of factors, including religion, social expectations, economic needs, and personal decisions. Despite China's one-child policy, for instance, pressure within segments of China's population to have more than one child shows a continuing desire to have larger families, and the problems associated with a rapidly aging population have forced the government to relax its fertility policy in some cases. In India, despite a half-century of promoting fertility reductions, fertility rates remain relatively high, with a TFR greater than 3.0.

Not surprisingly, population policy, and particularly fertility policy, whether meant to promote population growth or decline, is difficult to facilitate and has achieved varying degrees of success. From the set of policy levers that can be used to control population change, immigration policy has had the most direct effect by controlling who and how many can enter a country. Immigration has been assumed to be an important source of population growth, although it is also potentially associated with problems of immigrant adaptation, ethnic and racial divides, and national security issues. Incentives to increase or decrease fertility are also widespread but have met with mixed success. China's success with fertility reduction is largely due to its one-child policy. While it reduced the country's fertility rate, the reduction has largely occurred because of the state's tight control over the population. The one-child policy has also come with costs that are increasingly visible, including the preponderance of male births and the dramatically smaller working cohort that must support China's older population. Other cases of fertility control, such as India, have been far less successful. Likewise, fertility promotion has only been partially successful. Partially because of this limited success or other problems, countries have also explored alternatives to fertility promotion by looking at other policy alternatives, including delayed retirement to keep individuals within the labor force or delaying the start of welfare programs, as the United States has done.

FOCUS: POPULATION PLANNING IN SELECTED REGIONS

CHINA'S ONE-CHILD POLICY

Identified as one of the most successful, albeit controversial, fertility control programs, China's one-child policy has received considerable lay and academic attention.[1] Initially, China's government viewed family planning and fertility reduction programs as suspect, assuming instead that socialism would ensure the equitable distribution of resources across society. By the late 1960s, however, China's leadership recognized the limits to growth and the need for population control. With a TFR in excess of 7.0, rapid population growth was acknowledged to hinder attempts to improve the economy and raise the standard of living. Beginning in 1979, the Chinese government advocated its one-child program, with the goal of stabilizing the population at 1.2 billion, accomplished through a combination of social pressures including propaganda, local political activism and coercion, increased availability of contraception and family planning resources, and a series of economic incentives and disincentives. For those committing to the program, cash bonuses were paid, with one-child families given preference in school admission, housing, and job applications in urban areas. In rural areas, the program was altered slightly so that families would receive the same food rations as a two-child family and the same-sized plot for private cultivation as a two-child family. Disincentives to large families were also employed, requiring families having more than one child to repay all benefits received.

By the late 1990s, China's total fertility rate had dropped below replacement, and is currently 1.6. The apparent "success" of the program seemingly follows from the ability of the Chinese government to exert control over the population to limit births, a recognized feature of China's communist society. The program's success could also be attributed to the promotion of personal and national economic benefits and the program's link to broader health issues, which together engendered the desire for smaller families within the Chinese population.

Yet even though fertility rates declined and population growth slowed, the program has not been without its critics. Internally, a significant proportion of the Chinese population resisted the one-child policy, reflecting deeper cultural issues or economic necessity and the importance placed on the birth of male children. Although higher financial incentives were also attached to the birth of daughters among couples who endorsed the one-child policy and the government's allowance of more than one child in some rural areas, the prospect of a one-child family meant that approximately 50 percent of families would not have a son. Poverty further reinforced the importance and contribution of male children to family welfare. As a result, couples frequently opted to disregard the one-child policy in their efforts to have a son, and have also turned to prenatal scans and abortion to prevent the birth of unwanted daughters, leading to an imbalance in the number of boys relative to girls and the "missing girls" phenomenon.[2] In some parts of China, there are approximately 135 boys born for every 100 girls. The typical difference (the "sex ratio") is 105 boys for every 100 girls, raising fears of the potential for social unrest as males are unable to find partners. Equally disturbing, reports of female infanticide and abuse of women who give birth to girls are not uncommon,[3] and it was suggested that the set of disincentives for higher-order births deterred women from seeking appropriate prenatal and pregnancy-related care, increasing the risk of death for mother and child.[4]

The true success of the program has also been questioned since declines in fertility can be traced to the 1960s. Fertility decline was furthered in the 1970s with government policies of delayed marriage, longer spacing between births, and fewer children, so that by the early 1980s the TFR had already dropped below 3.0. In other words, the decline in fertility levels would appear to have been well established by the mid 1970s. Far from inducing fertility decline, the one-child program may therefore have simply enhanced the motivation for smaller families, codifying family size as a national goal through the provision of a set of incentives and disincentives.

Continued economic liberalization will likely promote small families in the coming years as the direct and opportunity costs of children are realized, particularly in urban

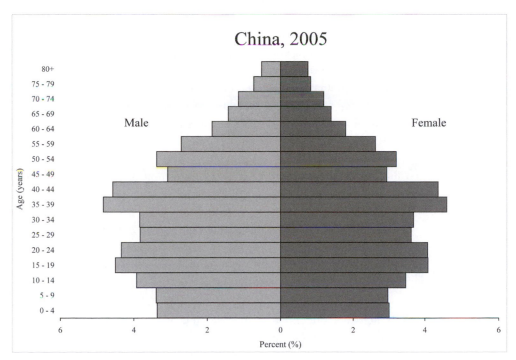

Figure 10F.1   China's Age Pyramid, 2005.

Note the larger proportion of young males and the population bulge as the labor force ages, with implications for the support of this aging population.

Source: US Census Bureau, IDB.

areas. Conversely, economic liberalization may also *promote* fertility among the poor as a means of ensuring their economic success in an economy that is increasingly separated by the rich and poor, leading observers to question whether the low rates of fertility can be maintained over the longer term. Even now, with China's estimated population of 1.3 billion in 2009, the original target population of 1.2 billion has been exceeded, owing to demographic momentum and the young age of the population. The government has already loosened its restrictions on early marriages and has relaxed its one-child policy, permitting two children in certain circumstances, suggesting that a substantial demand for larger families may remain within the population, particularly in rural areas where economic liberalization has increased pressure for children as a means of family support and production.

The Chinese have also recognized that the rapid reduction in fertility levels in just twenty-five years has resulted in a young population (aged fifteen years and less) that is substantially smaller than previous generations, creating a heavy burden of old-age dependency. Like many countries in the developed world, the Chinese government is trying to cope with an aging population and a shrinking labor force that supports the elderly.[5] Moreover, the erosion of traditional family structures means that children no longer care for their elderly parents, posing additional problems, making a further relaxation of the one-child policy to meet the problem of an aging population possible. At the same time, the Chinese government reaffirmed and codified the one-child policy in 2002, while also criminalizing coercive enforcement measures.[6] However, it is also a misconception that China has its population under control. Large-scale population movements from rural to urban areas have led to growing regional inequities, insufficient urban infrastructure, degradation of resources, and the potential for urban conflict given its Hukou system (see chapter 10).

PROMOTING FERTILITY IN QUEBEC, CANADA

Quebec, Canada's French-speaking province, provides an example of regional concerns associated with fertility and population size. Historically, birth rates within the province were higher than the Canadian average, as Quebecers resisted the adoption of contraception and fertility changes. Even in the late 1950s at the peak of the baby boom, Quebec's TFR was in excess of 4.0 children, giving the province one of the highest fertility rates in the industrialized world. The delayed uptake of newer fertility norms and contraceptive techniques reflected the control of the Roman Catholic Church and its traditional stance against contraception. In Quebec's case, the church also encouraged large families as a "demographic investment" that ensured the survival of French Canada within the Canadian Confederation.[7]

Quebec's demographic advantage was lost in the 1960s. The liberalization of the church and rapid emancipation of women contributed to declining fertility rates, enabling them to drop below the Canadian average. By the mid-1980s, Quebec had one of the lowest rates of fertility in the world

at that time (1.37),[8] and its share of the Canadian population dropped from 32.3 percent at the time of confederation in 1867 to 24 percent in 2001. Responding to this apparent crisis, Quebec's Commission de la Culture reported in 1985 that the province needed to take action to counter demographic trends that threatened the province's existence as a "distinct society," an issue that has dominated provincial politics since its foundation. The commission and other commentators pointed out that the demographic situation threatened the political strength of the province and its cultural sovereignty, in addition to the problems of providing for an aging population. Robert Bourassa, then premier of Quebec, echoed the concerns of the commission by declaring that increasing birth rates was the most important challenge for Quebec.[9] In response, Quebec initiated a series of pro-fertility programs, including more generous tax deductions for children, higher family allowances, longer parental work leaves, and more day care opportunities. Beginning in 1988, the Quebec government also offered baby bonuses based upon family size, with five hundred dollars for the first child, one thousand dollars for the second, and six thousand dollars for the third and subsequent children, along with extended maternity leaves and family allowances. Revisions to this policy in subsequent years raised the bonuses slightly,[10] while an overhaul of the system in 1997 refocused allowances based on the number of children under eighteen years and household income, increased maternity leave benefits, and provided highly subsidized day care.[11] Overall, the success of these policies has been limited. Statistics Canada, for example, identified a slight recovery in Quebec's fertility rates in the years following the introduction of pronatalist policies, with TFR reaching 1.6 in 1996 but dropping again to 1.5 in 1997 and remaining slightly below the Canadian average in 2000 with a TFR of 1.4.[12] By 2007, the TFR had reached 1.6, the highest rate in more than a decade.[13]

METHODS, MEASURES, AND TOOLS: PASS OR FAIL? EVALUATING POPULATION POLICIES

As evidenced by the discussion elsewhere in this chapter, population policies have offered mixed results at best. For instance, India's multiyear struggle to reduce fertility levels through various family planning programs and incentives has been problematic and piecemeal. Critics have charged that Indian programs have been inconsistent and have typically lacked direction, with demographic targets tied to oscillating rewards and disincentives. The program has also failed to offer more flexible birth control methods such as the pill or intrauterine device (IUD). Instead, it focused upon sterilization in a country that has historically low use of contraception. Other contraceptive techniques still represent only a small proportion of contraceptive use within India. India's lack of success runs deeper than inconsistent or narrow policy objectives by failing to account for the broader social context within which reproduction occurs, including the role of women, the interrelationship among classes, and the political consequences of fertility policies.

The failure of fertility reduction programs like India's is not unique, but is witnessed across the world and is more reflective of changing governments and their priorities than anything else. Even China's relative "success" in reducing fertility levels and constraining population growth must be viewed in the context of the dramatic and rapid shift in its age structure, which is rapidly becoming heavily skewed toward older generations, and the surplus of male births. Both problems may create social unrest and economic hardship in the coming years. More broadly, inconsistency in the application of family planning programs, undesired outcomes, or the failure to provide a range of contraception, for example, are seen elsewhere. Programs cannot be one size fits all and transplanted from place to place without recognition of differing morals and attitudes toward sex and contraception, as is the case in Africa. Instead, the reality is that different programs will likely need to be adopted for different locations and preferences.

Pronatalist policies and programs also have mixed outcomes.[1] Evidence suggests that the effects of pronatalist policies are short-lived and only moderately successful. Over the short term, fertility rates frequently increase, but the longer-term impact is less successful. If anything, most observers believe that incentives merely accelerate or alter the timing of the first birth, rather than changing the desired family size by increasing the number of "higher-order births" (i.e., second, third, or higher born children). Over the longer term, the relationship between financial incentives and other attitudinal factors related to fertility is difficult to measure and is unknown. Demographic factors, such as fewer women in their child-bearing years, mean that total births are likely to remain low. Restrictions on access to abortion services also have a short-term effect on fertility as couples quickly adjust their own practices or resort to illegal abortion.

The success of immigration policies is also variable, where the inconsistent application or setting of immigration targets and admissions can result in fluctuating patterns and numbers over time. To complicate matters, changing global economic conditions or options can alter immigrant numbers. At the same time, efforts to curb immigration have often led to increased illegal "backdoor" immigration. Countries are slowly awakening to the realization that immigration policy is problematic. Whichever way they turn—either to restrict immigration or promote particular components of immigration—is not guaranteed to achieve the desired results. Attempts to decrease immigrant flows have proven largely unsuccessful in the face of economic restructuring and globalization. Increasing immigration is problematic in its own way, threatening ethnic, racial, or social instability while creating a cadre of low-paid workers that would reduce wages and compete for positions with the native-born. Opening the doors may represent a slippery slope that governments would not be able to back away from, with immigration further spiraling beyond their control. Both measures carry the risk of mixed messages that condone immigration on the one hand while reducing it on the other. Ultimately, the future shape of immigration policy is unclear.

Chapter Eleven

Population Growth

Linking to Economic Development, Resource Scarcity, and Food Security

THE CONTINUED GROWTH of the human population is inevitable. Even if the demographic transition results in lower fertility and growth rates, population momentum will ensure a global population of 7.5 or 8 billion by 2025, bringing with it potentially significant societal and economic consequences. One question that remains, however, is whether a growing population has positive or negative implications for economic development, resource consumption, and food security, the topics of this chapter. The chapter begins by considering the work of Thomas Malthus, the eighteenth-century writer who first linked population and food resources. Following Malthus, the opposing approaches of Karl Marx and Friedrich Engels are introduced before examining links between population growth, economic development, resource scarcity, and food security. The chapter concludes with a discussion of the potential for conflict and instability. The "Methods, Measures, and Tools" section looks at the contributions of geographers to these areas of discussion, and the "Focus" section considers population growth and the potential for conflict over scarce resources.

THOMAS MALTHUS AND "ESSAY ON THE PRINCIPLE OF POPULATION"

Demographers and others struggle with the question of whether the world can feed itself. Writing in the 1960s, Paul Ehrlich's *The Population Bomb* alerted the public to the population crisis, bringing with it a sense of urgency.[1] But, Ehrlich's warnings were not new, with the population-food (resource) debate having a long history, dating to Thomas Malthus's 1798 writing "Essay on the Principle of Population" and later writings by Karl Marx and Friedrich Engels. Writing during a period of poor harvests and food shortages, Malthus argued that food supply would increase in a linear fashion (1, 2, 3 . . .), while population would increase geometrically (2, 4, 8 . . .).[2] Ultimately, population would exceed agricultural output, unless population growth was somehow "checked." Historically, Malthus argued that so-called positive checks, including famine, plague, and war, decreased the population. Alternatively, population growth could be controlled through "preventative checks," with individuals imposing their own limits on reproduction. With Malthus holding out little hope that humanity would be able to control its sexual and reproductive needs, he forecast a dismal future of population decline and widespread poverty. In opposition to Malthus, Marx and Engels argued that people were poor because economies and societies were organized in such a way that they did not have the opportunity to be anything else but poor. Influenced by the social and economic conditions of Europe during the Industrial Revolution, they promoted social and political change (often through revolution) and believed that a just and equitable distribution of resources aided by technology would allow unlimited population growth.

SETTING THE STAGE: THE DEBATE AND CURRENT PERSPECTIVES

Malthus's dire predictions remain a focal point of the debate over population growth, and the ability to feed the world's population remains an important question.[3] Time has proven the basic perspectives of Malthusian and Marxian theories both right and wrong—our mere presence on this planet points to the failings of Malthus's core thesis. While fertility has been reduced largely through personal choices as standards of living rose and new ideas filtered through society, technology, the green revolution (the application of fertilizers and pesticides to increase crop yields), and biotechnology have allowed the world to accommodate a population far larger than Malthus ever saw possible. Agricultural production has grown tremendously, allowing per-capita food supplies to increase despite continued population growth. Marx's position, on the other hand, seems vindicated in China. With a population in excess of 1.3 billion, China has proven that it can provide the basic needs of a large and rapidly growing population. At the same time, it has recognized that there are limits to growth, as it moved to reduce fertility through its one-child policy.

Even now, however, the Food and Agricultural Organization of the United Nations (UN FAO) estimates that over 920 million people were malnourished in 2007. While the majority of these were found in the developing world, many are also found in the developed world.[4] Millions more consume sufficient calories but fail to get the necessary proteins. Consequently, the world continues to grapple with the basic question of whether it can feed itself, both now and in the years to come. At the same time as agricultural production has increased, degradation of cropland through erosion, desertification, salinization, and urbanization have reduced the amount of land available for agriculture.[5] Created by poor farming practices, deforestation, and the use of ecologically marginal land, erosion can decrease average yields by reducing the soil's ability to retain moisture, by carrying away nutrients, and by degrading its physical qualities. Likewise, the salinization of crop land, whereby soils become increasingly salty because of saltwater infiltration, means the soil is unable to support agriculture. The expected impacts of climate change and the unequal distribution of food owing to distributional difficulties, conflicts, or politics within and among countries compound the problem.[6] With the world's population growing at a rate of 1.2 percent per year, and with over 130 million new souls each year requiring food and clothing and other resources, questions as to whether the earth can feed and sustain such a large population continue to be raised.[7]

Growing from the initial Malthusian/Marxian distinctions within the literature, three perspectives continue to underlie the current debate and influence public policy and commentary.[8] Pointing to growing carbon dioxide concentrations, the declining health of oceans, reductions in biodiversity, and degradation of land, *neo-Malthusians* argue that finite resources place strict limits on the growth of the human population and consumption.[9] If limits are exceeded, social breakdown occurs.[10] Recent food riots, caused by limited supplies and rapidly increasing costs, may be seen as a harbinger of future events, particularly as climate change redraws the agriculture map by reducing harvests.

Economic optimists, characterized by Julian Simon, see few limits to population growth and prosperity, provided the economic system and market mechanisms work correctly.[11] Following their reasoning, few societies face strict limits to growth or consumption, with optimists pointing to improvements in human health, life expectancy, and increasing food production to support their position. Finally, the *distributionist* viewpoint, which is favored by Marxists, focuses upon inequalities in the distribution of wealth and power within a society, and argues that the poor distribution of resources, poverty, and inequality are the causes, not consequences, of population growth and resource depletion.

While the neo-Malthusian, economic optimist, and distributionist perspectives are still identifiable within the literature, the debate has essentially become two-sided, with neo-Malthusians on one side and optimists on the other. Each argument contains grains of truth, but neither conveys the entire story. So, what went wrong and where do we currently stand? First, returning to the neo-Malthusian perspective, empirical and anecdotal evidence has failed to support the assumption that population growth is limited by resource barriers. In very general terms, the human population has grown beyond most of the barriers that were assumed by neo-Malthusians. Over the past two centuries, agricultural technology and capital have increased agricultural productivity tremendously, allowing agricultural output to increase. Similarly, neo-Malthusians forecasted energy shortfalls, predicting that energy prices would grow over fivefold between 1973 (the first oil crisis) and 2000. While the 1990s and early-to-mid-2000s marked a period of relatively inexpensive energy, prices skyrocketed in 2007 and early 2008 amid concerns of declining reserves, the inability to find new reserves of oil and gas, and rapidly increasing use of energy within the developing world, especially China and India, only to fall with the onset of the recession.

Economic optimists have been much better in explaining the ability of the world to adapt to these apparent barriers. For them, the operation of economic institutions, and particularly free markets, is key. Properly functioning institutions can facilitate conservation, substitution, innovation, and global trade of goods. Induced innovation theory argues that changes in endowments of land or labor, for example, are reflected in market price signals.[12] Through their ability to generate profit, markets induce innovations and stimulate technological innovations that loosen or remove constraints to population growth, and price changes encourage people to tap new resources or to substitute. Ester Boserup, for example, showed that scarcity of cropland stimulates greater labor specialization, increased productivity, and changes in agricultural practices.[13] Likewise, new lands may be opened to agriculture, conservation may be stimulated, or resource substitution may promote the increased use of fertilizers to increase agricultural output. Similarly, scarcities of nonrenewable resources can be overcome through resource substitution, conservation, improved production efficiencies, and enhanced resource extraction technologies. Economic optimists also argue that population growth has a key advantage in that it produces more geniuses, providing society with the means to resolve scarcities. For Julian Simon, resources are only limited by humanity's ability to invent. Thus, innovation and technical fixes allow societies to move beyond constraints to growth. Resource scarcity and degradation are therefore not due to population growth or increased consumption, but are instead due to market failure.

Like the neo-Malthusian perspective, however, the optimist framework is also flawed. A larger population does not, for instance, necessarily mean more discoveries or more Einsteins, but perhaps only that more people make the same discovery. Instead, the supply of scientists and other thinkers is constrained by the level and accessibility of education, limited capital, poor and incompetent bureaucracies, corruption, and weak governments. The brain drain from developing countries and into the developed world may have an especially pernicious effect, as the developed world's immigration policies are tailored to accept the educated and/or those with skills. This institutionalized brain drain poses further and long-term difficulties for the developing world in terms of maintaining human capital and its ability to generate, retain, and utilize the highly educated members of its populations, which will be necessary to solve impending problems.

Moreover, optimists' arguments rest on the free operation of the market, an assumption that is stretched in many cases. Free markets are far from universal. Even in America, the quintessential free-market economy, regulations at various government levels (state, national, and international) interfere with its free operation. In the developing world, the markets frequently become murkier. Institutional limitations, including market failure associated with unclear common property rights and inappropriate pricing for scarce resources (i.e., undervalued resources) limit the creation or substitution of alternatives. In addition, institutional biases may be present within markets, such that there is a tendency for institutions to favor some actors over others, leading to the marginalization of segments of the population. Consequently, a key caveat of the optimist viewpoint is the *quality* of institutions, policies, and technologies that are inherent within a society. Together, these effects, which are in turn modified by cultural, historical, and ecological factors, have direct bearing upon the ability to respond to resource scarcity. If markets are not able to identify or effectively incorporate the costs of scarcity so that resources or goods are undervalued, resources will be exploited and solutions to scarcity will not be forthcoming. Relatedly, it is unlikely that population growth can promote increases in agricultural output that will keep pace with population growth rates in Africa and parts of Asia.

For the most part, the debate between these three groups has stopped here, a debate that Homer-Dixon characterizes as sterile and with relatively little advancement.[14] Science, however, has better revealed the complexity and interconnectivity of ecological systems, with implications for the population. In the past, the earth's environmental systems were regarded as stable and resilient to our tampering. Instead, there is mounting evidence drawn from observation of ocean currents, ozone depletion, and fish stocks that environmental systems are not stable given human actions. What was previously considered slow or incremental changes to systems might be better described as nonlinear, with systems rapidly changing their character when some threshold is exceeded, making chaos and anarchy better descriptors of environmental systems.[15] There is increasing consensus that humanity—via population growth—is taxing the earth's resources to such a degree that complete ecosystems are disappearing. Global warming and the loss of biodiversity may, at some point, cascade to produce dramatic changes that humanity is ill-prepared to deal with.

LINKING TO ECONOMIC DEVELOPMENT, RESOURCE SCARCITY, AND FOOD SECURITY

In the coming decades, population growth, rising per-capita resource consumption, greater food demand, and inequalities in resource access guarantee that scarcities of renewable resources will become an issue. If population growth is taxing ecosystems, what is the prognosis for economic development, food security, and resources?

Population Growth and Economic Development

As the economies of the developing world, and particularly the poorest sub-Saharan countries, started to stagnate in the 1980s, social scientists scrambled to unearth the linkages between rapid growth and economic development.[16] After all, foreign investment and aid had poured into the developing world for years, and yet there was little to show for it. Instead, per-capita incomes had declined and an increasing proportion of the population lived in poverty. At the heart of the debate is the question of whether population growth favors economic development or hinders it, with the available data supporting a number of interpretations. On the surface, it is readily apparent that the richest countries are also those with slow population growth characterized by low rates of fertility and low mortality levels, while some of the poorest countries have high rates of population growth. The relationship is, however, not perfect, with oil-producing countries in the Middle East having high population growth (the fertility rate in Saudi Arabia and other Gulf states remains in excess of 2.1) as well as strong economic growth. The opposite is also true, with low population and low economic growth rates.

Muddying the waters are countering arguments that population growth promotes economic development. Recalling Boserup's argument (presented in chapter 9),[17] optimists have long asserted that population growth promotes economic development, assuming that it is a motivating force in the adaptation of societies, including the uptake or innovation of new technologies or economic reforms. The notion that population growth is in fact good for economic growth is well grounded. In Europe and North America, population growth and declining mortality levels are thought to have stimulated economic development and the Industrial Revolution. However, a different perspective is seen in the developing world. Building upon a much lower standard of living than Europe or the Americas at similar stages in their economic development, and having far greater rates of population growth, this group of countries is not, on average, following the lead of developed countries. In fact, they are slipping further into economic crisis, enhanced by the HIV/AIDS epidemic and its social and economic ramifications along with recessionary pressures.

Although the linkage between population and economic development is complex, emerging evidence reinforces the *negative* linkage between rapid population growth and economic development. The US National Research Council reinforced population's negative effect on economic growth, concluding that rapid population growth damages economic growth.[18] For economic development to occur, capital must be invested in such things as education, health, or infrastructure, a difficult proposition in much of the world, where poverty impedes the ability for governments and individuals to invest. For economies to grow, the level of capital investment must also grow, with higher rates of population growth necessitating higher rates of capital investment. Following a Malthusian line of reasoning, if the population growth rate exceeds the investment rate, countries will be trapped in poverty, unable to invest in themselves and provide the needed infrastructure. Although economic growth would occur under these situations, population growth is so high that economic growth is distributed throughout a larger population, meaning that individuals will receive a smaller proportional share.

This negative linkage can be viewed through a number of relationships linking rapid population growth and high fertility to economic growth.[19] First, rapid population growth tends to dampen the growth of per-capita GDP, a relationship that first appeared in the 1980s and appears strongest among the poorest countries.[20] The growth of GDP can be limited by high young dependency rates, reflective of high fertility rates. With a young population profile, the attendant costs associated with health and education for children are high, reducing household savings and increasing government expenditures. In turn, the growth of GDP is reduced, with the investment providing only long-term economic payoffs.[21] The impact on economic growth is also seen in the creation of new jobs. In countries with rapid population growth, labor markets are frequently unable to provide sufficient employment opportunities for the young, leading to underemployment or unemployment. This negative relationship has continued, ensuring that inequalities between the developed and developing world remain and providing little hope for their rapid amelioration.

Second, population growth and high fertility tend to aggravate poverty and promote its institutionalization from one generation to the next. In particular, population growth will likely reduce or slow wage growth among the least skilled and lowest-income groups. India, for example, has accommodated high population growth, but economic development policies have favored or improved the status of only 15 to 20 percent of the population. The poor in India have paid the highest price. Much of India's public education system, which is predominantly attended by lower socioeconomic classes, is underfunded and inadequate. The poor are progressively marginalized and increasingly unable to participate in the economy because of poor health, lack of nutrition, or illiteracy.[22] In addition, a cadre of low-skilled, low-wage workers may slow the adoption of more efficient technologies.

Third, high fertility inhibits household savings, forcing household expenditure on basic goods and services for a larger number of people while savings or expenditures upon education are postponed or neglected. Conversely, declining population growth and fewer children mean that households are able to invest in education and place more of their earnings in savings, a necessary condition for economic growth. The economic literature has, for example, largely attributed the growth of Asian economies such as South Korea during the 1980s to increased household saving rates as fertility dropped and incomes grew.[23] As families saved more, domestic savings increased and were invested both within the country and exported elsewhere.

Fourth, following Easterlin's reasoning, higher fertility rates mean that parents have less to invest in each child than those with smaller families. Similarly, children from larger families have less schooling on average than their counterparts from smaller families. In countries with rapid population growth, there is increased pressure placed on education and health care, requiring increased financial commitments. Unless rapid growth of government revenues is also occurring or governments are willing to shift spending priorities, expenditures on education and health are depressed.[24] Again, evidence in support of this can be drawn from Asia. In South Korea, decreasing fertility levels and young dependency rates meant that the government was able to quadruple real per-student educational expenditure between 1970 and 1989, even as it spent an approximately equivalent proportion of its national budget on education. If South Korea's share of school-aged children had grown as fast as Kenya's during the same period, it would have needed to spend more than double what it did.[25]

Finally, population growth threatens resources by placing increased pressure upon them, whether resource use is associated with increased per-capita consumption (i.e., through increasing incomes and demand) or through increasing demand generated by a growing population, even if per-capita demand remains the same. Forest products, fisheries, cropland, and freshwater resources are all vulnerable to human-induced pressures.

Rapid population growth and high fertility seemingly have the greatest negative impact in the poorest countries where national institutions are weak.[26] In these cases, population growth reinforces a downward economic spiral, reflective of several sub-Saharan countries with high fertility rates and lower average per-capita incomes today than two decades ago.[27] Poorly developed markets and/or ineffectual government programs and leadership fail to protect, invest in, or build the basic infrastructure that is needed. Without strong institutions to assist national programs associated with education, fertility and family planning, or infrastructure development, rapid population growth will decrease the supply of ingenuity, exacerbating resource scarcity and environmental degradation. In turn, failure to invest in infrastructure and the degradation of assets can cripple institutions and markets. Moreover, governments in developing countries often lack the financial or political ability to invest in institutions that will promote labor force development.

Population Growth and Resource Scarcity

The debate over the relationship between population growth and resources parallels that over population and economic development, pitting neo-Malthusians against economic optimists, with both groups claiming evidence to support their position. One point seems intuitive: the collective impact of 6.7 billion people on the Earth's ecosystems, measured through resource use, consumption, or pollution, is tremendous. Whether the current rate of resource consumption is sustainable is unknown, but it is suspected that current consumption patterns and human impacts are not sustainable over the long run. Already, many regions are faced with scarcities of cropland, water, and forests.

In his 1999 book, Homer-Dixon identified three sources of resource scarcity: supply-induced, demand-induced, and structural scarcity. Supply-induced scarcities occur when resources are depleted in quantity or have become degraded, perhaps through overexploitation or pollution. Demand-induced scarcity occurs when population growth and changes in consumption patterns boost the demand for a resource. Such scarcities occur only when a resource is rivalrous, meaning that its use by one economic actor reduces its availability for others, with examples including fisheries, water, or forests. Structural scarcity occurs when there is an imbalance in the distribution of the resource or in power and wealth within a society, such that certain groups get a proportionately larger share of the resource. If a resource is excludable (i.e., cropland), such that its use can be restricted or blocked through property rights or other institutions, some groups may be prevented from accessing the resource.

Not surprisingly, population growth is a key factor driving all three types of resource scarcity. Rather than operating independently, each of these sources of scarcity may interact and reinforce one another, either through *resource capture* or *ecological marginalization*.[28] Resource capture occurs when a scarce resource forces actors (i.e., governments or ethnic groups) to assert control over resources through legislation or other means. Poverty, desperation, and a lack of environmental knowledge to protect resources magnify the problem.

Whether the discussion is global or national, it is not just a question of feeding a large population, but also the tasks of providing health care, education, and infrastructure while finding employment and increasing the standard of living over the longer term in a sustainable fashion. Population growth also influences such diverse issues as increased energy consumption, global warming, ozone depletion, deforestation, loss of cropland, loss of biodiversity, and shrinking freshwater resources. Together, the requirements of a growing population may only be met by extracting a huge toll upon limited resources, which may only cripple future sustainability, a situation that is compounded by unequal access to resources and the marginalization of populations.

Population Growth and Food Security

Resource scarcity is closely linked with food security. It is questionable whether some countries, such as China, Egypt, and India, have the resources and economic ability to sustain their populations indefinitely, even if population growth was to cease immediately. Writing for the World Watch Institute in 1995, Lester Brown questioned the ability of China to feed itself in the coming decades.[29] Drawing from the experiences of other Asian countries, Brown forecasted a combination of rising standards of living and movement "up the food chain" from staples to more complex diets including animal proteins. Ultimately, increased food consumption, loss of cropland to urbanization, and declining water resources, among other factors, would mean that China would not be able to feed itself. The inability to domestically grow a sufficient food supply would force China to turn to world markets to purchase the necessary grains and other foodstuffs. The problem lies in its expected demand for grains, which Brown projected to exceed total world output, driving up prices globally and weakening the ability of smaller, poorer countries to purchase their requirements. Climate change may exacerbate food-supply issues by impacting crop production, food security and availability, and crop distribution. With the shifting precipitation patterns and decreased crop yields that are expected with climate change, many developing countries will become increasingly dependent on food imports. At the same time, pressure to cultivate marginal land or use unsustainable cultivation practices may lead to increased land degradation.

Food and resource scarcity is particularly problematic in the developing world, which is heavily reliant upon local resources for day-to-day survival. Already, many developing countries face a bleak future resulting from large-scale demographic, environmental, economic, and societal stresses.[30] The links between food supply and demand are complex,[31] with food supply affected by land and water constraints, lack of investment in agriculture, trade, weather, and lack of access to fertilizer and irrigation. Food demand, on the other hand, is affected by such factors as rising energy prices, population growth, globalization of food markets, changing diets, and the use of cropland for biofuel production. Beginning in 2000, food prices started to rise sharply, with some of the greatest price increases associated with the food crisis of 2007–2008, which saw the price of wheat and corn triple between 2005 and 2008, while rice rose fivefold.[32] Price increases reflected poor crops in parts of the developing world, the rapid increase in food demand, and a decline in the food supply:[33] fuel prices increased, droughts reduced harvests, and cropland was shifted from food to biofuel production. The result: not enough food, with the world's poorest being the most vulnerable. The UN FAO estimated that the escalating food prices increased the number of malnourished by 75 million,[34] with food riots in Haiti, Indonesia, Ivory Coast, Thailand, and other countries.[35] The world recession of 2009 further destabilized countries, with the United Nations estimating that twenty-seven nations were approaching instability with the loss of food security. Food aid from donor countries collapsed as the recession took hold, food prices remained high despite declines in fuel costs, investment in agriculture plummeted, and people in the developing world suddenly had less money to purchase food with as they too lost jobs or remittances from family members working in other countries.

Two broad processes pose concerns for global food security in the future. First, climate change could further jeopardize food crops and security as precipitation patterns are shifted and temperatures increase. The result, if not corrected, could be spreading violence and anarchy, perhaps making the riots of 2008 the opening paragraph for future unrest in the developing world. On its own, climate change is estimated to increase the number of malnourished between 40 and 170 million globally. Even slight increases in temperature are expected to reduce crop yields, particularly in tropical latitudes, including sub-Saharan Africa.[36] Agricultural land may be lost due to decreased precipitation and desertification, reducing food production. Compounding the problem are the generally lower intensity of agriculture and reduced availability of capital for agriculture in the developed world and limited funds to import increasingly expensive staple foods. In Africa, climate change could depress grain production by 2 to 3 percent by 2030,[37] while the UN FAO estimates that India could lose 18 percent of its total grain production. Poor and small-scale subsistence farmers will be especially vulnerable to income or food supply disruptions due to climate change given their limited capacity to adapt to changing climate. Consequently, countries will become more dependent on imported food supplies and/or be forced to cultivate marginal land or use unsustainable cultivation practices, increasing the likelihood of land degradation.

Second, population growth means more mouths to feed. World population is expected to reach seven billion by 2012, and the demand for food is expected to double by 2020, with about 20 percent of this increase attributed to population growth.[38] Compounding the problem are issues of land fragmentation (smaller farms that are not sustainable); the use of marginal lands for agricultural production in many areas of the developing world; increased urbanization, which is associated with the loss of agricultural lands; increased energy costs, which increase the cost of fertilizers and pesticides as well as increasing the demand for biofuels, which results in land shifted from agricultural production to biofuel production; and changes in food consumption practices, including the addition of more meat to traditional diets.

CONCLUSION: THE POTENTIAL FOR CONFLICT?

In his 1994 article "The Coming Anarchy," journalist Robert Kaplan painted a dire prediction of the world's future.[39] Robbed of their economic power by globalization, poor leadership, and environmental decay, peripheral states would disintegrate into smaller units defined by ethnicity or culture and ruled by warlords and private armies. Kaplan held out Africa and its seemingly endless list of war-ravaged countries as symbolizing the decay of the current world order, having already succumbed to environmental and demographic distress, leading to the breakdown of traditional civil government. Kaplan argued that violence and conflict have become the norm in many of these locations.

While perhaps sensationalized, the basic question within Kaplan's article is whether resource scarcity can prompt conflict. A short answer would be yes, with conflict potentially arising from scarcities and disputes over cropland, water, forests, or other resources. As we have seen, these are underlain by population issues. Resource scarcity may lead to harmful social effects, including constrained economic or agricultural production, migration, segmentation of society along ethnic or religious lines, and the disintegration of societal institutions, all of which can lead to conflict.[40] Effects are often causally linked, oftentimes with some feedback measure that tends to reinforce the initial negative consequences, such that resource capture arising from scarcity may induce further environmental degradation or greater scarcity of the resource.

Although the effects of resource scarcity are still poorly understood, there is a strong possibility and a growing body of evidence that they will affect social stability and ultimately underlie conflict, such as the food riots of 2008. While this is an intuitive assumption, questions remain as to what the exact relation-ship is and how it works. How, for example, does resource scarcity contribute to conflict? Most likely, it is through a complex set of interactions. Given that population growth will continue in the coming decades, and that scarcities of renewable resources caused by climate change, depletion, or degradation are relatively certain to occur, it is reasonable to assume that supply, demand, or structural scarcities could result in negative social effects, including reduced agricultural and economic output, migration and displacement, social segmen-tation, and institutional disruption. In turn, each of these could independently or collaboratively induce conflict.[41] In addition, resource scarcity can produce resource capture when actors seek to change the distribution of resources in their favor owing to a decline in the quality or quantity of a resource, leading to the ecological marginalization of weak groups. Both processes further envi-ronmental degradation, reinforce poverty, and increase the potential for con-flict as groups seek to control resources or address imbalances in the distribution of resources.

The not-so-trivial question that both neo-Malthusians and economic opti-mists consider is whether the world can provide sufficient food, water, and other resources in the face of continuing population growth. Intuitively, we can find relationships between population growth, resource use, and environmental scarcity. For example, in regions where population growth is high, resources such as food, fuel, and water are often scarce, and the risk of environmental degradation is increased. But this is not a perfect relationship. In fact, under-standing the linkages between population growth, environment, and resources is sketchy at best.[42] However, even if the most alarmist predictions are dis-counted, there is consensus that population growth slows economic growth and multiplies the damage created by other problems. That is, it is difficult not to conclude that population growth exacerbates land degradation: resource deple-tion promotes violence and conflict and places pressure upon institutions and governments. This is not to say that population growth is solely responsible for these problems. Environmental degradation, for example, is not just a function of the number of people, but how much and what they consume and how that consumption damages the environment. Nevertheless, population growth is an issue.

What of the broader resource and economic issues? Can the same logic be extended to include the impact of a growing population and increasing con-sumption upon other resources? Are current levels of resource consumption sustainable? The emerging consensus is that rapid population growth and high young dependency ratios relative to the size of the labor force reduce economic growth by increasing poverty and underemployment, weakening investment in human and physical assets (i.e., education, institutions, family planning, household savings), and decreasing and degrading resources. Worse, rapid population growth and poor economic growth appear to be self-reinforcing, making it exceedingly difficult for countries to pull themselves out of this downward spiral, given the lack of well-developed institutions in many of the poorest countries.

Finally, the developed world is not immune to the consequences of environmental scarcity, feeling the impact of induced migration from developing countries. Internal conflict or the disintegration of most any country would most likely produce large flows of displaced persons and migrants, potentially reinforcing environmental degradation and social segmentation. Much of the migration from rural Mexico or Haiti into the United States, Chinese immigration into North America, and migrations from North Africa into Europe can be attributed to resource scarcity in a broadly defined way. Many of these undocumented migrants are poor who are leaving behind economically or ecologically marginal areas. With few options in their homelands, they seek a new future elsewhere. For receiving countries, immigration alters the population composition of the country, and immigrants are most likely settling in urban areas. As discussed in chapter 7, governments are forced to react, limiting immigration or quelling anti-immigrant sentiments within the larger society. Similarly, the disintegration or political/economic destabilization of states would surely have implications for regional security and trade patterns, and ultimately the developed world. Countries and their governments may be precluded from effectively negotiating agreements, or may be completely excluded by the international community.

FOCUS: RESOURCE CONFLICT

In the past, national and international conflicts have frequently been predicated upon the territorial ambitions of governments and the concept of a nation-state.[1] In the twenty-first century, the nature of conflict is likely to represent the new realities of resource scarcity and population growth, a potential that is greatest where local institutions are weak, population growth is the greatest, and resources are the scarcest. Consequently, the number of conflicts linked to resource scarcity is likely to increase in the coming decades, with the developing world being at greatest risk. Having greater dependency upon local resources for economic and agricultural production and prosperity, frequently lacking the financial resources to buffer themselves from the negative effects of resource scarcity, and having fragile institutions, they are also less able to adapt.

If the emergence of resource scarcity potentially leads to conflict, what types of conflict are most likely to occur? Homer-Dixon[2] convincingly argued that population or resource scarcity issues will increasingly underlie conflicts in the coming years. In particular, he argued that disputes directly related to environmental degradation, ethnic conflicts due to migration and population displacement caused by environmental scarcities, and civil disorder and conflict caused by environmental scarcity that affects economic productivity and livelihood would be the most common in the developing world, where environmental scarcities would interact with and be contextualized by existing economic, cultural, political, or social factors, perhaps even reinforcing conflict and the decline of institutions.

RESOURCES AND CONFLICT

In their simplest case, resource conflicts are easily understood within the traditional paradigms of territory, power, and interstate relations, as states or other actors have commonly moved to secure nonrenewable resources such as oil. Conflicts related to oil include civil wars in Sudan and Angola and Iraq's invasion of Kuwait in 1990, which was partially based upon Iraq's desire to control major oil fields in the region.[3] With projections that known world oil supplies are likely to peak within the next twenty years, oil is likely to remain the "prize," a resource that is fought over in the coming years.[4]

Resource capture, whereby the decreasing quality or quantity of a resource interacts with population growth and increasing consumption and encourages groups to control a resource through trade or military conquest, can also be extended to renewable resources (i.e., resources that can be harvested and used up to some threshold without threatening their long-term viability) such as cropland, forests, or fresh water.[5] Scarcities of some of these resources are increasing rapidly in places,

leading to their potential seizure through military or other means, marginalizing groups and increasing resource scarcity or degradation.

Water may ultimately prove to be a key resource, critical for the survival of individuals as well as the state. While water is a renewable resource, its increasing scarcity, reduced not only through consumption but degraded through pollution and salinization and further compromised by climate change, threatens the livelihood and security of states, with the shortage defined as "water vulnerability."[6] But rather than directly causing conflict, water scarcity tends to limit economic development, promote resource capture, or lead to social segmentation, which in turn produces violence. Moreover, its transnational character, with rivers or underground aquifers crossing state borders, means that the use and actions of one country affect neighboring states. Various observers, including the United Nations,[7] have not missed the strategic importance of water. In 1995, the World Bank cautioned that wars in the coming century would be fought over water,[8] a statement that echoed a much earlier prediction by Jordan's King Hussein, who declared that only water issues could incite a war between Jordan and Israel. Years earlier, Egypt's former president Anwar Sadat indicated that he was prepared to use force if Ethiopia blocked or reduced Egypt's access to waters from the Nile, while Ethiopia chided Egypt for placing water from the Nile on the negotiating table during peace negotiations between Egypt and Israel in 1976.[9] At other times, water in the Middle East has been described as being more valuable than the oil pumped out of the ground. Still, conflict over scarce water resources is only valid in a limited number of circumstances where the downstream country is dependent on the water and the upstream country restricts its flow. Similarly, conflict is only likely to occur when the water supply is essentially finite (i.e., limited renewal), as it is in many Middle East countries, so that an increasing population means a decreasing per capita supply.

Despite the constraints of downstream and upstream geography, there are multiple examples of water's ability to induce conflict. When water resources and the relationship between states are contextualized by differences in religion and historical animosities, such as between Israel and its Arab neighbors or between Turkey and Syria, the potential for conflict between states is further increased (figure 11F.1). Water resources may have promoted Israel's military campaigns in south Lebanon. When Israel moved to create a security zone to protect its northern boundary, its invasion of southern Lebanon in 1982 placed the waters of the Litani River within Israel's borders for the duration of the occupation, echoing repeated calls dating from as early as 1919 for the Litani River to form the northern border of the Jewish state.[10] Likewise, water has colored relations between Egypt, which is dependent upon the Nile River for fresh water, and its upstream neighbor Ethiopia. Relations between Turkey, Syria, and Iraq have also been strained over control and access to the Euphrates and Tigris rivers, with Turkey's Great Anatolia Project, a massive complex of dams and irrigation systems in east Turkey, promising to significantly reduce the flow of the Euphrates when it is completed. What water does reach Syria will be contaminated with runoff laden with fertilizer, pesticides, and salts. Syria is already short of water, and its population growth (2.5 percent, doubling in approximately thirty years) complicates its need for water. Although Syria is weak relative to Turkey and therefore does not pose a likely military threat as a provoked downstream neighbor, these two countries have already exchanged threats over water resources. Syria has also allegedly sanctioned Kurdish guerillas fighting the Turkish government over control of eastern Turkey for the creation of a Kurdish state, the same area as the Great Anatolia Project.[11]

Elsewhere, water has been linked to conflict. In Africa, South Africa's support of a coup in Lesotho in 1986 has been linked to its desire to divert water out of Lesotho and into South Africa.[12] Also in Africa, the Senegal, Zambezi, and Niger rivers all flow through several countries, with the Senegal River the focus of conflict between Mauritania and Senegal. In the Lake Chad basin in North Africa, geophysicists have warned of the shrinkage of Lake Chad.[13] Since the 1960s, it has shrunk by 95 percent, with irrigation and drought the major causes. The loss of water in a region with a growing population of over 750,000, even as the diminished water supply threatens fish stocks and crops, could result in increased tensions between the four countries (Nigeria, Niger, Cameroon, and Chad) that utilize the lake's water. Finally, there are disputes over water rights in the former Soviet republics of Uzbekistan, Turkmenistan, Kazakhstan, Tajikistan, and Kyrgyzstan, which compete for the limited resources of the Amu and Syr rivers. Under the former Soviet Union, the government dammed and diverted the rivers, turning what was literally an arid desert into a huge cotton-growing region.[14] Since the end of the Soviet Union, competing rivalries between the five countries, capitalism, and waste have all but destroyed the system, leading to water shortages and increasing salinization of cropland, while the Aral Sea is literally choked of waters that might replenish it.

CONCLUSIONS

The combined effects of population growth and resulting resource scarcity may mean

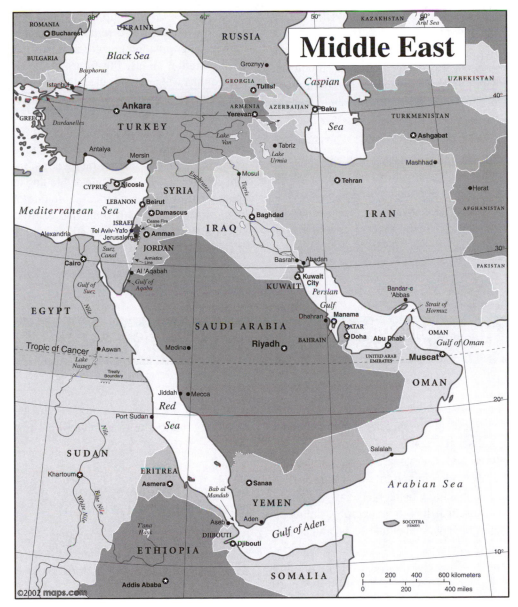

Figure 11F.1 Israel and Neighboring States.

Source: Maps.com.

that the world will witness an increase in conflict at various spatial scales, which may be underlain by issues pertaining to resource scarcity and population growth. Moreover, the speed and regularity with which resource conflicts will occur will in-crease in the future as resources become increasingly scarce and as populations grow. Developing countries dependent upon local resources but lacking the ability to mitigate scarcities are likely to be affected sooner, facing more regular, more complex, and more severe problems arising from environmental scarcities. If they do not have the abilities, measured by ingenuity or finances, to overcome these problems, scarcities can overwhelm the country and further erode its ability to overcome the scarcity.

While large-scale conflict is possible, environmental scarcity will generate chronic, diffuse violence, with conflicts increasingly at local or subnational scales. As a consequence of globalization, governments may be helpless in the face of environmental stress, escalating poverty and disease and social friction. For peripheral countries, which are already faced with few economic prospects, population growth, disease, and environmental stress, the future is bleak, and conflict will undoubtedly arise between groups over access to scarce resources. Weakened by globalization that has tended to bypass many of the poorest countries and the increased power of warlords, crime gangs, drug cartels, or guerrilla groups, future conflict may be "borderless," failing to conform to existing notions of interstate or intrastate conflict, with influence exerted not by a state, but instead by ethnic groups or clans.[15]

METHODS, MEASURES, AND TOOLS: WHAT HAVE GEOGRAPHERS CONTRIBUTED TO THE DEBATE?

Throughout the book, geography and the geographical perspective have underlain the discussion. In many instances, geographers and the geographical perspective have made important contributions in areas, including market location and analysis, medical/health geography, land-use planning, environmental issues, and analytical techniques commonly used by geographers. The contributions of population geographers have been noted in the introduction and throughout the book, particularly those contributions related to population mobility, while geographers have spent less time working with mortality and fertility. Geographers have also contributed to debates, including climate change (i.e., through the Intergovernmental Panel on Climate Change [IPCC]), water and other resources, food supply and security, international relations, and terrorism. While far from exhaustive, the following represents a sampling of the contributions made by geographers that relate to themes within this book.[1]

POLITICAL GEOGRAPHY AND INTERNATIONAL RELATIONS

Harm de Blij argues in his book *Why Geography Matters: Three Challenges Facing America*[2] that "geographic literacy is a matter of national security" and that

> Geographic knowledge constitutes a serious, perhaps critical, disadvantage in an increasingly competitive world. Geographic insights can be crucial in addressing geopolitical problems; they are needed also in decision making in spheres ranging from the cultural to economic.[3]

It's not surprising that geographers have long engaged such debates, given the inherently geographical nature of many of the problems identified by de Blij and others. Both Poulson (1995)[4] and Glassner (1996)[5] provide an overview of political geography and international relations. Some twenty geographers explored various issues, including socialism, capitalism, and problems of population growth and international migration, in *The Geographies of Global Change*.[6] Other geographers, including Cutter, Richardson, and Wilbanks (2003),[7] have explored the links between geography and terrorism, using geographical tools to prevent and prepare for terrorist attacks while also considering how terrorists mobilize across space and why terrorism develops in particular locations. Stump (2000)[8] explored religious fundamentalism as a phenomenon that has spread rapidly in recent decades, along with the social and cultural implications for societies.

POPULATION HEALTH AND HEALTH GEOGRAPHY

Population health has not escaped the interest of geographers, with work by Gatrell and Elliott[9] and Meade et al.[10] Spatial diffusion of disease is closely linked with epidemiology and has formed a cornerstone of work in this area. Later, the role of place was increasingly recognized. Work by Kearns and Gesler (1998),[11] for example, developed the importance of place as a determinant of health, an idea that now underpins much of the work in the subdiscipline, including work by Williams and Eyles.[12] Likewise, geographers, including authors such as Gould (1993)[13] and Kalipeni and Oppong (1996),[14] have made important contributions to the HIV/AIDS discussion and the understanding of the patterns of disease transmission. Advances in visualization tools and methods, particularly GIS and spatial analysis, have contributed to

this area, but the use of qualitative methods demonstrates the nuances of health geographies.[15]

RESOURCE ISSUES

Resource production and use raises multiple issues, including those related to conflict, sustainability, location, and climate change. As such, research in this area often cuts across geographical dimensions, incorporating physical, human, and environmental branches of the field. A large body of geographical work has built around land and resource use, including water resources, which intersect both physical and human geography. Insight and solutions require knowledge of the hydrologic cycle as well as the relationship between human impacts and the cycle. Amery and Wolf (2000), for instance, have discussed Middle East water resources and links to conflict.[16] Discussion of water resources at other geographic scales, including within the United States, is also of importance and interest, including water laws and groundwater depletion, water rights, and water management, particularly in the Great Plains.[17] The relationship between population growth and energy use, and its relationship to global climate change, has also attracted the attention of geographers, including that of physical geographers and earth scientists.

AGRICULTURE AND FOOD SUPPLY

A dominating issue throughout the geographic (and other) literature is that of the relationship between population and food supply. Food production might continue to grow faster than the population, and the world will likely be able to feed a much larger population, but the question is how many can the world really feed? It may yet have difficulty feeding its population. Not surprisingly, much of the recent geographical work has also focused on population growth and transformation of agriculture, land tenure, resource conflict, and environmental issues. Turner et al. (1993),[18] for instance, explored the relationship between population growth and agricultural transformation in Africa, concluding that while population growth has spurred change, it also reflects differences in the environment, land tenure systems, technology, and politics. Another geographer, Vaclav Smil, has explored the ability to feed the world's population. Based on data from the mid-1990s, he concluded that there was more than enough food to feed the world's population based on a daily caloric intake equivalent to that of the average North American. However, Smil also cautioned that the carrying capacity of the earth had already been exceeded, if all six billion were fed a diet similar to that of an average American, particularly given the emphasis on meat proteins in the average American diet.[19] Fortunately, many in the developed world tend to be overfed, the Western diet is wasteful, and there are global inefficiencies in the way food is produced, distributed, and consumed. By correcting these inefficiencies and altering the diet, for example by decreasing or removing animal proteins (which tend to be less efficient users of agricultural resources), Smil estimated that a population of 8.4 billion could be supported, with no new land required for cultivation and no new technologies that dramatically increase agricultural output. Increasing the daily caloric intake would reduce the final population size the earth could support.

THEORY

A discussion of the contributions to the field of population geography would not be complete without recognizing the role of theory. For much of its history, population geography has been rooted in positivistic frameworks and emphasized data and methods, reflecting the impact of formal demography on the field. Empirical work and data have dominated theory formation, meaning that research, and consequently theoretical advances, has tended to concentrate in data-rich areas, with the implication that theory formation has been disadvantaged.

Recent discussions have, however, attempted to move the theoretical basis of population geography, so that it has, for example, engaged social geography, as witnessed by authors including Graham and Bailey, Halfacree, and Boyle.[20] Critical population geography, such as Tyner's 2009 "War, Violence, and Population: Making the Body Count,"[21] will also influence the field of population geography and influence future work. Moreover, the book connects fertility, migration, and mortality with war and conflict.

Conclusion

Doing Population Geography

A S OF 2009, world population was approximately 6.8 billion and continued to grow at a rate of 1.2 percent. Theoretically, this allows the world's population to double in slightly more than fifty years, meaning that the world's demographic situation remains critical by almost any measure. This book has sought to provide an overview of population geography tools and methods by exploring the major demographic issues that the world now faces. It has discussed current knowledge and emerging themes and issues and how they are interrelated: how population affects resources and environmental degradation, how population growth may be related to conflict, the implications of low fertility and an aging society, the impact of HIV/AIDS, and relationships between fertility and population change. But it is also unlikely that anyone will commonly use the techniques discussed here, at least immediately. Instead, most will wait until they enter the labor force to apply some of the knowledge learned here. Even then, it is unlikely that you will be employed as a "population geographer" and hired just because of your knowledge of population techniques.

So, where (and how) can the tools of population geography be applied? That is, how do you "do" population geography? Perhaps the most immediate way is through knowledge of population issues. While this may sound somewhat self-serving, it is important for individuals to know how population interfaces with issues, including resource use, conflict, climate change, and general population dynamics. In essence, you have become informed consumers of population knowledge and better able to participate in conversations relating to population. Domestically, issues such as population aging and immigration will continue to mold political discussions including social security, education, and training, and it is important to have a grasp of some of the basic demographic foundations of these issues.

Rather than being hired as a "population geographer" following graduation, it is more than likely that you will be hired in business, local government, education, or some related field. In fact, it is probably extremely rare to see a job ad that screams "Wanted: One Population Geographer!" But, as a population geographer, you would bring two important qualities to the table. First, you bring your knowledge of population issues and their relationships with related disciplines, including economics, finance, marketing, and policy. Second, your geographic background would enable analysis of problems from a geographic perspective, recognizing the importance of space and geographic relationships.

Population geography also meshes with social and cultural geography, transportation studies, economic geography, and health geography, along with other studies and disciplines. It is, for example, difficult to look at the changing social geography of our cities without considering the population trends that are at work in transforming them. Are, for example, immigrants moving in? Are the native-born staying or moving on? What are the settlement patterns and fertility practices of new immigrants? Do some areas of a city have, on average, older populations, which mean that services may need to be aligned differently than in areas with a comparatively young population? Clearly, such questions also impinge on the economic and political functioning of the city. The following discusses a few of the "real-world" applications using the basics of population geography.

MARKETING

Perhaps one of the most interesting and influential uses of population information is found in marketing, where knowledge of population structures is more than just useful: it could mean the success or failure of a product line or company. For example, the successful pitch of a new product or service that is geared toward teenagers would not find traction in a retirement community. That is, knowledge of population structure, including its sociodemographic and socioeconomic composition, allows companies to target their products toward those most likely to purchase them. Similarly, segmentation of a market refers to the packaging or promotion of a product directly toward specific groups, including the use of advertising or products in particular languages (i.e., Spanish for a Hispanic population).

Marketing of goods and services through population targeting and market segmentation could be accomplished with basic demographic and economic data available from the US Census Bureau and related sources, such as the Bureau of Labor Statistics or the *Statistical Abstract of the United States* (with most of these resources available through the Internet). Information on population descriptors such as age, births, gender, race or ethnic status, and income enable targeting of products given that individuals have different needs and taste across these dimensions. Small-scale information, including at the scale of the neighborhood, provides more fine-grained analysis of the local population, although such information is not often freely available and must be purchased.

A widely used demographic tool is Potential Rating Index for Zip Markets (PRIZM) (Claritas Corporation), a tool which divides the nation based on shared demographic traits, lifestyle preferences, and consumer behaviors.[1] That is, it works from the principle that people with similar lifestyles tend to live near each other. PRIZM divides the country up into sixty-six lifestyle groups (based on 2008 segmentation), describing each neighborhood in the United States to enable marketing to specific groups. For example, a component of the well-known 90210 zip code (Beverly Hills, CA) includes the "blue blood estates." This segment is described as older, wealthy families with children living in multimillion-dollar homes with manicured lawns. Many of those living here hold advanced professional degrees or are in management and have a median household income (2008) of $119,475, representing some of the wealthiest of US households. Other neighborhoods in the same 90210 zip code include "money and brains," "movers and shakers," and the "young digerati." Elsewhere in the nation, neighborhoods may be characterized as "Asian affluence" or "tools and trucks."

POPULATION PROJECTIONS: HEALTH CARE, EDUCATION, AND TRANSPORTATION

Earlier on, the "Methods, Measures, and Tools" discussion in chapter 1 focused on population projection techniques. Increasingly, such tools are found in a variety of applications. Marketers may want, for example, to know what the demographics of an area will be like ten, twenty, or thirty years down the road, so that companies can start planning for changing demographics. Similarly, financial planners may want to know the age and gender structure of future populations, with the corresponding implications for savings rates and consumption of goods and services. Population projections are also required in education and health care planning. How, for instance, can health care planners decide on the location of a new hospital or clinic? How can educators and boards of education respond to local demographic change? Can they close or open new schools? Where do they locate new schools? How are new schools to be paid for?

Regardless of perspective or background, the key issue turns on population structure and aging. Aging populations, for example, mean greater demand on health care facilities and greater time spent in care, while the overall number of students engaged in school decreases. Likewise, older populations will have different marketing and financial needs than younger ones. But, while population aging is a national phenomenon, not all areas or neighborhoods will experience population aging and decline. Instead, population aging and growth will be irregular over local areas, with new suburban areas concentrating growth and older areas more likely to be associated with older populations.

In all cases, the key questions are therefore based on knowledge of the underlying demographic structure and its future dimensions. Clearly, school board planners do not want to spend large amounts of money to build a new school in an area that cannot support its current or future use. Consequently, school boards will use projections and surveys to see where population growth is occurring to derive enrollment projections. Faced with a smaller cohort of young, college/university administrators have looked to university participation rates and population change to highlight if particular groups or regions are underrepresented in the nation's postsecondary education system. Likewise, the health care industry is unlikely to invest in new maternity facilities in locations with aging populations and low birth rates, while urban and transportation planners may need to project the population to evaluate future transportation and housing scenarios.

Population projection therefore offers a way to look into the future, enabling urban planners and others to make informed decisions about their future plans. For instance, as part of the Places to Grow legislation (chapter 9, "Focus"), local municipalities were required by the Ontario provincial government to project their urban populations under different planning assumptions, such as increased population density at particular locations in the city. In another case, concerns with aging populations have led to the analysis of what aging populations mean for transportation sustainability. Recent research provides evidence suggesting that as people age they become more dependent on the automobile.[2] This suggests that in the coming decades there will be a significant increase in both the number and the percentage of older drivers in urban areas. Despite these observations, the relationship between the aging population and the sustainability of the transportation system has not been fully addressed.

As part of a large project looking at the relationship between population aging and transportation needs in Hamilton, Ontario, Canada, the future age structure and distribution of Hamilton's population at the census tract scale needed to be modeled.[3] For example, given internal migration in and out of a metropolitan area, population aging, and declining births, where would the old be concentrated in the future, and what would the relationship to services and transportation look like? The authors proposed a demographic model based on the Rogers model, but applied it to small areas (census tracts) by adjusting migration data that was typically available only at more aggregate levels. While not all population projection models are as complex as this was, they will become increasingly valuable as the need for small-area data increases.

POLITICAL PLANNING

Another demonstration of the use of population geography lies in political planning. As noted earlier, the US Census is used to determine how membership in the House of Representatives (and state legislatures) should be apportioned (i.e., the number of representatives each state has). Both US congressional and state legislative districts must be drawn so residents have fair representation, necessitating geographically detailed data.[4] The need for careful analysis is even greater in the age of the Internet: beginning with reapportionment after the 1990 census, individuals participated in the discussion like never before, with the availability of demographic data giving individuals and groups the opportunity to comment on reapportionment and to present their own plans.

CONCLUSION

Aspects of population geography and demography also underlie broad, lay-based discussions. In Canada, David Foot's 1996 book *Boom, Bust, and Echo: How to Profit from the Coming Demographic Shift*[5] grounded the discussion of Canada's changing demographics and what they would mean for such things as finance, property values, marketing, and urban planning. More recently, Richard Florida linked population trends, and specifically human capital (as a measure of the level of education or creativity in a population),[6] with city growth and economic performance. Underlying many of his assumptions and work was that migration flows underlie variations in human capital across geographic space, although the impact of internal migration is tempered by the role of international migration and a city's ability to generate human capital amongst its own population, all of which vary by geographic scale.[7] In the Canadian context, immigration was a key supplier of new human capital for the largest metropolitan areas, while domestic migration was much more important at the local scale.

The point of this discussion is that knowledge of population geography underlies so many of the debates and policies in today's world. Moreover, the rapidly increasing availability of population and geographic data in the United States and in other countries, along with the computational abilities and analytical techniques to work with the data, has meant an explosion in the area of population geography or more formal demography. Businesses, governments, educators, and nongovernment organizations all put population to work so that they can better understand current and future trends.

Glossary of Key Terms and Acronyms

age pyramid: Representation of a population distributed by age and sex.

aging: An increase in the proportion of population in older age groups.

AIDS: Acquired immunodeficiency syndrome.

alien: A person resident in a country who has not acquired citizenship by naturalization.

antinatalist: Positions or policies that discourage fertility and childbearing. Disincentives may include reduced child benefits or other, more repressive options.

antiretroviral drugs: The class of drugs that are used to suppress the HIV virus, inhibiting the development of HIV into AIDS. Also know as the "triple cocktail."

assimilation: The economic, social, cultural, and political processes of adjustment undergone by immigrants, transforming them into citizens of the host country.

asylees: Individuals forced out of their country of origin and seeking refuge in the new country in which they are living.

asylum: The act of seeking refuge and protection within a country.

baby boom: The rise in birth rates in many Western countries between 1946 and 1964.

bracero: Mexicans who were admitted legally into the United States for labor between 1942 and 1964.

BSI: Border Safety Initiative. Run by the Border Patrol to educate would-be illegal entrants of the dangers of crossing the border and to provide medical assistance if needed.

carrying capacity: The maximum number of organisms that can be theoretically supported in a habitat for an indefinite period of time; dependent upon the social, economic, political, and natural systems as well as upon the level of consumption.

CIC: Citizenship and Immigration Canada.

cohort: A group of individuals born in the same calendar year or group of years.

counterurbanization: The shift in net migration flows away from large metropolitan centers toward nonmetropolitan areas.

demographic transition (DTT): Process whereby a country moves from high to low mortality and fertility rates, accompanied by rapid population growth.

dependency ratio: The ratio of people of dependent rate (zero to fourteen, sixty-five-plus) to the economically active population (fifteen to sixty-four). The young dependency ratio is the ratio of those aged zero to fourteen to those in the labor force, and is usually associated with rapid population growth.

developed world: Following UN classification, the developed world includes Europe, North America, Australia, Japan, and New Zealand.

developing world: All countries and regions outside the developed world.

doubling time: The number of years it will take the population to double assuming a constant rate of natural increase.

ecological footprint: A measure of environmental sustainability, based upon past and present demands of the earth's natural resources.

ecological marginalization: The forced movement of individuals or groups into ecologically marginal areas.

economic optimists: Individuals who believe that population growth stimulates economic development.

emigrant: A person who leaves one country to settle in another.

epidemiological transition: Shifts in health and disease patterns as mortality moves from high to low rates.

FAO: United Nations Food and Agricultural Organization.

fecundity: The physiological ability of individuals to have children.

fertility: The ability to reproduce.

fertility transition: The shift from high to low fertility.

green revolution: The improvement in agricultural productivity in the 1940s and 1950s associated with new high-yield crop strains, fertilizer, irrigation, and pesticide use.

gross domestic product (GDP): The total value of goods and services produced by a country, not including international trade.

HIV: Human immunodeficiency virus, the virus that causes AIDS.

illegal migrants: Individuals entering a country without proper documentation or approval.

immigrant: A person who moves into a country where she or he is not a native to take up residence.

immigration gap: The differential between states' immigration policy and their outcomes.

infant mortality rate (IMR): Annual number of deaths of infants under one year of age per one thousand live births.

INS: US Immigration and Naturalization Service.

interdiction: The policy of stopping would-be refugee or asylee claimants before they enter a country and initiate the refugee claim process.

internally displaced persons (IDPs): Individuals or groups forced to flee homes to escape armed conflict, violence, human rights abuses, or disaster. Unlike refugees, they are not residing outside their country of nationality.

IRB: Immigration Review Board (Canada).

IRCA: Immigration Reform and Control Act (1986).

least developed countries: Defined by the United Nations, those countries where per-capita income is less than $900 (US) per year.

life expectancy: The average number of years beyond age x an individual can expect to live under current mortality levels. Usually expressed as life expectancy at birth.

lifespan: The longest period over which a person may live.

logical positivism: A school of philosophy that combines rationalism based on mathematical and logical constructs with empiricism (the idea that observational evidence is indispensable for knowledge of the world).

Malthusian: References the writings of Malthus, who believed that population grows geometrically but food supplies grow linearly, resulting in an inadequate food supply and population decline through famine, disease, or war (positive checks).

Marxist: Adherent to the theories of Karl Marx.

Maquiladoras: Assembly plants employing Mexicans where parts are shipped to Mexico, assembled, and then re-exported for sale, allowing companies to benefit from the cheaper labor.

megacity: A city with a population over ten million.

morbidity: Sickness.

mortality (death) rate: The annual number of deaths per one thousand people. This rate is not age standardized to account for differential death rates across age groups.

natural increase: The birth rate minus the death rate, indicating the annual rate of population growth (without migration) expressed as a percentage.

neo-Malthusian: An individual who accepts Malthusian principles, but who believes birth control methods can be used to reduce population growth.

nonrefoulement: The basic tenet of United Nations Refugee Convention that prohibits states from returning refugees against their will to their origin.

nonrenewable resources: Finite resources, such as oil or minerals.

over-stayers: Individuals who enter a country legally, but who remain in the country after their permission to do so expires.

population explosion: The rapid growth of the world's population.

population momentum: The potential for population growth that is present within the age/sex structure of a population, even if fertility rates were to drop to replacement level.

prevalence: The number of people in a population sick with a disease at a particular time, regardless of when the illness began.

pronatalist: Policies that favor a high birth rate. May include tax incentives, cash bonuses for number of children born in excess of the first, day-care provision, or parental leaves.

Proposition 187: Legislation in California meant to limit access to education and health services among illegal immigrants, passed by a majority in 1994 but ruled unconstitutional by a federal judge.

quota system: US immigration policy that imposed quotas on the number of immigrants based upon a defined base (northern European) population.

refugees: Individuals or groups who, owing to well-founded fear of being persecuted for reasons of race, religion, nationality, membership in a particular group, or political opinion, are outside the country of nationality and are unable or unwilling to return.

renewable resource: Resources such as water, cropland, or forests that can be used indefinitely, provided a threshold of sustainability is not exceeded.

replacement fertility level: The fertility rate (2.1) that is required to exactly replace a generation, accounting for death before completion of childbearing years.

resource capture: Control of a scarce resource through the use of legislation or other means.

rivalrous resources: Resources that are used by one or more actors, which reduce their availability for others.

social segmentation: The division of society, typically along class, ethnic, or religious lines.

STDs: Sexually transmitted diseases, including syphilis, gonorrhea, or HIV.

sustainable development: The level of human activity that meets the needs of the present without compromising the ability of future generations to meet their own needs, subject to constraints.

TFR: Total fertility rate. The average number of children a woman would have assuming that current age-specific birth rates remain constant through the childbearing years (ages fifteen to forty-nine).

transmigrant: Refers to the relocation of individuals from one area to another. Typically refers to the relocation of Indonesians out of Java to other regions or Russians to other republics or satellite states.

UNAIDS: United Nations program on HIV/AIDS.

UNHCR: United Nations High Commissioner on Refugees.

UNICEF: United Nations Children's Fund.

urban: Describes a concentration of people in space whose livelihoods are organized around nonagricultural activities. Different countries will define the urban threshold differently.

USAID: United States Agency for International Development.

USCRI: United States Committee for Refugees and Immigrants.

WHO: World Health Organization.

ZPG: zero population growth. The situation in which the population does not change in size from year to year.

Population Websites

Websites are current as of August 2009. Note that websites are not necessarily permanent, so the correct address cannot be guaranteed.

GENERAL

www.population.com
Population provides world news related to demography.

www.iom.int
The International Organization for Migration (IOM) is an intergovernmental organization that promotes migration for economic development, the understanding of migration issues, and humanitarian programs to assist refugees and displaced persons. Among its publications, IOM publishes *International Migration*, a quarterly peer-reviewed journal.

www.cis.org
The Center for Immigration Studies (CIS) is a nonprofit organization devoted to research on and policy analysis of immigration. Site includes recent numbers, background reports, and news, reflecting a diversity of issues and opinions.

www.populationinstitute.org
The Population Institute provides information about population issues and promotes programs to reduce population growth.

www.populationconnection.org
Population Connection is an organization that has actively promoted a reduction in population growth. Website includes many topical links and information as well.

www.npg.org
Negative Population Growth (NPG) is an organization that educates the American public on the dangers of population growth. The website provides alternate

perspectives to population issues, advocating a smaller US population and reduced immigration levels in order to create a sustainable future. The site provides links to like-minded organizations, such as Californians for a Sustainable Population, along with mainstream agencies or groups such as the US Citizenship and Immigration Services (USCIS).

www.refugees.org
The United States Committee for Refugees is a private organization that helps refugees. The site includes information on refugees and asylees throughout the world.

www.acf.hhs.gov/programs/orr/
This is the website of the US Office of Refugee Resettlement (ORR), providing information on refugee legislation and resettlement within the United States.

www.popcouncil.org
The Population Council is an international, nonprofit organization devoted to biomedical, social science, and public health research related to population issues.

www.psi.org
Population Services International, a nonprofit organization, seeks to increase the availability of health and population control products/services in low-income areas of the world.

SOURCES OF DEMOGRAPHIC STATISTICS

www.world-gazetteer.com
World Gazetteer provides population statistics for cities, towns, and places, along with related data.

www.aecf.org
The Annie E. Casey Foundation has worked to promote opportunities for and the environments of children and families in the United States. The website includes demographic data on children within the United States.

www.prb.org
This is the website for the Population Reference Bureau (PRB). It is a very useful site for both lay and academic interests in population issues, including data, information, publications, and other services relating to the United States and the world.

www.ciesin.org
The Center for International Earth Science Information Network (CIESIN) at Columbia University is a nonprofit, nongovernmental organization. The website includes detailed demographic information, including interactive mapping from the US Census Bureau, census data, and other data sources, including environmental information and social indicators of development.

www.census.gov
The home page for the US Census Bureau. It includes information on the 2000 census and downloadable information and data on the United States at a variety of spatial scales. It also contains links to international statistical agencies, such as Mexico, the United Kingdom, or Germany.

www.census.gov/ipc/www/idb/
The International Data Base (IDB) section of the US Census Bureau is particularly useful for demographic and socioeconomic data on other countries.

www.statcan.ca/start.html
This is the Statistics Canada home page. The site is available in both French and English, with information and data that are downloadable.

www.cic.gc.ca
Citizenship and Immigration Canada (CIC) maintains information on immigrant and refugee arrivals in Canada, along with current policy information and some historical records.

www.dhs.gov/index.shtm
The US Department of Homeland Security (DHS) website includes links to Border Patrol and Management, and recent statistics on the origin of immigrants, immigrant class, and the settlement of arrivals, including the immigration yearbook.

www.usaid.gov
The United States Agency for International Development (USAID) website includes information on current programs, missions, and statistics.

www.cdc.gov
The Centers for Disease Control and Prevention (CDC) is the lead federal agency for prevention of disease and promotion of health. The site includes information on health topics and statistics for the United States and the world.

www.cdc.gov/nchs

The CDC provides links to the National Center for Health Statistics (NCHS), which includes vital statistics, including data on births, deaths, and marriages. Links to state health units are provided.

www.worldbank.org

The World Bank has a large amount of comparative world data, including population.

UNITED NATIONS

www.unaids.org

This website is operated by the United Nations and other health groups. It contains up-to-date information on the HIV/AIDS epidemic and links to other sources.

www.who.int

The home page for the World Health Organization (WHO), which monitors world health. Includes updates on world health and health initiatives, and the WHO Statistical Information System (WHOSIS) provides access to the latest world health data.

www.unhcr.ch

Website for the United Nations High Commissioner on Refugees. Includes publications and up-to-date statistics.

www.un.org/unrwa/

This is the home page of the UN Relief and Works Agency for Palestine Refugees in the Near East.

www.unicef.org

United Nations Children's Fund website. Includes resources and statistics related to children's health.

www.undp.org

The United Nations Population Information Network coordinates population information activities at a variety of scales. Resources include links to other sites as well as an electronic library.

www.un.org/esa/population/

The United Nations runs its own population division, responsible for providing current data on population and development.

www.unfpa.org
The United Nations Population Fund helps developing countries with population issues. The UNFPA website includes information on recent programs.

www.fao.org
The Food and Agricultural Organization of the United Nations website includes information and statistics relating to nutrition, food, forestry, fisheries, and agriculture.

BIBLIOGRAPHIC DATABASES

http://canada.metropolis.net
This is the website for the Canadian Metropolis project, linking researchers who focus on immigration issues at institutions across Canada and throughout the world. The site has a digital library of papers produced by its associates, many of which are downloadable free of charge.

http://db.jhuccp.org/popinform/basic.html
Billed as the world's largest online bibliographic database on population issues, POPLINE is based at Johns Hopkins University.

ACADEMIC SITES

www.ccis-ucsd.org
The Center for Comparative Immigration Studies at the University of California, San Diego includes information on programs and research areas and links to other sites.

www.cpc.unc.edu
The Carolina Population Center is a community of scholars and professionals collaborating on interdisciplinary research and methods.

www.psc.isr.umich.edu
The Population Studies Center at the University of Michigan focuses on both domestic and international population issues.

www.iussp.org
The International Union for Scientific Study in Population promotes scientific studies of demography and population-related issues.

www.uu.nl/uupublish/onderzoek/onderzoekcentra/ercomer/24638main.html
The European Research Center on Migration and Ethnic Relations (ERCOMER) is a European research center that focuses upon comparative migration analysis, ethnic relations, and ethnic conflict, based at the Utrecht University in the Netherlands.

opr.princeton.edu/archive/
The Office of Population Research websites offer links to demographic centers throughout the world, as well as links to other statistical resources and organizations.

www.popassoc.org
The Population Association of America is a society of professionals working in the population field. Links include publications.

SELECTED JOURNALS

Demography (the official journal of the Population Association of America)
www.popassoc.org/i4a/pages/index.cfm?pageid=3576

European Journal of Population
www.springer.com/social+sciences/population+studies/journal/10680

Journal of Population Research
www.springer.com/social+sciences/population+studies/journal/12546

Immigrants and Minorities
www.tandf.co.uk/journals/titles/02619288.asp

International Journal of Family Planning Perspectives
www.globalhealth.org/sources/view.php3?id=1105

International Migration Review
www.wiley.com/bw/journal.asp?ref=0197-9183

Journal of Ethnic and Migration Studies
www.tandf.co.uk/journals/carfax/1369183X.html

Population and Environment
www.springer.com/social+sciences/population+studies/journal/11111

Population Bulletin
www.prb.org

Population Development Review
www.wiley.com/bw/journal.asp?ref=0098-7921

Population Research and Policy Review
www.springer.com/social+sciences/population+studies/journal/11113

Population, Space, and Place
www3.interscience.wiley.com/journal/106562735/home?CRETRY=1&
SRETRY=0

Population Studies
www.lse.ac.uk/collections/PIC/populationStudies/

The Professional Geographer
Although not a population geography journal per se, it often carries population
papers.
www.aag.org

Studies in Family Planning
www.popcouncil.org/publications/sfp/default.htm

Notes

POPULATION GEOGRAPHY: AN INTRODUCTION

1. *World Population Data Sheet* (Washington DC: Population Reference Bureau, 2009), www.prb.org. Unless otherwise noted, population statistics throughout this text are drawn from this source.

2. Following UN classification, the developed world includes Europe, North America, Australia, Japan, and New Zealand. The developing world includes all countries and regions outside the developed world.

3. Kathleen Newland, "Refugees: The New International Politics of Displacement," in *Perspectives on Population*, ed. Scott W. Menard and Elizabeth W. Moen (New York: Oxford University Press, 1987), 314–21.

4. See the United Nations High Commissioner on Refugees website, www.unhcr.org (accessed 31 October 2008).

5. Of course, people were doing "population geography" well before this time, and the field of demography has also existed for a much longer time period.

6. Patricia Gober and James A. Tyner. "Population Geography," in *Geography in America at the Dawn of the Twenty-First Century*, ed. Gary L. Gaile and Cort J. Willmott (Oxford: Oxford University Press, 2005), 185–99.

7. The AAG (www.aag.org) is the national academic organization of geographers. This group holds annual meetings and publishes the *Annals of the AAG* and *The Professional Geographer*. The Population Specialty Group sits within the AAG and is a group of researchers interested in population studies. Trewartha's text is reprinted in Glen T. Trewartha, "A Case for Population Geography," *Annals of the Association of American Geographers* 43 (1953): 71–97.

8. David A. Plane, "The Post-Trewartha Boom: The Rise of Demographics and Applied Population Geography," *Population, Space, and Place* 10 (2004): 285–88.

9. Wilbur Zelinsky, *A Prologue to Population Geography* (Englewood Cliffs, NJ: Prentice-Hall, 1966).

10. Peter E. Ogden, "Population Geography," *Progress in Human Geography* 22, no 1 (1998): 352–54.

11. Gober and Tyner, "Population Geography."

12. Curtis Roseman, Hans-Dieter Laux, and Gunter Thieme, eds., *EthniCity* (London: Rowman & Littlefield, 1996).

13. Kavita Pandit and Suzanne Davies-Withers, eds., *Migration and Restructuring in the US: A Geographic Perspective* (Boulder, CO: Rowman & Littlefield, 1999).

14. K. Bruce Newbold and John Spindler, "Immigrant Settlement in Metropolitan

Chicago," *Urban Studies* 38, no. 11 (2001): 1903–19; K. Bruce Newbold, "Spatial Distribution and Redistribution of the Foreign-Born in the US: 1980 and 1990," *Economic Geography* 75, no. 3 (1999): 254–71; Kevin McHugh, Emily Skop, and Ines Miyares, "The Magnetism of Miami: Segmented Paths in Cuban Migration," *Geographical Review* 897 (1997): 504–19; Wei Li, *Ethnoburb: the New Ethnic Community in Urban America* (Honolulu: University of Hawaii Press, forthcoming).

15. James P. Allen and Eugene Turner, "Spatial Patterns of Immigrant Assimilation," *The Professional Geographer* 48, no. 2 (1996): 140–55.

16. Ellen Percy Kraly, "Emigration: Implications for US Immigration Policy Research," in *Mexico/US Migration Patterns, Research Papers*, ed. E. Loaza and S. Martin (Washington DC: Commission on Immigration Reform, 1997), 105–19; Kevin McHugh and Richard Mings, "The Circle of Migration: Attachment to Place in Aging," *Annals of the Association of American Geographers* 86 (1996): 530–50.

17. D. H. Kaplan, "The Creation of an Ethnic Economy: Indochinese Business Expansion in Saint Paul," *Economic Geography* 73, no. 2 (1997): 214–33; Thomas D. Boswell, "Racial and Ethnic Segregation Patterns in Metropolitan Miami, Florida, 1980–1999," *Southeastern Geographer* 33, no. 1 (1993): 82–109.

18. David Ley, "Transnationalism," in *International Encyclopedia of Human Geography*, ed. Rob Kitchin and Nigel Thrift (Oxford: Elsevier, forthcoming).

19. Jonathon Crush and David A. McDonald, eds., *Transnationalism and New African Immigration to South Africa* (Kingston, Ontario: Southern African Migration Projection [SAMP] and Canadian Association of African Studies [CAAS], 2002).

20. Matthew Foulkes and K. Bruce Newbold, "Poverty In-migration to Impoverished Rural Illinois Places," *Environment and Planning A* 37 (2005): 845–60.

21. Rachel Franklin and David A. Plane, "A Shift-Share Method for the Analysis of Regional Fertility Change: An Application to the Decline of Childbearing in Italy, 1952–1991," *Geographical Analysis* 36 (2004): 1–20.

22. Sarah Blue, "State Policy, Economic Crisis, Gender, and Family Ties: Determinants of Family Remittances to Cuba," *Economic Geography* 80, no. 1 (2004): 63–82.

23. Alan Findlay and F. L. N. Li, "The Meaning of Migration: A Biographical Approach to Understanding Hong Kong Emigration," *Area* 29 (1997): 33–44.

24. Kevin E. McHugh, "The 'Ageless Self'? Emplacement of Identities in Sun Belt Retirement Communities," *Journal of Aging Studies* 14, no. 1 (2000): 103–15.

25. Rachel Silvey, "Consuming the Transnational Family: Indonesian Migrant Domestic Workers to Saudi Arabia," *Global Networks* 6, no. 1 (2006): 1–18; Rachel Silvey, "Geographies of Gender and Migration: Spatializing Social Difference," *International Migration Review* 40, no. 1 (2006): 64–81.

26. Richard Morrill, *Political Redistricting and Geographic Theory, Resource Publications in Geography* (Washington DC: Association of American Geographers, 1981).

27. William A. V. Clark and Paul A. Morrison, "Demographic Paradoxes in the Los Angeles Voting Rights Case," *Evaluation Review* 15, no. 6 (1991): 712–26.

28. See Barbara Entwisle, "Putting People into Place," *Demography* 44, no. 4 (2007): 687–703.

29. Vaclav Smil, "How Many People Can the Earth Feed?" *Population and Development Review* 20, no. 2 (1994): 225–92.

30. See, for example, Hussein Amery and Aaron T. Wolf, *Water in the Middle East: A Geography of Conflict* (Austin: University of Texas Press, 2000).

31. Thomas Homer-Dixon, *Environment, Scarcity, and Violence* (Princeton, NJ: Princeton University Press, 1999). See also Michael T. Coe and Jonathan A. Foley, "Human and Natural Impacts on the Water Resources of the Lake Chad Basin," *Journal of Geophysical Research* 106, no. D4 (2001): 3349–56.

32. Roger-Mark de Souza, John S. Williams, and Frederick A. B. Meyerson, "Critical Links: Population, Health, and the Environment," *Population Bulletin* 58, no. 3 (September 2003).

33. David Foot, *Boom, Bust, and Echo: How to Profit from the Coming Demographic Shift* (Toronto: Macfarlane Walter and Ross, 1996); Richard Florida, *The Rise of the Creative Class: And How It's Transforming Work, Leisure, Community and Everyday Life* (New York: Basic Books, 2002).

34. Jane Menken, "Demographic-Economic Relationships and Development," in *Population—the Complex Reality: A Report of the Population Summit of the World's Scientific Academies*, ed. Francis Graham-Smith (Golden, CO: The North American Press, 1994). Also Richard P. Cincotta and Robert Engelman, *Economics and Rapid Change: The Influence of Population Growth* (Washington, DC: Population Action International, 1997).

Focus: The Importance of Spatial Scale

1. Ernest George Ravenstein, "The Laws of Migration," *Journal of the Royal Statistical Society* 52 (1889): 241–301.

2. Peter A. Rogerson, "Buffon's Needle and the Estimation of Migration Distances," *Mathematical Population Studies* 2 (1990): 229–38. See also K. Bruce Newbold, "Spatial Scale, Return and Onward Migration, and the Long-Boertlein Index of Repeat Migration," *Papers in Regional Science* 84, no. 2 (2005): 281–90.

Methods, Measures, and Tools: Tools of the Population Geographer

1. Adrian Bailey, *Making Population Geography* (London: Hodden Arnold, 2005).

2. See "Focus: Multi-Method Research in Population Geography," *Professional Geographer* 51, no. 1 (1999).

3. For further discussion, see K. Bruce Newbold, "Using Publicly Released Data Files to Study Immigration: Confessions of a Positivist," in *Research Methods in Migration Studies: War Stories of Young Scholars* (New York: SSRC Press, 2007). Available online at www.ssrc.org (accessed 3 June 2008).

CHAPTER 1: WORLD POPULATION

1. Alene Gelbard, Carl Haub, and Mary M. Kent, "World Population beyond Six Billion," *Population Bulletin* 54, no. 1 (March 1999). See also Lori S. Ashford, Carl Haub, Mary M. Kent, and Nancy V. Yinger, "Transitions in World Population," *Population Bulletin* 59, no. 1 (March 2004); Joseph A. McFalls Jr., "Population: A Lively

Introduction," *Population Bulletin* 62, no. 1 (March 2007); and Massimo Livi-Bacci, *A Concise History of World Population*, 3rd ed. (Oxford: Blackwell, 2001).

2. J. A. Ross, ed., *International Encyclopaedia of Population* (New York: Free Press and Center for Population and Family Health, Columbia University, 1982).

3. Gelbard, Haub, and Kent, "World Population." The PRB has a number of useful reports on population issues, most of which are available online at www.prb.org.

4. Tom Edwards, "World Population Approaches 7 Billion," US Census Bureau, www.census.gov/Press-Release/www/releases/archives/population/012112.html (accessed 1 December 2008).

5. International Data Base (IDB), "World Fertility Indicators by Development Status," www.census.gov/ipc/www/idb/ (accessed 6 April 2009).

6. Martin T. Brockerhoff, "An Urbanizing World," *Population Bulletin* 55, no. 3 (September 2000).

7. United Nations, *World Urbanization Prospects: The 2003 Revision* (New York: United Nations, 2000), www.un.org/esa/population/publications/wup2003/WUP2003 Report.pdf (accessed 15 February 2008).

8. Fertility rates tend, on average, to be lower in urban areas in the developing world, but remain greater than replacement in many cases.

9. John C. Caldwell, "Toward a Restatement of Demographic Transition Theory," in *Perspectives on Population*, ed. Scott W. Menard and Elizabeth W. Moen (New York: Oxford University Press, 1987), 42–69.

10. China is frequently excluded from population indicators because its one-child policy has dramatically altered its demographic future and sets it apart from other developing nations.

11. See, for example, Barbara Crossett, "How to Fix a Crowded World: Add People," *Sunday New York Times*, 2 November 1997, Week in Review, 1; Ben Wattenberg, "The Population Explosion Is Over," *New York Times Magazine*, 23 November 1997, 60–63; Lori Ashford, "New Population Policies: Advancing Women's Health and Rights," *Population Bulletin* 56, no. 1 (March 2001).

12. Phillip Longman, *The Empty Cradle: How Falling Birthrates Threaten World Prosperity* (New York: Basic Books, 2004). See also *World Population Ageing: 1950–2050* (New York: United Nations, 2002).

13. Carl Haub and O. P. Sharma, "India's Population Reality: Reconciling Change and Tradition," *Population Bulletin* 61, no. 3 (September 2006).

14. The decline in Argentina's fertility rate could be short-term and a reflection of the country's difficult economic situation in the early 2000s, when the government nearly went bankrupt. For a discussion of stationary fertility rates elsewhere, see Carl Haub, "Flat Birth Rates in Bangladesh and Egypt Challenge Demographers' Projections," *Population Today* 28, no. 7 (October 2000): 4.

15. Warren Sanderson and Sergei Scherbov, "Rethinking Age and Aging," *Population Bulletin* 63, no. 4 (December 2008).

16. Longman, *The Empty Cradle*.

17. Philip Martin and Gottfried Zurcher, "Managing Migration: The Global Challenge," *Population Bulletin* 63, no. 1 (March 2008).

18. Jason DeParle, "World Banker and His Cash Return Home," *New York Times* 17 March 2008, A7.

Focus: Population Growth Regimes in India, Germany, and the United States

1. Carl Haub and O. P. Sharma, "India's Population Reality: Reconciling Change and Tradition," *Population Bulletin* 61, no. 3 (September 2006).

2. Haub and Sharma, "India's Population Reality."

3. Haub and Sharma, "India's Population Reality."

4. Carl Haub, "Global Aging and the Demographic Divide," *Public Policy and Aging Report* 17, no. 4 (2007).

5. European Commission, "Childbearing Preferences and Family Issues in Europe," *Eurobarometer* 65, no. 1 (2006).

6. Philip L. Martin, "Germany: Reluctant Land of Immigration," in *Controlling Immigration: A Global Perspective*, ed. Wayne A. Cornelius, Philip L. Martin, and James F. Hollifield (Stanford, CA: Stanford University Press, 1992): 189–226.

7. For additional discussion of the determinants of fertility, see chapter 4.

8. Mary M. Kent and Mark Mather, "What Drives US Population Growth?" *Population Bulletin* 57, no. 4 (December 2002).

9. AmeriStat, "US Fertility Rates Higher among Minorities" (Washington, DC: Population Reference Bureau, 2003), www.prb.org/Articles/2003/USFertilityRatesHigher AmongMinorities.aspx (accessed 10 June 2008). See also J. A. Martin et al., "Births: Final Data for 2001," *National Vital Statistics Report* 51, no. 2 (2001) and S. J. Ventura et al., "Births: Final Data for 1997," *National Vital Statistics Report* 47, no. 18 (1999).

10. Laura E. Hill and Hans P. Johnson, *Understanding the Future of Californians' Fertility: The Role of Immigrants* (San Francisco: Public Policy Institute of California, 2002).

Methods, Measures, and Tools: Graphical Representation

1. The John Snow website can be found at www.ph.ucla.edu/epi/snow.html.

2. See www.worldmapper.org (accessed 3 November 2008).

3. Sandy Holland and David A. Plane, "Methods of Mapping Migration Flow Patterns," *Southeastern Geographer* 41 (2001): 89–104.

4. A good discussion of design of color maps can be found at www.personal.psu .edu/cab38/ColorBrewer/ColorBrewer_intro.html.

5. Mark Monmonier, *How to Lie with Maps*, 2nd ed. (Chicago: University of Chicago Press, 1996).

6. Further information on GeoDA can be found at geodacenter.asu.edu/. R is a freeware-based program. S-Plus information can be found at www.insightful.com/prod ucts/splus/. Other resources, including the Center for Spatially Integrated Social Sciences (CSISS), www.csiss.org/, or www.spatialanalysisonline.com are available.

Methods, Measures, and Tools: Population Estimates and Projections

1. Readers may also want to turn to the US Census Bureau, who also use population estimation and projection (www.census.gov/population/www/projections/index .html).

2. For a full discussion of these methods, see Andrei Rogers, *Regional Population Projection Models* (Beverly Hills, CA: Sage, 1995).

3. K. Bruce Newbold and Martin Bell, "Return and Onwards Migration in Canada and Australia: Evidence from Fixed Interval Data," *International Migration Review* 35, no. 4 (2001): 1157–84.

CHAPTER 2: POPULATION DATA

1. In the 2000 census, the US Census Bureau employed 860,000 temporary workers. Census 2010 was field tested in 2003, 2004, 2005, and 2006, and a final "dress rehearsal" was held in 2008.

2. Robert Goldenkoff and David A. Powner, *2010 Census: Little Time Remains to Address Operational Challenges* (Washington, DC: US Government Accounting Office, 5 March 2009).

3. Most statistic books will include a discussion of basic sampling techniques, their differences, and advantages and disadvantages. Books written by geographers include J. Chapman McGrew Jr., and Charles B. Monroe, *An Introduction to Statistical Problem Solving in Geography,* 2nd ed. (Boston: McGraw-Hill, 2000); Peter A. Rogerson, *Statistical Methods for Geography: A Student's Guide,* 2nd ed. (Thousand Oaks, CA: Sage, 2006); and James E. Burt, Gerald M. Barber, and David Rigby, *Elementary Statistics for Geographers,* 3rd ed. (New York: Guilford Press, 2009).

4. One excellent source that provides information on data sets is www.icpsr.org. Also, reference the website documentation in this book for additional links to data sources.

5. Links to other national statistical agencies can be found at www.census.gov/aboutus/stat_int.html (accessed 29 May 2009).

6. See, for example, David A. Plane, C. J. Henrie, and M. J. Perry, "Migration Up and Down the Urban Hierarchy and Across the Life Course," *Proceedings of the National Academy of Sciences* 102 (2005), 15313–18.

7. IPUMS: international.ipums.org/international/. Population Reference Bureau: www.prb.org (accessed 2 December 2008).

8. ciesin.org/index.html (accessed 29 May 2009).

9. Matthew Foulkes and K. Bruce Newbold, "Using Alternative Data Sources to Study Rural Migration: Examples from Illinois," *Population, Space, and Place* 14 (2008), 177–88.

10. US Census Bureau, www.census.gov (accessed 3 June 2008).

11. See, for example, Kristin G. Esterberg, *Qualitative Methods in Social Research* (Boston: McGraw-Hill, 2002) and Anselm Strauss and Juliet Corbin, *Basics of Qualitative Research: Techniques and Procedures for Developing Grounded Theory,* 2nd ed. (London: Sage Publications, 1998).

12. Mark Ellis and Richard Wright, "When Immigrants are not Migrants: Counting Arrivals of the Foreign-born Using the US Census," *International Migration Review* 32 (1998),127–44.

13. Geographers have long grappled with how best to define neighborhoods. Recent commentary can be found in Ana V. Diez Roux, "Investigating Neighborhood and Area

Effects on Health," *American Journal of Public Health* 91, no. 11 (2001): 1783–89; Nancy A. Ross, Stéphane Tremblay, and Katie Graham, "Neighbourhood Influences on Health in Montreal, Canada," *Social Science and Medicine* 59, no. 7 (2004): 1485–94.

Focus: Census Data and the ACS

1. Readers can consult the PRB discussion regarding the 2010 census (www.prb .org/Topics/Census2010.aspx). The page includes links to the questions that will be asked in the 2010 census, the ACS, and the history of the census.

2. For further discussion, see Louis DeSipio, Manuel Garcia y Griego, and Sherri Kossoudji, eds., *Researching Migration: Stories from the Field* (New York: Social Science Research Council, 2007), online at www.ssrc.org/blog/2007/12/21/researching-migration-stories-from-the-field (accessed 17 March 2008).

3. See www.ipums.umn.edu (accessed 2 December 2008).

4. See Mark Mather, Kerri L. Rivers, and Linda A. Jacobsen, "The American Community Survey," *Population Bulletin* 60, no. 3 (September 2005).

5. See factfinder.census.gov (accessed 17 March 2008).

6. Interested readers should consult www.census.gov/acs/www/ for up-to-date discussion of the ACS, along with data handbooks, FAQs, and related information (accessed 11 June 2008). The 2006 handbook can be found at www.census.gov/acs/www/Downloads/Handbook2006.pdf (accessed 11 June 2008).

7. Rachel S. Franklin and David A. Plane, "Pandora's Box: The Potential and Peril of Migration Data from the American Community Survey," *International Regional Science Review* 29, no. 3 (2006): 231–46. This paper gives an excellent overview of the ACS, its potential, and its challenges.

8. Andrei Rogers, James Raymer, and K. Bruce Newbold, "Reconciling and Translating Migration Data Collected over Time Intervals of Differing Widths," *Annals of Regional Science* 37 (2003): 581–601.

9. K. Bruce Newbold, "Counting Migrants and Migrations: Comparing Lifetime and Fixed-Interval Return and Onward Migration," *Economic Geography* 77, no. 1 (2001): 23–40.

10. Philip H. Rees, "The Measurement of Migration from Census Data and Other Sources," *Environment and Planning* A 9 (1977): 247–72.

Methods, Measures, and Tools: Working with Data

1. See also the discussion of migration theory in chapter 6.

2. Caroline B. Brettell and James F. Hollifield, *Migration Theory: Talking across Disciplines*, 2nd ed. (New York: Routledge, 2007).

3. 2010.census.gov/2010census/about_2010_census/007621.html (accessed 2 April 2009).

4. Most statistical texts include a discussion of sampling methods.

5. See, for example, Kristin G. Esterberg, *Qualitative Methods in Social Research* (Boston: McGraw-Hill, 2002) and Anselm Strauss and Juliet Corbin, *Basics of Qualita-*

tive Research: Techniques and Procedures for Developing Grounded Theory, 2nd ed. (London: Sage Publications, 1998).

6. Strauss and Corbin, *Basics of Qualitative Research*.

7. Strauss and Corbin, *Basics of Qualitative Research*, 146.

CHAPTER 3: POPULATION DISTRIBUTION AND COMPOSITION

1. Readers can also consult Arthur Haupt and Thomas T. Kane, *Population Handbook*, 5th ed., available online at www.prb.org.

2. *Atlas of Canada*, available at atlas.nrcan.gc.ca/site/english/index.html (accessed 21 May 2008).

3. *World Population Data Sheet* (Washington, DC: Population Reference Bureau, 2009).

4. Terry A. Slocum, Robert B. McMaster, Fritz C. Kessler, and Hugh H. Howard, *Thematic Cartography and Geographic Visualization*, 2nd ed. (New York: Prentice Hall, 2008). See also John Krygier and Denis Wood, *Making Maps: A Visual Guide to Map Design for GIS* (New York: Guilford Press, 2005).

5. Marc G. Weisskopf, Henry A. Anderson, Lawrence P. Hanrahan et al., "Maternal Exposure to Great Lakes Sport-Caught Fish and Dischlorodiphenyl Dichloroethylene, but Not Polychlorinated Biphenyls, Is Associated with Reduced Birth Weight," *Environmental Research* 97, no. 2 (2005): 149–62. See also William H. James, "Was the Widespread Decline in Sex Ratios at Birth Caused by Reproductive Hazards?" *Human Reproduction* 13, no. 4 (1998): 1083–84.

6. Peter H. Jongbloet, "Over-Ripeness Ovopathy: A Challenging Hypothesis for Sex Ratio Modulation," *Human Reproduction* 19, no. 4 (2004), 769–74.

7. Alfonso Gutierrez-Adan, Belen Pintado, and Jose de la Fuente, "Demographic and Behavioral Determinants of the Reduction of Male-to-Female Birth Ratio in Spain from 1981 to 1997," *Human Biology* 72, no. 5 (2000), 891–98.

8. Eric Baculinao, "China Grapples with Legacy of Its 'Missing Girls,'" NBC, 14 September 2004, www.msnbc.msn.com/id/5953508 (accessed 6 November 2008); Jeremy Hsu, "There Are More Boys than Girls in China and India," *Scientific American* 4 August 2008, www.scientificamerican.com/article.cfm?id=there-are-more-boys-than-girls (accessed 29 May 2009). Jeffrey Wasserstrom, "Resistance to the One-Child Family," in *Perspectives on Population*, ed. Scott W. Menard and Elizabeth W. Moen (New York: Oxford University Press, 1987), 269–76.

9. Lena Edlund and Douglas Almond, "Son-Biased Sex Ratios in the 2000 United States Census," *Proceedings of the National Academy of Sciences* 105 (2008): 5681–82.

10. Kristen J. Navara, "Humans at Tropical Latitudes Produce More Females," *Biological Letters* (published online, 1 April 2009), rsbl.royalsocietypublishing.org/content/early/2009/03/31/rsbl.2009.0069.abstract.

11. US Census Bureau, *US Population Projections*, table 12, "Projections of the Population by Age and Sex for the United States: 2010 to 2050," www.census.gov/population/www/projections/summarytables.html (accessed 2 April 2009).

12. Mary M. Kent and Mark Mather. "What Drives US Population Growth?" *Population Bulletin* 57, no. 4 (December 2002).

13. Kevin Kinsella and David R. Phillips. "Global Aging: The Challenge of Success," *Population Bulletin* 60, no. 1 (March 2005).

14. Gary L. Gaile and Cort J. Willmott, eds., *Geography in America at the Dawn of the Twenty-first Century* (New York: Oxford University Press, 2003), 9.

Focus: The Changing Face of the US Population

1. For a broader discussion of the nation's changing demographic profile, including housing and race, see *The Population Profile of the United States: 2000* (Internet release), www.census.gov/population/www/pop-profile/profile2000.html (accessed 17 June 2008).

2. David A. Plane and Peter A. Rogerson, *The Geographical Analysis of Population with Applications to Planning and Business* (New York: Wiley, 1994).

3. Population density reflects land area and changes in the amount of land area over time. See www.census.gov/population/censusdata/table-2.pdf (accessed 17 June 2008).

4. www.census.gov/population/www/censusdata/density.html. Historic density figures taken from US Census Bureau, *Population, Housing Units, Area Measurements, and Density: 1790 to 1990*, table 2 (accessed 6 April 2009).

5. US Census Bureau, censtats.census.gov/data/US/01000.pdf (accessed 17 June 2008).

6. The US Census Bureau has often defined the young dependency ratio as the number of persons under age eighteen to those aged eighteen through sixty-four, different from the definition used here and elsewhere. Historical figures drawn from Mary M. Kent and Mark Mather, "What Drives US Population Growth?" *Population Bulletin* 57, no. 4 (December 2002).

7. Sam Roberts, "In a Generation, Minorities May Be the US Majority," *New York Times*, 14 August 2008, A7.

8. US Census Bureau, *Age and Sex Distribution in 2000*, www.census.gov/population/pop-profile/dynamic/AgeSex.pdf (accessed 17 July 2008).

9. US Census Bureau, *Profile of Selected Social Characteristics: 2000*, censtats.census.gov/data/US/01000.pdf (accessed 17 June 2008).

10. Migration Policy Institute, www.migrationinformation.org/DataHub/charts/fb.2.shtml (accessed 17 June 2008).

11. Audrey Singer, Susan W. Hardwick, and Caroline B. Brettell, eds., *Twenty-First Century Gateways: Immigrant Incorporation in Suburban America* (Washington, DC: The Brookings Institution Press, 2008). See also Audrey Singer, Samantha Friedman, Ivan Cheung, and Marie Price, *The World in a Zip Code: Greater Washington, D.C., as a New Region of Immigration* (Washington, DC: The Brookings Institution Press, 2001).

12. US Census Bureau, "An Older and More Diverse Nation by Midcentury," www.census.gov/Press-Release/www/releases/archives/population/012 496.html (accessed 15 October 2008).

Methods, Measures, and Tools: Life Tables

1. The World Health Organization has life tables for all member states. See www
.who.int/whosis/database/life_tables/life_tables.cfm (accessed 11 June 2008).

CHAPTER 4: FERTILITY

1. For example, the Population Reference Bureau projects Latvia's current population of 2.3 million to decline to 1.8 million by 2050. Germany's population, currently 82 million, is projected to decline to 71.4 million by 2050. Other Eastern European countries, including Romania and Hungary, had TFRs of just 1.3 in 2009.

2. US Bureau of the Census, *Historical Statistics of the United States* (Washington, DC: Government Printing Office, 1975).

3. See, for example, David Foot, *Boom, Bust, and Echo* (Toronto: McFarlane, Walters, and Ross, 1996); Doug Owram, *Born at the Right Time: A History of the Baby Boom Generation* (Toronto: University of Toronto Press, 1996).

4. Sergi Maksudov, "Some Causes of Rising Mortality in the USSR," in *Perspectives on Population*, ed. Scott W. Menard and Elizabeth W. Moen (New York: Oxford University Press, 1987), 156–74.

5. John R. Weeks, *Population: An Introduction to Concepts and Issues*, 7th ed. (Belmont, CA: Wadsworth, 1999).

6. Kingsley Davis and Judith Blake, "Social Structure and Fertility: An Analytical Framework," *Economic Development and Cultural Change* 4, no. 3 (1956). S. Philip Morgan and Miles G. Taylor, "Low Fertility at the Turn of the Twenty-First Century," *Annual Review of Sociology* 32 (2006): 375–99.

7. John Bongaarts, "A Framework for Analyzing the Proximate Determinants of Fertility," *Economic Development and Cultural Change* 4 (1978): 211–35.

8. *World Population Data Sheet* (Washington, DC: Population Reference Bureau, 2009).

9. Peter Gould, *The Slow Plague: A Geography of the AIDS Pandemic* (Oxford: Blackwell, 1993).

10. Weeks, *Population*.

11. Gilda Sedgh, Stanley Henshaw, Susheela Singh, Akinrinola Bankole, and Joanna Drescher, "Legal Abortion Worldwide: Incidence and Recent Trends," *International Family Planning Perspectives* 33, no. 3 (2007): 106–16.

12. Stanley Henshaw, "Induced Abortions: A World Review, 1990," *Family Planning Perspectives* 22, no. 2 (1990): 76–89.

13. Weeks, *Population*.

14. Karen Oppenheim Mason, "Explaining Fertility Transitions," *Demography* 34, no. 4 (November 1997): 443–54.

15. Richard A. Easterlin, "An Economic Framework for Fertility Analysis," *Studies in Family Planning* 6 (1975): 54–63; Richard A. Easterlin and Eileen M. Crimmins, *The Fertility Revolution: A Supply-Demand Analysis* (Chicago: The University of Chicago Press, 1985).

16. Weeks, *Population*.

17. Although this is discussed later, fertility was already starting to decline (predominately in the upper classes) in Europe at the time of Malthus's writings. Had he foreseen that fertility decline was to occur across all classes, his writings might not have been so dark.

18. John Cleland and Christopher Wilson, "Demand Theories of the Fertility Transition: An Iconoclastic View," *Population Studies* 41 (1987): 5–30.

19. Nancy E. Riley, "Gender, Power, and Population Change," *Population Bulletin* 52, no. 1 (May 1997).

20. Joseph A. McFalls Jr., "Population: A Lively Introduction," 4th ed., *Population Bulletin* 58, no. 4 (December 2003).

21. Alene Gelbard, Carl Haub, and Mary M. Kent, "World Population beyond Six Billion," *Population Bulletin* 54, no. 1 (March 1999).

22. Thomas J. Espenshade, Juan C. Guzman, and Charles F. Westoff, "The Surprising Global Variation in Replacement Fertility," *Population Research and Policy Review* 9 (2003): 575–83.

23. Wairagala Wakabi, "Population Growth Continues to Drive Up Poverty in Uganda," *The Lancet* 367, no. 9510 (2006): 558.

24. Morgan and Taylor, "Low Fertility at the Turn of the Twenty-first Century."

25. Peter McDonald, "Low Fertility Not Politically Sustainable," *Population Today*, August/September 2001.

26. Eric G. Moore and Mark W. Rosenberg, *Growing Old in Canada*, cat. no. 96-321-MPE (Ottawa: Statistics Canada, 1997).

27. Judith Treas, "Older Americans in the 1990s and Beyond," *Population Bulletin* 50, no. 2 (May 1995).

28. Erin Anderssen, "Now's Not the Time for a Happy Surprise: As the Economy Falters, Couples Delay Making Babies," *Globe and Mail* 9 May 2009, A8. Also Sam Roberts, "Birth Rate Is Said to Fall as a Result of Recession," *New York Times* 7 August 2009, A9. The PRB has also joined the discussion.

29. Fred R. Harris, ed., *The Baby Bust: Who Will Do the Work? Who Will Pay the Taxes?* (Lanham, MD: Rowman & Littlefield Publishers, 2005).

30. Ester Boserup, *Population and Technological Change: A Study of Long-term Trends* (Chicago: University of Chicago Press, 1981); Ester Boserup, *The Conditions of Agricultural Growth* (Chicago: Aldine, 1965).

31. See, for example, Moore and Rosenberg, *Growing Old*; Victor W. Marshall, *Aging in Canada*, 2nd ed. (Markham, ON: Fitzhenry and Whiteside, 1987); Judith Treas, "Older Americans."

32. Geoffrey McNicoll, "Economic Growth with Below-Replacement Fertility," *Population and Development Review* 12 (1986): 217–37; Kingsley Davis, "Low Fertility in Evolutionary Perspective," *Population and Development Review* 12 (1986): 397–417.

33. Review of Demography, *Charting Canada's Future* (Ottawa: Canada Health and Welfare, 1989).

34. Carl Haub, "Flat Birth Rates in Bangladesh and Egypt Challenge Demographers' Projections," *Population Today* 28, no. 7 (October 2000): 4.

35. Thomas J. Goliber, "Population and Reproductive Health in Sub-Saharan Africa," *Population Bulletin* 52, no. 4 (December 1997).

36. Birth spacing also plays an important role in the nutritional status of young children, with short intervals (less than two years) between births increasing the risk for stunted growth and underweight. See James N. Gribble, Nancy Murray, and Elaine P. Menotti, "Reconsidering Childhood Under Nutrition: Can Birth Spacing Make a Difference? An Analysis of the 2002–2003 El Salvador National Family Health Survey," *Maternal and Child Nutrition* 5, no. 1 (2008).

37. Grace Dann, "Sexual Behavior and Contraceptive Use among Youth in West Africa," Population Reference Bureau, February 2009.

38. Up-to-date statistics on the HIV/AIDS epidemic are available at www.unaids .org/en/KnowledgeCentre/HIVData/GlobalReport/Default.asp (accessed 10 June 2008).

39. Goliber, "Population and Reproductive Health."

40. *Women of Our World Data Sheet* (Washington: Population Reference Bureau, 2005). This discussion should not imply that women's reproductive health is not an issue in the developed world. Instead, issues in the developed world tend to focus more on the pharmaceutical market, contraceptive choices, and infertility treatment rather than on negative health outcomes for mother and child. Still, debates in countries such as Canada and the United States with respect to access to abortion services and attempts to limit access may push direct health outcomes to the surface once again.

41. In addition to the PRB, the World Health Organization and the United Nations Population Fund (UNFPA) have a number of resources that are available online. See www.who.int/topics/reproductive_health/en/ and www.unfpa.org/ (accessed 29 May 2009). The journal *Reproductive Health Matters* is also a useful source.

42. Farzaneh Roudi-Fahimi, "Women's Reproductive Health in the Middle East and North Africa" (Washington, DC: Population Reference Bureau, 2003).

43. Ranjita Biswas, "Maternal Care in India Reveals Gaps between Urban and Rural, Rich and Poor" (Washington, DC: Population Reference Bureau, 2005).

44. Heathe Luz McNaughton, Marta Maria Blandon, and Ligia Altamirano, "Should Therapeutic Abortion Be Legal in Nicaragua: The Response of Nicaraguan Obstetrician-Gynaecologists," *Reproductive Health Matters* 2002, no. 10:111–19.

45. Liz C. Creel and Rebecca J. Perry, "Improving the Quality of Reproductive Health Care for Young People" (Washington, DC: Population Reference Bureau, 2003).

46. Lori S. Ashford, "Good Health Still Eludes the Poorest Women and Children" (Washington, DC: Population Reference Bureau, 2005) and Lori S. Ashford, "Unmet Need for Family Planning: Recent Trends and Their Implications for Programs" (Washington, DC: Population Reference Bureau, 2003).

Focus: Contrasting Fertility Rates and Choices in North America and Uganda

1. For a comprehensive examination of estimates of fertility and related indicators, see *World Fertility Report*, United Nations, 2003.

2. Sam Roberts, "Birth Rate is Said to Fall as a Result of Recession," *New York Times* 7 August 2009, A9.

3. Alain Belanger and Genevieve Ouellet, "A Comparative Study of Recent Trends

in Canadian and American Fertility, 1980–1999," in *Report on the Demographic Situation in Canada 2001* (Ottawa: Statistics Canada, 2002).

4. Mary M. Kent and Mark Mather, "What Drives U.S. Population Growth?" *Population Bulletin* 57, no. 4 (December 2002).

5. Kent and Mather, "What Drives US Population Growth?"

6. Kent and Mather, "What Drives US Population Growth?"

7. Laura E. Hill and Hans P. Johnson, *Understanding the Future of Californians' Fertility: The Role of Immigrants* (San Francisco: Public Policy Institute of California, 2002).

8. John Blacker, Collins Opiyo, Momodou Jasseh, Andy Sloggett, and John Ssekamatte-Ssebuliba, "Fertility in Kenya and Uganda: A Comparative Study of Trends and Determinants," *Population Studies* 59, no. 3 (2005): 355–73.

9. *World Population Data Sheet* (Washington: Population Reference Bureau, 2009).

10. U.S. Census Bureau, International Data Base, www.census.gov/ipc/www/idb/ (accessed 18 June 2008).

11. Lori Ashford, *Unmet Need for Family Planning: Recent Trends and Their Implications for Programs* (Washington DC: Population Reference Bureau, 2003).

12. Ashford, *Unmet Need*.

Methods, Measures, and Tools: Measuring Fertility

1. J. A. Martin, B. E. Hamilton, P. D. Sutton, S. J. Ventura, et al. "Births: Final Data for 2006," *National Vital Statistics Reports* 57, no. 7 (Hyattsville, MD: National Center for Health Statistics, 2009).

CHAPTER 5: MORTALITY

1. Alene Gelbard, Carl Haub, and Mary M. Kent, "World Population beyond Six Billion," *Population Bulletin* 54, no. 1 (March 1999).

2. For a discussion of the geographical diffusion of illness, see Andrew Cliff and Peter Haggett, "Spatial Aspects of Epidemic Control," *Progress in Human Geography* 13 (1989): 315–47; Andrew Cliff and Peter Haggett, *Atlas of Disease Distributions: Analytical Approaches to Disease Data* (Oxford: Blackwell, 1988); Peter Gould, *The Slow Plague: A Geography of the AIDS Pandemic* (Oxford: Blackwell, 1993).

3. Michael Bliss, *A Living Profit* (Toronto: McCelland and Stewart, 1974); Terry Copp, *The Anatomy of Poverty* (Toronto: McCelland and Stewart, 1974).

4. Thomas McKeown, *The Role of Medicine: Dream, Mirage, or Nemesis* (Princeton, NJ: Princeton University Press, 1979).

5. *World Population Data Sheet* (Washington, DC: Population Reference Bureau, 2009).

6. Thomas J. Goliber, "Population and Reproductive Health in Sub-Saharan Africa," *Population Bulletin* 52, no. 4 (December 1997).

7. Abdel Omran, "The Epidemiological Transition: A Theory of the Epidemiology of Population Change," *Milbank Memorial Fund Quarterly* 49 (1971): 509–38.

8. In 2005, for example, the United States spent 15.2 percent of its GDP on health care. www.who.int/countries/en/#C (accessed 18 June 2008).

9. Marian F. MacDorman and T. J. Mathews, "Recent Trends in Infant Mortality in the United States," NCHS Data Brief, no. 9 (Hyattsville, MD: National Center for Health Statistics, 2008).

10. Readers can refer to Linda Pickles, Michael Mungiole, Gretchen K. Jones, and Andrew R. White, *Atlas of United States Mortality* (Hyattsville, MD: US Department of Health and Human Services, 1996). See also Rogelio Saenz, *The Growing Color Divide in US Infant Mortality* (Washington DC: Population Reference Bureau, 2008).

11. Readers can refer to www.omhrc.gov/.

12. MacDorman and Mathews, "Recent Trends in Infant Mortality in the United States."

13. NCHS, *Health, United States, 2007*, available online at www.cdc.gov/nchs/data/hus/hus07.pdf (accessed 18 February 2008).

14. Toshiko Kaneda and Dia Adams, *Race, Ethnicity, and Where You Live Matters: Recent Findings on Health and Mortality of US Elderly* (Washington, DC: Population Reference Bureau, 2008).

15. T. J. Mathews and Marian F. MacDorman, "Infant Mortality Statistics from the 2004 Period Linked Birth/Infant Death Data Set," *National Vital Statistics Reports* 55, no. 14 (2007). Available online at www.cdc.gov/nchs/data/nvsr/nvsr55/nvsr55_14.pdf (accessed 18 February 2008).

16. Illinois Department of Public Health, "Health Statistics," www.idph.state.il.us/health/statshome.htm#Leading%20Causes (accessed 18 February 2008).

17. Carmen DeNavas-Walt, Bernadette D. Proctor, and Jessica Smith, *Income, Poverty, and Health Insurance Coverage in the United States: 2006* (Washington, DC: US Department of Commerce Economics and Statistics Administration, 2007), available online at www.census.gov/prod/2007pubs/p60-233.pdf (accessed 18 February 2008).

18. DeNavas-Walt, Proctor, and Smith, *Income, Poverty, and Health Insurance Coverage.*

19. DeNavas-Walt, Proctor, and Smith, *Income, Poverty, and Health Insurance Coverage.*

20. Norman J. Waitzman and Ken R. Smith, "Separate but Lethal: The Effects of Economic Segregation on Mortality in Metropolitan America," *The Milbank Quarterly* 76, no 3. (1998): 341–73.

21. Sheryl Gay Stolberg, "After Two Centuries, Washington Is Losing Its Only Public Hospital," *New York Times* 7 May 2001, A1.

22. Sally Macintyre, Anne Ellaway, and Steve Cummins, "Place Effects on Health: How Can We Conceptualise, Operationalise, and Measure Them?" *Social Science and Medicine* 55 (2002): 125–39. Sally Macintyre and Anne Ellaway, "Neighbourhoods and Health: Overview," in *Neighbourhoods and Health*, ed. I. Kawachi and L. Berkman (Oxford: Oxford University Press, 2003), 20–42.

23. Katherine Baicker, Amitabh Chandra, and Jonathan S. Skinner, "Geographic Variation in Health Care and the Problem of Measuring Racial Disparities," *Perspectives in Biology and Medicine* 48, no. 1 (2005): S42–53.

24. See also Michael Marmot, *The Status Syndrome: How Social Standing Affects*

Our Health and Longevity (New York: Times Books, 2004) and William Cockerham, *The Social Causes of Health and Disease* (Cambridge, UK: Polity Press, 2007).

25. Sergei Maksudov, "Some Causes of Rising Mortality in the USSR," in *Perspectives on Population*, ed. Scott W. Menard and Elizabeth W. Moen (New York: Oxford University Press, 1987), 156–74.

26. John Haaga, "High Death Rate among Russian Men Predates Soviet Union's Demise," *Population Today* 28, no. 3 (April 2000): 1.

27. Christopher Davis and Murray Feshbach, *Rising Infant Mortality in the USSR in the 1970s* series P-95, no. 74 (Washington, DC: US Census Bureau, September 1980).

28. Maksudov, "Some Causes," 156.

29. See Laurie Garrett, *The Coming Plague: Newly Emerging Diseases in a World Out of Balance* (London: Penguin, 1994).

30. S. Jay Olsahansky, Bruce Carnes, Richard G. Rogers, and Len Smith, "Infectious Diseases—New and Ancient Threats to World Health," *Population Bulletin* 52, no. 2 (July 1997).

31. This is not to imply that attempts to control malaria are not occurring. See www.rollbackmalaria.org/ (accessed 31 May 2009).

32. Acute respiratory infections and malaria are also major killers amongst children less than five years old, accounting for 19 percent and 8 percent of all deaths to children. See Jennifer Bryce, Cynthia Boschi-Pinto, Kenji Shibuya, and Robert E. Black, et al., "WHO Estimates of the Causes of Death in Children," *The Lancet* 365, no. 9465 (March 2005): 1147–53.

33. World Health Organization, "Progress in Global Measles Control and Mortality Reduction, 2000–2007," *Weekly Epidemiological Record* 83, no. 49 (2008): 441–48, www.who.int/wer (accessed 6 December 2008).

34. Kreeston M. Madson et al., "A Population-Based Study of Measles, Mumps, and Rubella Vaccination and Autism," *New England Journal of Medicine* 347, no. 19 (2002): 1477–82.

35. World Health Organization, www.who.org (accessed 21 February 2008).

36. Worobey et al., "Direct Evidence of Extensive Diversity of HIV-1 in Kinshasa by 1960," *Nature* 455 (2008): 661–64.

37. Gould, *The Slow Plague*.

38. Gardner Harris, "Detailed Study on Spread of HIV in US," *New York Times*, 12 September 2008, A9.

39. UNAIDS, *AIDS Epidemic Update, 2008*, www.unaids.org (accessed 18 February 2008).

40. In Somalia, the adult prevalence rate is less than 1.0 percent, with low infection rates associated with isolation due to its civil war and a devout Muslim population. While low, 1 percent is viewed by UNAIDS as a critical takeoff point, where infections could quickly rise if controls are not in place. Moreover, testing and reporting is difficult given ongoing conflict. However, within the country, HIV/AIDS is not seen as a problem, echoing denials in the 1990s from other countries, and observers question whether the low incidence rate is truly representative.

41. See the edited volume *African Rural and Urban Studies* 3, no. 2 (1996) for a

discussion of AIDS in sub-Saharan Africa. See also www.unaids.org/ (accessed 18 February 2008).

42. Lawrence K. Altman, "The AIDS Questions That Linger," *New York Times*, 30 January 2001, D1D. For an academic analysis of the spread of HIV/AIDS in Africa, see Bakama B. BakamaNume, "The Spatial Patterns of HIV/AIDS Infection in Uganda: 1987–1994," *African Rural and Urban Studies* 3, no. 2 (1996): 141–62; Veronica Ouma, "A Spatial-Temporal Analysis of HIV/AIDS Diffusion in Kenya: 1986–1993," *African Rural and Urban Studies* 3, no. 2 (1996): 113–40.

43. Ezekiel Kalipeni and Joseph Oppong, "Rethinking and Reappraising AIDS, Health Care Systems, and Culture in Sub-Saharan Africa—Introduction," *African Rural and Urban Studies* 3, no. 2 (1996): 7–11.

44. See, for example, Helen Schneider and Joanne Stein, "Implementing AIDS Policy in Post-Apartheid South Africa," *Social Science and Medicine* 52 (2001): 723–31.

45. Pride Chigwedere, George R. Seage III, Sofia Gruskin, Tun-Hou Lee, and M. Essex, "Estimating the Lost Benefits of Antiretroviral Drug Use in South Africa," *Perspective: Epidemiology and Social Science* 49, no. 4 (2008), 410–15.

46. Geoffrey York, "Drug Shortages Roll Back the Clock on Beating AIDS in Africa," *Globe and Mail* 10 April 2009, A9.

47. Geoffrey York, "How the World Broke Its Promise to Millions of Mothers," *Globe and Mail* 22 May 2009, A1.

48. Gould, *The Slow Plague*.

49. Thomas J. Goliber, "Population and Reproductive Health in Sub-Saharan Africa," *Population Bulletin* 52, no. 4 (December 1997).

50. Projected life expectancies, mortality rates, and infant mortality rates included within this chapter are drawn from the US Census Bureau's IDB (follow the HIV/AIDS link), www.census.gov/ipc/www/idb/ (accessed 18 February 2008).

51. *World Population Data Sheet*, 2009.

52. *AIDS Epidemic Update, 2008.*

53. *AIDS Epidemic Update, 2008.*

54. *AIDS Epidemic Update, 2008.*

55. See *USAID Efforts to Address the Needs of Children Affected with HIV/AIDS* (Washington: USAID, 2000). It can be found at www.usaid.gov/pubs/hiv_aids/ (accessed 18 February 2008).

56. For a more general discussion of the impacts, see UNAIDS, *2004 Report on the Global AIDS Epidemic*, www.unaids.org/bangkok2004/GAR2004_html/GAR2004_00_en.htm.

57. *AIDS Epidemic Update, 2008.*

58. Thomas Homer-Dixon, *Environment, Scarcity, and Violence* (Princeton, N.J.: Princeton University Press, 1999).

59. UNAIDS/WHO, *AIDS Epidemic Update, 2008*, data.unaids.org/pub/EpiReport/2006/2006_EpiUpdate_en.pdf.

60. Trudy Harpham and Carolyn Stephens, "Urbanization and Health in Developing Countries," *World Health Statistics Quarterly* 44, no. 2 (1991): 62–69.

61. Referenced from Martin Brockerhoff, "An Urbanizing World," *Population Reference Bulletin* 55, no. 3 (September 2000): 23.

62. Nkepile Mabuse, "Zimbabwe Cholera Epidemic Worsening," CNN, broadcast February 17, 2009.

63. Olsahansky, Carnes, Rogers, and Smith, "Infectious Diseases."

64. Robert G. Evans and Gregory L. Stoddart, "Producing Health, Consuming Health Care," *Social Science and Medicine* 31, no. 12 (1990): 1247–1363.

65. See: K. Bruce Newbold, "Problems in Search of Solutions: Health and Canadian Aboriginals," *Journal of Community Health* 23, no. 1 (1998): 59–73.

Focus: Mortality Differences—The United States, Mexico, and Zimbabwe

1. Joseph A. McFalls Jr., "Population: A Lively Introduction," *Population Bulletin* 58, no. 4 (December 2003).

Methods, Measures, and Tools: Measuring Mortality

1. H. C. Kung, D. L. Hoyert, J. Q. Xu, and S. L. Murphy. "Deaths: Final Data for 2005," *National Vital Statistics Reports* 56, no. 10 (2008).

CHAPTER 6: INTERNAL MIGRATION

1. K. Bruce Newbold, "Counting Migrants and Migrations: Comparing Lifetime and Fixed-interval Return and Onward Migration," *Economic Geography* 77, no. 1 (2001): 23–40.

2. Wilbur Zelinsky, "The Hypothesis of the Mobility Transition," *Geographical Review* 61, no. 2 (1971): 1–31.

3. The West includes the states of Montana, Wyoming, Colorado, New Mexico, Arizona, Utah, Idaho, Nevada, California, Oregon, Washington, Hawaii, and Alaska. Data from Rachel S. Franklin, "Domestic Migration across Regions, Divisions, and States, 1995–2000," Census 2000 Special Reports, CENSR-7 (Washington, DC: US Census Bureau, 2003).

4. Jason P. Schachter, Rachel S. Franklin, and Marc J. Perry, "Migration and Geographic Mobility in Metropolitan and Non-Metropolitan America: 1995–2000," Census 2000 Special Reports, CENSR-9 (Washington, DC: US Census Bureau, 2003).

5. Andrei Rogers, James Raymer, and K. Bruce Newbold, "Reconciling and Translating Migration Data Collected over Time Intervals of Differing Widths," *Annals of Regional Science*, 37 (2003): 581–601.

6. The exception is the 1950 census, which asked place of residence one year prior. Five years prior, many Americans would have still been mobilized for the war effort.

7. Canada has also included a one-year migration question since the 1991 census.

8. Larry Long, *Migration and Residential Mobility in the United States* (New York: Russell Sage Foundation, 1988). See also K. Bruce Newbold and Kao-Lee Liaw, "Characterization of Primary, Return, and Onward Interprovincial Migration in Canada: Overall and Age-Specific Patterns," *Canadian Journal of Regional Science* 13, no. 1 (1990): 17–34.

9. K. Bruce Newbold, "Spatial Scale, Return, and Onward Migration, and the Long-Boertlein Index of Repeat Migration," *Papers in Regional Science* 84, no. 2 (2005): 281–90.

10. Elspeth Graham, "What Kind of Theory for What Kind of Population Geography?" *International Journal of Population Geography* 6 (2000): 257–72.

11. Ernest George Ravenstein, "The Laws of Migration," *Journal of the Royal Statistical Society* 52 (1889): 241–301.

12. Everet S. Lee, "A Theory of Migration," *Demography* 3 (1966): 47–57.

13. Zelinsky, "Hypothesis of the Mobility Transition."

14. John Richard Hicks, *The Theory of Wages* (London: Macmillan, 1932).

15. See George H. Borts and Jerome L. Stein, *Economic Growth in a Free Market* (New York: Columbia University Press, 1965); see also Michael J. Greenwood, "Research on Internal Migration in the United States: A Survey," *Journal of Economic Literature* 13 (1975): 397–433.

16. Thomas J. Courchene, "Interprovincial Migration and Economic Adjustment," *Canadian Journal of Economics* 3, no. 4 (1970): 550–76.

17. Courchene, *Interprovincial Migration and Economic Adjustment*. See also R. Paul Shaw, *Intermetropolitan Migration in Canada: Changing Determinants over Three Decades* (Toronto: New Canadian Publications, 1985).

18. See Brian Cushing, "Migration and Persistent Poverty in Rural America," in *Migration and Restructuring in the United States: A Geographic Perspective*, ed. Kavita Pandit and Suzanne Davies-Whithers (Lanham, MD: Rowman & Littlefield, 1999).

19. Shaw, *Intermetropolitan Migration in Canada*. See also William P. Anderson and Yorgos Y. Papageorgiou, "Metropolitan and Non-metropolitan Population Trends in Canada, 1966–1982," *Canadian Geographer* 36, no. 2 (1992): 124–43; Kao-Lee Liaw, "Joint Effects of Personal Factors and Ecological Variables on the Interprovincial Migration Patterns of Young Adults in Canada," *Geographical Analysis* 22 (1990): 189–208.

20. Andrei Rogers, "Requiem for the Net Migrant," *Geographical Analysis* 22, no. 4 (1990): 283–300.

21. Jacques Ledent and Kao-Lee Liaw, "Interprovincial Migration Outflows in Canada, 1961–1983: Characterization and Explanation," QSEP Research Report 141 (Hamilton, ON: McMaster University, 1985).

22. Long, *Migration and Residential Mobility in the United States*. See also K. Bruce Newbold, "The Role of Race in Primary, Return, and Onward Migration," *Professional Geographer* 49, no. 1 (1997): 1–14.

23. Larry A. Sjaastad, "The Costs and Returns of Human Migration," *Journal of Political Economy* 70 (1962): 80–93.

24. Ian Molho, "Theories of Migration: A Review," *Scottish Journal of Political Economy* 33, no. 4 (1986): 396–419.

25. Peter Rossi, *Why Families Move*, 2nd ed. (Beverly Hills, CA: Sage Publications, 1980).

26. See William A. V. Clark and Jun L. Onaka, "Life Cycle and Housing Adjustment as Explanations of Residential Mobility," *Urban Studies* 20 (1983): 47–57; William A. V. Clark and Jun L. Onaka, "An Empirical Test of a Joint Model of Residential

Mobility and Housing Choice," *Environment and Planning A* 17 (1985): 915–30; Patricia Gober, "Urban Housing Demography," *Progress in Human Geography* 16, no. 2 (1992): 171–89; Kevin E. McHugh, Patricia Gober, and Neil Reid, "Determinants of Short- and Long-Term Mobility Expectations for Home Owners and Renters," *Demography* 27, no. 1 (1990): 81–95.

27. See Larry A. Brown and Eric G. Moore, "The Intra-Urban Migration Process: A Perspective," *Geografiska Annaler* 52, no. 1 (1970): 1–13; Eric Moore, *Residential Mobility in the City* (Washington, DC: Commission on College Geography, 1972).

28. Charles F. Longino, "From Sunbelt to Sunspot," *American Demographics* 16 (1994): 22–31; Charles F. Longino and William J. Serow, "Regional Differences in the Characteristics of Elderly Return Migrants," *Journal of Gerontology: Social Sciences* 47, no. 1 (1992): S38–S43; Robert F. Wiseman, "Why Older People Move: Theoretical Issues," *Research on Aging* 2, no. 2 (1980): 141–54.

29. Kao-Lee Liaw and Pavlos Kanaroglou, "Metropolitan Elderly Out-Migration in Canada, 1971–76: Characterization and Explanation," *Research on Aging* 8, no. 2 (1986): 201–31.

30. Elspeth Graham, "Breaking Out: The Opportunities and Challenges of Multi-Method Research in Population Geography," *Professional Geographer* 51 (1999): 76–89; Kenneth H. Halfacree and Paul J. Boyle, "The Challenge Facing Migration Research: The Case for a Biographical Approach," *Progress in Human Geography* 17 (1993): 333–48; James H. McKendrick, "Multi-Method Research: An Introduction to Its Application in Population Geography," *Professional Geographer* 51 (1999): 40–50.

31. Keven E. McHugh, "Inside, Outside, Upside Down, Backward, Forward, Round and Round: Migration in the Modern World," paper presented at the Roundtable Symposium on Migration and Restructuring in the US: Towards the Next Millennium, Athens, GA, 1997.

32. See, for example, Douglas S. Massey, Luin Goldring, and Jorge Durand, "Continuities in Transnational Migration: An Analysis of Nineteen Mexican Communities," *American Journal of Sociology* 99, no. 6 (1994): 1492–1533.

33. Keven E. McHugh and Robert C. Mings, "The Circles of Migration: Attachment to Place and Aging," *Annals of the Association of American Geographers* 86, no. 3 (1996): 530–50; Keven E. McHugh, Timothy D. Hogan, and Stephen K. Happel, "Multiple Residence and Cyclical Migration: A Life Course Perspective," *Professional Geographer* 47, no. 3 (1995): 251–67.

34. Anthony Fielding, "Migration and Culture," in *Migration Processes and Patterns*, vol. 1, *Research Progress and Prospects*, ed. Tony Champion and Anthony Fielding, 201–12 (London: Belhaven Press, 1992).

35. Alejandro Portes and Ruben G. Rumbaut, *Immigrant America: A Portrait* (Berkeley, CA: University of California Press, 1990). Alejandro Portes and Min Zhou, "The New Second Generation: Segmented Assimilation and Its Variants," *Annals of the Academy of Political and Social Science* 530 (1993): 74–96.

36. Peter H. Rossi, *Why Families Move: A Study of the Social Psychology of Urban Residential Mobility* (Glencoe, IL: Free Press, 1955).

37. Sjaastad, "The Costs and Returns of Human Migration."

38. Paul Boyle, Thomas J. Cooke, Keith Halfacree, and Darren Smith, "The Effect

of Long-Distance Family Migration and Motherhood on Partnered Women's Labour Market Activity Rates in GB and the US," *Environment and Planning A*, 35 (2003): 2097–114.

39. Jim Huff and William A. V. Clark, "Cumulative Stress and Cumulative Inertia: A Behavioral Model of the Decision to Move," *Environment and Planning A* 10 (1978): 1101–19. See also John Miron, "Demography, Living Arrangements, and Residential Geography," in *The Changing Social Geography of Canadian Cities*, ed. Larry S. Bourne and David F. Ley (Montreal: Queens University Press, 1993).

40. Larry A. Brown and Eric G. Moore, "The Intra-Urban Migration Process: A Perspective," *Geografiska Annaler* 52, no. 1 (1970): 1–13.

41. See, for example: William A. V. Clark and Jun L. Onaka, "Life Cycle and Housing Adjustment as Explanations of Residential Mobility," *Urban Studies* 20 (1983): 47–57; Patricia Gober, "Urban Housing Demography," *Progress in Human Geography* 16, no. 2 (1992): 171–89; Dowell Myers, S. Simon Choi, and Seong Woo Lee, "Constraints of Housing Age and Migration on Residential Mobility," *Professional Geographer* 49, no. 1 (1997): 14–28.

42. Long, *Migration and Residential Mobility in the United States*. See also K. Bruce Newbold and Martin Bell, "Return and Onwards Migration in Canada and Australia: Evidence from Fixed Interval Data," *International Migration Review* 35, no. 4 (2001): 1157–84.

Focus: Contemporary Internal Population Movement in the United States

1. Mark Mather, "Population Losses Mount in US Rural Areas," press release, Population Reference Bureau, March 2008, available online at www.prb.org/Articles/2008/populationlosses.aspx (accessed 21 July 2008).

2. Robert Lalasz, "Americans Flocking to Outer Suburbs in Record Numbers," press release, Population Reference Bureau, May 2006, available online at prb.org/Articles/2006/AmericansFlockingtoOuterSuburbsinRecordNumbers.aspx (accessed 21 July 2008).

3. Mark Mather, "Population Losses Mount in US Rural Areas."

4. John Iceland, *Where We Live Now: Immigration and Race in the United States* (Los Angeles: University of California Press, 2009).

5. David A. Plane, Christopher J. Henrie, and Marc J Perry, "Migration Up and Down the Urban Hierarchy and Across the Life Course," *Proceedings of the National Academy of Sciences* 102, no. 43 (2005): 15313–18.

6. David A. McGranahan and Calvin L. Beale, "Understanding Rural Population Loss," *Rural America* 17, no. 4 (2002): 2–11.

7. Kenneth Johnson, "Rural America Undergoing a Diversity of Demographic Change," press release, Population Reference Bureau, May 2006, available online at prb.org/Articles/2006/RuralAmericaUndergoingADiversityofDemographicChange.aspx (accessed 21 July 2008).

8. Lalasz, "Americans Flocking."

9. Kimberlee Shauman and Mary Noonan, "Family Migration and Labor Force

Outcomes: Sex Differences in Occupational Context," *Social Forces* 85 (2007): 1735–64.

10. Peter S. Goodman, "Fuel Prices Shift Math for Life in Far Suburbs," *New York Times* 25 June 2008, A10.

Methods, Measures, and Tools: Measuring Migration

1. Rachel S. Franklin, "Domestic Migration across Regions, Divisions, and States, 1995–2000," *Census 2000 Special Reports* (Washington, DC: US Bureau of the Census, 2003).

2. Larry Long, *Migration and Residential Mobility in the United States* (New York: Russell Sage Foundation, 1988).

3. Andrei Rogers, "Requiem for the Net Migrant," *Geographical Analysis* 22 (1990): 283–300.

4. This term is also known as demographic effectiveness or demographic efficiency. Dorothy Swaine Thomas, *Social and Economic Aspects of Swedish Population Movements: 1750–1933* (New York: MacMillan, 1941). See also Henry S. Shryock, *Population Mobility within the United States* (Chicago: University of Chicago, 1964).

CHAPTER 7: INTERNATIONAL MIGRATION FLOWS

1. The US Census Bureau, for example, maintains information on foreign-born populations in the country: www.census.gov/population/www/socdemo/foreign/STP-159-2000tl.html (accessed 31 May 2009).

2. Philip Martin and Gottfried Zürcher, "Managing Migration: The Global Challenge," *Population Bulletin* 63, no. 1 (2008).

3. Population Reference Bureau, *World Population Highlights: Key Findings from PRB's 2007 World Population Data Sheet* (Washington, DC: Population Reference Bureau, 2007).

4. Following the collapse of the Soviet Union and its satellite states, ethnic Russians who had been relocated to other republics for political and economic control have been returning to Russia. Interestingly, housing and the provision of employment for returning Russians pose a difficulty for the Russian government at a time of economic restructuring. If the expectations of its citizens are not met, this has the potential to create civil unrest.

5. DHS, *Yearbook of Immigration Statistics*, www.dhs.gov/files/statistics/publications/yearbook.shtm (accessed 18 August 2009).

6. For summaries of these theories, see Douglas Massey, Joaquin Arango, Graeme Hugo, Ali Kouaouci, Adela Pellegrino, and J. Edward Taylor, "Theories of International Migration: A Review and Appraisal," *Population and Development Review* 19, no. 3 (1993): 431–66; Douglas Massey, Joaquin Arango, Graeme Hugo, Ali Kouaouci, Adela Pellegrino, and J. Edward Taylor, "An Evaluation of International Migration Theory: The North American Case," *Population and Development Review* 20, no. 4 (1994): 699–752.

7. Michael P. Todaro, "A Model of Labor Migration and Urban Unemployment in

Less-Developed Countries," *American Economic Review* 59 (1969): 138–48; Arthur W. Lewis, "Economic Development with Unlimited Supplies of Labor," *Manchester School of Economic and Social Studies* 22 (1954): 139–91.

8. Oded Stark and David E. Bloom, "The New Economics of Labor Migration," *American Economic Review* 75, no. 2 (1985): 173–78.

9. Michael J. Piore, *Birds of Passage: Migrant Labor in Industrial Societies* (Cambridge: Cambridge University Press, 1979).

10. Gunnar Myrdal, *Rich Lands and Poor* (New York: Harper and Row, 1957).

11. Trends in US opinion toward immigrants and guest-worker policies can be found in Shayerah Ilias, Katherine Fennelly, and Christopher M. Federico, "American Attitudes toward Guest Worker Policies," *International Migration Review* 42, no. 4 (2008): 741–66; Roberto Suro, "Attitudes toward Immigrants and Immigration Policy: Surveys among Latinos in the US and in Mexico," Pew Hispanic Center (16 August 2005), available online at pewhispanic.org/reports/report.php?ReportID=46 (accessed 15 November 2008); Thomas J. Espenshade and Charles A. Calhoun, "An Analysis of Public Opinion toward Undocumented Immigration," *Population Research and Policy Review* 12 (1993): 189–224; Rita J. Simon and Susan H. Alexander, *The Ambivalent Welcome: Print Media, Public Opinion, and Immigration* (Westport, CT: Praeger, 1993).

12. James P. Smith and Barry Edmonston, *The New Americans* (Washington, DC: The National Academy Press, 1997). In Canada, a similar review of the costs and benefits of immigration was carried out in the late 1980s: *Demographic Review, Charting Canada's Future* (Ottawa: Health and Welfare, 1989).

13. www.census.gov (accessed 10 June 2008).

14. John Isbister, *The Immigrant Debate: Remaking America* (West Hartford, CT: Kumarian Press, 1996); K. Bruce Newbold, "Immigration: Prospects and Policy," *Policy Options* 15, no. 8 (October 1994): 42–45; Smith and Edmonston, *The New Americans*.

15. Smith and Edmonston, *The New Americans*.

16. Similar conclusions have been found in Canada. See Roderic Beaujot, *Population Change in Canada* (Toronto: McCelland Stewart, 1991).

17. Michael Janofsky, "Illegal Immigration Strains Services in Arizona," *New York Times* 11 April 2001, A10.

18. Dollar values based on 2007 remittances. World Bank, *Migration and Remittances Factbook 2008*.

19. Jason DeParle, "World Banker and His Cash Return Home," *New York Times* 17 March 2008, A7.

20. Carl Haub, "US Population Could Reach 438 Million by 2050, and Immigration Is Key," Population Reference Bureau, February 2008.

21. Barbara Boyle Torrey and Carl Haub, "Diverging Mortality and Fertility Trends: Canada and the United States," Population Reference Bureau, 2003, www.prb.org/Articles/2003/DivergingMortalityandFertilityTrendsCanadaandtheUnitedStates.aspx?p=1.

22. Haub, "US Population Could Reach 438 Million by 2050."

23. Stanley Lieberson and Mary C. Waters, "The Location of Ethnic and Racial Groups in the United States," *Sociological Forum* 2, no. 4 (1987): 780–810.

24. Cornelius, Martin, and Hollifield, eds., "Introduction," *Controlling Immigration: A Global Perspective* (Palo Alto, CA: Stanford University Press, 1994), 1.

25. Ginger Thompson and Steven Greenhouse, "Mexican 'Guest Workers': A Project Worth a Try?" *New York Times* 3 April 2001, B1.

26. Julie R. Watts, *An Unconventional Brotherhood: Union Support for Liberalized Immigration in Europe* (La Jolla, CA: Center for Comparative Immigration Studies, 2000).

27. Julia Preston and Steven Greenhouse, "Immigration Accord by Labor Boosts Obama Effort," *New York Times* 13 April 2009, A1.

28. Ginger Thompson and Steven Greenhouse, "Mexican 'Guest Workers.'"

29. Steven Greenhouse, "Los Angeles Warms to Labor Unions as Immigrants Look to Escape Poverty," *New York Times* 9 April 2001, A7.

30. For an expanded discussion of the history of US immigration policy, numbers, and origins, see Kitty Calavita, "US Immigration and Policy Responses: The Limits of Legislation," in *Controlling Immigration: A Global Perspective*, ed. Wayne A. Cornelius, Philip L. Martin, and James F. Hollifield (Stanford, CA: Stanford University Press, 1994): 55–82; Roger Daniels and Otis L. Graham, *Debating American Immigration, 1882–Present* (Lanham, MD: Rowman & Littlefield, 2001); John Isbister, *The Immigration Debate* (West Hartford, CT: Kumarian Press, 1996); Philip Martin and Elizabeth Midgley, "Immigration to the United States," *Population Bulletin* 50, no. 2 (June 1999); Philip Martin and Elizabeth Midgley, "Immigration: Shaping and Reshaping America," *Population Bulletin* 58, no. 2 (June 2003).

31. Immigrant flows in 1998 from Canada, which has traditionally been a major exporter of immigrants to the United States, totaled just 1.5 percent. Therefore, the majority of flows from the Americas were from South and Central America and the Caribbean.

32. Calavita, "US Immigration and Policy," 55.

33. Cornelius, Martin, and Hollifield, "Introduction," 1.

34. Calavita, "US Immigration and Policy," 55.

35. See, for example, Damien Cave, "States Take New Tack on Illegal Immigration," *New York Times* 9 June 2008, A7.

36. See www.ice.gov/ (accessed 3 April 2009).

37. Philip Martin, "Proposition 187 in California," *International Migration Review* 29, no. 1 (Spring 1995): 255–63; William A. V. Clark, *The California Cauldron* (New York: Guilford Press, 1998).

38. In 1882, anti-Chinese sentiments in California led to the National Exclusion Act. See Alexander Saxton, *The Indispensable Enemy: Labor and the Anti-Chinese Movement in California* (Berkeley: University of California Press, 1971).

39. Clark, *The California Cauldron*.

40. Deborah L. Garvey and Thomas J. Espenshade. "State and Local Fiscal Impacts of New Jersey's Immigrant and Native Households," in *Keys to Successful Immigration: Implications of the New Jersey Experience*, ed. Thomas J. Espenshade (Washington, DC: Urban Institute Press, 1997).

41. Clark, *The California Cauldron*.

42. George J. Sanchez, "Face the Nation: Race, Immigration, and the Rise of Nativ-

ism in Late-Twentieth-Century America," in *The Handbook of International Migration: The American Experience*, ed. Charles Hirschman, Philip Kasinitz, and Josh DeWind (New York: Russell Sage Foundation, 1999): 371–82.

43. See "Arizona's Proposition 200," Immigrationonline.org, www.immigrationline.org/feature.asp?issueid=%7B19AAAD22-5EEF-4523-90FB-F8738D74BABD%7D (accessed 8 April 2009).

44. Audrey Singer, Jill H. Wilson, and Brooke DeRenzis, *Immigrants, Politics, and Local Response in Suburban Washington* (Washington, DC: Brookings Institution, 2009).

45. James P. Smith and Barry Edmonston, *The New Americans* (Washington, DC: The National Academy Press, 1997).

46. TANF replaced Aid for Families with Dependent Children (AFDC) benefits.

47. Demetrios G. Papademetriou and Aaron Terrazas, *Immigrants and the Current Economic Crisis: Research Evidence, Policy Challenges, and Implications* (Washington, DC: Migration Policy Institute, 2009).

48. DHS, *Yearbook of Immigration Statistics*.

49. Understandably, apprehensions are the only measure of the success of Border Patrol operations. They are only a rough approximation for the number of individuals who try to cross the border, and may include multiple attempts by the same persons.

50. Frank D. Bean, "Illegal Mexican Immigration and the United States/Mexico Border: The Effects of Operation Hold-the-Line on El Paso/Juarez," report prepared for the US Commission on Immigration Reform, July 1994.

51. Dennis Wagner, "Illegals Dying at Record Rate in Arizona Desert," *USA Today* 19 August 2005, A1A. See also James Sterngold, "Devastating Picture of Immigrants Dead in Arizona Desert," *New York Times* 25 May 2001, A1.

52. Michael Hoefer, Nancy Rytina, and Bryan C. Baker, *Estimates of the Unauthorized Immigrant Population Residing in the United States: January 2007* (Washington, DC: Office of Immigration Statistics, 2008), available at www.dhs.gov/xlibrary/assets/statistics/publications/ois_ill_pe_2007.pdf (accessed 17 November 2008). Also Jeffrey S. Passel, "Estimates of the Size and Characteristics of the Undocumented Population," Pew Hispanic Center, 2005, pewhispanic.org/reports (accessed 10 June 2008).

53. Nina Glick-Schiller, Linda Bash, and Cristina Blanc, "From Immigrant to Transmigrant: Theorizing Transnational Migration," *Anthropological Quarterly* 68, no. 1 (1995): 48–63.

54. David Ley and Audrey Kobayashi, "Back to Hong Kong: Return Migration or Transnational Sojourn?" *Global Networks* 5, no. 2 (2005): 111–27.

55. Johanna L. Waters, "Flexible Families? 'Astronaut' Households and the Experiences of Lone Mothers in Vancouver, British Columbia," *Social and Cultural Geography* 3, no. 2 (2002): 117–34.

Focus: The "Immigration Gap"

1. Michael Hoefer, Nancy Rytina, and Bryan C. Baker, "Estimates of the Unauthorized Immigrant Population Residing in the United States: January 2007" (Washington, DC: Office of Immigration Statistics, 2008), www.dhs.gov/xlibrary/assets/statistics/pub

lications/ois_ill_pe_2007.pdf (accessed 17 November 2008). See also Jeffrey S. Passel, "Estimates of the Size and Characteristics of the Undocumented Population" (Washington, DC: Pew Hispanic Center, 2005), pewhispanic.org/reports (accessed 10 June 2008).

2. Jeffery S. Passel, "Unauthorized Migrants: Numbers and Characteristics," Pew Hispanic Center (14 June 2005), pewhispanic.org/reports/report.php?ReportID = 46 (accessed 15 November 2008).

3. Julie R. Watts, *An Unconventional Brotherhood: Union Support for Liberalized Immigration in Europe* (La Jolla, CA: Center for Comparative Immigration Studies, 2000).

4. Wayne A. Cornelius, Philip L. Martin, and James F. Hollifield, eds., *Controlling Immigration: A Global Perspective* (Palo Alto, CA: Stanford University Press, 1994).

5. Manuel Garcia y Griego, "Canada: Flexibility and Control in Immigration and Refugee Policy," in *Controlling Immigration: A Global Perspective*, ed. Wayne A. Cornelius, Philip L. Martin, and James F. Hollifield (Palo Alto, CA: Stanford University Press, 1992): 119–42.

Methods, Measures, and Tools: Counting Immigrants, Illegal Immigrants, and Emigrants

1. Jeffery S. Passel, "Unauthorized Migrants: Numbers and Characteristics," Pew Hispanic Center (14 June 2005). Available online at pewhispanic.org/reports/report.php?ReportID = 46 (accessed 8 May 2008).

2. Guillermina Jasso, Douglas S. Masey, Mark R. Rosenzweig, and James P. Smith, "From Illegal to Legal: Estimating Previous Illegal Experience among New Legal Immigrants to the United States," *International Migration Review* 42, no. 4 (2008): 803–43.

CHAPTER 8: REFUGEES AND INTERNALLY DISPLACED PERSONS

1. The 1951 UN Convention was meant only to deal with European refugees associated with pre-1951 events at the end of World War II. The 1967 Protocol removed the provisions associated with geography and the requirement that only victims of pre-1951 events could be defined as refugees.

2. Asylees are individuals forced out of their country of origin who are seeking refuge in the new country in which they are living.

3. www.unhcr.org (accessed 28 November 2008).

4. See www.unhcr.org/cgi-bin/texis/vtx/home (accessed 31 May 2009).

5. The Spring 2001 (vol. 35) issue of *International Migration Review* is a special issue that deals with the UNHCR: "UNHCR at 50: Past, Present, and Future of Refugee Assistance."

6. Kathleen Newland, "Refugees: The New International Politics of Displacement," in *Perspectives on Population*, ed. Scott W. Menard and Elizabeth W. Moen (New York: Oxford University Press, 1987), 314–21.

7. Newland, "Refugees," 314.

8. Farzaneh Roudi, "Final Peace in the Middle East Hinges on Refugee Population," *Population Today* 29, no. 3 (April 2001): 1. Readers can also find information applicable to Palestinian refugees through the UN Relief and Works Agency for Palestine Refugees in the Near East, www.un.org/unrwa/ (accessed 28 November 2008).

9. Ray Wilkinson, "The Heart of Darkness," *Refugees* 110 (Winter 1997): 3–8.

10. Holly Reed, "Kosovo and the Demography of Forced Migration," *Population Today* 27, no. 6 (June 1999): 4–5.

11. Carlotta Gall, "Crisis in the Balkans: In Macedonia; At Wit's End, A Neighbor Turns Back the Refugees," *New York Times* 31 March 1999, A1.

12. Misha Glenny, "When Victims Become a Threat," *New York Times* 6 April 1999, A2; Anthony DePalma, "Crisis in the Balkans: Neighbor; Kosovo Crisis Strains Already Struggling Albania," *New York Times* 26 May 1999, A4.

13. Roger Cohen, "Crisis in the Balkans: The Europeans; Already Burdened, Western Europe Is Reluctant to Take in Kosvo's Outcasts," *New York Times* 2 April 1999, A3.

14. Following the resolution of the war in Kosovo, many refugees who had been resettled to North America chose to return home. Many others stayed.

15. UNHCR, *UNHCR Statistical Yearbook 2007*, www.unhcr.org (accessed 28 November 2008).

16. Jacqualine Desbarats, "Ethnic Differences in Adaptation: Sino-Vietnamese Refugees in the United States," *International Migration Review* 20, no. 2 (1986): 405–27. See also K. Bruce Newbold, "Refugees into Immigrants: Assessing the Adjustment of Southeast Asian Refugees in the US, 1975–1990," *Canadian Studies in Population* 29, no. 1 (2002): 151–71.

17. David W. Haines, *Refugees as Immigrants* (Totowa, NJ: Rowman & Littlefield, 1986).

18. Alejendro Portes and Reuben Rumbaut, *Immigrant America: A Portrait* (Berkeley: University of California Press, 1996).

19. K. Bruce Newbold and Matthew Foulkes, "Geography and Segmented Assimilation: Examples from the New York Chinese," *Population, Space, and Place* 10 (2004): 3–18.

20. Sara Corbett, "The Long Road from Sudan to America," *New York Times Magazine* 1 April 2001, 1–6. For an academic discussion of the adjustment of refugees to the host society, see Reginald P. Baker and David S. North, *The 1975 Refugees: Their First Five Years in America* (Washington, DC: New TransCentury Foundation, 1984); Haines, *Refugees*; Alejendro Portes, "Economic Sociology and the Sociology of Immigration: A Conceptual Overview," in *The Economic Sociology of Immigration*, ed. Alejendro Portes (New York: Russell Sage, 1995): 1–41.

21. Kelly Woltman and K. Bruce Newbold, "Of Flights and Flotillas: Assimilation and Race in the Cuban Diaspora," *Professional Geographer* 61 no. 1 (2009): 70–86; Emily Skop, "Race and Place in the Adaptation of Mariel Exiles," *International Migration Review* 35, no. 1 (2001): 449–71.

22. UNHCR, *UNHCR Statistical Yearbook 2007*, www.unhcr.org (accessed 10 June 2008).

23. UNHCR, *UNHCR Statistical Yearbook 2007*, www.unhcr.org (accessed 10 June 2008).

24. Ray Wilkinson, "IDPs: The Hot Issue for a New Millennium: Who's Looking After These People?" *Refugees* 117 (1999): 3–8.

25. UNHCR, 2007 *Global Trends: Refugees, Asylum-Seekers, Returnees, Internally Displaced and Stateless Persons*, 17, www.unhcr.org (accessed 10 June 2008).

26. Approximately eleven thousand to twelve thousand a year seek protection in Canada after passing through the United States. The flow in the opposite direction—into the United States—is much smaller, at about two hundred asylum seekers per year.

27. Arthur C. Helton and Eliana Jacobs, "Harmonizing Immigration and Refugee Policy Between the US and Canada," *Population Today* 30, no. 2.

28. CBC News, "Refugee Claims Down 40% in Deal's Wake," 27 July 2005, www.cbc.ca/canada/story/2005/07/27/refugee-claims050727.html (accessed 10 August 2009).

29. Judith Kumin, "A Multi-Billion Dollar Trade in Humans," *Refugees* 119 (2000): 18–19.

30. Farzaneh Roudi, "Final Peace in the Middle East Hinges on Refugee Population," *Population Today* 29, no. 3 (April 2001): 1.

31. IPPC, *Climate Change 2007*, IPPC Fourth Assessment Report, 2007, www.ipcc.ch/index.htm (accessed 3 December 2008).

32. IPPC, *Climate Change 2007*.

33. Elisabeth Rosenthal, "Water Is a New Battleground in Spain," *New York Times* 3 June 2008, S1.

Focus: The United States: Welcoming Refugees?

1. I use this term with caution, since US refugee policy has frequently been a tool of foreign policy and many more could be resettled.

2. Not all refugee groups have been granted entry. The United States, for instance, blocked the admission of European Jews during the 1930s and 1940s.

3. Hania Zlotnik, "Policies and Migration Trends in the North American System," in *International Migration, Refugee Flows, and Human Rights in North America*, ed. Alan B. Simmons (New York: Center for Migration Studies, 1996), 81–103.

4. Ray Wilkinson, "Give Me. . . . Your Huddled," *Refugees* 119, no. 2 (Summer 2000): 5–21.

5. DHS, 2008 *Yearbook of Immigration Statistics*, www.dhs.gov/files/statistics/publications/yearbook.shtm (accessed 18 August 2009).

6. Each year, the number of applications for asylum exceeds the number granted following the determination of the veracity of the refugee claim. Calculating an average approval rate would be misleading, since approval rates vary significantly by country, being higher in the 1980s and 1990s for aliens from the former Soviet Union and lower for Central Americans.

7. T. Alexander Aleinikoff, "United States Refugee Law and Policy: Past, Present, and Future," in *International Migration, Refugee Flows, and Human Rights in North*

America*, ed. Alan B. Simmons (New York: Center for Migration Studies, 1996), 245–57.

8. US Department of Justice, Executive Office for Immigration Review, *Asylum Statistics by Nationality, FY 2008*, www.usdoj.gov/eoir/efoia/foiafreq.htm (accessed 18 August 2009).

9. Lucas Guttentag, "Haitian Refugees and US Policy," in *International Migration, Refugee Flows, and Human Rights in North America*, ed. Alan B. Simmons (New York: Center for Migration Studies, 1996), 272–89.

10. Kathleen Newland, "Refugees: The New International Politics of Displacement," in *Perspectives on Population*, ed. Scott W. Menard and Elizabeth W. Moen (New York: Oxford University Press, 1987), 314–21.

11. T. Alexander Aleinikoff, "United States Refugee Law and Policy: Past, Present, and Future," in *International Migration, Refugee Flows, and Human Rights in North America*, ed. Alan B. Simmons (New York: Center for Migration Studies, 1996), 245–57.

12. Aleinikoff, "Refugee Law and Policy," 245.

13. Wilkinson, "Give Me," 5.

Methods, Measures, and Tools: Counting Refugees and IDPs

1. Holly Reed, "Kosovo and the Demography of Forced Migration," *Population Today* 27, no. 6 (June 1999): 4–5.

2. Definitions of these terms can be found in the *2007 UNHCR Statistical Yearbook*.

3. www.refugees.org (accessed November 28, 2008).

CHAPTER 9: URBANIZATION

1. United Nations, *World Urbanization Prospects: The 2003 Revision* (New York: United Nations, 2000), www.un.org/esa/population/publications/wup2003/WUP2003 Report.pdf (accessed 14 June 2005).

2. Fertility rates tend, on average, to be lower in urban areas in the developing world, but remain greater than replacement in many cases.

3. As of 2006, London's population was 7.5 million.

4. Richard Florida, *The Rise of the Creative Class: And How it is Transforming Work, Leisure, and Everyday Life* (New York: Basic Books, 2002).

5. Jane Jacobs, *The Economy of Cities* (New York: Random House, 1969).

6. Ernest George Ravenstein, "The Laws of Migration," *Journal of the Royal Statistical Society* 52 (1889): 241–301.

7. Ravenstein, "The Laws of Migration," 191.

8. Wilbur Zelinsky, "The Hypothesis of the Mobility Transition," *Geographical Review* 61, no. 2 (1971): 1–31.

9. Trudy Harpham and Carolyn Stephens, "Urbanization and Health in Developing Countries," *World Health Statistics Quarterly* 44, no. 2 (1991): 62–69.

10. Referenced from: Martin P. Brockerhoff, "An Urbanizing World," *Population Bulletin* 55, no. 3 (September 2000).

11. Robert E. Lang and Dawn Dhavale, *Beyond Megalopolis: Exploring America's New "Megapolitan" Geography*, Metropolitan Institute Census Report Series, census report 05:01 (Blacksburg, VA: Virginia Tech, 2005).

12. Lang and Dhavale, *Beyond Megalopolis*, 1.

13. Jean Gottmann, *Megalopolis Revisited: Twenty-Five Years Later* (College Park, MD: The University of Maryland Institute for Urban Studies, 1987), 52.

14. For a review of the links between health and urban poverty in the developing world, see Mark R. Montgomery, "Urban Poverty and Health in Developing Countries," *Population Bulletin* 64, no. 2 (June 2009).

15. Brockerhoff, "An Urbanizing World."

16. For additional discussion, see Blair Badcock, *Making Sense of Cities: A Geographical Survey* (London: Arnold, 2002).

17. See, for example, Richard E. Bilsborrow, *Migration, Urbanization, and Development: New Directions and Issues* (New York: United Nations Population Fund and Kluwer Academic Publishers, 1998); Brockerhoff, "An Urbanizing World"; Gavin W. Jones and Pravin M. Visaria, *Urbanization in Large Developing Countries: China, Indonesia, Brazil, and India* (Oxford: Clarendon Press, 1997); Josef Gugler, *The Urban Transformation of the Developing World* (Oxford: Oxford University Press, 1996); Eugene Linden, "Megacities," *Time* 11 January 1993, 28–38.

Focus: Planning for Growth

1. www.smartgrowth.org/about/default.asp (accessed 16 October 2008).

2. www.metro-region.org/index.cfm/go/by.web/id=277 (accessed 16 October 2008).

3. Government of Ontario, Ministry of Public Infrastructure Renewal, 2006, Places to Grow: Growth Plan for the Greater Golden Horseshoe (Toronto: Government of Ontario).

4. Government of Ontario, Ministry of Municipal Affairs and Housing, 2005, Greenbelt Plan (Toronto: Government of Ontario).

5. Jun Myung-Jin, "The Effects of Portland's Urban Growth Boundary on Urban Development Patterns and Commuting," *Urban Studies* 41, no. 7 (2004): 1333–48.

6. Deborah Howe, "The Reality of Portland's Housing Markets," in *The Portland Edge: Challenges and Successes in Growing Communities*, ed. Connie P. Ozawa, 184–205 (Portland, OR: Portland State University, Island Press, 2004).

Methods, Measures, and Tools: Defining "Urban" across Countries

1. See also the interesting work using GIS by the Center for International Earth Science Information Network (CIESIN) at sedac.ciesin.columbia.edu/gpw/.

2. See US Census Bureau, "Differences between the 1990 Census and Census 2000 Urbanized Area Criteria," www.census.gov/geo/www/ua/uac2k_90.html (accessed 24 September 2008).

1. Lori S. Ashford, "New Population Policies: Advancing Women's Health and Rights," *Population Bulletin* 56, no. 1 (March 2001).

2. Mary Mederios Kent, "Shrinking Societies Favor Procreation," *Population Today* 27, no. 12 (December 1999): 4–5.

3. Pew Hispanic Center, *US Population Projections: 2005–2050*, pewhispanic.org/files/reports/85.pdf (accessed 7 August 2008).

4. Alain Bélanger, Laurent Martel, and Éric Caron-Malenfant, *Population Projections for Canada, Provinces and Territories, 2005–2031*, catalogue 91-520-XIE (Ottawa: Statistics Canada, 2005).

5. See the discussions by James F. Hollifield, Phillip L. Martin, Rogers Brubaker, Elmar Honekopp, and Marcelo M. Suarex-Orozco in *Controlling Immigration: A Global Perspective*, ed. Wayne A. Cornelius, Philip L. Martin, and James F. Hollifield (Stanford, CA: Stanford University Press, 1992).

6. Keith Crane, Beth Asch, Joanna Zorn Heilbrunn, and Danielle C. Cullinane, *The Effect of Employer Sanctions on the Flow of Undocumented Immigrants to the United States* (Lanham, MD: University Press of America, 1990).

7. Philip Martin, "Labor and Unauthorized US Migration," Population Reference Bureau, May 2005.

8. Julia Preston, "Obama to Push Immigration Bill as One Priority," *New York Times* 9 April 2009, A1; Julia Preston and Steven Greenhouse, "Immigration Accord by Labor Boosts Obama Effort," *New York Times* 13 April 2009, A1.

9. Jana Mason, *Shadow Plays: The Crisis of Refugees and IDPs in Indonesia* (Washington, DC: United States Committee for Refugees, 2001).

10. Chun-Chung Au and J. Vernon Henderson, "Are Chinese Cities Too Small?" *Review of Economic Studies* 73 (2006): 549–76.

11. Arjan de Haan, "Livelihoods and Poverty: The Role of Migration—A Critical Review of the Migration Literature," *Journal of Development Studies* 36, no. 2 (2000): 1–23.

12. Judith Treas, "Older Americans in the 1990s and Beyond," *Population Bulletin* 50, no. 2 (May 1995).

13. Jean-Claude Chesnais, "The Demographic Sunset of the West," *Population Today* 25, no. 1 (January 1997): 4–5.

14. *Demographic Review, Charting Canada's Future* (Ottawa: Health and Welfare, 1989). Peter McDonald, "Low Fertility Not Politically Sustainable," *Population Today*, August/September 2001.

15. Henry P. David, "Eastern Europe: Pronatalist Policies and Private Behavior," in *Perspectives on Population*, ed. Scott W. Menard and Elizabeth W. Moen (New York: Oxford University Press, 1987), 250–58.

16. Effective July 1, 2005, the bonus was increased to $4,000 per child. Robert Lalasz, "Baby Bonus Credited with Boosting Australia's Fertility Rate," *Population Reference Bureau*, 2005.

17. Marlene A. Lee and Mark Mather, "US Labor Force Trends," *Population Bulletin* 63, no. 2.

18. Alene Gelbard, Carl Haub, and Mary M. Kent, "World Population beyond Six Billion," *Population Bulletin* 54, no. 1 (March 1999).

19. Gelbard, Haub, and Kent, "World Population."

20. Peter H. Kostmayer, "Bush 'Gags' the World on Family Planning," *Chicago Tribune* 25 January 2001, A2. Note that Kostmayer was, at the time that the *Tribune* article was written, the president of Zero Population Growth (now Population Connections). Additional references can be found on the Population Connections website, www .populationconnection.org/ (accessed 10 June 2008). See also Liz Creel and Lori Ashford, "Bush Reinstates Policy Restricting Support for International Family Planning Programs," Population Reference Bureau, 2001, www.prb.org/Articles/2001/BushRein statesPolicyRestrictingSupportforInternationalFamilyPlanningPrograms.aspx (accessed 18 June 2008).

21. Peter Baker, "Obama Reverses Rules on US Abortion Aid," *New York Times* 23 January 2009, A13.

22. Liz Creel and Lori Ashford, "Bush Reinstates Policy." (accessed 1 June 2009).

23. Timothy King, *Population Policies and Economic Development* (Baltimore: Johns Hopkins University Press, 1974).

24. Barbara Shane, "Family Planning Saves Lives, Prevents Abortion," *Population Today* 25, no. 3 (March 1997): 1.

25. Sarah Curtis and Ann Taket, *Health and Societies: Changing Perspectives* (London: Arnold, 1996).

Focus: Population Planning in Selected Regions

1. For additional information on China's one-child policy, see Jim P. Doherty, Edward C. Norton, and James E. Veney, "China's One-child Policy: The Economic Choices and Consequences Faced by Pregnant Women," *Social Science and Medicine* 52 (2001): 745–61; Johns Hopkins University Population Information Program, "Population and Birth Planning in the People's Republic of China," *Population Reports* 1, no. 25 (1982); Jeffrey Wasserstrom, "Resistance to the One-child Family," in *Perspectives on Population*, ed. Scott W. Menard and Elizabeth W. Moen (New York: Oxford University Press, 1987), 269–76. For a broader discussion of China's population policies, see Nancy E. Riley, "China's Population: New Trends and Challenges," *Population Bulletin* 59, no. 2 (June 2004).

2. See Ansley Coale and J. Bannister, "Five Decades of Missing Females in China," *Demography* 31 (1994): 459–80. See also Jim Yardley, "Fearing Future, China Starts to Give Girls Their Due," *New York Times*, 31 January 2005, 2C, and Eric Eckholm, "Desire for Sons Drives Use of Prenatal Scans in China," *New York Times*, 21 June 2002, 4A.

3. Wasserstrom, "Resistance to the One-child Family," 269.

4. Doherty, Norton, and Veney, "China's One-Child Policy," 745.

5. Nancy E. Riley, "China's Population: New Trends and Challenges," *Population Bulletin* 59, no. 2 (June 2004).

6. Lori S. Ashford, Carl Haub, Mary M. Kent, and Nancy V. Yinger, "Transitions in World Population," *Population Bulletin* 59, no. 1 (March 2004).

7. Gary Caldwell and Daniel Fournier, "The Quebec Question: A Matter of Population," *Canadian Journal of Sociology* 12, nos. 1–2 (1987): 16–41; Roderic Beaujot, *Population Change in Canada* (Toronto: McClelland and Stewart, 1991).

8. Caldwell and Fournier, "The Quebec Question," 16.

9. Beaujot, *Population Change in Canada*.

10. Jean Dumas, *Report on the Demographic Situation in Canada 1990*, cat. no. 91-209 (Ottawa: Statistics Canada).

11. Catherine Krull, "Quebec's Alternative to Pronatalism," *Population Today*, www.prb.org/Articles/2001/QuebecsAlternativetoPronatalism.aspx (accessed 19 August 2008).

12. Alain Belanger, *Report on the Demographic Situation in Canada 2002*, cat. no. 919-209-XPE (Ottawa: Statistics Canada).

13. www.stat.gouv.qc.ca/salle-presse/communiq/2007/avril/avril0703a_an.htm (accessed 19 August 2008).

Methods, Measures, and Tools: Pass or Fail? Evaluating Population Policies

1. See, for example, Henry P. David, "Eastern Europe: Pronatalist Policies and Private Behavior," in *Perspectives on Population*, ed. Scott W. Menard and Elizabeth W. Moen (New York: Oxford University Press, 1987), 250–58; Jim P. Doherty, Edward C. Norton, and James E. Veney, "China's One-child Policy: The Economic Choices and Consequences Faced by Pregnant Women," *Social Science and Medicine* 52 (2001): 745–61; Johns Hopkins University Population Information Program, "Population and Birth Planning in the People's Republic of China," *Population Reports* 1, no. 25 (1982); Jeffrey Wasserstrom, "Resistance to the One-Child Family," in *Perspectives on Population*, ed. Scott W. Menard and Elizabeth W. Moen (New York: Oxford University Press, 1987), 269–76; Gary Caldwell and Daniel Fournier, "The Quebec Question: A Matter of Population," *Canadian Journal of Sociology* 12, nos. 1–2 (1987): 16–41.

CHAPTER 11: POPULATION GROWTH

1. Paul Ehrlich, *The Population Bomb* (New York: Ballantine Books, 1968).

2. Thomas Robert Malthus, "An Essay on the Principle of Population," reprinted in Scott W. Menard and Elizabeth W. Moen, *Perspectives on Population* (New York: Oxford University Press, 1987).

3. Paul Ehrlich, Anne Ehrlich, and Gretchen Daily, "Food Security, Population, and Environment," *Population and Development Review* 19, no. 1 (1993): 1–32.

4. Based upon 2008 data drawn from the UN FAO website, www.fao.org/sof/sofi/index_en.htm (accessed 26 November 2008).

5. William Bender and Margaret Smith, "Population, Food, and Nutrition," *Population Bulletin* 51, no. 4 (February 1997); Paul Ehrlich, Anne Ehrlich, and Gretchen Daily, "Food Security, Population, and Environment," *Population and Development Review* 19, no. 1 (1993): 1–32; Robert Livernash and Eric Rodenburg, "Population Change, Resources, and the Environment," *Population Bulletin* 53, no. 1 (March 1998).

6. Frances Lappe and Joseph Collins, *Food First* (Boston: Houghton Mifflin, 1977).

7. Digby J. McLaren, "Population and the Utopian Myth," *Ecodecision* 21 (June 1993): 59–63.

8. In particular, the popular press and green movement have adopted neo-Malthusian perspectives, while the viewpoints of economic optimists inform the governments of most developed nations and are found in the policies of the World Bank.

9. In his original writings, Malthus did not believe in birth control, nor did modern methods exist. Neo-Malthusians are distinguished from true Malthusians in their belief that birth control can be used as a check against population growth.

10. Numerous authors have contributed to this debate. Two of the most famous are Paul Ehrlich and Anne Ehrlich, *The Population Explosion* (New York: Touchstone, 1991).

11. Julian L. Simon, *The Ultimate Resource* (Princeton, NJ: Princeton University Press, 1981).

12. John Richard Hicks, *The Theory of Wages* (London: Macmillan, 1932).

13. Ester Boserup, *The Conditions of Agricultural Growth: The Economics of Agrarian Change under Population Pressure* (Chicago: Aldine, 1965).

14. Thomas Homer-Dixon, *Environment, Scarcity, and Violence* (Princeton, NJ: Princeton University Press, 1999). Much of the following discussion is derived from his writing.

15. See, for example, Wallace Broecker, "Unpleasant Surprises in the Greenhouse?" *Nature* 328, no. 6126 (9 July 1987): 123–26; William Clark, *On the Practical Implications of the Carbon Dioxide Question* (Laxenburg, Austria: International Institute of Applied Systems Analysis, 1985).

16. Jane Menken, "Demographic-Economic Relationships and Development," in *Population—the Complex Reality: A Report of the Population Summit of the World's Scientific Academies*, ed. Francis Graham-Smith (Golden, CO: North American Press, 1994).

17. Ester Boserup, *Population and Technological Change: A Study of Long-Term Trends* (Chicago: University of Chicago Press, 1981); Boserup, *Conditions of Agricultural Growth*.

18. National Research Council, Committee on Population, *Population Growth and Economic Development: Policy Questions* (Washington, DC: National Academy Press, 1986).

19. Richard P. Cincotta and Robert Engelman, *Economics and Rapid Change: The Influence of Population Growth* (Washington, DC: Population Action International, 1997).

20. Allen C. Kelley and Robert M. Schmidt, *Population and Income Change: Recent Evidence* (Washington, DC: World Bank, 1994).

21. Edward M. Crenshaw, Ansari Z. Ameen, and Matthew Christenson, "Population Dynamics and Economic Development: Age-Specific Population Growth Rates and Economic Growth in Developing Countries, 1965 to 1990," *American Sociological Review* 62, no. 6 (1997): 974–84.

22. Cincotta and Engelman, *Economics and Rapid Change*.

23. See, for example, Kenneth H. Kang, "Why Did Koreans Save So 'Little' and Why Do They Now Save So 'Much,'" *International Economic Journal* 8, no. 4 (1994): 99–111. See also World Bank, *The East Asian Miracle* (Oxford: University of Oxford Press, 1993).

24. Allen C. Kelley, "The Consequences of Rapid Population Growth on Human Resource Development: The Case of Education," in *The Impact of Population Growth on Well-Being in Developing Countries*, ed. Dennis Ahlburg, Allen C. Kelley, and Karen Oppenheim Mason (New York: Springer, 1996), 67–137; T. Paul Schultz, "School Expenditures and Enrollments, 1960–1980: The Effects of Incomes, Prices and Population Growth," in *Population Growth and Economic Development: Issues and Evidence*, ed. D. Gale Johnson and Ronald D. Lee (Madison, WI: University of Wisconsin Press, 1985), 413–36.

25. Cincotta and Engelman, *Economics and Rapid Change*.

26. Cincotta and Engelman, *Economics and Rapid Change*.

27. United Nations Development Program (UNDP), *Human Development Report 2000* (New York: UNDP, 2000).

28. Homer-Dixon, *Environment*.

29. Lester R. Brown, *Who Will Feed China? Wake-up Call for a Small Planet* (New York: W. W. Norton, 1995). See also Lester R. Brown, "Averting a Global Food Crisis," *Technology Review* (November/December 1995): 44–53.

30. Canadian Broadcasting Corporation, "The Crisis the World Forgot," aired April 2, 2009.

31. Audrey Dorélien, "Population's Role in the Current Food Crisis: Focus on East Africa," Population Reference Bureau, August 2008, www.prb.org/Articles/2008/food securityeastafrica.aspx.

32. Joel K. Bourne Jr., "The End of Plenty," *National Geographic* 215, no. 6 (June 2009): 26–59.

33. The June 2009 *National Geographic* reports that the world has been consuming more food than farmers have been producing for the past decade. Essentially, the cupboard is bare.

34. UNFAO, *The State of Food Insecurity in the World, 2008* (Rome: UNFAO, 2008).

35. Keith Bradsher, "A Drought in Australia, A Global Shortage of Rice," *New York Times* 17 April 2008, A4.

36. Bradsher, "A Drought in Australia."

37. IPCC, *Climate Change 2007*, Fourth Assessment Report (AR4) (New York: IPCC, 2007).

38. United Nations Population Fund, "Statement of the UNFPA on the Global Food Crisis, Population and Development," news release, June 3, 2008, www.unfpa .org/public/News/pid/1083 (accessed 9 April 2009).

39. Robert D. Kaplan, "The Coming Anarchy," *Atlantic Monthly* (February 1994): 44–76. Much of Kaplan's article was based on Thomas Homer-Dixon's work, albeit reinterpreted in a very pessimistic and journalistic manner. While pointing out the potential for conflict, Homer-Dixon also provided an important "out" for humanity by pointing out potential interventions to alleviate scarcities and reduce the potential for conflict.

40. Much of the discussion in this chapter is derived from Thomas Homer-Dixon, *Environment, Scarcity, and Violence* (Princeton, NJ: Princeton University Press, 1999). For additional insights into population and resource scarcity, see also Nicholas Polunin, *Population and Global Security* (Cambridge, UK: Cambridge University Press, 1998).

41. Homer-Dixon, *Environment*.

42. See Roger-Mark De Souza, John S. Williams, and Frederick A. B. Meyerson, "Critical Links: Population, Health, and the Environment," *Population Bulletin* 58, no. 3 (September 2003).

Focus: Resource Conflict

1. Martin Ira Glassner, *Political Geography*, 2nd ed. (New York: John Wiley, 1996).

2. Thomas Homer-Dixon, *Environment, Scarcity, and Violence* (Princeton, NJ: Princeton University Press, 1999).

3. In addition, other significant factors, including Iraq's historic claim to Kuwait based upon the former Ottoman Empire and access to the Persian Gulf, were used to "justify" the invasion.

4. Clayton Jones, "Paradise Islands or an Asian Powder Keg," *Christian Science Monitor*, 1 December 1993; Daniel Yergin, "Oil: The Strategic Prize," in *The Gulf War Reader*, ed. Micah L. Sifry and Christopher Serf (New York: Times Books, 1991).

5. In fact, Homer-Dixon was interested solely in the role of renewable resources as generators of conflict. It should be noted, however, that states will be just as eager to capture scarce nonrenewable resources.

6. Alanna Mitchell, "The World's 'Single Biggest Threat,'" *Globe and Mail*, 4 June 2001, 8–9A.

7. William J. Broad, "With a Push from the UN, Water Reveals Its Secrets," *New York Times*, 25 June 2005, 1S.

8. Ismail Serageldin, "Earth Faces Water Crisis," press release, World Bank, Washington, 6 August 1995.

9. Terje Tvedt, "The Struggle for Water in the Middle East," *Canadian Journal of Development Studies* 13, no. 1 (1992): 13–33. Egypt ultimately backed away from its offer to provide Israel with water from the Nile, realizing its own tenuous supply.

10. Terje Tvedt, "The Struggle for Water in the Middle East."

11. See John Kolars and William Mitchell, *The Euphrates River and the Southeast Anatolia Development Project* (Carbondale, IL: Southern Illinois University Press, 1991); Nurit Kliot, *Water Resources and Conflict in the Middle East* (London: Routledge, 1994).

12. Patrick Laurence, "Pretoria Has Its Way in Lesotho," *Africa Report* 31, no. 2 (1986): 50–51.

13. Michael T. Coe and Jonathan A. Foley, "Human and Natural Impacts on the Water Resources of the Lake Chad Basin," *Journal of Geophysical Research* 106, no. D4 (2001): 3349–56.

14. In doing so, it also largely drained the Aral Sea, once the world's sixth-largest inland ocean, in a huge environmental disaster.

15. See, for example, Robert D. Kaplan, "Countries Without Borders," *New York Times*, 23 October 1996, 8A; Paul L. Knox and Sallie A. Marston, *Human Geography: Places and Regions in Global Context*, 2nd ed. (Upper Saddle River, NJ: Prentice Hall, 2001).

Methods, Measures, and Tools: What Have Geographers Contributed to the Debate?

1. The contributions are far too numerous to summarize adequately. Interested readers are directed to Gary L. Gaile and Cort J. Willmott, eds., *Geography in America at the Dawn of the Twenty-First Century* (New York: Oxford University Press, 2003). See also Peter Gould, *The Geographer at Work* (Boston, MA: Routledge, 1985).

2. Harm de Blij, *Why Geography Matters: Three Challenges Facing America* (New York: Oxford University Press, 2005).

3. de Blij, *Why Geography Matters*, x.

4. Thomas M. Poulson, *Nations and States: A Geographic Background to World Affairs* (Englewood Cliffs, NJ: Prentice Hall, 1995).

5. Martin Ira Glassner, *Political Geography*, 2nd ed. (New York: John Wiley, 1996).

6. Ronald J. Johnston, Peter J. Taylor, and Michael J. Watts, *The Geographies of Global Change* (Oxford: Blackwell, 1995).

7. Susan L. Cutter, Douglas B. Richardson, and Thomas J. Wilbanks, *The Geographical Dimensions of Terrorism* (New York: Routledge, 2003).

8. Roger W. Stump, *Boundaries of Faith: Geographical Perspectives on Religious Fundamentalism* (Lanham, MD: Rowman & Littlefield, 2000).

9. Anthony C. Gatrell and Susan J. Elliott, *Geographies of Health: An Introduction* (Malden, MA: Wiley-Blackwell, 2009).

10. Melinda Meade, John Florin, and Wilbert Gesler, *Medical Geography* (New York: Guilford Press, 1998).

11. Robin A. Kearns and Wibert M. Gesler, eds., *Putting Health into Place: Landscape, Identity, and Well-Being* (Syracuse, NY: Syracuse University Press, 1998).

12. John Eyles and Allison Williams, eds., *Sense of Place, Health and Quality of Life* (Bodmin, UK: Ashgate, 2008).

13. Peter Gould, *The Slow Plague: A Geography of the AIDS Pandemic* (Oxford: Blackwell, 1993).

14. Ezekiel Kalipeni and Joseph Oppong, "Rethinking and Reappraising AIDS, Health Care Systems, and Culture in Sub-Saharan Africa—Introduction," *African Rural and Urban Studies* 3, no. 2 (1996): 7–11.

15. Susan J. Elliott, "Focus: Qualitative Approaches in Geography," *The Professional Geographer* 51, no. 2 (1999): 240–320.

16. Hussein Amery and Aaron T. Wolf, *Water in the Middle East: A Geography of Conflict* (Austin, TX: University of Texas Press, 2000).

17. See "Water Resources" in *Geography in America at the Dawn of the Twenty-First Century*, ed. Gaile and Willmott.

18. Brian L. Turner II, Goran Hyden, and Robert Kates, eds., *Population Growth and Agricultural Change in Africa* (Gainesville, FL: University of Florida Press, 1993).

19. Vaclav Smil, "How Many People Can the Earth Feed?" *Population and Development Review* 20, no. 2 (1994): 225–92.

20. Adrian Bailey, *Making Population Geography* (London: Hodden Arnold, 2005); Elspeth Graham, "Breaking Out: The Opportunities and Challenges of Multi-Method Research in Population Geography," *The Professional Geographer* 51, no. 1 (1999): 76–89; Keith Halfacree and Paul Boyle, "The Challenge Facing Migration Research: The Case for Biographical Approach," *Progress in Human Geography* 27 (1993): 333–48.

21. James A. Tyner, *War, Violence and Population: Making the Body Count* (New York: Guilford Press, 2009).

CONCLUSION: DOING POPULATION GEOGRAPHY

1. See www.claritas.com. The PRIZM system is also available in other countries, including Canada, through Environics Analytics (http://www.environicsanalytics.ca).

2. Sandra Rosenbloom, "Sustainability and Automobility among the Elderly: An International Assessment," *Transportation* 28 (2001): 375–408.

3. Pavlos Kanarolgou, Hanna Maoh, K. Bruce Newbold, Darren M. Scott, and Antonio Paez, "A Demographic Model for Small Area Population Projections: An Application to the Census Metropolitan Area (CMA) of Hamilton in Ontario, Canada," *Environment and Planning A*, 41 (2009): 965–79.

4. See www.census.gov/rdo/data/009919.html

5. David Foot, *Boom, Bust and Echo: How to Profit from the Coming Demographic Shift* (Toronto: Macfarlane Walter and Ross, 1996).

6. Richard Florida, *The Rise of the Creative Class: And How It's Transforming Work, Leisure, Community, and Everyday Life* (New York: Basic Books, 2002).

7. Des Beckstead, Mark Brown, and K. Bruce Newbold, *Cities and Growth: In Situ versus Migratory Human Capital Growth*, catalogue #11-622-M, no. 019 (Ottawa: Statistics Canada, 2008).

Index

About the Author

K. Bruce Newbold is professor of geography at McMaster University, where he received his PhD in 1994. He taught at the University of Illinois (1994–2000) before returning to McMaster in 2000. He has held guest scholar positions at the University of California San Diego's Center for Comparative Immigration Studies (CCIS) and at the University of Glasgow's Social and Public Health Sciences Unit, where he held a Journal of Urban Studies Fellowship. His research interests include migration, immigration, health, and aging, and he has received funding from NSF, SSHRC, SSRC, and CIHR. He is currently the director of the McMaster Institute of Environment and Health. He has authored numerous peer-reviewed papers, along with *Six Billion Plus*, which is now in its second edition.